Pro NetBeans™ IDE 5.5 Enterprise Edition

Adam Myatt

Pro NetBeans™ IDE 5.5 Enterprise Edition

Copyright © 2007 by Adam Myatt

ISBN-13 (pbk): 978-1-59059-788-0

ISBN-10 (pbk): 1-59059-788-5

Printed and bound in the United States of America 9 8 7 6 5 4 3 2 1

Lead Editor: Steve Anglin
Technical Reviewer: Sumit Pal
Editorial Board: Steve Anglin, Steve Anglin, Ewan Buckingham, Gary Cornell, Jason Gilmore,
    Jonathan Gennick, Jonathan Hassell, James Huddleston, Chris Mills, Matthew Moodie,
    Jeff Pepper, Paul Sarknas, Dominic Shakeshaft, Jim Sumser, Matt Wade
Project Manager: Beth Christmas
Copy Edit Manager: Nicole Flores
Copy Editor: Marilyn Smith
Assistant Production Director: Kari Brooks-Copony
Production Editor: Katie Stence
Compositor: Susan Glinert
Proofreader: Linda Marousek
Indexer: Julie Grady
Cover Designer: Kurt Krames
Manufacturing Director: Tom Debolski

Distributed to the book trade worldwide by Springer-Verlag New York, Inc., 233 Spring Street, 6th Floor, New York, NY 10013. Phone 1-800-SPRINGER, fax 201-348-4505, e-mail orders-ny@springer-sbm.com, or visit http://www.springeronline.com.

For information on translations, please contact Apress directly at 2560 Ninth Street, Suite 219, Berkeley, CA 94710. Phone 510-549-5930, fax 510-549-5939, e-mail info@apress.com, or visit http://www.apress.com.

The source code for this book is available to readers at http://www.apress.com in the Source Code/Download section.

To my wonderful wife, Morgan, for all her love and support.

Contents at a Glance

PART 1 ■■■ Creating and Managing Projects

PART 2 ■■■ The NetBeans Coding Experience

PART 3 ■■■ NetBeans and Professional Software Development

Contents

PART 1 ■■■ Creating and Managing Projects

PART 2 ■■■ The NetBeans Coding Experience

PART 3 ■■■ NetBeans and Professional Software Development

About the Author

ADAM MYATT currently works as the Principal Technologist of Software Development for GE Global Research, the worldwide R&D headquarters of General Electric, located in Niskayuna, New York. Adam is an experienced Java developer, with Sun Microsystems Certified Java Programmer certification. His work entails leading globally developed Java software and web applications through a rigorous software development life-cycle process, researching new technologies, and setting long-term strategies.

Adam is an active participant in a local Java users group and an avid enthusiast of open source software. He has also worked for several software firms prior to joining General Electric. Adam is a graduate of the Computer Science department at the State University of New York College at Potsdam.

In what little free time he has, Adam enjoys traveling to new and interesting places, fishing, and playing poker. He also enjoys working on his house and driving his wife crazy by talking about work nonstop.

About the Technical Reviewer

 **SUMIT PAL** has about 12 years of experience with software architecture design and development on a variety of platforms, including J2EE. Sumit has worked in the SQL Server Replication group while with Microsoft for two years, and with Oracle's OLAP Server group while with Oracle for seven years.

Along with certifications like IEEE-CSDP and J2EE Architect, Sumit also has an MS in Computer Science from the Asian Institute of Technology, Thailand.

Sumit has a keen interest in database internals, algorithms, and search engine technology. He has invented some basic generalized algorithms to find divisibility between numbers and also invented divisibility rules for prime numbers less than 100.

Currently, Sumit loves to play as much as he can with his daughter. He also likes to swim and play badminton.

Acknowledgments

I would like to thank the many people without whom this book would not have been possible. A team of very dedicated people greatly assisted me in creating this work.

First, I want to thank my editor, Steve Anglin, for bringing me together with Apress for this project and taking a chance on me. His advice and guidance in this project were invaluable.

I want to express sincere gratitude to my project manager, Beth Christmas, for working ever so hard to keep me on schedule and on time. Her experience and professionalism helped make the book writing process far easier than it might have been.

Thanks to my technical reviewer, Sumit Pal, who helped make this a stronger, more accurate book. You have my appreciation for all your insightful suggestions and comments.

A huge thanks goes out to my copy and production editors Marilyn Smith and Katie Stence for the fantastic job they did on making what I wrote actually read well and look good. Marilyn somehow made sense of my ramblings and helped organize my thoughts to make the excellent book this turned out to be.

I greatly appreciate the entire Apress team and all the efforts of its members.

I would also like to express my thanks to the entire GEGR ITMS organization for the support at work. Balancing work and personal projects can be difficult at times, but having a great team to work with certainly made it easier.

There have also been several people and groups during my academic and professional career that have imparted their wisdom on me in one way or another. Thanks to Dr. John Dalphin, all the past and present CIS faculty at SUNY Potsdam, the CIS Board of Advisors, Chris Thompson and Anthony Debonis from my old shadow IT organization, and the CDJDN.

Finally, I would like to express my heartfelt thanks to my wife, Morgan, who put up with me working nights and weekends on this book for far too long. Her love and support during this project made it all possible.

Introduction

This book explores the many features of NetBeans IDE 5.5. Developers can focus on a variety of technologies and areas when learning NetBeans. With the latest release, developers have access to an impressive array of features for working with JavaServer Faces (JSF), Ajax, Unified Modeling Language (UML) modeling, Enterprise JavaBeans (EJB 3.0), the Java Persistence API, web services, Business Process Execution Language (BPEL), and more. I wanted to write a book that really showcased the fantastic tools for working with these technologies.

Pro NetBeans IDE 5.5 Enterprise Edition is designed for all levels of developers. Whether you are new to NetBeans, a student programmer, or an experienced professional, you will find this book provides direct explanations of features and straightforward examples. It also focuses on many of the core features of NetBeans that assist professional software developers: Ant, JUnit, Concurrent Versioning System (CVS), Subversion, the developer collaboration tools, code coverage, and so on.

My personal web site, www.ProNetBeans.com, contains a variety of content, such as Java and NetBeans news, articles, tutorials, and more. It will also contain updates, corrections, and errata to this book. If you have any questions or would like to provide feedback, please feel free to contact me at adam@pronetbeans.com.

PART 1

■ ■ ■

Creating and Managing Projects

CHAPTER 1

■ ■ ■

Integrated Development Environments

In the beginning, code was written using simple text-based tools like Notepad. For the purposes of this discussion, I'll define "beginning" as the early to mid-1990s, when Java first started to become popular. Using the combination of a text editor and command prompt, users could write and compile code.

It was quickly determined that this approach did not provide the most efficient development environment. For example, if you made a code syntax mistake in the text editor, there was no way to identify the problem until you saved and compiled the file. You would then review the compilation error, locate the offending line in the code, and attempt to determine the cause. Compilation errors are not always entirely helpful in diagnosing the problem with your code.

Many novice programmers start out using the Notepad and command-prompt environment. There is nothing inherently wrong with this approach, since some professionals still do the same thing. For an absolute beginner learning Java, using a plain text editor can sometimes be the easiest and fastest approach. However, text editors do not provide assistance with language syntax, compiler integration, intelligent refactoring support, or other code writing capabilities.

One of the useful features most text editors possess is called Find and Replace. Using this simple capability, programmers could replace occurrences of a word or phrase with another. This worked for certain situations, but could cause problems. Suppose you created the following class:

```java
public class SomeCode {

    public void myMethod1(String var) {

        String FirstName = var.toUpperCase();

        // do something with FirstName
    }
```

```
public void myMethod2(String var) {

    String FirstName = var.toLowerCase();

    // do something else with FirstName
}

}
```

The SomeCode class includes two methods: myMethod1 and myMethod2. If you later needed to rename the FirstName variable in myMethod1, you could manually edit each line of code to alter the name. Obviously, this is a simple example, but if myMethod1 happened to be a hundred lines long and FirstName appeared in many places, then manual editing of the code could take quite a long time. You could also use the text editor's Find and Replace functionality to quickly replace all occurrences of FirstName with the new variable name. However, the original change request specified only the FirstName variable in the myMethod1 method and *not* in the myMethod2 method. Using Find and Replace could incorrectly replace the wrong occurrences of FirstName in myMethod1 and myMethod2. Of course, it's possible to replace occurrences one by one, but that can take time and be prone to human error.

Some text editors offer more advanced support for programming languages. The popular Unix-based tool Emacs offers many interesting features. Emacs offers advanced text matching and replacement capabilities. Through plug-ins, it can also provide Java syntax highlighting, code indentation, basic debugging, and compilation support. These are great pieces of functionality, but still do not offer the most flexible and productive environment.

Why Use an IDE?

The first question anyone who uses Emacs or text editors might ask is, "Why use an IDE?" Some programmers tend to grow attached to a specific tool set or programming language and are resistant to change. An important quality in today's ever-changing world is the ability to adapt to new technology.

New tool sets can help professional programmers in many ways. A programmer's time should be spent writing code, rewriting code, and testing code. You shouldn't need to waste time trying to figure out how to rename methods across your code, generate project documentation, or correctly compile all the classes in a package. Once you have identified the action you need to perform, your tool should easily do it for you.

Integrated development environments (IDEs) literally provide an entire environment for your work. They bring together many different tools in a coherent way, so that the services and actions you need are seamlessly integrated together.

Some technical benefits of IDEs include the following:

- Graphical user interface (GUI) for performing actions

- Grouping of source code and configuration files into the concept of a *project*

- Tight integration with the compiler

- Coupling with a source code repository

- Ability to performance tune, analyze, and load test code

- Integration with reusable test frameworks

- Capability to utilize third-party plug-ins and tools

- Ability to debug code by executing one line at a time

- Quick access to and ease of generating project documentation

Some of the more tangible business benefits of using an IDE include the following:

- Reduces the cycle time of development

- Increases the quality and reliability of your code

- Standardizes your software development processes

- Provides a common platform for programming staff to reduce training time

Some of these benefits are definitely arguable and can sometimes be realized only after careful analysis, implementation, and execution. Many other factors come into play, but a really good Java IDE tool can be the foundation for accomplishing important milestones such as the examples I provided.

NetBeans vs. Other IDE Tools

NetBeans is my Java IDE of choice. This might be obvious since I wrote this book, but I have many valid reasons for loving and using NetBeans. My experience with development tools covers a wide range of products, such as Notepad, TextPad, Emacs, vi, Macromedia Ultradeveloper, Macromedia Dreamweaver, Oracle JDeveloper, IntelliJ IDEA, Borland JBuilder, Microsoft Visual Studio, and Eclipse.

Each of these tools has its own pros and cons. They all have devoted users and entire communities centered around them. After a while, distinguishing between the tools can be difficult, since they offer many similar features. I was on the fence deciding between IntelliJ IDEA and Eclipse. After only a few hours of working with NetBeans and viewing various tutorials, I was convinced. I downloaded, installed, and started working with it. I quickly discovered that the features were located in places I expected them to be, they functioned as I thought they would, and there were few or no configuration issues. In my opinion, that is how a tool should function out of the box.

In no particular order, the top ten reasons I think programmers should use NetBeans over another Java IDE are summarized as follows:

Intuitive and easy-to-use Matisse GUI designer for Swing development: With little or no Swing knowledge, users can be up and running dragging-and-dropping elements into a WYSIWYG design window. The Matisse GUI designer actually generates real Swing code and not the usual boilerplate fluff code many tools tend to create. At the last JavaOne conference I attended, I sat next to a gentleman who used the GUI design capabilities of JBuilder. After only two minutes of watching me use Matisse, he was completely blown away and ran off to download it for himself.

Strong refactoring support: This is particularly true for the Jackpot engine, allowing for Java type-aware refactoring using a regular expression-like query language. Designed by James Gosling, the query language is quite simple to use and allows for pattern matching and replacement. The interesting aspect to the queries is that they can be tested to match specific Java types or instances of objects.

One of the best code profilers: Given I haven't used every code profiler out there, but with an amazing array of options, the NetBeans Profiler is among the best. Users can profile for memory, CPU, and performance problems, as well as monitor threads. The Profiler can also be attached and detached from a currently running process or application. It provides 32-bit and 64-bit support, as well as allowing you to profile Enterprise JavaBeans (EJB) modules and enterprise applications. For those Mac fans in the crowd, it also supports profiling on Mac OS X Intel systems.

UML project support: Programmers can create a Unified Modeling Language (UML) project for modeling code, process steps, or design patterns. UML projects can be linked directly to Java projects. As a user creates and modifies the UML objects and diagrams, the corresponding Java code is automatically generated. If the source code in the linked Java project is changed, the diagram is also updated automatically. With the ability to export diagrams, generate code, and create web-based project reports, the UML project feature is one of the coolest additions to NetBeans that I have enjoyed using.

Ant integration: Java projects in NetBeans are structured using Ant build files. When a project is first created, the IDE generates the build script and associated targets. Users can then trigger specific targets or completely customize the structure of their build file to suit the needs of their project. For users that are not familiar with Ant, there is almost no impact, since execution of Ant targets is linked directly to the menus and buttons in NetBeans. Many users will also find it easy to import existing build files from external projects and quickly get up to speed. For beginners, it is ridiculously easy to use. For experts, it is ridiculously easy to customize.

J2ME mobile application support: Even if you don't do much mobile application development, after viewing the samples and reading an introductory tutorial, you should quickly see the power of NetBeans mobile tools. The sample applications provided are impressive enough as it is. With support for Java 2 Micro Edition (J2ME) Mobile Information Device Profile (MIDP) 2.0, a visual mobile designer, a wireless connection wizard, and over-the-air download testing, mobile application developers have some impressive and powerful tools.

Developer collaboration tools: Developers can log in to a public or private environment and share code. You can join public conversations or start your own restricted private ones. One of the greatest features I've seen in a while is the ability to drag-and-drop code or entire projects in the chat window and share code between one or more programmers. NetBeans supports multiuser team coding. As one user starts to change a block of code, it is highlighted and locked for the other users sharing it. In the current global economy, where development teams are spread across numerous locations, this tool can prove very beneficial.

Easy-to-use Update Center: The NetBeans Update Center allows you to quickly select which update distribution sites you wish to check for changes, updates, and new modules. You can also choose to install modules that you previously downloaded, but chose not to install. The Update Center is more intuitive than many other Java IDE update tools and makes updating NetBeans a snap.

Out-of-the-box JSP and Tomcat support: NetBeans comes bundled with Apache Tomcat. Once you have used the new project wizard to create a web application project, you can create your JavaServer Pages (JSP) files. Then you can right-click any JSP file and select Run File. The bundled Tomcat server immediately starts, your default Internet browser opens, and the JSP file executing in Tomcat is displayed. NetBeans is even smart enough to activate the HTTP Monitor.

NetBeans HTTP Monitor: I do a lot of web-related Java development. To me, this is one of the coolest and most unique features of any Java IDE on the market. The HTTP Monitor can be activated during the debugging or execution of a web application. It allows you to monitor the request, HTTP headers, cookies, session, servlet context, and client/server parameters. You no longer need to write server-side code to read these variables, output them to a log, and view the log file. Inside NetBeans, you can debug your code, step line by line through it, and watch the attributes you need.

These features are only a sampling of some of what NetBeans has to offer. Other Java IDEs may provide some of the capabilities described here, but none can match the NetBeans IDE's intuitive interface and integrated tool set. To learn about everything NetBeans has to offer, I invite you to continue reading the rest of the chapters in this book.

Summary

In this chapter, we discussed the high-level evolution of programming using text editors and tools. Obviously, many tools have been introduced and many milestones have been reached during the past 50 years of software development, but I wanted to cover the basic reasons why developers use full-blown IDEs.

There are many benefits to using a modern development environment like NetBeans. It offers more productivity enhancements and conveniences than competing tools, such as Notepad, TextPad, Emacs, and vi. Users can take advantage of features like an advanced GUI designer, integrated testing with JUnit, performance profiling, debugging tools, and full compilation and packaging support.

Many of the NetBeans features briefly covered in this chapter offer significant improvements over other Java IDEs. For these reasons, and many more, I believe NetBeans should be the Java IDE of choice for development teams.

■■■

CHAPTER 2

Installing and Customizing NetBeans

To start using NetBeans, you just need to download and install it. This chapter describes how to do that, as well as check for updates and customize some NetBean settings to suit your own preferences. Finally, we'll take a quick look at the NetBeans window you'll use most often.

Downloading Files

To download the NetBeans files, go to netbeans.org. The web site provides several different links for downloading the NetBeans software and related tools. The main features are typically listed under a section named Latest Downloads. A Downloads link also appears near the top of the page.

Depending on which path you follow to get to the download section, you may be presented with several choices. Select the desired Operating System and Localization Language options for the build you wish to download. You may also be asked to select Build Type and Version options. Unless you are feeling adventurous, you will want to always select Release as the Build Type.

The main products you want to make sure you download are theNetBeans IDE and the NetBeans Profiler

Installing the NetBeans IDE and Core Add-Ons

Since NetBeans can be installed across numerous platforms, I will mention only the important installation concepts. NetBeans can be installed on almost any operating system for which there is a Java Virtual Machine (JVM). I am running NetBeans using Java 6, unless otherwise specified.

On the download page at netbeans.org, a list of Release Documents is provided. In this list is a link to the Installation Instructions as recommended by NetBeans. These instructions cover the basic installation process for Windows, Solaris, Linux, and Macintosh OS X. The Release Documents section also contains links for the Profiler Java Development Kit (JDK) 1.4 add-on and the Profiler Remote Agents.

As of version 5.0 of the Profiler, it is recommended that you run it with JDK 1.5.04 or later. It *is* possible to profile against JDK 1.4, but an experimental add-on is needed to allow this functionality. The add-on is not supported by Sun and should be used at your own risk. If your application is written for Java 1.4, I recommend that you install the latest release of Java 6.0 and set the source compatibility in NetBeans to 1.4. This should resolve any issues with running the Profiler, as well as maintain your Java 1.4-based code. To set the source compatibility for a project, right-click the project name and select Properties from the context menu. With the Sources category selected, you should see a field called Source Level. Using the drop-down list, you can set the version of Java with which your source code should be compatible.

The first time I downloaded and installed NetBeans, I used Sun's Java 5 on Windows XP, but have since upgraded to Java 6. After executing the Windows installer, I clicked the Next button, accepted the license agreement, and selected a directory to install NetBeans. Personally, I like to group all my Java-related products in one location. I typically start with a c:\java directory. Within that directory, I will install several JDKs, Java tools like NetBeans or Eclipse, as well as a directory for all my Java-related projects and applications. I usually end up with the following:

- c:\java\1.5.0.10

- c:\java\1.4.2.11

- c:\java\netbeans\5.5

- c:\java\projects

The installation process will search for and ask about which JDK you want to use. If you have multiple JDKs installed, you should see a list of them in the bottom portion of the window. Select the JDK you wish you use (I recommend installing and picking JDK 1.6.0) and click the Next button. Continue through the installer until it has finished.

Next you will need to install the NetBeans Profiler. The Profiler installation is quite standard. On Windows, once you have executed the installer and accepted the license agreement, you are prompted to select a suitable NetBeans IDE. Select the version of the IDE you have just installed and continue clicking the Next button until the installation is complete.

Customizing the NetBeans JVM Startup Options

One thing most people will probably never think to use is the ability to customize the NetBeans JVM startup options. By including several arguments in a NetBeans configuration file, you can tweak the memory usage settings for the JVM in which NetBeans starts up. You can also change the type of garbage-collection algorithm that is used.

If you are working on a semi-standard computer (32-bit single processor), you probably won't benefit from changing the garbage-collection routine the JVM uses. However, if you use a JVM other than the Sun JVM or have a machine that is either multiprocessor or 64-bit, you might want to consider these options. Your JVM vendor should provide some sort of documentation regarding the garbage-collection routines that run and how to configure them via command-line arguments. These can be passed along to NetBeans during startup.

In NetBeans, you can configure JVM startup arguments by editing the file /etc/netbeans. conf in your NetBeans home directory. In this file, you should see a property named netbeans_ default_options. This property allows you to pass JVM customization arguments to NetBeans. The first two arguments you should see that are set by default and are the ones we will focus on:

- The -J-Xms32m argument specifies that the initial heap size allocated to the JVM should be 32MB.

- The -J-Xmx128m argument specifies that the maximum heap size that can be allocated to the JVM should be 128MB.

Increasing the value of the Xms argument can improve performance in some applications, since the JVM would not have to keep reallocating heap space each time it needed to increase the available space. There is a lot of discussion in the Java industry about the correct way to set these parameters. The safest bet is to set the Xms argument to 64MB or 128MB and set the Xmx argument as high as possible (usually between 50 to 75 percent of the total memory on your system). You should also note that the Xms and Xmx arguments only specify the heap size of the JVM and not the total amount of memory the JVM will use, since there are items in the JVM that do not live inside the heap.

Setting a Proxy

Many programmers, whether they are in corporations or on college campuses, need to work behind a proxy. The NetBeans IDE uses an Internet connection for numerous operations, such as downloading updates, linking to help documentation, and connecting to external database and web servers.

To configure the proxy settings for NetBeans, select Tools ➤ Options. The Basic Options window is displayed by default, and it contains a Proxy section. If it is not visible, click the General tab to see the proxy settings, as shown in Figure 2-1.

You can also access and modify the same proxy settings in the Advanced Options section by clicking the Advanced Options button and selecting IDE Configuration ➤ System ➤ System Settings. The proxy settings will appear in the right pane of the window. An additional field named Non Proxy Hosts will also appear in the list. This field allows you to specify an ignore list of hosts that can be accessed by NetBeans without going through the proxy.

For the Web Proxy field, select the HTTP Proxy option. Enter a proxy host and port number, and then click the OK button.

It is possible to use a SOCKS proxy, but you will need to pass a command-line switch to the JVM when starting NetBeans. In the NetBeans installation root, look in the etc directory and find the netbeans.conf file. In the configuration file, edit the netbeans_default_options property and add the following to the end of the line:

```
-J-DsocksProxyHost=mysocksservername -J-DsocksProxyPort=mysocksserverportnum
```

Save the changes to the configuration file. Before you close it, notice the other properties in the file, as it is useful to occasionally change things here if certain situations come up (such as changing the default JDK NetBeans is configured to use, tuning JVM startup options, and so on.

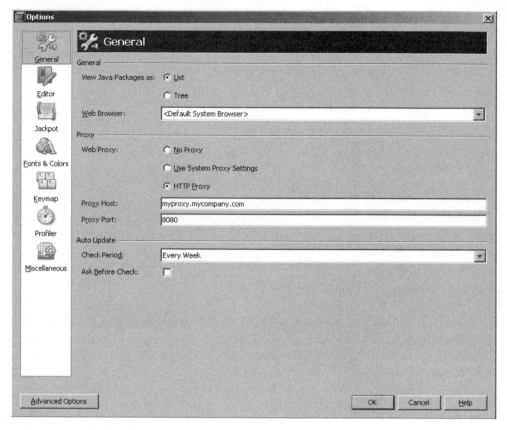

Figure 2-1. *Proxy settings section*

Checking for Updates

One of the most important aspects of a Java IDE tool is the ability to receive updates and fixes. Anyone who has ever written code knows that no program is ever perfect. Mistakes and bugs happen, and when they do, the most important thing that can occur (other than fixing the bug) is to deliver the updated code to the users.

NetBeans allows you to check for, download, and install updates to the tools and plug-ins that are installed within your distribution through the Update Center. It is an integrated tool that checks one or more remote sites for any software updates that may be available. You can also check a remote site for new plug-ins, as well as manually install an update module that was previously downloaded.

Using the Update Center

To access the Update Center, select Tools ➤ Update Center. In the window that opens, you should see a list of Update Centers that are currently configured in your NetBeans distribution, as shown in Figure 2-2.

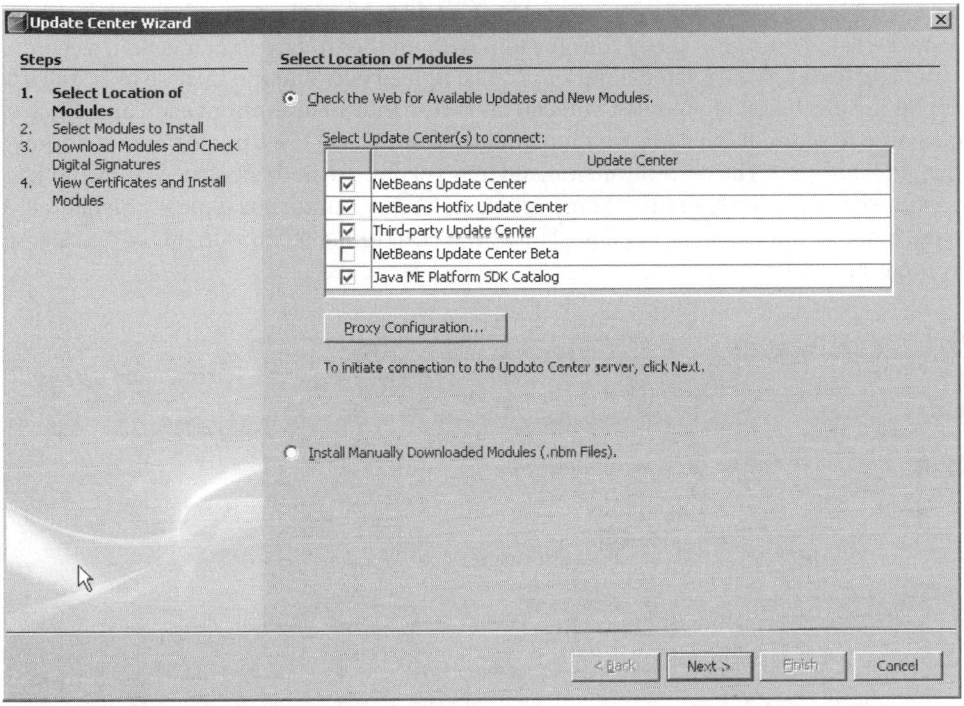

Figure 2-2. *The NetBeans Update Center window*

The Check the Web for Available Updates and New Modules option should be selected by default. The Update Center window also includes a button labeled Proxy Configuration. If you have not already done so, you can set or adjust the proxy setting NetBeans will use to connect to the Update Center(s). To check an Update Center for available updates and new features, place a check mark next to it in the list. Then click the Next button.

Note The NetBeans Update Center Beta listing is for tools and features that are not quite ready for production use and/or have not been completely battle-tested. In my NetBeans distribution on my work computer, I don't use this Update Center, because I need to maintain a consistent and stable development environment. However, on my home computer, I frequently check this Update Center and experiment with the tools it provides.

After checking the various sites, NetBeans will display the results it found. The results are grouped together by Update Center and can be displayed in folders. The NetBeans Update Center site groups items into two folders:

- The Features folder contains the core tools.

- The Libraries folder contains the supporting APIs and code that support features.

To add a feature, select it in the list and click the Add button. The feature you selected will appear in the list of the right. One of the nice things about the Update Center is that, as you select and add features, the related libraries are also moved over into the Include in Install list.

As you review the list of modules, you can find more information about each one. Click a module name to see additional information in the bottom half of the Update Center window, as shown in Figure 2-3. The current version and new version are both displayed, allowing you to determine if the update is a minor or major release. A description box typically displays the size of the module, the actual release date, and a brief description of the contents of the release or new module.

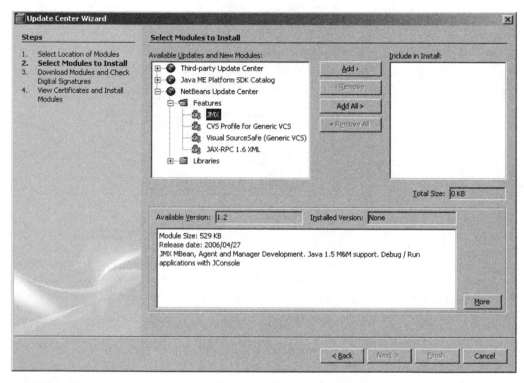

Figure 2-3. *Module description and version information in the Update Center window*

Notice the More button to the bottom right of the description box. Clicking it opens an Internet browser and directs it to the web site for the specified module you currently have selected. This is especially useful before installing third-party plug-ins and tools, as you are able to find out more information about them before proceeding with the installation.

■**Note** Several important features that are initially available from the NetBeans Update Center are the Eclipse Project Importer, JBuilder Project Importer, and Collaboration tools. In later chapters, I cover how to use these tools, so you may want to make sure they are included in your list of modules to install.

Once you have specified the complete list of modules you want to install, click the Next button. For most modules, you will be presented with a window asking you to accept a license agreement. After you have selected each license agreement, the modules will immediately begin to download. Once they have downloaded, the progress bar will read 100 percent, and you will be able to click the Next button.

The next window, View Certificates and Install Modules, allows you to view each module's security certificate. Here, you can make a final decision on whether you wish to install the module. None of the modules are marked to be included by default. However, if during a previous module installation you selected to Always Accept or Accept the certificate from a publisher, then the Include check box next to those modules will be checked. You can remove the check next to the module name if you do not want to install it.

You may want to download a module, but install it at a later date. The Update Center allows you to do so by working with modules in the form of files with the *.nbm extension. In the list of modules in Figure 2-4, you can select a module and click the Save Copy button. This allows you to save the downloaded module as an .nbm file to be later installed. You can install downloaded modules at any time by going to the Update Center and selecting the Install Manually Downloaded Modules option (see Figure 2-2).

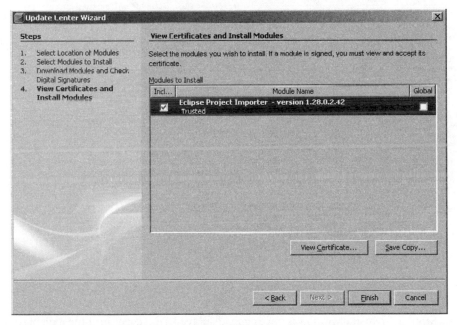

Figure 2-4. *List of downloaded modules in the View Certificates and Install Modules window*

One last option available on the View Certificates and Install Modules window is a Global check box next to each downloaded module. This feature is for use in multiuser IDE environments. Selecting the Global option for a module will enable it for each user of NetBeans. If the Global option is not selected, the module is installed only for the current user. This feature is especially important to note for anyone updating NetBeans on a computer that is typically a shared machine, such as in computer labs.

Once you have finished determining the final list of modules to install, click the Finish button. The Update Center window will disappear. Look at the NetBeans status bar in the lower-left corner. It will display the current status as NetBeans installs and activates the various modules. When it is finished, you will see a message saying "Done," or you may be prompted to restart NetBeans immediately or postpone the restart for later. If you do not need to restart the IDE, the installed modules should be active and ready for use.

Installing Previously Downloaded Modules

To manually install modules that were previously downloaded, select Tools ➤ Update Center. The second option displayed is Install Manually Downloaded Modules (.nbm Files). Select this option and click the Next button. In the following window, you will need to navigate your local file system and select which .nbm files you wish to install, as shown in Figure 2-5. Click the Add button to see a file system browser window. After selecting each .nbm file you want to install, click the Next button.

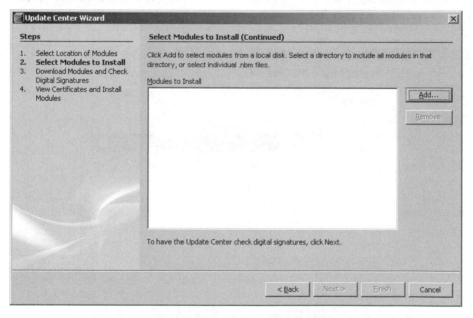

Figure 2-5. *Installing manually downloaded modules through the Update Center*

The Select Modules to Install window is once again displayed. However, this time it displays a Manually Downloaded Modules list instead of a list of Update Center sites. The module(s) you previously selected as .nbm files should be displayed in the Include in Install list. The remaining installation steps are similar to those for updating and downloading modules, as described in the previous section.

Activating Features Through the Module Manager

An important feature of NetBeans is the Module Manager. The Module Manager allows you to
enable, disable, and uninstall features and modules. You can access it by selecting Tools ➤
Module Manager. The Module Manager window displays the entire list of installed modules for
your distribution of NetBeans, as shown in Figure 2-6.

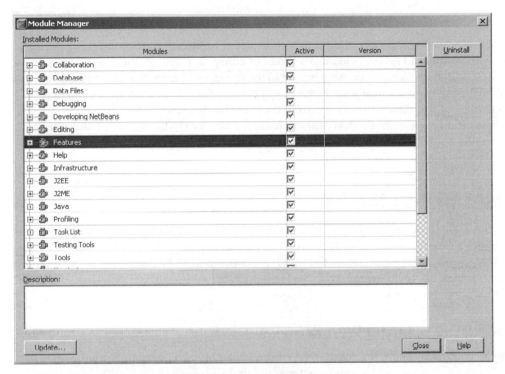

Figure 2-6. *The list of installed modules in the Module Manager window*

In the Module Manager, the features and modules are categorized by types, such as J2EE,
J2ME, Java, Editing, and so on. Click the plus next to each category type to see the list of modules
belonging to that type.

Along with the module name and parent type, the module status and version are displayed.
The Active column contains a check box that allows you to either enable (checked) or disable (not
checked) a particular module. The Active check box next to the parent type allows you to enable or
disable all modules and features belonging to that type. Disabling a feature does *not* mean it
has been uninstalled. It simply means that it is not currently available for use in the IDE. If you
attempt to disable a module that has a dependency on another module, NetBeans will ask if it
is acceptable to disable the dependent module.

■Tip Disabling modules or features that you rarely use can improve the startup time and memory usage of NetBeans. When NetBeans opens, its splash screen displays several status messages, such as "Reading module storage," "Turning on modules," "Loading modules," and "Starting modules." Much of the processing and work that goes on behind the scenes during startup involve activating modules. The fewer modules NetBeans must activate, the better.

The Module Manager also allows you to completely uninstall modules. Navigate the list of types and modules to find the module you want to uninstall. Highlight the module by clicking its name, and then click the Uninstall button in the upper-right corner of the window. You will then be prompted to confirm your decision. After confirmation, the module is immediately deactivated, uninstalled, and removed from the list of modules.

The Module Manager also has a button for accessing the Update Center. This is the same as selecting Tools ➤ Update Center, and is convenient if you need to uninstall modules and then download a fresh copy.

Customizing the IDE

Many Java IDE tools allow a wide array of customizations. NetBeans is no exception. Users can customize a variety of settings, such as fonts, colors, text messages, coding preferences, menus, toolbars, shortcuts, and much more. You could spend an exhaustive amount of time examining each and every possible customization, so I have highlighted several key items that I feel are most relevant and useful.

Setting the Internal Web Browser

I personally do a lot of development with web-based content, so I need to be able to view that content in a web browser in a convenient manner in the browser of my choice. Sometimes I need to test web content in different browsers, especially if I am writing cross-browser JavaScript code. One of the nice features of NetBeans is the ability to set which Internet browser is used to view web content.

If you have a JSP file named index.jsp open and want to run it, select Run ➤ Run File ➤ Run and choose index.jsp. In the Output window, you will first see the application compiled, packaged, and deployed. Then the bundled Java application server will start, and finally, a web browser will open.

NetBeans is initially configured to use the default browser for your system. You can change this by selecting Tools ➤ Options and selecting General in the left pane of the Options window (see Figure 2-1). The Web Browser drop-down list offers Default System Browser, Swing HTML Browser, and any browsers you have installed on your system. If you always prefer to test your web applications with Firefox, you could select it from the list.

If you choose a normal Internet browser, it will open outside the NetBeans tools, as you would expect. However, if you set NetBeans to use the Swing HTML Browser, you get a different result. This is an internal browser with limited functionality, but there is an advantage of running a browser inside NetBeans as a tabbed window in the Source Editor section. You are then able to easily toggle back and forth within NetBeans between your code and the visual browser-based representation of it.

Note The internal Swing HTML Browser does allow you to navigate to external web sites, just like a regular browser, but it does not support as much DHTML, layers, CSS, and so on. Try navigating to sites like Msnbc.com or Espn.com, and you will see what I mean.

Setting Code Editor Indentation

NetBeans allows some flexibility when configuring code indentation and formatting. When NetBeans formats source code (select Source ➤ Reformat Code) or autogenerates code, it applies several code styles. You can modify these by choosing Tools ➤ Options ➤ Editor and clicking the Indentation tab. As shown in Figure 2-7, this tab contains the code formatting options and a preview that displays how your code would be formatted if you toggled each of the available options. The following sections cover some of the more important settings.

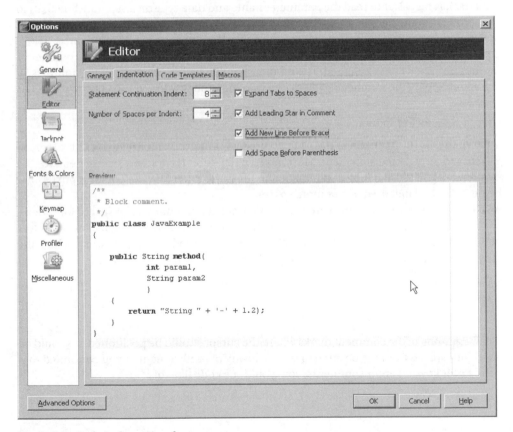

Figure 2-7. *Code indentation features*

Statement Continuation Indent

When writing code such as a method declaration with parameters, the line of characters can become quite long, as in this example:

```
public void setEmployeeData(String FirstName, String LastName)
```

Some coders believe it a best practice to leave the entire method declaration and defined parameters on one line. Popular practice is to separate long lines:

```
public void setEmployeeData(String FirstName,
                            String LastName)
```

or:

```
public void setEmployeeData(
        String FirstName,
        String LastName
        )
```

This type of syntax formatting is especially useful if you are defining a method with many parameters. It is far easier to read the parameter name and data type on a separate line than to have to scroll far to the right in a very long line.

In NetBeans, you can control the amount of space the continued code is indented. The Statement Continuation Indent option on the Indentation tab allows you to set the number of spaces the continued line is indented. The minimum indent is 1 space, and the maximum is 50 spaces. Try changing the number of spaces and watching the preview at the bottom of the tab.

Number of Spaces Per Indent

Part of writing easy-to-maintain and legible code is indenting statements such as `if-else`, `switch-case`, or any nested statement. Most modern IDE tools have some level of default indentation. As you finish typing a statement and press the Enter key, the cursor is positioned on the next line and indented one or more spaces.

In NetBeans, you can customize this formatting. the default number of spaces for indentation is four. The Number of Spaces Per Indent option on the Indentation tab allows you to adjust this setting from 1 to 50. To see this in action, type a line of code like `if(myBooleanValue)`, the opening curly brace, and press Enter. You should see the following:

```
if(myBooleanValue) {
    //start here
}
```

The beginning of the comment marks where the cursor should be positioned. It should be indented four spaces from the position of the enclosing parent element. If you continued to press the Enter key and enter comments, you would see code like this:

```
if(myBooleanValue) {
    //start here
    //comment2
    //comment3
    //comment4
    //comment5
}
```

Notice that the line spacing for each of the lines inside the `if` block is the same. The IDE monitors the fact that all the statements you are typing have the same scope (I use this term loosely) and attempts to maintain similar spacing. After the fifth comment line, add another `if` block and see how the spacing is maintained. After typing `if(myNextBooleanValue)`, an opening curly brace, and pressing Enter, add several lines of comments. The following code should appear:

```
if(myBooleanValue) {
    //start here
    //comment2
    //comment3
    //comment4
    //comment5
    if(myNextBooleanValue) {
        // comment 6
        // comment 7
    }
}
```

If you want to see a better example of this, try setting the Number of Spaces Per Indent option to 20 and typing several nested `if-else` blocks of code.

Expand Tabs to Spaces

When indenting code, some developers like to add tabs and some like spaces. For many people, this is not a huge issue, but if you open code in different tools, it can cause formatting problems. If your development team develops on a variety of operating systems or uses a variety of tools like Emacs, vi, NetBeans, or Notepad, you may have run into this issue.

The Expand Tabs to Spaces option in NetBeans automatically converts any tab characters into an equivalent number of spaces. One tab character is the number of spaces set for the Number of Spaces Per Indent option. This can help reduce formatting issues and spacing problems.

Add New Line Before Brace

A lot of development shops enforce a set of standard coding practices. One element of good coding is using a consistent method of placing curly braces after method declarations, `if` blocks, `else` blocks, `switch` statements, `for` loops, and so on.

If you've ever worked on code that another developer created, you've probably seen bad coding styles. A typical piece of code for a method might look like this:

```
public int calculate(int x, int y, int z)
{
    int total = 0;
    if(x<y) {
        total = x + y;
    }
    else if(x > y)
    {
        total = x + z;
    }
    else {
        total = x+ y + z;
    }
    return total;
}
```

Notice that the opening curly brace for each block is either on the same line immediately following the statement or on the following line. Depending on how intricate your code is, this can lead to hard-to-read files, especially if numerous code blocks are embedded within code blocks embedded within code blocks.

I remember a previous project where I inherited code from another developer. I needed to trace what happened throughout a very long method. In the method were numerous loops and if-else blocks. Lining up curly braces to see where one block ended and another started soon grew frustrating. Using the NetBeans Add New Line Before Brace option and applying the formatting to the source code would have saved me a lot of headaches.

Choosing Fonts and Colors

NetBeans provides the ability to customize the overall appearance of fonts and colors. With the variety of development tools on the market, many developers are familiar with a different look and feel. For example, if you've been coding in Emacs and now are making the move to NetBeans, perhaps you want the code syntax to reflect the color scheme you used in Emacs. NetBeans provides several levels of customization.

Fonts and Color Profiles

The font and color customizations are grouped into a color profile. The profile contains the settings for customizing colors for language-specific syntax, highlighting, and annotations. Color profiles allow you to change numerous settings and toggle back and forth between them.

To customize color profiles, select Tools ➤ Options ➤ Fonts & Colors and select the Syntax tab. This tab displays the relevant settings, as shown in Figure 2-8.

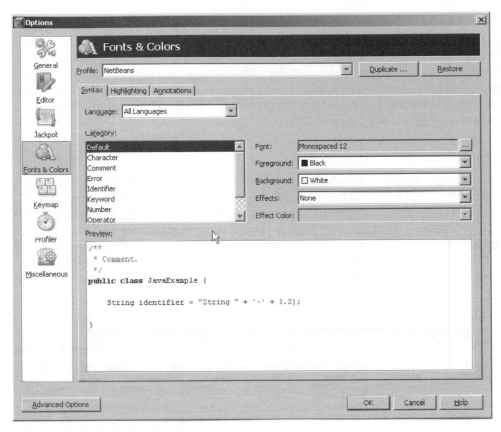

Figure 2-8. *Fonts & Colors window*

NetBeans provides two color profiles, named NetBeans and City Lights. These can be modified as frequently as you wish and later restored to their initial settings by clicking the Restore button next to the Profile drop-down list. I recommend creating a copy of the NetBeans color profile and modifying it as you see fit. You can do so by selecting the profile and clicking the Duplicate button to the right of the Profile drop-down list. This is useful since a profile that is a copy of another profile cannot be restored. It can only be deleted.

I use color profiles most often when giving presentations. For writing code, I typically use a color profile similar to the system default profile. When giving presentations, where I need to project my screen, I switch to an alternate profile that uses a larger font size and darker font color scheme.

Language-Specific Color Settings

For each color profile in the Fonts & Colors section, a list of language-specific settings is available. The list includes settings like Java, JSP, HTML, SQL, XML, and more. By selecting one item from the list, you can customize the language-specific syntax elements. For example, if you select JSP, you will see a category list of items such as EL, HTML, JSP, and XML elements. Once you have selected an item from the category list, you can change the font size, color, and other attributes using the options on the right (see Figure 2-8).

Highlighting

Through the Highlighting tab of the Fonts & Colors window, you can customize the foreground and background colors for elements that appear highlighted in various places in NetBean's Source Editor window. One possible use of this includes changing the color of the line numbers in the line number bar so they are easier to see at a glance. I like is to set the Code Folding Bar foreground to red so the lines that appear next to each method stand out and are easier to trace when I am scrolling quickly through a class.

Annotation Coloring

The Annotations tab of the Fonts & Colors window allows you to customize several items related to glyphs that appear in the glyph margin. The glyph margin is the gray vertical strip that appears in the Source Editor to the immediate left of any source code. If you select View ➤ Show Line Numbers, the line numbers are also displayed in the glyph margin. You can change the foreground and background color of annotations, as well as set the color of the Wave Underlined property for the Parser Annotation (Error) category. The Wave Underlined property pertains to the wavy line that appears under parser errors in your code, such as statements that will not compile.

■Tip If you really want a parser error to stand out, you can set the background color to black, the foreground color to green, and the Wave Underlined property to red. Once you have done this, it should not be too difficult to spot compilation errors.

Configuring Keymaps

Every good software tool should provide shortcut keys (also known as hotkeys). NetBeans is no exception. Since the majority of the work carried out in NetBeans involves typing code, it is obviously convenient to not need to take your hands off the keyboard very often. Many menu commands, actions, and tools can be activated using keyboard shortcuts. NetBeans categorizes a group of shortcuts as a *keymap*.

Keymaps can be configured in the Basic Options window. Select Tools ➤ Options and choose Keymap from the left pane in the Options window. The default set of keyboard shortcuts (the keymap) is named NetBeans. You can copy any of the existing keymaps by selecting one from the Profile drop-down list and clicking the Duplicate button. The new keymap profile can then be customized any way you wish.

To modify a specific keyboard shortcut, select the profile and locate which action you want to change. For example, you may want to change the shortcut used to compile a single file. To modify the shortcut, do the following:

1. Select the profile in the Keymap section of the Options window.

2. Click the plus sign next to the Build node.

3. Select the Compile File node under the Build node.

4. In the Shortcuts section at the bottom of the window, click the Remove button.

5. Click the Add button.

6. In the window that opens, press the key or keys that you want as the shortcut. The text representing those keys should be added to the Shortcut field.

7. Click the OK button.

NetBeans will prevent you from adding a duplicate keyboard shortcut. If the key or keys you pressed in the Shortcut pop-up window match another shortcut, after clicking the OK button, you will receive an error message. If the shortcut was successfully assigned to the action, it will be displayed in the Shortcuts list, as shown in Figure 2-9.

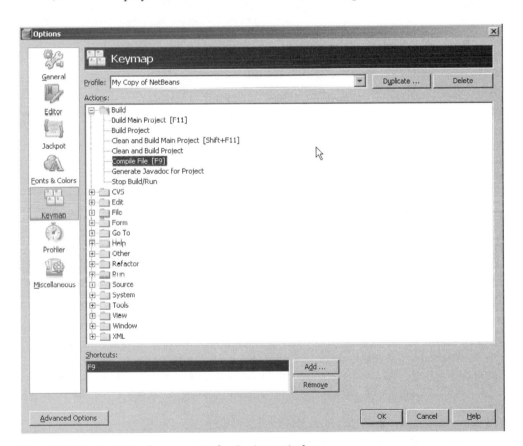

Figure 2-9. *Customizing keymaps in the Options window*

Setting Advanced Options

In the Basic Options section (select Tools ➤ Options), you'll find a button to access the Advanced Options window. From the Advanced Options section, you can customize a wider variety of features than is possible through the Basic Options section. The settings for toolbars and menu bars are covered here. Other Advanced Options settings, such as those for system and external tools, MIME, and file types, are covered in later chapters.

Menu Bars

NetBeans allows you to customize the system menu bars. In the Advanced Options section, select IDE Configuration ➤ Look and Feel ➤ Menu Bar. Here, you can rename the menu options such as File, Edit, View, and so on. If you really wanted to, you could rename the View menu to Look At Stuff.

By right-clicking menu names, you can delete menus, change menu-item ordering, and add menu separators. By right-clicking menu items, you can cut or copy a menu item and paste it into another menu.

A useful application of this feature is to reorder menu items to be grouped in a manner that makes more sense to you. For example, on the Refactoring menu, I have rearranged the items I use most often to appear on the top, followed by a separator and the rest of the items. I have also found this functionality useful on the Run and Window menus.

Toolbars

NetBeans also allows you to customize toolbars in much the same way as menu bars. You can create new toolbars, reorder the elements of a toolbar, and copy and paste elements from one toolbar to another. Being able to create custom toolbars is an important feature if you have installed a lot of plug-ins that are similar and want to group quick-access icons in one toolbar location.

Navigating the IDE

Once NetBeans has been installed and customized to your liking, it is time to start working on projects. But first, you need to become familiar with the general layout of the NetBeans IDE. It provides numerous windows that enable you to view specific items or pieces of data.

Projects Window

The Projects window displays all the currently opened projects. Projects are the main entry point for NetBeans to categorize and group files for use in an application. A project can be a Java Application, an EJB Module, a Web Application, a Mobile Class Library, a NetBeans Module Project, or another type. If you need to quickly jump to the Projects window, you can toggle to it by pressing Ctrl+1.

The layout and usage of elements in the Projects window is covered in more detail in the next chapter, where you'll create a Java Application project.

Files Window

The Files window provides a more normal file-based view of open projects. It contains the same information that is displayed in the Projects window, but is organized in a manner that may be more familiar to you. The files in a project are organized in a folder and file structure that represents how your project would look if you used a file explorer outside NetBeans to view it. If the Files window is not active, you can toggle to it by pressing Ctrl+2.

Runtime Window

The Runtime window is where you can find important resources such as HTTP servers, database servers, web services, DTD and XML schema catalogs, and processes. You can access the Runtime window by selecting Window ➤ Runtime or pressing Ctrl+5.

Navigator Window

The Navigator window provides a quick and easy view of a node that has been selected in the Projects window or Source Editor. It can display the methods, constructors, and fields in a class in a traditional list view or as an inheritance tree. For classes with numerous methods, this can be a convenient way to jump back and forth between methods or fields. You can display the Navigator window by selecting Navigator from the Window menu or by pressing Ctrl+7.

Source Editor

The Source Editor window is where you edit code and other files. This is where the "magic" happens. When you open files, they appear in the Source Editor window as a tabbed view. The files displayed in this window can be arranged in several different ways (more on this in the next chapter, where you'll create your first Java application). If you have a file already open in the Source Editor, you can quickly toggle to it by pressing Ctrl+0.

■Tip Pressing and holding Ctrl+Tab allows you to select and switch back and forth between open tabs in the Source Editor window, similar to how you can toggle between open applications in Windows using Alt+Tab.

Output Window

The Output window can display a variety of information. If you choose to build your project, compile a single file, or run a file that outputs text to the standard output or standard error stream, the information and results are displayed in the Output window. If the Output window is not displayed, you can select Window ➤ Output or press Ctrl+4 to open it.

Properties Window

The Properties window displays the attributes and properties of either the element currently selected in the Projects window or the item that is highlighted in the Source Editor. To see this in action, open the Properties window by selecting Window ➤ Properties or pressing Ctrl+Shift+7.

Once the Properties window opens, navigate through the Projects window and select a Java source file in an open project. The Properties window will display several attributes for the Java file, such as the filename, size, last modified date, and classpath.

Double-click the source file. Once it opens in the Source Editor, select any method by clicking the method name. Notice that the Properties window changes to display the attributes of the method, such as the method name, access modifier, parameters, return type, any exceptions, and Javadoc comments.

The Properties window can be very convenient when used in conjunction with the Projects window for quickly navigating file structures and viewing attributes.

Palette Window

The Palette window displays a context-sensitive list of elements that are useful for the current file you are editing in the Source Editor. You can open the Palette window by selecting Window ➤ Palette or pressing Ctrl+Shift+8. If you selected a JSP file, the Palette window would display HTML, JSP, JSTL, and database elements. If you open a Java Swing source file in the Source Editor, the Palette window is filled with visual elements to be used in Swing projects.

Summary

This chapter discussed topics such as installing NetBeans, updating features, and customizing internal properties.

We covered installing NetBeans into standard directory structures, associating the correct JDK, and installing the desired add-on packs. Performance considerations for the tool's startup time were also discussed. We reviewed several suggested settings that you may want to tweak to obtain optimal performance.

You can configure a variety of NetBeans settings based on your preferences. In this chapter, we also discussed how to use the Options window (accessible from the Tools main menu) to set these properties. Everything from code formatting, to fonts and colors, to menus and toolbars can be configured.

Lastly, we reviewed some of the windows that programmers will see and use most often. These windows provide various pieces of information and quick access to certain features. Understanding where and how to use them is critical to becoming an expert user of NetBeans.

CHAPTER 3

■■■

Creating a Java Project

In the NetBeans IDE, all Java development takes place within a project. Projects allow a developer to relate or group a set of application files together, whether those files are Java sources, XML configuration files, or bitmap images. NetBeans uses the Ant tool to internally compile and build its projects, as discussed in Chapter 14.

In this chapter, we will cover how to create and work with a Java application project.

Creating a Java Application

When you create a project in NetBeans, you are essentially telling the IDE what type of functionality and abilities you intend to use.

To start a new project, select File ➤ New Project. In the New Project window, you can choose from several categories of projects. The General category is selected by default. Two of the project types that are listed in this category are Java Application and Java Class Library. These are similar in nature, except that a Java Application project is intended to be a standard Java 2 Standard Edition (J2SE) application with a main class. A main class is the class that will execute when the project is run. A Java Class Library project is not intended to have a main class and will most likely be packaged into a Java Archive (JAR) file for distribution or usage in other applications. For this chapter's example, we will use the Java Application project type.

In the New Project window, select Java Application from the General category and click the Next button. In the following window, you will need to name the project and specify its file location. One minor annoyance is that as you name the project, the project folder is also given the same name. Some developers like to assign extended names to their project, but might not want the directory structure to reflect the long name. If you name your project Finance Department Report Viewer Application with a root project location of c:\projects, the path to your project will end up as c:\projects\Finance Department Report Viewer Application.

Tip If you want your project to have a nice long name, but not an identical directory structure, you can rename the project. When creating your project, start by picking a short name, such as FinanceDRV. When the project is created, you will see a path structure of c:\projects\FinanceDRV (assuming your root location is c:\projects). Then in the Projects window, right-click the project name and select Rename Project. Enter the full name you want to assign to the project. The project structure will stay the same, but the project name displayed in the Projects window will have the long name you originally wanted.

Once you have specified a project name and location, there are two additional features to note. The Set As Main Project check box allows you to designate this project as the entry point for the application in case your source code is split across multiple projects. The next option is the Create Main Class field. Enabling this check box directs NetBeans to autogenerate an empty main class once the project has been completed. More important, it also allows you to define the initial source package structure for the main class by typing com.mypackage.mysite. MainClass instead of just the name of the main class. The name of the project acts as the initial package name by default. You should change this field to reflect your desired package structure and the name of your main class, such as com.mycompany.projectname.MyMain.

After you have set the options to your liking, click the Finish button. The new Java Application project will now be displayed in the Projects window. The autogenerated source code for your main class will also be displayed in the Source Editor, as shown in Figure 3-1. You are now ready to start developing your Java code.

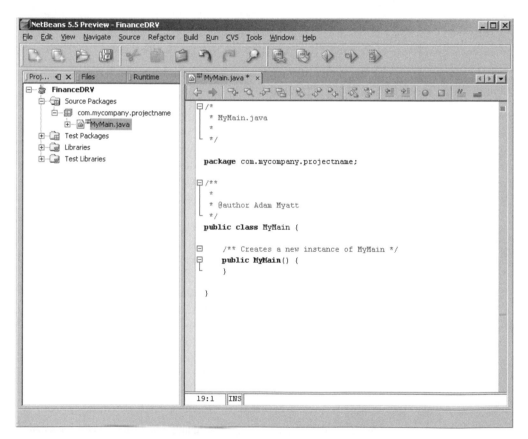

Figure 3-1. *Initial project window layout*

Working in the Projects Window

The Projects window is the primary location where you can view the files associated with your application. It is structured as a parent-child tree, where the parent node is the project and the child nodes are the categories into which NetBeans organizes the files.

For the Java Application project type, the files are sorted into four groups:

- Source Packages
- Test Packages
- Libraries
- Test Libraries

Source Packages

The Source Packages location is where you define the Java source code to be used in your application. Here, you can add and maintain the package statements you would normally use, such as com.mycompany.projectname. Adding packages is extremely easy. Right-click Source Packages and select New ➤ Java Package. In the New Java Package window, you can specify the name of the new package, such as com.yourcompany.product. Once you have decided on the name for your package, click the Finish button, and the new package name is added under Source Packages in the Projects window.

Tip Notice the icon next to the package name. If the icon is gray (which it is after you add a new package), then it is empty of classes. Once you have added at least one class into a package, the icon becomes orange. This small feature is useful once you have multiple hierarchies of package names.

A useful piece of functionality in the Projects window is the ability to view the elements of a class in an outline format. Click the plus sign next to the class name, and a node will appear that represents the class. Clicking the plus sign next to this node will display Fields, Constructors, Methods, and Bean Patterns nodes for the class, as shown in Figure 3-2.

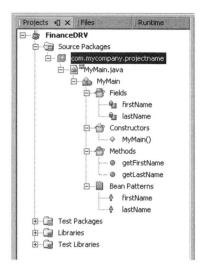

Figure 3-2. *Elements of the MyMain class*

Each of these categories allows you to view the corresponding elements in a grouping that is easy to understand. In addition to letting you quickly review the elements in the class without having to read code, these nodes also allow context-sensitive right-clicking to add new elements, as follows:

Fields: Right-clicking the Fields node brings up a menu that allows you to add a field. If you select that option, the Add New Field wizard starts. Using this wizard, you can enter the field's name, data type, modifier, access level, and select an initial value—all without having to actually modify the code in the Source Editor. If you do not want to use one of the data types in the Type drop-down list, you can type your own value, such as `java.util.HashMap` or `MyCustomObject`.

Constructors: Right-clicking the Constructors node displays a menu allowing you to add a new constructor or static initializer. The wizard also gives you the ability to add parameters and exceptions.

Methods: Right-clicking the Methods node brings up the Add New Method wizard. As you can probably guess, this wizard allows you to add methods to the class and specify input parameters, return types, exceptions, and access modifiers. Using the wizard, you can select or type the names of input parameters, return types, and exceptions.

Bean Patterns: If you were working on an EJB project, the Bean Patterns node might be useful. For a simple Java class file, it is useful if you want to add a class member and associated getter and setter methods. Right-click the Bean Patterns node and select Add ➤ Property. In the wizard that opens, you can specify the class member you want to add and specify that the related setter and getter methods for the class are also generated. This can save time if you will be adding several class members and know you will want the associated setter and getter methods.

Test Packages

The Test Packages node in the Projects window is nearly identical to the Source Packages node. However, the Test Packages node specifies the package structure for your application's test classes and JUnit tests. If you were to execute the project tests by going to the Run menu and selecting Test *MyProjectName*, the classes in the Test Packages node would be executed.

The source code for Test Packages is separate from the regular source code from the Source Packages. You can see the difference by right-clicking the project name and selecting Properties. Make sure the Sources option is selected. In the Sources section in the Project Properties window, you will see a section for defining Source Package folders and a different section for defining Test Package folders, as shown in Figure 3-3. This allows you to reference one or more locations for source and test packages.

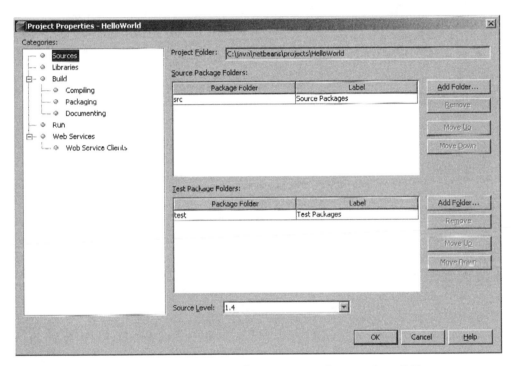

Figure 3-3. *Project Properties window specifying source and test package folders*

Libraries

The Libraries node in the Projects window is for defining class libraries that your application will use. If you need to use nonstandard libraries or classes from an external project, you can define them under the Libraries node. To add a JAR file to the libraries for your project, right-click the Libraries node and select Add JAR/Folder.

Test Libraries

Similar to the Libraries node, the Test Libraries node contains class files or JAR files that your project test classes need to reference. You can add files to your test libraries by right-clicking the Test Libraries node and selecting Add JAR/Folder. The JAR file for JUnit exists by default in the Test Libraries section.

Working in the Source Editor

The Source Editor window is where programmers will spend most of their time. This is where file contents are displayed when opened through the other windows or locations in NetBeans. The Source Editor displays all files, such as Java source files, XML files, text files, and so on. The Source Editor provides a different set of tools and functionality based on the file type that is currently displayed or active.

Displaying Files

To display a file in the Source Editor, double-click the file in the Projects or Files window. It should open in the Source Editor portion of the IDE, as shown in Figure 3-4.

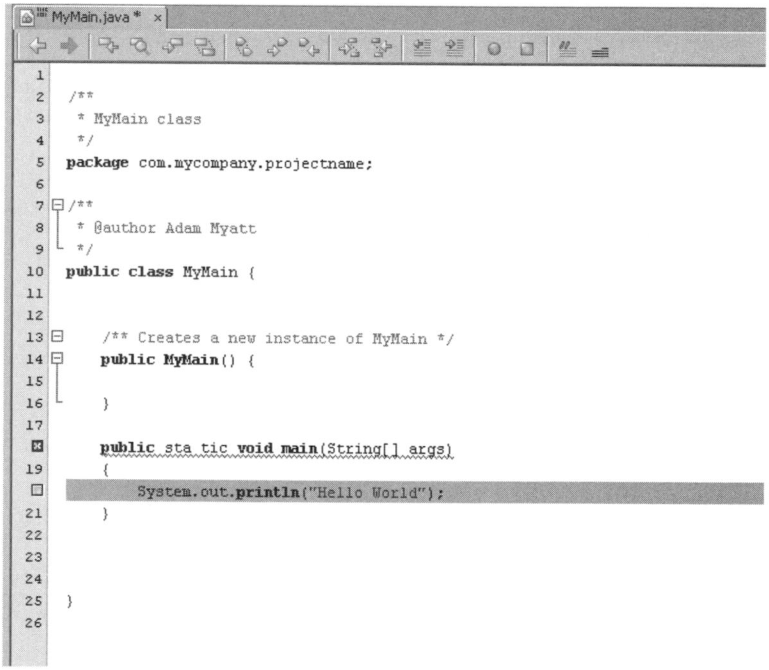

Figure 3-4. *A file in the Source Editor*

A toolbar at the top of the window allows for some convenient links to IDE functionality. It contains icons for searching for words, indenting code, and commenting lines of text. The icons displayed in this toolbar vary depending on the type of file that is displayed. The same features can also be activated by viewing the corresponding menu items on the Edit, Navigate, and Source menus. Most of the features have keyboard shortcuts, which are noted on those main menus.

Line Numbers

In the Source Editor, line numbers are displayed along the left column. The line numbers provide a great way to track where certain pieces of code are, as well as provide a quick way to trace the location of exceptions that are thrown. If the line numbers are not displayed, you can enable them by selecting View ➤ Show Line Numbers.

Code Folding

The next feature in the Source Editor to notice is code folding. For each section of Javadoc comments and each method name, notice the minus icon and the line extending below it. This denotes a piece of text that can be folded, or hidden. The obvious question from any user new to a modern Java IDE is "Why do I need this?"

If you have ever worked with a very long Java source file, you can start to see where I'm going with this. All too often, to edit code, I have needed to scroll up and down through a file between two methods. Every time you edit source code, you don't want to be rearranging where methods are in a file just to make it easier to work with them. With code folding, you can hide large blocks of code that you do not need to see.

Code folding can be enabled or disabled depending on your personal preference. To disable code folding in NetBeans, select Tools ➤ Options ➤ Editor. On the top of the General tab is a check box labeled Use Code Folding. Uncheck this box and click OK. The code folding lines and minus icons will disappear from the Source Editor.

In the same section in the Basic Options, you can also configure the default folding properties of Java source files. Below the Use Code Folding check box is a section called Collapse by Default. Here, you can enable folding for methods, inner classes, imports, Javadoc comments, and initial class comments. I typically enable code folding by default for methods and Javadoc comments, but leave the rest of the options disabled. This is useful when you open a lot of Java source files and know exactly which method you need to find and edit.

If you have enabled code folding, several menu items in the IDE can be useful. Once you have opened a Java source file with all the methods and Javadoc folded, select View ➤ Code Folds. In this submenu are options for expanding all sections that are folded (Expand All), collapsing all sections that can be folded (Collapse All), expanding or collapsing just Javadoc comments, and expanding or collapsing all Java code blocks. This allows a great deal of flexibility when working with code folding in a file and saves you from manually scrolling through the file and collapsing each method.

■**Tip** The best shortcuts to remember when working with code folding are Ctrl+Shift+– (minus) to collapse all folds and Ctrl+Shift++ (plus) to expand all folds. If the cursor is inside a method, section of Javadoc, or other element where cold folding applies, you can also press the Ctrl+key combination to collapse or expand just that code block.

Current Line Highlighting

A trivial but useful feature of the NetBeans Source Editor is current line highlighting. The line that contains the cursor is lightly highlighted, so you always know exactly which line is being edited. You can see this by clicking anywhere in a Java source file and then using the up and down arrow keys to navigate through the file.

Code Syntax Error Highlighting

In my humble opinion, code syntax error highlighting might just be the greatest feature of modern Java IDE tools. As you type Java code and progress line by line, the IDE scans the text of your source code in the background to determine if it will compile, and if not, shows the possible errors and warnings.

For example, if you were to open a Java source file, type `System.out.printlnnn("Hi");`, and press the Enter key, you would see a red wavy line appear under that piece of code. If you position the mouse over the line with the red wavy underline, a window will pop up with the message "cannot find symbol, symbol : method printlnnn(java.lang.String)."

Why is this one of the greatest features? Because it allows you to immediately spot code syntax errors, see exactly where in the code they occur, and get a helpful message telling you why the error exists. You do not have to wait until you compile the file and read the compiler output to discover that there is a problem.

Annotation Glyphs and the Error Stripe

The annotation glyph margin (also called the glyph gutter) and the error stripe are two incredible features in NetBeans that allow a developer to perform fast error identification and resolution.

On the left side of the Source Editor, small icons, or glyphs, can appear in a vertical gray bar or in place of line numbers, if the line number feature is enabled. For example, in Figure 3-4, glyphs are displayed instead of the line numbers for lines 18 and 20. The annotation glyph margin displays icons denoting the following:

- Errors

- Breakpoints for debugging

- Bookmarks

- Compiler warnings

- Suggestions

- Tasks

- Other code syntax notifications

The icons that appear in the glyph margin allow you to mouse over and read a brief description of the identified issue.

On the far-right side of the Source Editor window is a slim, vertical gray bar, which is the error stripe. The error stripe goes hand in hand with the glyph margin and code syntax highlighting. The error stripe displays small, color-coded rectangles for specific issues that correspond to the glyphs in the glyph margin. The main difference is that as you scroll through a long file, the glyph margin and line numbers on the left scroll with you, while the error stripe bar on the right stays fixed. Displayed on the error stripe are all syntax errors and warnings, highlighted items, breakpoints, and bookmarks. You can instantly get a view of any errors and mouse over them to read about the error. Another nice feature is the ability to click the rectangles in the error stripe and immediately jump to that line of code in the Source Editor.

Arranging Files in the Source Editor

The Source Editor allows you to arrange files in many different ways, giving you the maximum flexibility in working with files. The default viewing option for files is a tabbed approach, where all the files open in the same window with the names of each file appearing in a tab.

A different option is dual file editing, where one file is displayed in the left portion of the Source Editor and another file is displayed in the right portion, as shown in Figure 3-5. I use this occasionally when I am writing code that is subclassing another class. I display the superclass on the right and the subclass on the left. This way, I can line up method implementations and compare code, without having to repeatedly toggle between two tabs.

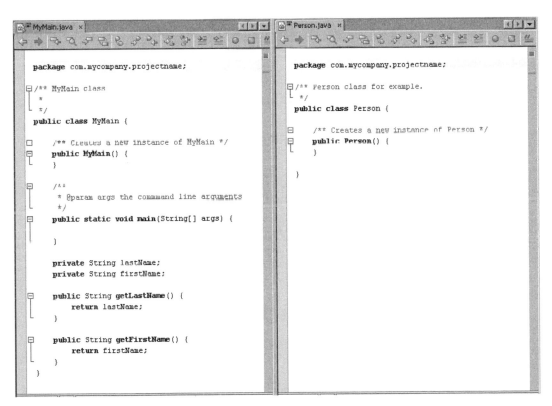

Figure 3-5. *Dual window file display using left and right panels*

An additional method for displaying files in the Source Editor is top-bottom. Sometimes I need to edit one file and find myself constantly scrolling back and forth between two methods. Code folding comes in handy here, but may not be convenient enough. If I could only view the same file in two places at once, my life would be much easier.

You can do this in the NetBeans Source Editor by right-clicking the filename tab and selecting Clone Document. A second instance of the file will open in the Source Editor. Click and hold the filename tab for the second file, and move your mouse to the lower half of the Source Editor. A highlighted outline of the file should be visible. Once you have it positioned correctly, release the mouse button. The result will be a split screen, as shown in Figure 3-6.

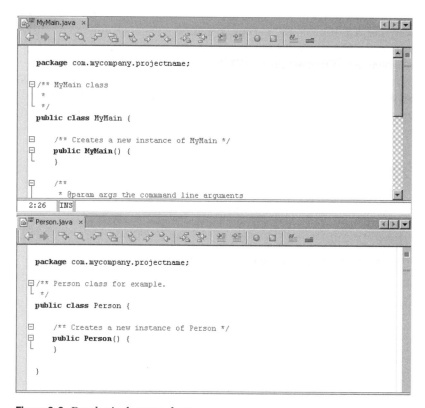

Figure 3-6. *Dual window top-bottom*

Working in the Files Window

As discussed in Chapter 2, the Files window displays the same data as the Projects window, but in a more traditional file and folder view. In Figure 3-7, you can see a set of project files displayed in the Files window. The Files window shows a src folder for the Source Packages, a test folder for the Test Packages, and an nbproject folder, which contains the internal project-related settings NetBeans uses.

Now that you have seen the traditional method of creating a Java project and how it is laid out in NetBeans, let's look at other ways to start a project in NetBeans.

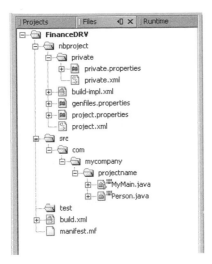

Figure 3-7. *Files window layout*

Importing Projects and Code

Not all projects in NetBeans are *new* projects. Most developers have an existing set of projects and source code that they will need to import and use in the NetBeans environment.

Creating a Java Project from Existing Sources

When you import an existing project, the New Project wizard allows you to specify multiple source and test folders. Typically, if your project spans multiple source folders, you may want to consider creating multiple projects and setting dependencies between them to keep your code structured cleanly and efficiently.

To begin the process, select File ➤ New Project. In the New Project window, make sure the General category is selected. In the list of Project Types, choose the Java Project with Existing Sources option.

Note If your existing project also has an Ant build script, you will most likely want to select Java Project with Existing Ant Script for the Project Type option.

You will then need to specify the name and location of the new project, and indicate if you want to set this as the main project. In the following window, you can select the source and test packages, as shown in Figure 3-8. Once you have picked the existing files from your project, click the Finish button. Your new project will be generated and opened in the Projects window in the IDE.

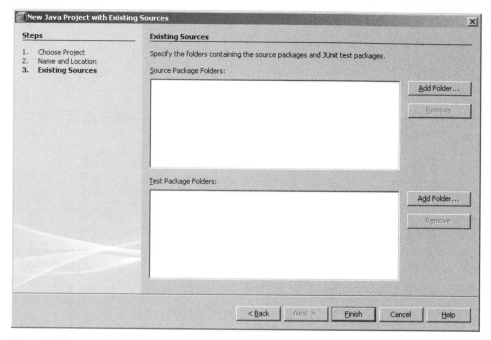

Figure 3-8. *Importing a Java project with existing sources*

Importing an Existing Project from Eclipse

If you used the Java IDE plug-in from Eclipse to develop your project, this is the section for you. NetBeans has a plug-in that offers a wizard for converting Eclipse projects into NetBeans projects. It is not installed by default (as of the time of this writing), so you'll need to download it using the Update Center, as described in Chapter 2.

To use the Import Eclipse Project wizard, select New ➤ Import Project ➤ Eclipse Project. The window that opens provides two options, as shown in Figure 3-9:

- The first option asks you to specify the Eclipse workspace from where you will import projects. If you traditionally develop stand-alone projects with no dependencies, you will want to select this option.

- The second option asks if you want to import project ignoring any project dependencies that may have been established in Eclipse.

Click the Browse button and select the folder that represents the Eclipse workspace where the Eclipse projects reside on your file system. Once you have selected the workspace location and clicked the Next button, the wizard will display the recognized Eclipse projects that you will be able to import. The next action you will need to take is to check the check box next to each project you wish to import into NetBeans, as shown in Figure 3-10.

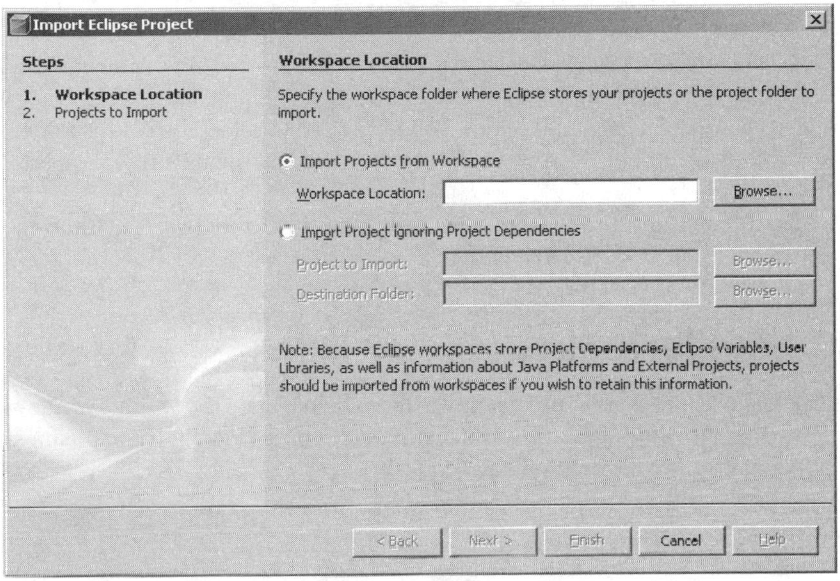

Figure 3-9. *Importing a project from Eclipse*

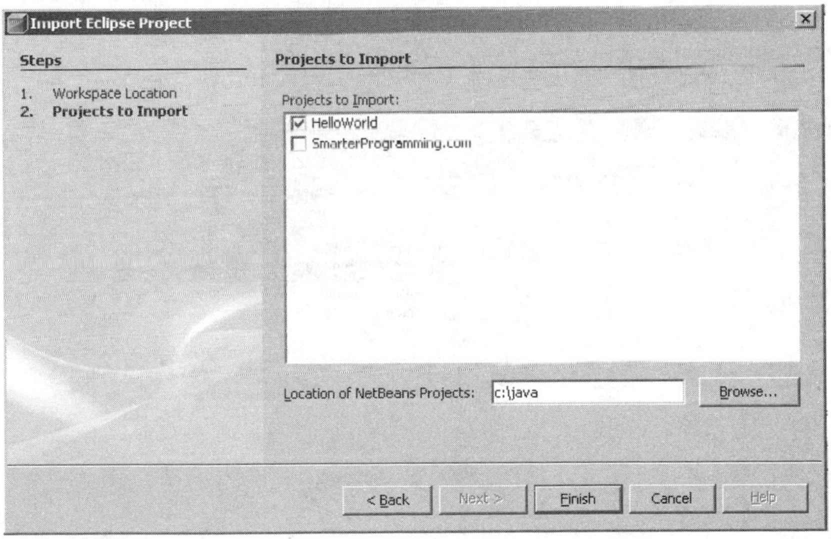

Figure 3-10. *List of Eclipse projects available to import*

At the bottom of the Projects to Import window, you will need to specify the location of NetBeans projects. This location is where the Eclipse projects being imported will end up on your file system. Once you are ready, click the Finish button.

The import tool will process the project files, NetBeans will scan the classpath briefly, and your old Eclipse projects will now appear as regular NetBeans projects in the Projects window.

Importing an Existing Project from JBuilder

Importing JBuilder 2005 projects is even easier than importing Eclipse projects. After you have installed the JBuilder import tool through the Update Center, select File ➤ Import Project ➤ JBuilder2005 Java Project. In the wizard that opens, you only need to select the source folder the JBuilder project resides in and the destination folder where the NetBeans project will be imported.

This plug-in currently supports projects from JBuilder 2005, but other Java IDE import plug-ins exist and can be installed for use in NetBeans.

Building HelloWorld.java

You have now learned how install NetBeans, customize the IDE, navigate the various windows in the IDE, create projects, and import existing projects. Now it's time to get down to business. Let's start using NetBeans for what is intended: writing code.

Adding Java Files to a Project

In your Java Application project, you can add Java source files in several different ways. Select File menu ➤ New File (or press Ctrl+N) to start the New File wizard.

Since you want to create a Java class file, select the category Java Classes and the file type Java Class, as shown in Figure 3-11. Before clicking the Next button, make sure you have selected the correct project from the Project drop-down list at the top of the window.

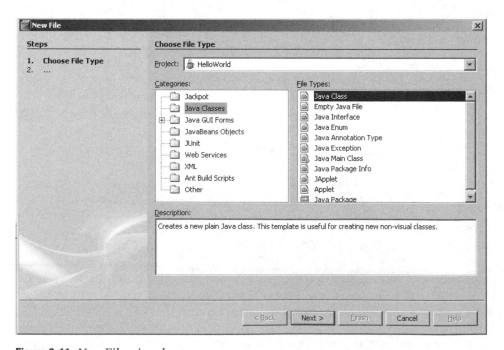

Figure 3-11. *New File wizard*

Next, the wizard will prompt you for several fields related to the new class. In the Class Name field, enter HelloWorld. This will be the name of the new class and the name of the Java source file. The Project field should be already filled in and uneditable. For the Location field, Source Packages should be selected by default, but you can change this setting to Test Packages if you want this class to be a test for your project.

The last field—one of the most important—is the Package field. This field allows you to specify in which package hierarchy you want the Java source file to belong. I strongly advise against using the default package (used when no package name is specified). If you leave the package name blank, the wizard warns you with a yellow warning icon and message at the bottom of the window.

Once you are finished specifying the class file options, click the Finish button. The new class you have just created is immediately displayed in the Source Editor. Notice the code that was automatically created for you, as shown in Listing 3-1.

Listing 3-1. *Automatically Generated Class File*

```
package com.mycompany.product;

/**
 *
 * @author Adam Myatt
 *
 */
public class HelloWorld
{
    /** Creates a new instance of HelloWorld */
    public HelloWorld()
    {
    }

}
```

The New File wizard not only generated the empty file, but also created the default constructor and some Javadoc comments. If you had selected a File Type of Java Main Class instead of Java Class, the wizard would have also generated an empty Main method for the file. This seems trivial, but can save you time as you create a lot of Java classes.

An alternate method of creating new Java classes is through the Projects window. You can right-click the name of any package under the Source Packages node and select New ➤ Java Class. In the New File wizard, the Package field is already set to the name of the package you originally right-clicked.

Compiling and Running the Project

Once you have created your Java source files, you need to compile and run them to see how they function. In your HelloWorld file, add a Main method, if you haven't already done so, and enter the following within it:

```
System.out.println("Hello World!");
```

If there are no compile errors visible in the error stripe in the Source Editor, then your file can be compiled (and already has been in the background).

Select Run ➤ Run File ➤ Run HelloWorld.java. The Output window will appear, and the compilation output text will be displayed. You should see the text "Hello World!" as shown in Figure 3-12.

If the class you want to run is set to the main class for your project, you can also select Run ➤ Run Main Project or press F6.

To build the entire project, select Build ➤ Build Main Project or press F11. This will compile all the files in the project and package them into a distributable JAR file. This will be covered in more detail in Chapter 14, which describes managing compilation and projects with Ant.

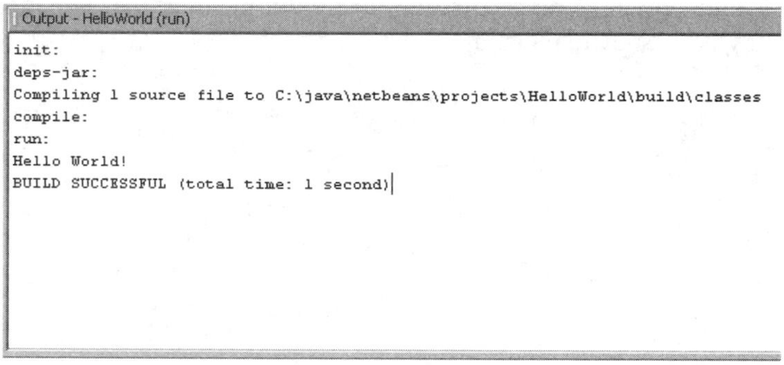

```
Output - HelloWorld (run)
init:
deps-jar:
Compiling 1 source file to C:\java\netbeans\projects\HelloWorld\build\classes
compile:
run:
Hello World!
BUILD SUCCESSFUL (total time: 1 second)
```

Figure 3-12. *The compilation and run statements in the Output window*

Summary

In the chapter, we covered how to create a *very* simple Java project. You started to work with the various windows, editors, and tabs. You also saw it is possible to import projects and code from various other Java IDE tools. Throughout the rest of the book, we will expand on this basic project and cover many issues regarding working with projects, such as Concurrent Versioning System (CVS), running tests, and more.

CHAPTER 4

■ ■ ■

Creating a Web Application Project

Several options are available in NetBeans for creating and working with web applications. The first and most traditional is the Web Application project type. Prior to NetBeans 5.5, this was the only type of web project you could use. NetBeans 5.5 added support for a new project type called Visual Web Application, which is covered in the next chapter.

This chapter focuses on the Web Application project type, which should be familiar to web developers. It supports HTML, Cascading Style Sheets (CSS), JSP, Servlets, Struts, and other frameworks. NetBeans provides various wizards and tools to make working with your web project files easier, as you will learn in this chapter.

Creating a Web Application

To create a new web application, select File ➤ New Project. In the New Project window, choose the Web category. You will see the following project type choices:

- Visual Web Application

- Web Application

- Web Application with Existing Sources

- Web Application with Existing Ant Script

As mentioned at the beginning of the chapter, the first type, Visual Web Application, will be discussed in Chapter 5. The second type is the one we will focus on in this chapter. The third and fourth types are the same as the Web Application type. They differ only in how the project is created.

Follow these steps to create a Web Application project:

1. In the New Project window, select Web Application from the list, and then click the Next button to continue. As you can see in Figure 4-1, several options are available when creating a Web Application project.

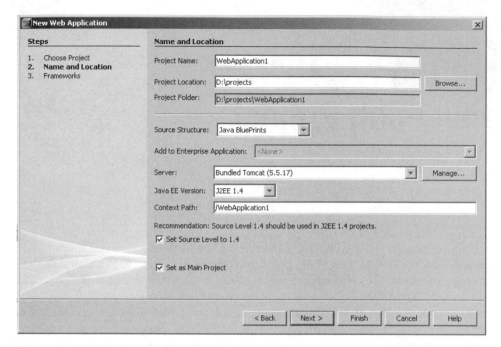

Figure 4-1. *Web Application properties in the New Web Application wizard*

2. The first few items to set in the wizard are the project name and location. Enter a value in the Project Name field. It will be appended to the value in the Project Location field to create what is displayed in the third field, Project Folder. You will want to pick a generic location for the Project Location field. In Figure 4-1, you can see that I selected the folder D:\projects.

■**Tip** If you want your project to have a long meaningful name, but not an identical directory structure, you can do that. When creating your project, start by picking a short name, such as surveytool. When the project is created, you will see a path structure like c:\projects\surveytool (assuming your root location was c:\projects). Then in the Projects window, right-click the project name and select Rename Project. Enter the full name you want to assign the project, such as MyCustomer Survey Tool. The project structure will stay the same, but the project name displayed in the Projects window will have the long name you originally wanted.

---

3. Set the Source Structure field. This tells NetBeans which file and directory structure to use when generating the initial web application. The drop-down list contains two options:

- Java Blueprints is basically the Sun recommendation for structuring a web application, especially if it is going to be deployed to the Sun Java System Application Server.

- Jakarta is the suggested format for web applications that will be deployed to the Tomcat application server.

Note The Source Structure options are only suggestions; they are not requirements.

The only real difference between the two directory structures is that the Java Blueprints structure places a conf directory under the root src directory. The Jakarta structure places the same conf directory at the same root level as the src directory.

4. Set the Server field to specify to which application server you will deploy the project. This can easily be changed through the Project Properties window later, so don't panic if you feel you've selected the wrong server. The options that appear in the Server field drop-down list may vary depending on the NetBeans bundle you downloaded and installed. For the most part, NetBeans comes bundled with Tomcat. If you installed the Enterprise Pack, the Sun Java System Application Server will also appear in the list. If the server you wish to use does not appear in the list, click the Manage button to use the Server Manager tool. See the "Defining Java Application Servers" section later in this chapter for details on setting up an application server.

5. Fill in the Context Path field to define the URL where your application can be accessed once deployed to the application server.

6. Set the other fields to specify the Java Enterprise Edition (EE) version of the application, the source level, and that the new project should be the main project.

7. Once you have set the configuration options for your application, click the Next button.

8. In the next window, the New Project wizard prompts you to add a framework to the web application. This list will vary depending on which modules you have installed and activated. By default, you should see JavaServer Faces and Struts in the list. This chapter will focus on using the Struts framework. Using the JavaServer Faces framework is discussed in the next chapter. Click the check box next to the Struts option, and you should see additional fields appear in the bottom half of the window, as shown in Figure 4-2.

9. The Struts Configuration section allows you to set the main high-level properties that the Struts framework will use for your web application. You can set the Action URL Pattern field, which is initialized by default to *.do. This is the pattern that your web application will use to map file URLs to Struts actions, as defined in the Struts configuration files. Before continuing, you should also modify the package structure in the Application Resource field to conform to the Java package structure your application will use.

10. Once you're satisfied with the settings, click the Finish button to generate the web application.

Once the new web application has been created, you can browse the nodes in the Projects window.

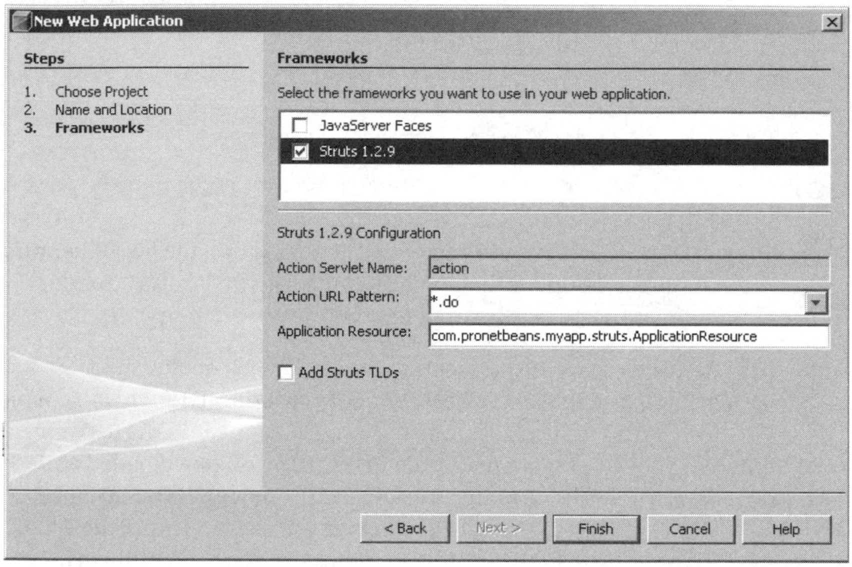

Figure 4-2. *Specifying the framework and properties for the Java web application*

Navigating the Web Application Project

Like every other project type, Web Application projects are structured as a set of parent-child nodes with special designations. For the Web Application project type, the files are sorted into the following nodes:

- Web Pages

- Configuration Files

- Server Resources

- Source Packages

- Test Packages

- Libraries

- Test Libraries

This structure is how NetBeans arranges the files. The Source Packages, Test Packages, Libraries, and Test Libraries items should look familiar. These are the same as a regular Java Application or Class Library project, as discussed in the previous chapter. They contain the Java source files, the source of the test files, any project libraries, and any test-specific libraries, respectively. The new nodes you have not seen before are Web Pages, Configuration Files, and Server Resources.

Web Pages

The Web Pages node in the Projects window defines where the actual web content should be located. This is where you can add HTML, JSP, CSS, images, and folders to your application.

If you look at the project structure in the Files window, you will see a top-level directory named web. This directory is where the content in the Web Pages node is located.

You will see that it contains a sample index.jsp file, as well as the standard WEB-INF directory. If you look in the WEB-INF directory, you will also find a web.xml file and the struts-config.xml file.

Configuration Files

Configuration Files is a special node that does not represent an actual folder in the project structure. The items that appear under this node are categorized as items that you would normally need access to when making configuration changes to the application. It also contains the deployment descriptor for the web application.

The Configuration Files node contains the web.xml, struts-config.xml, and other project configuration files. These are the same files that appear under the WEB-INF directory in the Web Pages node.

■**Note** The files under the Configuration Files node are not copies of the files under other nodes. They simply represent an alternative method for viewing and accessing them. If you find it confusing, you don't even need to use the Configuration Files node.

If you have captured any database schemas, you will be able to view the schema file under this node as well. You will learn how to do so in Chapter 18, which covers the NetBeans database tools.

Server Resources

The Server Resources node is primarily used with Enterprise projects; however, there are a few uses for it in Web Application projects. Several files and objects are placed under this node after they have been created.

If you define a JDBC Resource, JDBC Connection Pool, JMS Resource, Persistence Resource, or JavaMail Resource, it will be listed under the Server Resources node. This is handy, since it gives you quick access to related resources. The items under the Server Resources node appear under the Setup directory in the Files window.

Adding Web Application Files

NetBeans allows you to add numerous types of files to a standard Web Application project. The New File window recognizes some of the file types and provides wizards that allow you to set several options specific to that file type. HTML, XML, and other file types can be added to almost any type of project type in NetBeans, as described in the following sections.

Adding HTML Files

To add a new HTML file, right-click the Web Pages node in the Projects window and select New. On the New submenu, the top option is File/Folder, with several suggested file types below it. The HTML file type should appear on the list. Select it to start the New HTML File wizard, as shown in Figure 4-3. If HTML is not listed on the New submenu, select File/Folder. In the New File wizard window, select the Web category, and the list of file types on the right of the window will contain the HTML item. Select the HTML file type and click the Next button to see the options shown in Figure 4-3.

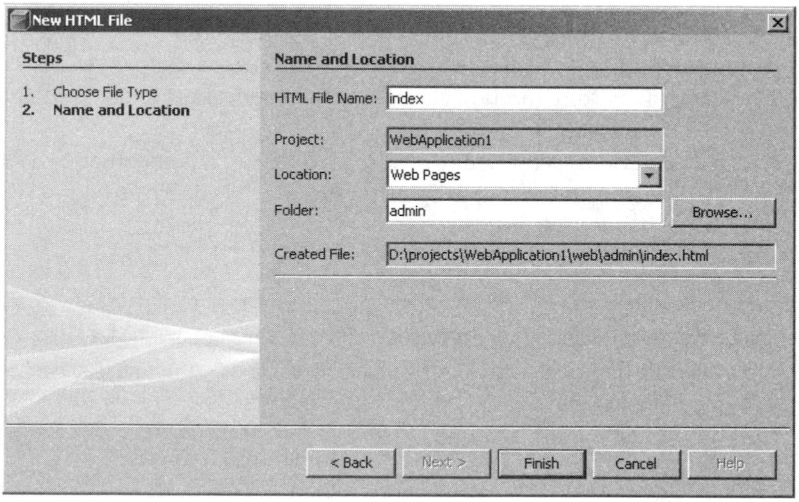

Figure 4-3. *Adding a new HTML file*

The file created is shown in Figure 4-4. The file contains some bare-bones HTML content. You can work with the HTML file in the Source Editor, similar to how you can work with a Java source file. The Source Editor provides basic syntax coloring and code-completion capabilities.

You can type an HTML element such as <td> and use the code completion tool to add the attributes. For example, after typing <td on, you can activate code completion by pressing Ctrl+spacebar. Options such as onclick, ondblclick, and onkeydown appear in the list. This capability can save you time coding HTML tags, as well as remind you of the attributes of each tag. Code completion is discussed in more detail in Chapter 10.

As shown in Figure 4-4, the Palette window displays some HTML-specific items. You can drag-and-drop these items from the Palette window and add them into the HTML document. NetBeans does not provide a What You See Is What You Get (WYSIWYG) editor like Dreamweaver. However, you can use the components in the Palette window, and NetBeans will provide some utility wizards.

Note If the Palette window is not visible, select Window ➤ Palette or press Ctrl+Shift+8.

Figure 4-4. *The new HTML file in the Source Editor*

For example, if you add a Table component from the Palette, you will see a dialog box like the one shown in Figure 4-5. Here, you can enter the number of rows, number of columns, border size, width, cell spacing, and cell padding. If you select the Form component, the wizard will prompt you for the form name, action, method, and encoding, as shown in Figure 4-6. You could manually type these fields into the HTML code in the Source Editor, but the wizards save time, and you do not have to remember the exact attribute names (something that is increasingly difficult the more programming/scripting languages you learn). The Palette window is discussed in more detail in Chapter 9.

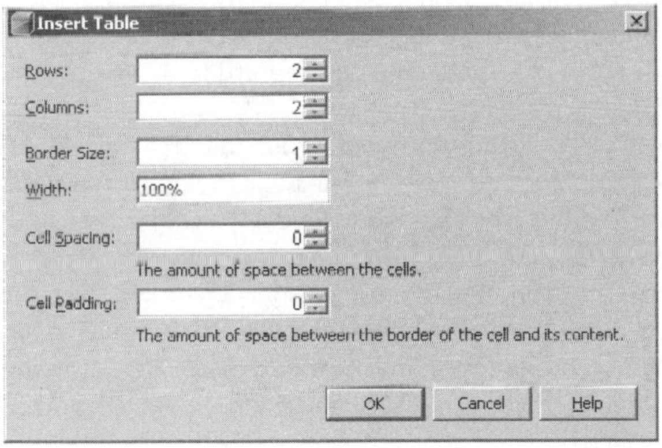

Figure 4-5. *Prompt for specifying table attributes*

Note You cannot record a macro using the HTML component wizards. I initially thought it would be convenient to use the wizards to generate some sections of useful HTML to be later recalled by a macro. Unfortunately, the HTML component wizards do not register during the macro-recording session.

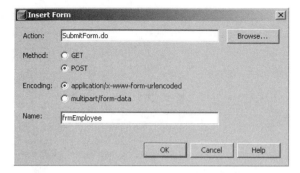

Figure 4-6. *Prompt for specifying form attributes*

Adding CSS Files

Out of the box, NetBeans provides only basic support for CSS files. You can use the New File wizard to add a CSS file to your project, but it is treated like a plain text file. You'll see some basic syntax coloring of the tokens that appear in the file, but there are no editors or visual tools to edit it.

If you are developing a web application, as a best practice, you make frequent use of CSS files. Any tools that can assist you in working with them are very valuable.

When you install the Visual Web Pack (as described in the next chapter), it provides some additional CSS support. You do *not* need to be working with a Visual Web Application project to use the improved CSS tool support. You can also use it in Web Application projects, as described here. In the near future, the CSS tools will most likely be a standard part of NetBeans, rather than a separate module.

To add a new CSS file to your current Web Application project, select File ➤ New File. In the New File window, select the XML category, choose the Cascading Style Sheet file type, and then click Next. Enter the filename. Do *not* add the .css extension. Select the folder in which the file will be located, and then click Finish.

The CSS file will be added to your project and will open in the Source Editor window. The file contains a comment block that lists the name of the file, the date it was originally created, the author, and a sample explanation of the purpose of the file. It also contains a TODO directive suggesting the initial text in the file be modified. You can see this listed in the To Do window by selecting Window ➤ To Do or by pressing Ctrl+6.

Figure 4-7 shows the CSS file is the Source Editor with the comments removed. The toolbar along the top of the window includes two CSS-specific options added by the Visual Web Pack: Create Rule and Style Builder.

■**Tip** In the NetBeans IDE, you can see the function for each icon by placing the mouse over it and reading the tooltip that is displayed.

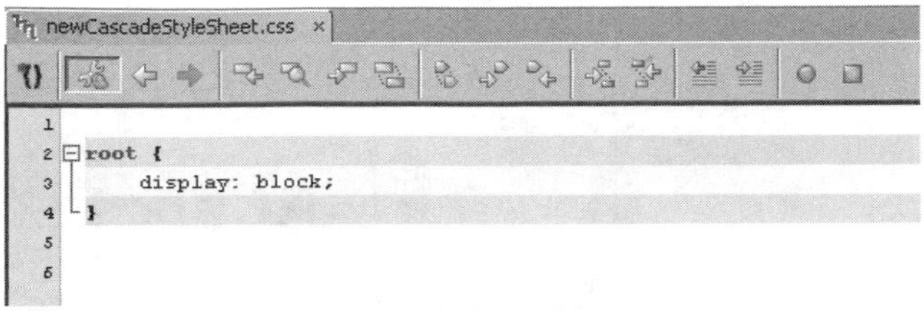

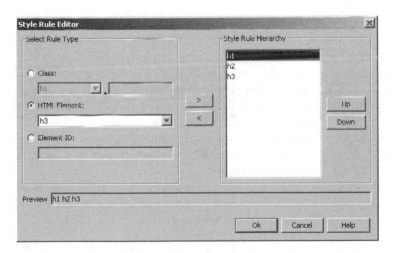

Figure 4-7. *Default content in new CSS file*

The Create Rule button is on the far-left side of the toolbar (with two curly brackets and a green asterisk). When you click the Create Rule icon, the Style Rule Editor dialog box appears. It allows you to define a new style class or element definition. You can use the Style Rule Editor to define a set of styles for an HTML element. The dialog box provides a drop-down list of HTML elements and allows you to choose multiple HTML elements. To add elements to the Style Rule Hierarchy list on the right, click the > button. For example, in Figure 4-8, the <h1>, <h2>, and <h3> elements were chosen from the HTML Element drop-down list and added to the Style Rule Hierarchy list. Once you have created a Style Rule Hierarchy list to your liking, click the OK button. The new style rule is then added to the CSS file, but does not contain any style definitions, like this:

```
h1 h2 h3 {

}
```

Figure 4-8. *The Style Rule Editor dialog box*

Once you have created the empty style rule, you need to define styles. You can do so manually in the text displayed in the Source Editor, or you can use the Style Builder. The second icon in the Source Editor toolbar is for the Style Builder. The icon should be selected by default, and the Style Builder window should be visible along the bottom of the screen, as shown in Figure 4-9. (This may vary slightly depending on how many windows you have open at the time.)

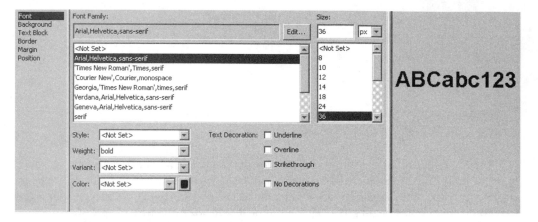

Figure 4-9. *Editing styles in the Style Builder*

The Style Builder provides a graphical interface for editing styles. You can use it to set font attributes, margins, borders, background attributes, and more. To use the Style Builder for a specific element in a CSS file, place the cursor anywhere inside the corresponding style. As you select different properties from the list, the preview pane on the right will show you what the text will look like with the style applied. (If you are defining a style for a nontext HTML element, the preview pane will not display anything.)

As you set the various properties for the style, you will see the text in the Source Editor change to correspond to your selections. Once you are finished, you can close the CSS file from the Source Editor window. The Style Builder will also close.

Adding Deployment Descriptors

Another important part of a Java web application is the deployment descriptor (the web.xml file). NetBeans provides an easy-to-use visual editor for working with the web.xml file. It helps ensure that the file does not contain syntax errors, since a web application often cannot function without a correct web.xml file.

The visual editor interface helps by allowing you to enter the various properties and settings without having to remember the precise tag name for the XML elements. It also helps enforce that the XML tags appear in the file in the suggested order.

The web.xml file for a Web Application project can be found in the Projects window under the Configuration Files node. Double-click the file to open it in the Source Editor with the special NetBeans interface. The visual editor neatly divides the web.xml file into the following sections:

- General

- Servlets

- Filters

- Pages

- References

- Security

- XML

Each section in the list represents a category where you can add and edit elements directly to the XML file without having to know the proper XML syntax.

If you create a Web Application project and add the Struts framework, NetBeans typically adds code to the web.xml file to define the Struts action servlet and several related parameters. The Servlets section, shown in Figure 4-10, allows you convenient access to the parameters without having to edit code such as this:

```
<servlet>
    <servlet-name>action</servlet-name>
    <servlet-class>org.apache.struts.action.ActionServlet</servlet-class>
    <init-param>
        <param-name>config</param-name>
        <param-value>/WEB-INF/struts-config.xml</param-value>
    </init-param>
    <init-param>
        <param-name>debug</param-name>
        <param-value>2</param-value>
    </init-param>
    <init-param>
        <param-name>detail</param-name>
        <param-value>2</param-value>
    </init-param>
    <load-on-startup>2</load-on-startup>
</servlet>
<servlet-mapping>
    <servlet-name>action</servlet-name>
    <url-pattern>*.do</url-pattern>
</servlet-mapping>
```

The other tabs in the deployment descriptor visual editor allow you to edit the other parameters in the file. If you are not used to working with the visual editor and want to directly edit the XML, click the XML tab to see the XML content of the deployment descriptor in the Source Editor window. Any changes made directly to the XML will be reflected immediately in the other sections (General, Servlets, Filters, and so on).

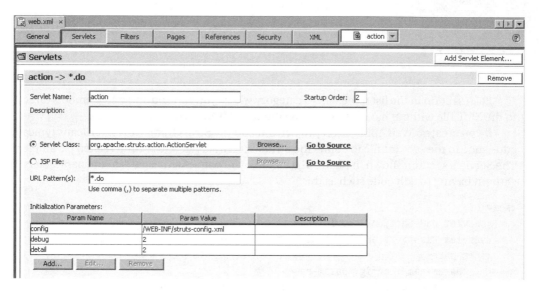

Figure 4-10. *Editing the Servlets section of the web.xml file in the NetBeans visual editor*

If you look closely at Figure 4-10 (or open a web.xml file in NetBeans), you will see a code folding bar extending down the page. This allows you to collapse the servlet definition for ease of viewing in case there are multiple servlets defined in the file. (See Chapter 3 for more information about the NetBeans code folding feature.)

You can add new servlet definitions by clicking the Add Servlet Element button in the upper-right corner of the editor window. You can set servlet variables like the servlet name, description, class, startup order, and initialization parameters.

Adding JSP Files

If you are developing a web application, then you need to know how to work with JSP files in a NetBeans project. You can add a JSP file to a web application in the same way that you add any other new file.

Right-click the project name in the Projects window and select New ➤ File/Folder from the context menu. In the New File window, select the Web category, choose the JSP file type, and then click the Next button. The Name and Location window includes several properties you may set for the new JSP file, as shown in Figure 4-11. Specify the JSP filename, the folder it will be located in, and what type of JSP file should be generated.

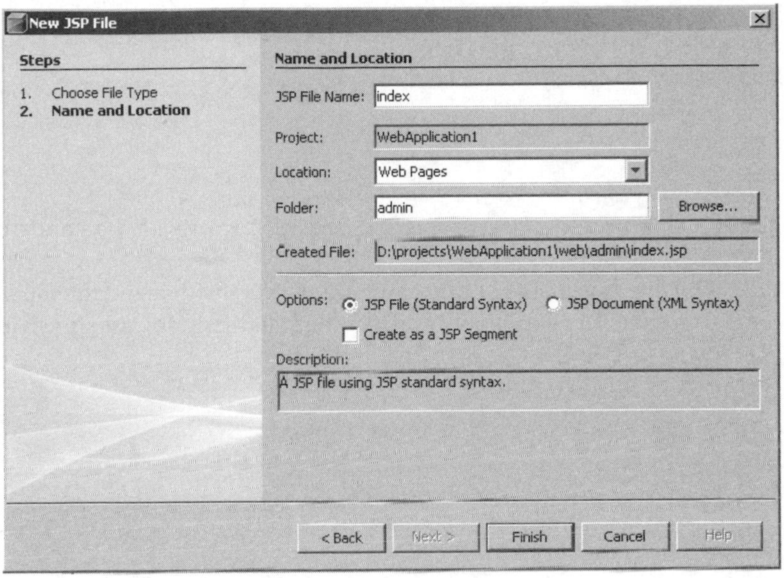

Figure 4-11. *Properties that need to be set when creating a new JSP file*

The Options field allows you to select either a JSP File (Standard Syntax) or a JSP Document (XML Syntax). The Create As a JSP Segment check box lets you modify each of those file types so it is created as a JSP segment (page fragment) that will be statically included by other JSP files. If you create a new JSP page using the standard syntax, it will look like the following:

```
<%@page contentType="text/html"%>
<%@page pageEncoding="UTF-8"%>

<!DOCTYPE HTML PUBLIC "-//W3C//DTD HTML 4.01 Transitional//EN"
    "http://www.w3.org/TR/html4/loose.dtd">

<html>
    <head>
        <meta http-equiv="Content-Type" content="text/html; charset=UTF-8">
        <title>JSP Page</title>
    </head>
    <body>
        <h1>JSP Page</h1>
    </body>
</html>
```

If you create a new JSP page using the XML syntax, it will look like this:

```
<?xml version="1.0" encoding="UTF-8"?>
<jsp:root xmlns:jsp="http://java.sun.com/JSP/Page" version="2.0">

    <jsp:directive.page contentType="text/html;charset=UTF-8"/>
```

```
<jsp:element name="text">
    <jsp:attribute name="lang">EN</jsp:attribute>
    <jsp:body>Sample text</jsp:body>
</jsp:element>

</jsp:root>
```

Either syntax is perfectly valid; however, most people find it easier to work with the standard JSP syntax.

Once you have added a JSP file to the project, you can begin to work with it and the tools NetBeans provides. One of the first things you should notice is the Palette window, as shown in Figure 4-12.

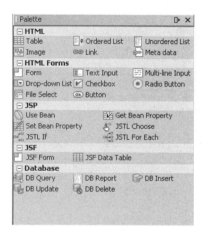

Figure 4-12. *The HTML and JSP components in the Palette window*

■**Note** If you create a JSP file with the XML syntax, the Palette window will not display any available components. This is because the file extension is `jspx`. At the time of this writing, the NetBeans Palette window does not treat `jsp` and `jspx` files the same.

One of the nicest features of NetBeans is its JSP support. You can use NetBeans to debug JSP files in the same way that you debug Java source files. With a JSP file open in the Source Editor, you can click in the margin to toggle a breakpoint. Then, as you run or debug the application, the breakpoints are hit, just as in regular Java source files. You can debug JSP files by right-clicking the filenames in the Project window and selecting Debug File from the context menu.

Another nice feature when working with JSP files is the ability to compile and validate the file. When the application server parses a JSP file, it is converted to a Java source file and then compiled into a Java class file. You can choose to compile a single JSP file rather than building the entire application. To compile a single JSP file, right-click the filename in the Projects window and select Compile File. You can also use the keyboard shortcut F9.

Once you have compiled the JSP file, you can view the generated Java source content. To view the source code, right-click the filename in the Projects window and select View Servlet from the context menu. A new tab will appear in the Source Editor, displaying the Java source file for the parsed JSP file.

Suppose you start with the following original JSP file:

```
<html>
    <head>
        <title>JSP Page</title>
    </head>
    <body>
    <%
        for(int i=0;i<5;i++) {
            out.println("Hello World!");
        }
    %>
    <h1>JSP Page</h1>
    </body>
</html>
```

If you use the View Servlet option, you will see the following Java code extracted from the _jspService method of the Java source file:

```
out.write("\n");
out.write("<html>\n");
out.write("    <head>\n");
out.write("        <title>JSP Page</title>\n");
out.write("    </head>\n");
out.write("    <body>\n");
out.write("    ");

for(int i=0;i<5;i++) {
    out.println("Hello World!");
}

out.write("\n");
out.write("    <h1>JSP Page</h1>\n");
out.write("    </body>\n");
out.write("</html>\n");
```

It is occasionally useful to be able to view the generated Java source code for a JSP file. If a JSP file throws an exception during the file's execution, it is difficult to know where the error occurred. The stack trace will list a line number, but it does not match a line number in the original JSP file. You need to view the Java source code file to find the offending line of code.

When working in JSP files, you can use the NetBeans code template feature. Code templates are essentially short abbreviations that allow you to quickly access larger blocks of code. You can type two or three letters, press the spacebar, and immediately see the extended block of code. This saves time, saves keystrokes, and helps programmers be more efficient when working in NetBeans. There is an entire set of JSP code template abbreviations, and you can easily add to the list. This means that if there are Java code templates you frequently use, you can copy them into the JSP template category as well. Code templates are discussed in detail in Chapter 10.

■**Caution** Code templates are language-specific. The same set of templates you use for Java source files does not necessarily work inside a JSP file (even though you may embed sections of Java code within it).

Leveraging Struts

Craig McClanahan originally kicked off the Apache Struts framework around mid-2000. The first major version was released in 2001, providing a Java Model-View-Controller (MVC) framework. Since then, Java developers have been using it to build web applications that cleanly separate business logic, control flow, and presentation.

This section assumes you have a working knowledge of Struts. If you are new to Struts, I strongly suggest learning about its capabilities. You can find information at the official web site (http://struts.apache.org) or refer to a book on the topic, such as *Beginning Apache Struts: From Novice to Professional* by Arnold Doray (Apress, 2006).

Adding Struts Support

Earlier in this chapter, you saw how to add Struts support to a new application that you created. You can also add Struts support to an existing web application. To add the Struts framework to an existing web application, follow these steps:

1. Right-click the project name in the Project window and select Properties.

2. Click Frameworks in the Categories section, and then click the Add button on the right side of the window.

3. Select Struts in the list of options and click the OK button.

4. Customize the text in the Action URL Pattern field if necessary.

5. Customize the package hierarchy text in the Application Resource field.

6. Optionally, select the Add Struts TLDs check box.

7. Click the OK button.

Once Struts support has been added to the project, you will notice additional files under the various nodes in the Projects window. A welcomeStruts.jsp file is listed under the Web Pages node. The default index.jsp page will also be modified to include a link to the new welcomeStruts.jsp page using the Struts action URL pattern Welcome.do, which maps to welcomeStruts.jsp.

You will also see a file named struts-config.xml listed under the Configuration Files node. This file contains the basic Struts configuration information, the action mappings, plug-in definitions, and so on. The web.xml file has also been modified to include references to the necessary

Struts servlets. Some additional XML configuration files may appear in the WEB-INF directory, but do not appear under the Configuration Files node.

The Struts resource file ApplicationResource.properties will appear in a package hierarchy under the Source Packages node. This file contains name/value pairs used throughout the application code and the Struts superclasses.

The Struts JAR file and supporting JAR files will be listed in the Libraries node.

If you chose to add Struts TLD files when you added the Struts framework support to the project, a few changes are made to the project. The files struts-logic.tld, struts-bean.tld, struts-html.tld, struts-nested.tld, and struts-tiles.tld are added to the WEB-INF directory under the Web Pages node. These files contain basic configuration information for the various Struts constructs. The web.xml file is also modified to include the correct references to the local TLD files. You should see the following added to the web.xml file:

```
<jsp-config>
    <taglib>
        <taglib-uri>/WEB-INF/struts-bean.tld</taglib-uri>
        <taglib-location>/WEB-INF/struts-bean.tld</taglib-location>
    </taglib>
    <taglib>
        <taglib-uri>/WEB-INF/struts-html.tld</taglib-uri>
        <taglib-location>/WEB-INF/struts-html.tld</taglib-location>
    </taglib>
    <taglib>
        <taglib-uri>/WEB-INF/struts-logic.tld</taglib-uri>
        <taglib-location>/WEB-INF/struts-logic.tld</taglib-location>
    </taglib>
    <taglib>
        <taglib-uri>/WEB-INF/struts-nested.tld</taglib-uri>
        <taglib-location>/WEB-INF/struts-nested.tld</taglib-location>
    </taglib>
    <taglib>
        <taglib-uri>/WEB-INF/struts-tiles.tld</taglib-uri>
        <taglib-location>/WEB-INF/struts-tiles.tld</taglib-location>
    </taglib>
</jsp-config>
```

Note One of the negatives of the NetBeans Struts support is that you cannot change the overall settings after initial setup. When you add Struts support to a project, you can set the various parameters. Once you have clicked OK, you are locked into the settings you have chosen. If you go back to the Frameworks node in the Project properties, you will see the fields grayed out. If you need to make any changes to those parameters, you must make them directly in the configuration files. Perhaps this feature will be improved in a future version.

Adding Forms

As you build a Struts-based web application, you may need to create your own `ActionForm` classes. In Struts, when you need to validate and store the input data from users, you create a subclass of `org.apache.struts.action.ActionForm`. These classes are used to transfer data between JSP pages and other Struts classes such as `Actions`.

To create a new Struts `ActionForm` class, follow these steps:

1. Right-click the project name in the Projects window, select New, and choose File/Folder.

2. Select the Web category from the list on the left and choose the Struts ActionForm Bean from the File Types list on the right. Click the Next button to move to the next step of the wizard, as shown in Figure 4-13.

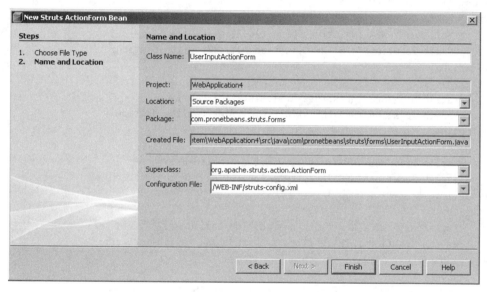

Figure 4-13. *Customizing ActionForm Bean fields*

3. Most of the `ActionForm` Bean fields are already filled out for you. The Project, Location, Superclass, and Configuration File fields are preset to the suggested values. All you need to specify is the Class Name and the Location values. Then click the Finish button.

■**Tip** When naming Struts classes, I usually end the names of `ActionForm` Beans with the word `Form` and end Struts actions with the word `Action`. It also helps to separate them into separate packages, such as `com.mydomain.projectname.forms` and `com.mydomain.projectname.actions`.

Once the file has been created, it should open in the Source Editor window. You will notice that the `ActionForm` class has several default properties and basic content in the standard `validate` method.

Adding Actions

Actions are Struts way of handling the Request and Response objects in the web application server container. You can use Struts actions to read information to the request, respond back to the calling client, and dispatch work to other classes.

To create a new Struts Action class, follow these steps:

1. Right-click the project name in the Projects window, select New, and choose File/Folder.

2. Select the Web category from the list on the left and Struts Action from the File Types list on the right. Click the Next button to move to the next step of the wizard, as shown in Figure 4-14.

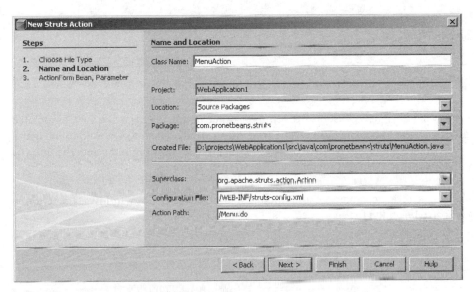

Figure 4-14. *Adding a new Struts action*

3. In the example in Figure 4-14, the class name has been set to MenuAction. The Superclass field is set to org.apache.struts.action.Action. The Configuration File field references the struts-config.xml file that was generated when you added Struts support to the project. When the Action class is created, its definition and action mapping will be listed in the struts-config.xml file. Once the properties are set, click the Next button.

4. You can choose to associate an ActionForm Bean with the Struts action you are about to create. If you select the Use ActionForm Bean check box, the remaining properties will be enabled, as shown in Figure 4-15.

5. Select an ActionForm Bean to associate with the Struts action. The ActionForm Bean Name field is a drop-down list of existing ActionForm Beans in the project. You must select an existing ActionForm Bean; otherwise, you cannot proceed.

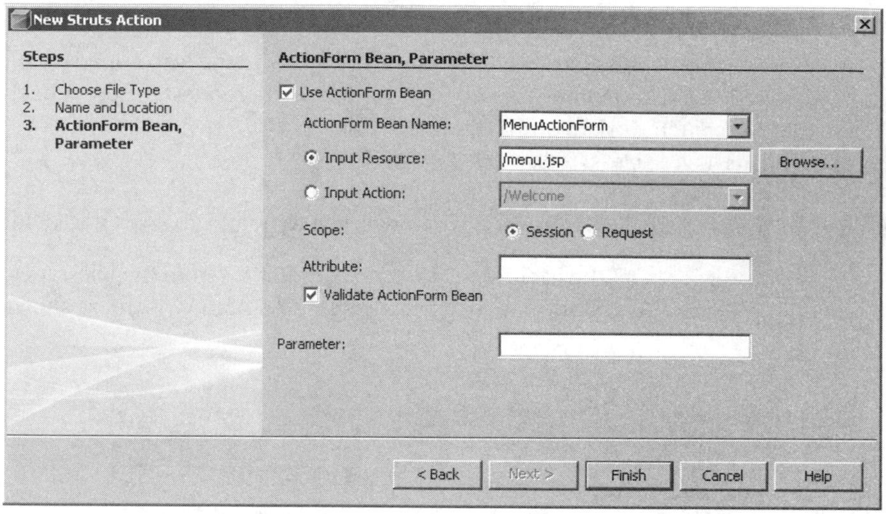

Figure 4-15. *Associating an ActionForm Bean with a Struts action*

6. The last field you need to set is the Input Resource text box. This is the view associated with the `ActionForm` Bean. You can use the Browse button next to the field to navigate the list of files under the Web Pages node in the Projects window and select the one you wish to use. Once you are finished, click the Finish button.

The new action will be generated and opened in the Source Editor window. The action mapping will also be added to the `struts-config.xml` file:

```
<action-mappings>
    <action input="/menu.jsp" name="MenuActionForm"
                path="/menu.do" scope="session"
                type="com.pronetbeans.struts.forms.MenuAction"/>
    <action path="/Welcome" forward="/welcomeStruts.jsp"/>
</action-mappings>
```

You will see that the path for the `welcomeStruts.jsp` file is `/Welcome` instead of `/Welcome.do`. This is due to the `forward` attribute, which specifies that requests for the path `/Welcome` should be immediately forwarded to the `welcomeStruts.jsp` file instead of to a Struts action.

■**Tip** One problem with using Struts `Action` classes is with testing. In Chapter 15, you will learn about using JUnit in NetBeans to create tests for your code. The problem with trying to use JUnit to test Struts actions is that you need to be able to simulate the internal state of the Struts application. This is extremely difficult to do. Instead, you can use an open source project available from SourceForge.net called StrutsTestCase. This tool effectively extends JUnit and allows you to test Struts `Action` classes. For more detailed information on the project, visit the web site at `http://strutstestcase.sourceforge.net/`.

Configuring Struts

As previously mentioned, the `struts-config.xml` file is where many of the overall configuration settings for Struts are defined. It is also where navigation rules such as forwards and action mappings are defined.

The file allows a variety of tags, but the sections you will use most often are `form-beans`, `global-exceptions`, `global-forwards`, and `action-mappings`. If you read the previous sections on `Action` and `ActionForm` classes, the `form-beans` and `action-mappings` sections should look familiar. The `global-exceptions` section allows you to map an error response to a specific action. The `global-forwards` section allows you to map a URL pattern to an action. This is handy if you want to map a URL like `www.mydomain.com/tv` to a longer or more complicated action-mapping name.

NetBeans does not provide the same sort of interface for the `struts-config.xml` file as it does for the `web.xml` file (at least, not yet). However, it does provide a few wizards, which are available from the context menu. With the `struts-config.xml` file open in the Source Editor, right-click anywhere in the file. You should see a Struts option on the context menu. The Struts menu will contain options such as Add Action, Add Forward, Add Exception, and so on. These wizards allow you to define new actions, forwards, and so on for existing Struts components without creating new classes. For example, use the Add Action menu item to access a wizard that allows you to specify a new action mapping, as shown in Figure 4-16. In this dialog box, set the Action Class and Action Path values. You can then customize the other fields in the same manner as discussed previously. Then click the Add button. You should see the new action defined in the `struts-config.xml` file.

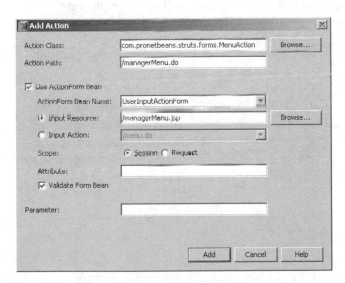

Figure 4-16. *The Add Action dialog box*

Building a Web Application

In NetBeans, you can choose to compile and build an entire web application without necessarily having to deploy it to an application server. Building an application in NetBeans is quite simple. Select the Build ➤ Build Main Project menu option. This assumes the project you want to build is set as the main project. If it is not, you can set it to the main project by right-clicking the project name in the Projects window and choosing Set Main Project. You can also right-click a project name and choose Build Project from the context menu if you want to build a specific project.

Once you have started the project build process, the Output window will appear. You will see a number of lines scroll through the Output window. The output lines are caused by the actions that are taking place in the background based on the project's build configuration (in other words, the project's Ant build file). Choosing the Build menu option actually activates an Ant target for the current project. For more details on how NetBeans projects are structured and integration with Ant, see Chapter 14.

The basics of what happened during the build are abstracted away for the most part. You should see a "Build Successful" message as one of the last lines in the Output window. This tells you that the Java source files compiled correctly and the web application was packaged as specified in the project properties. You can now run the application, work with the compiled application files externally from NetBeans, or continue with your development work.

Cleaning and Building a Project

You may also choose the Build ➤ Clean and Build Main Project menu option. This does the same set of tasks as the Build option, with one difference: all content inside the `build` directory in the NetBeans project structure is deleted. This ensures that there are no class files or other resource files present.

After deleting the content of the build directory, the project is then recompiled into the `build` directory. This is sometimes necessary if you have built an application and made numerous code changes, and want to feel confident that the compiled code is using the most current version of the source files. This also comes in handy after updating your application from a source code repository like CVS.

■Caution In NetBeans, you may occasionally have a problem cleaning and building a running web application. If JAR files in the `WEB-INF/lib` directory are in use by the application server, they often cannot be deleted by the clean operation. You need to go to the Runtime window and stop the running application server (as described in the "Defining Java Application Servers" section later in this chapter) before initiating the clean and build operation.

Compiling JSP Files

For web applications, you may also want to make sure that all the JSP files are compiled during the project build operation. This is a configurable option that is disabled by default. It is highly recommended that you enable it, since it will let you know if your JSP files will compile correctly. To enable this property, do the following:

1. Right-click the project name in the Projects window and select Properties.

2. Under the Build category, choose Compiling.

3. Select the check box next to the Test Compile All JSP Files During Builds field.

4. Click the OK button.

The next time you build your project, you should notice some additional text in the Output window under the heading `compile-jsps`. With each project build, all the JSP files will be compiled.

Repeating and Stopping Builds

Two new features added as of NetBeans 6 are the ability to repeat a build and to stop a currently running build. These menu options appear on the main Build menu.

If you initiated at least one build or run operation, you should be able to select Repeat Build/Run *AppName* (*operation*) from the main Build menu. The *AppName* will be the name of the application in which the last build or run operation occurred, and the *operation* will be either Build or Run. This helps clear any confusion, especially if you are working in multiple open projects.

The Build ➤ Stop Build/Run option is useful when the build operation takes a long time and you need to stop it. This saves you from having to wait through the entire build process.

You will also see new icons in the Output window as of NetBeans 6, as shown in Figure 4-17. These represent the Repeat Build and Run and Stop Build/Run options. The two green triangles activate the repeat build/run operation, and the square under it will stop a currently running build or run operation.

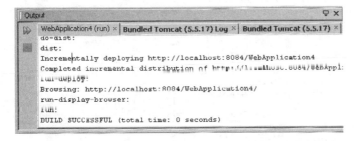

Figure 4-17. *The Repeat Build/Run and Stop Build/Run icons in the Output window*

Running a Web Application

A large component of developing web applications is being able to test and run them in an application server. During the regular course of development, most programmers will run a JSP page dozens of times to make sure it functions as expected.

When a web application is run, it is first built, packaged, and deployed. If the associated Java application server is not started, NetBeans attempts to start and deploy the application to it. When you choose to run an application, NetBeans uses the project's Ant build file to compile, package, and run the application files.

To run the web application, select Run ➤ Run Main Project, or press F6. The Output window will appear. As the various steps in the build configuration process, you will notice a separate tab for the run operation in the Output window.

The various build steps will execute—compiling any Java source files, compiling JSP files, copying files to the project build directory, and so on. Before the application actually runs, you will notice the application files are packaged into a distribution file. For a Java Application project, a JAR file is created. For Web Application projects, a WAR file is created. The WAR file is a glorified JAR file that allows the entire web application to be packaged and distributed together. You can then take this WAR file and deploy it to one or more servers.

If the application WAR file is not created, you can set the project to create one. To force a web application project to generate a WAR file, perform the following steps:

1. Right-click the project name in the Projects window and select Properties.

2. Select Packaging from the Categories list on the left.

3. Check the Create WAR File property check box.

Once the run and run/deploy steps in the build process execute, the target application server will be started. Additional tabs will open in the Output window for the application server. Figure 4-18 shows an example of the tabs and output for an application running and deployed to the Tomcat application server.

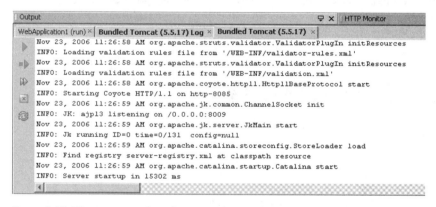

Figure 4-18. *The output tabs when running a JSP page*

The five icons along the left margin of the tab shown in Figure 4-18 allow quick access to the application server and the ability to start, stop, and restart it. From top to bottom, the icons are Start the Server, Start the Server in Debug Mode, Restart the Server, Stop the Server, and Refresh the Server Status. The Refresh the Server Status option is useful when the application server takes a long time to stop or shut down. Sometimes application servers can hang or time out, and the ability to refresh the status can save you some headaches.

Defining Java Application Servers

Web applications can be deployed to a variety of Java application servers. Among that list are Tomcat, BEA WebLogic, the Sun Java Application Server, JBoss, and others. Web applications can be associated only with application servers that have been identified in NetBeans through the Server Manager tool.

The Server Manager tool allows you to define an application server, reference the root directory where it is installed, and configure a variety of server properties. Once this process is complete, you can manage the server directly in NetBeans, control it (starting, stopping, restarting, and so on), and deploy web applications to it.

To access the tool, select Tools ➤ Server Manager. The initial list of servers registered with NetBeans will vary depending on your NetBeans version. However, it should at least include Tomcat, as that application server is bundled with most new versions of NetBeans.

The Server Manager will list the currently configured application servers in the left pane. If a specific server is selected, its properties appear in the right pane. Click the Add Server button on the lower-left side of the window to define a new application server for use with your NetBeans Web Application projects. When adding a new server, you will need to know the base directory location for the installed server as well as some additional parameters.

Once an application server is configured, you will see it listed under the Servers node in the Runtime window. From there, you can control the server, view information about it, and access the various web applications that may be deployed.

With an application server configured for use in NetBeans, you can configure web applications to use it through the project properties for the application.

The following sections discuss how to add specific types of servers, and then how to set your web applications to deploy to your configured servers.

Using Tomcat

NetBeans currently ships with a bundled version of the Tomcat Java application server. Tomcat is a de facto standard widely used by the programming industry to deploy Java applications.

Setting Tomcat Properties

You can use the Tomcat properties available in the Server Manager to configure the server. As shown in Figure 4-10, the Server Manager displays multiple tabs for the bundled Tomcat server: Connection, Startup, Platform, Classes, Sources, and Javadoc. Each tab contains a set of properties you can modify. For example, on the Connection tab, you can change the port that the server listens on, the username and password for the manager role, and so on.

■**Note** If you plan on running multiple instances of Tomcat on your machine, you will need to change the value in the Server Port field. The default is 8080, but can be set to any port that is not in use. If you accidentally set the server port to one in use, you will see an error message in the Server Output tab in the Output window when the server starts up.

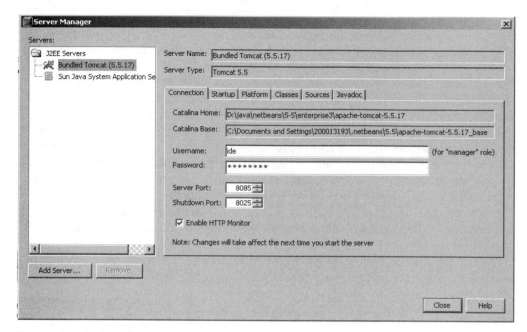

Figure 4-19. *The bundled Tomcat server selected in the Server Manager*

Click the Platform tab to view two very important fields:

Java Platform: Allows you to select in which version of Java the application will run. If you have a heterogeneous development environment, you may need to be able to test Tomcat in different versions of the JVM.

VM Options: Allows you to pass command-line parameters to the JVM during startup. One issue you may encounter is memory constraints. You may be testing or profiling your application code in Tomcat and receive an out of memory error. This happens when your application code uses up the maximum amount of memory the JVM is allowed to allocate. You can adjust the initial and upper limit for memory allocation by passing parameters to the JVM via the VM Options field. The value -Xms200m -Xmx500m sets the initial amount of memory allocated to the JVM to around 200MB and the maximum amount it can expand to consume to around 500MB.

Once you have modified the properties, click the OK button to close the Server Manager. You will need to restart the Tomcat application server for the changes to take effect.

Working with Applications Deployed to Tomcat

The bundled Tomcat server should appear in the Server Manager tool and under the Servers node in the Runtime window. In the Runtime window, you'll see a Web Applications node under the Bundled Tomcat listing. (Other servers may have different nodes available.) Tomcat simply lists the applications that have been deployed in the server instance, as shown in Figure 4-20.

Figure 4-20. *The web applications deployed to the bundled Tomcat server listed in the Runtime window*

For each deployed web application listed under the Web Applications node, you have several options. Right-click the application name to see a context menu with the following options:

Start: Allows you to explicitly start a web application instance that is deployed to Tomcat. The Tomcat server itself may be started, but that does not mean every web application instance has also been started. When you run a web application in NetBeans, it is deployed to the application server and started by default. It should not be stopped unless you have done so explicitly.

Stop: Allows you to stop a running web application. This will make the application unavailable via a web browser, but does *not* undeploy it from Tomcat. Tomcat will still recognize it, and you can restart the application whenever you wish.

Undeploy: Stops the web application and undeploys it from the server. The server will no longer list the application under the Web Applications node. You will need to redeploy it to Tomcat to be able to view it.

Open in Browser: Opens the NetBeans default web browser and navigates to the URL for the web application. This is basically the same as using the Run Main Project option for a web application, in that it opens the application in the browser.

Controlling the Tomcat Server

NetBeans also provides the ability to control the Tomcat server in the Runtime window. Right-click the server name in the Runtime window to see a context menu with the following options:

Start, Start in Debug Mode, and Start in Profile Mode: Allow you to start the Tomcat application server for the specified purposes.

Stop: Allows you to shut down the application server so no web applications can be accessed. Note that this does not explicitly stop each individual web application as does the Stop option on the context menu for an application under the Web Applications node. The next time you start Tomcat, the web applications will all be available, unless you explicitly used the Stop option for a specific application.

Restart: Stops and restarts the Tomcat server. This is useful if you want to clear any sessions in progress or clean up any potential memory leaks caused by your application code.

Refresh: Polls the application server to see what state it is in and refreshes the menu items that may be available.

Edit server.xml: Opens Tomcat's main configuration file, server.xml, in the Source Editor. If you need to make changes to the overall server configuration, you can conveniently access it directly in NetBeans.

View Admin Console: Opens a new web browser window and navigates to the Tomcat admin console. You can log in to this web application and perform administrative functions for Tomcat.

View Server Log and View Server Output: Open the Output window in NetBeans and give focus to the Server Log tab and Server Output tab, respectively.

Properties: Opens the Server Manager tool with the Tomcat server selected. This allows you quick access to the Tomcat configuration properties that you are allowed to change directly in NetBeans, as described earlier.

Using the Sun Java System Application Server

Depending on your version of NetBeans and the add-on packs you have installed, the Sun Java System Application Server (SJSAS) may be registered with NetBeans in the Server Manager. If an instance of the SJSAS is configured, it will appear under the J2EE Servers node in the left pane of the Server Manager window.

If the SJSAS is not configured in the Server Manager, you need to define a new instance. Click the Add Server button and select Sun Java System Application Server in the Add Server Instance window. Once you have selected SJSAS as the server, click the Next button.

You will be prompted to select the base directory location where the server is installed. The Server Manager should automatically discover and populate many of the necessary settings, such as the domain registration fields. Depending on your selection, you may need to provide additional values for domain-related properties.

■**Note** I've glossed over some of the details of adding a new SJSAS, since it should already be registered in the Server Manager. If you are unsure of what settings to specify, the rule of thumb is to keep the suggested defaults that NetBeans provides and click the Next button until the wizard finishes.

Setting SJSAS Properties

Select the SJSAS in the Server Manager to see its properties displayed on the right side of the Manager window, as shown in Figure 4-21.

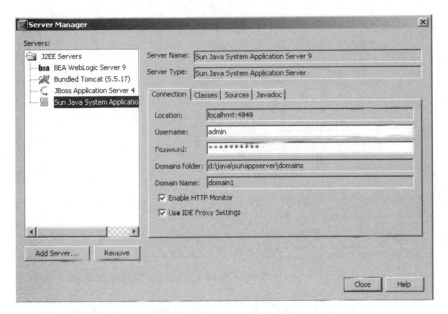

Figure 4-21. *The SJSAS selected in the Server Manager*

You can set properties like the username and password for administrative access. You can also choose to enable the HTTP Monitor (discussed in the "HTTP Monitoring" section later in this chapter) and to use IDE proxy settings. The Classes, Sources, and Javadoc tabs allow you to see and modify the resources available at a server level.

Controlling the SJSAS

Open the Runtime window to see the SJSAS listed under the Server node. Right-click the server name to display a context menu with a variety of actions. These actions are nearly identical to the ones available for the Tomcat application server, described in the previous section. You can start, stop, and restart the SJSAS, as well as view the log and admin console.

Using JBoss

Starting with the 5.5 release, NetBeans provides a bundled installation of the JBoss application server. Using this release, you can install NetBeans and JBoss through the same installer. However, you do not need this bundled version to use JBoss with NetBeans. You can install NetBeans through the standard download process and configure it to work with JBoss through the Server Manager.

The 5.5 version does not provide a preconfigured instance of JBoss that appears in the Server Manager (as it does with the standard NetBeans installation that comes bundled with Tomcat). You still need to define a JBoss instance in the Server Manager.

To add JBoss support through the Server Manager, click the Add Server button and select JBoss from the list of available options. You will be prompted to enter the base directory location where the JBoss application server is installed. Once you have selected the correct location, click the Next button. You will see the Instance Properties window, as shown in Figure 4-22.

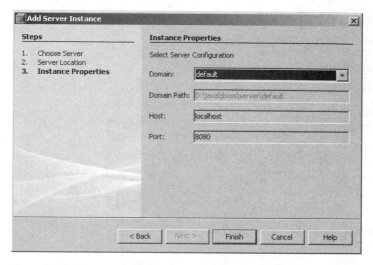

Figure 4-22. *JBoss server properties in the Server Manager when adding a new instance*

The only property you can set is the Domain. Choose from the drop-down list of available domains that have been created in the JBoss application server (default is a common choice). Then click the Finish button. JBoss will be added to the list under the Servers node in the Server Manager.

Working with Applications Deployed to JBoss

After the JBoss server has been started, you can expand the plus icon next to the name to view additional nodes under it, as shown in Figure 4-23. You will see nodes labeled Enterprise Applications, EJB Modules, and Web Applications. If a project of those types has been deployed to the JBoss server, it will appear under the respective node.

Figure 4-23. *The JBoss node in the Runtime window*

Right-click the name of an application under the JBoss node to see a context menu with options to view the application in a web browser or undeploy it. When the application is undeployed, it is removed entirely from JBoss, and you will need to redeploy it if you wish to run it again.

Controlling the JBoss Server

You can also control the server through the Runtime window. Right-click the server node in the Runtime window to see the standard server control options in the context menu. You can select to start, stop, and restart the server, as well as view the server's admin console and log. JBoss also has an option to view the JMX Console. This is a JBoss-specific feature, which is why you will not see this option on the context menu for Tomcat and other application servers.

Using BEA WebLogic

NetBeans also allows you to configure a server instance for BEA WebLogic in the Server Manager. In the Server Manager tool, click the Add Server button, select BEA WebLogic Server from the Server drop-down list, and click the Next button. In the following step of the Add Server Instance wizard, you need to select the Server Location for BEA WebLogic. Use the Browse button to locate the directory on your machine where WebLogic is installed, and then click the Next button.

The last step in the Add Server Instance wizard displays some additional properties you may want to set for WebLogic, as shown in Figure 4-24. You must select a value from the Local Instances field. This allows you to specify which instance/domain of WebLogic you wish to register. It will also allow you to specify the administrative password.

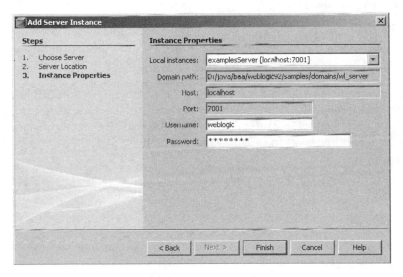

Figure 4-24. *Setting BEA WebLogic Server instance properties*

■**Tip** By default, WebLogic sets the username and password to weblogic. If you have a default server installation, you should set the username and password fields to weblogic as well in the Add Server Instance wizard.

Once you have finished setting the WebLogic properties, click the Finish button. The application server will be added to the list of servers and available for use by projects.

Controlling the WebLogic Server

As with the other application servers, in the Runtime window, you can right-click the BEA WebLogic Server node to view the context menu options. You should see menu items such as Start, Stop, Restart, View Admin Console, and View Server Log. The Properties menu item allows you to jump directly to the Server Manager with the BEA WebLogic Server selected.

Adjusting WebLogic Memory Usage

One issue I have with running NetBeans and WebLogic 9 on the same machine is memory usage. The computer I have NetBeans installed on runs Windows XP (hold the jeers and catcalls please). When I am running NetBeans with several projects open, the amount of memory utilized on my machine is around 350MB to 400MB. Keep in mind that Windows XP gobbles up between 230MB to 260MB of this total before I even open NetBeans.

Once I use the NetBeans Runtime window to start the WebLogic application server, the memory usage jumps through the roof to consume almost 1GB (the maximum I have available). This memory usage makes the computer very sluggish.

When WebLogic starts up, you should monitor server debugging information that appears in the Output window. You will probably see a line that states:

```
Java Memory arguments: -Xms256m -Xmx512m
```

This is a setting for the WebLogic server that was automatically configured during installation. Experienced WebLogic users can configure this setting to raise or lower the maximum amount of memory allocated to the JVM. For the average person who may not be an expert in configuring WebLogic, here is a big tip.

Search the domain directory that you defined in the instance properties through the Server Manager (see Figure 4-24). This domain directory should contain a `bin` subdirectory. In the `bin` directory, you should find a file named `setDomainEnv.cmd` (for Windows) or `setDomainEnv.sh` (for Unix). The file will contain the line to set the memory options for the JVM:

```
set MEM_ARGS=-Xms256m -Xmx512m
```

You can change the values to something more reasonable, such as the following:

```
set MEM_ARGS=-Xms128m -Xmx300m
```

The next time you start that domain in the WebLogic server, it should consume far less memory on your system, providing for a better overall user experience.

Setting Advanced Server Options

For some application servers, you may also be able to modify properties through the Advanced Options window. To access this window, select Tools ➤ Options. In the Basic Options window, click the Advanced Options button in the lower left.

In the Advanced Options window, the IDE Configuration node appears in the left pane. Underneath the node, you will see a listing for Server and External Tool Settings. Expand this node as well, and you will see a listing for J2EE Servers. Expand the J2EE Servers node, and you will see a list of applications that are available to be edited. Select the server in the left pane, and its properties should be visible in the right pane. In the example shown in Figure 4-25, only the SJSAS has properties exposed to the Advanced Options window.

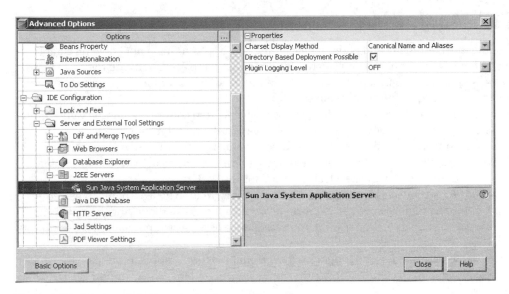

Figure 4-25. *Advanced Options in the Server Manager*

As application servers release new versions, there may be more properties listed in this section in the future. For now, you should adjust the advanced properties only if you know exactly what they do.

Setting the Application Server for a Project

After you have added an application server in the Server Manager, it is available for use. You can modify which application server a project will use by doing the following:

1. Right-click the name of a project in the Projects window and select Properties

2. Select the Run category in the left pane.

3. Select the desired application server from the Server field drop-down list.

4. Click the OK button.

Once you have switched the application server in the project properties, no further actions are necessary.

NetBeans makes it extremely easy to toggle the application server a project will use. This is invaluable if you need to test your application across different types of servers to ensure compatibility. It can also come in handy if you must develop an application that will be deployed onto one server for development and testing purposes, but deployed to a different server for production.

HTTP Monitoring

One of the most annoying things about developing web applications is not knowing what is going on behind the scenes when you are testing a particular page. Often, you read and write from the Request, Response, and Session objects and need to know what the values for session attributes were for a specific page request.

At one time or another, many web developers have written code that grabs the values from the Session or Request objects, iterates through the names, and prints out the current values. This is often done in an attempt to know the precise values passed to a JSP page or servlet. The HTTP Monitor can help make that type of debugging a thing of the past. In my humble opinion, the HTTP Monitor is one of the best features available in NetBeans.

The HTTP Monitor allows you to view all the state information for a particular page request directly within the IDE. You can also perform powerful actions like modifying the state information, replaying a specific page request from a sequence of requests, and saving a page request for later viewing.

The HTTP Monitor must be supported by and enabled for the application server to which you are deploying. At the time of this writing, only Tomcat and the SJSAS support the HTTP Monitor.

Enabling the HTTP Monitor

You can enable the HTTP Monitor for a server in the Server Manager tool as follows:

1. Select Tools ➤ Server Manager.

2. In the Server Manager window, select a server from the left pane.

3. In the server properties displayed in the right pane, you will see an Enable HTTP Monitor check box if the server supports the HTTP Monitor (see Figures 4-19 and 4-21, earlier in this chapter). Check this box, and then click Close.

Using the HTTP Monitor

Once you configure an application server to work with the HTTP Monitor, you can start using the tool. When you run a single JSP page or an entire web application, the HTTP Monitor will automatically activate. After the browser has finished processing the initial request, the HTTP Monitor window will open and display any results, as shown in Figure 4-26.

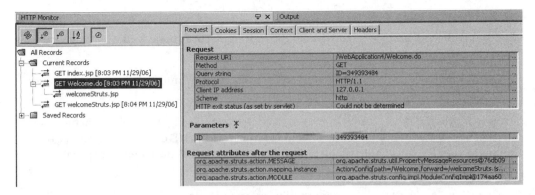

Figure 4-26. *Sample output in the HTTP Monitor*

Viewing Record Information

In the example in Figure 4-26, the HTTP Monitor displays three records under the Current Records node on the left side of the window. The current records are HTTP requests that have been made in the application you have deployed to the server. You can click any record to view the data for it.

Once you select a record, the fields and values for that specific record will display in several tabs on the right side of the HTTP Monitor window:

Request: Displays request information, such as the URI, method, protocol, and client IP address. Also shows an individual listing of parameters and values from the query string. Additionally, it displays request attributes that exist after the request.

Cookies: Displays the incoming and outgoing cookies.

Session: Displays general information about the session like the session ID, the time it was created, and the time it was last accessed. This tab also displays the session attributes that existed before the request and the attributes that exist after the request.

Context: Displays general servlet context data as well as context attributes and initialization parameters.

Client and Server: Displays client information such as the protocol, client IP address, character encoding, locale, software used, and accepted file formats. Also displays server information such as the hostname, port, application server platform, and Java version.

Headers: Displays the typical HTTP headers such as user-agent, host, connection, and cookie.

You can use the data displayed in the HTTP Monitor to perform a forensic analysis of all the request-related variables. If you examine the records displayed in Figure 4-26, you will see they are formatted as HTTP protocol, page name, and date/time. The three records listed in the figure were all done via a GET request. You may notice the second record has a child node listed beneath it. This is due to the fact that the original request to Welcome.do redirected to the child request of welcomeStruts.jsp.

Manipulating Records

When you right-click a single request under the Current Records node, you will see several options on the context menu:

Delete: Permanently deletes the request record. There is no undo for this type of operation, so make sure you really want to delete the record.

Save: Moves the record under the Saved Records node (see Figure 4-26). It will then be saved for further examination. Once you close the NetBeans IDE software, the items under the Current Records node will be lost. Only the records that have been saved will be accessible.

Replay: Directs NetBeans to automatically perform the exact HTTP request again. All request attributes, session variables, context parameters, and cookies are put in place to exactly simulate the original request. A web browser window will open, and the requested page will load. After the request is completed, a new record will appear at the end of the Current Records list. The fields and values that result from the request may or may not be identical to the original request. You may have changed application code before replaying the request, which may affect the values.

Edit and Replay: Allows you to select a request record, alter some of the fields and values, and replay the request in the web application. This is invaluable for testing things like query string parameters, cookies, and header variables. This is one of the particularly interesting features I use most often, as described next.

Editing and Replaying Records

When you select the Edit and Replay item from the record's context menu, the Edit and Replay window appears. Using the Add Parameter button, you can specify a name/value pair for a new query string parameter. You can also edit or delete any of the existing query string parameters. Figure 4-27 shows an example of three query string parameters displayed in the Edit and Replay window.

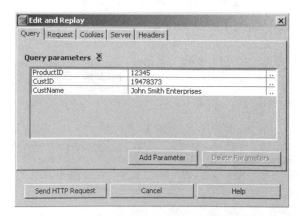

Figure 4-27. *Editing the query string in the HTTP Monitor*

Once you have added, modified, or deleted the request parameters, you can trigger the replay operation by clicking the Send HTTP Request button. If you change your mind and decide to not replay the request, click the Cancel button.

Here are several scenarios where the Edit and Replay feature may come in handy:

- You need to test a JSP page that displays different data based on the value of a query string parameter.

- You want to add a cookie value to test a "remember my username" feature on a login form.

- You want to change the server hostname that the request will be sent to during a test of a clustered server.

- You need to change the HTTP header accept-language to an alternate value to test the internationalization capabilities of your web application.

- You want to change the HTTP header user-agent to test the cross-platform, cross-browser capabilities of some JavaScript in a web application.

There are many reasons for using the HTTP Monitor. It is a simple yet powerful tool, which every web application programmer should get to know. I encourage you to try it out and experiment.

Exploring the Sample Web Projects

Many of the tools and technologies for developing Java web applications can be very confusing at times. NetBeans tries to alleviate this by providing a rich variety of sample projects that can be created as stand-alone projects in the IDE. The samples cover almost every type of NetBeans project, such as Java Application, SOA, EJB Module, NetBeans Plug-in, Web Application, and so on.

You can access the sample projects through the New Project wizard. Select File ➤ New Project. In the New Project window, expand the nodes under the Samples category to see the various sample projects that NetBeans provides. For example, under the Web node, you will see the following project types:

- JSTL Example

- Tomcat JSP Example

- Tomcat Servlet Example

Each project type contains a full set of examples and source code.

Select a project type and click the Next button. You will be prompted to enter a project name and location. Click the Finish button, and the project will be generated.

The sample applications serve as hands-on tutorials for developers who like to learn by picking apart code. You can look at real source code, see how things work, modify any code you wish, and run the application to see the results. You can then apply the best practices you learned to your own projects.

There is also a category under the Samples node in the New Project wizard titled Java Blueprints Solutions. Under this category are numerous professional examples of applications from Sun Microsystems. One of the child nodes is Blueprints for EE 1.4. This node is the parent node for the Web Tier Design category. Select the Web Tier Design category to see the following project types:

- Making Web Applications Accessible

- Client-side Validation

- Client Session State

- Handling Command Submissions

- Server-side Validation

■Note The list of examples will most likely change with each version of NetBeans. New best practice projects are created, and existing ones may be modified.

These sample projects can be a valuable resource in learning ways to implement web applications. The Making Web Applications Accessible project should be of particular interest to many developers, particularly those who create web applications for local, state, and federal government organizations. Many government organizations require public-facing web applications to conform to the World Wide Web Consortium (W3C) Web Content Accessibility Guidelines (WCAG). The sample application demonstrates many of the best practices to assist you with this task.

Summary

This chapter focused on creating web applications in NetBeans. We covered how to create a web application and manage its properties and settings, and the overall structure and layout of its files. We discussed building, running, and deploying an application, along with the various properties and tools for controlling those operations.

We reviewed working with web application files, such as HTML, CSS, JSP, and the deployment descriptor. You learned that NetBeans provides common Java and JSP tools, such as code completion, code templates, syntax highlighting, debugging, and so on.

The chapter also provided an overview of the NetBeans tools for working with Struts in a web application. It covered how to use the IDE wizards to add actions and forms, as well as make modifications to the overall Struts configuration.

As you learned in this chapter, before you can deploy an application to a Java application server, that server must be registered in NetBeans. We covered how to set up Tomcat, WebLogic, JBoss, and the Sun Java System Application Server.

Next, you learned about one of my favorite NetBeans tools, the HTTP Monitor. The HTTP Monitor is a valuable tool for examining HTTP request data, modifying values such as query string parameters and HTTP headers, and replaying specific HTTP requests.

Lastly, we briefly discussed the sample projects NetBeans provides for learning best practices in developing web applications.

CHAPTER 5

Creating Visual Web Applications: JSF, Ajax, and Data Binding

The Visual Web Pack (VWP) is a recent addition to the NetBeans family of tools. Starting with NetBeans 5.5, you can add powerful features for working with JSF, Ajax, and data binding.

The VWP includes support for an impressive array of technology standards, including JSF 1.2, Struts, EJB 3.0, Java Servlets 2.5, JSP Standard Tag Libraries, Java API for XML Web Services (JAX-WS) 2.0, and a variety of XML and web service-related APIs. Bundled with the NetBeans IDE, these technologies greatly enhance your ability to effectively develop cutting-edge Java applications.

This chapter will discuss how to install the VWP, create NetBeans Visual Web Application projects, and work with the different tools the VWP provides.

Getting Started with the VWP

One of the biggest gaps in functionality of earlier versions of NetBeans was its lack of a good WYSIWYG web design tool. Java Studio Creator contained a pretty reasonable tool for performing visual JSF development, and many developers, including myself, secretly wished for it to become part of NetBeans.

At the JavaOne 2006 conference, I visited many of the Sun booths in the pavilion area. One of the NetBeans development team members was present and mentioned that the different Sun IDE products were being modularized for inclusion in other tools. He also made the comment that a visual web design tool was coming soon for the next major release of NetBeans, version 5.5. Suffice it to say, I was delighted at this news.

The VWP was delivered with NetBeans 5.5 at the end of October 2006 as a technology preview. It was later released as a production-ready version in December 2006. Based on the JSF Visual Designer from Studio Creator, the VWP has been updated and made available as an add-on pack for NetBeans. At the time of this writing, plans are underway to fully open source the VWP by early 2007 or by JavaOne 2007.

The VWP provides a variety of time-saving and productivity-improving features that make working with JSF easy and fun. For example, you can drag-and-drop JSF components from a palette onto a JSP page. The NetBeans VWP offers the usual types of components—buttons, form elements, text fields, and so on—but it also provides some nonstandard components, such as Tree, Tab Sets, Add Remove Lists, Breadcrumbs, and more. All of these components can be configured visually in the Visual Designer window or textually in the Properties window. They can also be bound to data without having to write a single line of code.

In the past, tools like Macromedia UltraDeveloper provided similar capabilities. However, as you used the automated capabilities, they generated multiple lines of obtuse code that was difficult to understand, hard to maintain, and not always the optimal method for obtaining the desired functionality. The automatic code generated by the NetBeans VWP is quite different. It actually looks like Java code a programmer would write. This makes software written with the VWP easier to work with and more maintainable.

The VWP also comes with the Visual Database Query Editor. This tool is very similar to Microsoft SQL Server's Enterprise Manager tool for working with SQL. It is bundled with the VWP add-on, but in the near future will be extracted as either a separate downloadable module or a core part of the database tools in NetBeans 6.0.

All these tools are brought together in NetBeans. When combined with the overall ease of use that NetBeans provides, you have an extremely powerful software development platform.

Installing the VWP

The VWP can be installed in NetBeans 5.5. It provides Java EE 5 and JSF 1.2 capabilities that are currently supported by only the Sun Java System Application Server 9.1. To use the VWP with any other server, you must use Java EE 1.4 and JSF 1.1.

Before installing the VWP, you must have JDK 1.5.0.06 or higher installed. You should also have a Java application server supported by NetBeans configured for use in the IDE.

To install the VWP, download the NetBeans Visual Web Pack installation file from the NetBeans download page at http://www.netbeans.org. Run the installer and click the Next button on each screen. You will be prompted to accept a license agreement, select the installation directory for the NetBeans IDE to which you are installing the VWP, and select a JDK to use. On the final screen of the installation wizard, click the Finish button to complete the process.

Configuring VWP Options

The NetBeans VWP allows you to configure several options that affect its operation. You can view and modify the VWP properties by selecting Tools ➤ Options and clicking the Advanced Options button. In the left pane of the Advanced Options window are two categories for the VWP properties: Visual Designer and Data Source Drag and Drop.

Visual Designer Properties

Select Visual Designer in the left pane of the Advanced Options window to see the corresponding properties in the right pane, as shown in Figure 5-1.

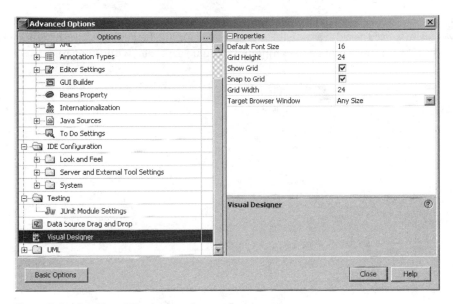

Figure 5-1. *The Visual Designer advanced properties*

The Visual Designer is the WYSIWYG interface for working with JSF in NetBeans. You can set the following properties for it:

Default Font Size: This is the size of fonts for text components that are dropped onto the Visual Designer window for a JSP page. The font size displayed in the Visual Designer may differ from what is rendered in a web browser due to default browser settings. You can set the default font size value for the Visual Designer to any standard font size.

Grid Height and Grid Width: These properties control the number of pixels between grid lines in the Visual Designer window. They define the height and width of each square that appears in the grid. This is a very important element to review, especially if the Snap to Grid property is enabled.

Snap to Grid: This property instructs the Visual Designer to automatically snap components to the nearest grid line. This affects almost all the work you do in the Visual Designer.

Show Grid: This property, enabled by default, determines if the grid lines are displayed in the Visual Designer window.

Target Browser Window: This property determines the specific screen resolution size for the web pages you develop. If you set to the smallest size, 640x480 (600x300 page), and open a JSP page in the Visual Designer, the page visually denotes the shape and size. This allows you to add and arrange components according to the window size of your user community.

In Figure 5-2, I have arranged a number of Text Field components to demonstrate the effect of the grid size. The JSP page shown in the figure is divided into three sections. In the first section, the four components were arranged as close as possible without overlapping. Notice how the Text Field component labeled Textbox 2 starts almost exactly where the Text Field component labeled Textbox 1 ends. However, there is a small amount of space between the edges of the two components. The third and fourth Text Field components are in a row below the first two. They are vertically spaced as close as possible without overlapping. Regardless of the height and width of the grid, this is how Text Field components can be arranged without overlap.

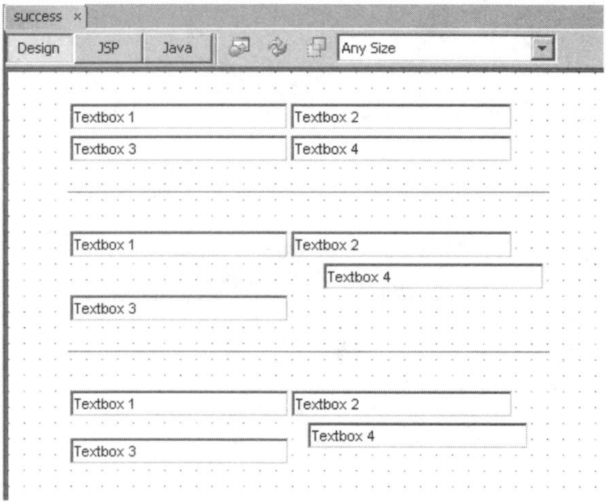

Figure 5-2. *Sample Text Field layouts in the Visual Designer window grid*

Note The components in Figure 5-2 were arranged using different grid sizes, but once you change the grid size, it is used by all components on the page. You cannot have different grid sizes on the same page.

The second section displayed in Figure 5-2 is arranged according to the default grid size of 24 pixels. In this section, I clicked the Text Field component labeled Textbox 3 and pressed the down arrow key. The component moved down one grid position, which was 24 pixels in this case. I also moved the Text Field component labeled Textbox 4 to the right by one grid position.

The third section of Text Field components in Figure 5-2 is arranged exactly like the second section. The only difference is that I set the grid size to 12 pixels instead of 24. I moved the two components in the second row in the same manner as the matching components in the second section.

Once you have arranged the components with the correct spacing, you can run the page or preview it in a web browser. You'll see that the components appear very similar to how they were arranged, but contain some additional space between them. This is related to the default settings for each component and how the VWP renders it for the browser.

Tip Using the grid can make arranging components easy, but sometimes it can be annoying as well. If you are attempting to arrange a component and the grid doesn't allow you to make the adjustment you want, you do not need to turn off the Snap to Grid property in the Advanced Options window. Instead, when moving the component, just hold down the Shift key. This temporarily disables the components' adherence to the grid lines.

Data Source Drag and Drop Properties

The Data Source Drag and Drop properties in the Advanced Options window control some of the attributes of the VWP data binding. When you bind a database table to a component, several Java objects are created. (Data binding is covered later in this chapter.) The Data Source Drag and Drop properties affect the creation of those Java objects.

Click the Data Source Drag and Drop node in the Advanced Options window to see the following properties:

Create RowSets in Session: This property affects where a CachedRowSet object is created, regardless of where you drag-and-drop it. The property is enabled by default. If you unselect it, binding a database table to a component will result in the rowset being created where you bind the data.

Check for Duplicate RowSets: This property affects the creation of rowsets as you drop them onto components. If you bind a database table to a component, the VWP first attempts to determine if a matching rowset already exists. If the property is selected, which it is by default, NetBeans will prompt you to either reuse the existing rowset or to create a new one. If the property is unselected, NetBeans will automatically generate a new rowset.

Suffix for Data Providers: This property specifies the text that is added to the name of the data provider class that is generated during a data-binding operation. If you drop a database table onto a component, a data provider class is created using the name of the database table combined with the value of the Suffix for Data Providers property. For example, if you created a data binding for a table named customers, the data provider would be named customersDataProvider.

Suffix for RowSets: This property specifies the suffix for the rowset class that is created. For example, the rowset created for the customers table would be named customersRowSet.

After you have set the VWP properties, click the Close button in the Advanced Options window. You have now installed and configured the VWP and are ready to create your first Visual Web Application project.

Creating a Visual Web Application

The VWP adds one type of project to NetBeans: the Visual Web Application. This project type allows you to access the VWP's powerful drag-and-drop capabilities. In this section, you'll learn the basics of working with Visual Web Application projects.

Creating a Visual Web Application Project

After you've installed the VWP and configured it to suit your preferences, you can select the Visual Web Application project type in NetBeans. Follow these steps to start a new Visual Web Application project:

1. Select File ➤ New Project from the main menu.

2. In the New Project window, select Web from the categories section on the left, select Visual Web Application from the list of projects on the right, and then click the Next button.

3. Fill out the Project Name and Project Location fields.

4. Specify a Java package in the Default Java Package field.

5. Select a source code structure from the Source Structure drop-down list.

6. Make sure that Sun Java System Application Server is selected in the Server drop-down list.

7. Make sure that the Java EE Version field is set to Java EE 5.

8. The Name and Location window should look similar to Figure 5-3. Click the Finish button.

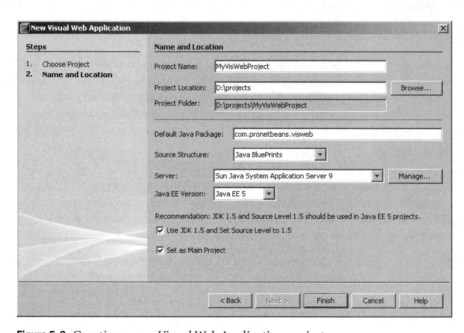

Figure 5-3. *Creating a new Visual Web Application project*

As you can see, creating a new Visual Web Application project is very similar to creating a regular Web Application project. The only real difference is specifying the value of the Java EE Version drop-down field.

Your new project will be listed in the Projects window. Let's review the project structure in the Projects window.

Navigating the Visual Web Application Project Structure

Like a Web Application project, the Visual Web Application project type is structured as a set of parent-child nodes, as shown in Figure 5-4. This structure allows you to access the core content of your project. It also organizes the different components that make up a Visual Web Application project into easy-to-understand sections.

Let's take a look at what each of these nodes contains.

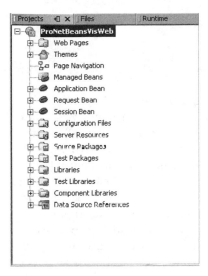

Figure 5-4. *The Visual Web Application nodes in the Projects window*

Web Pages

The Web Pages node is where the web-related content is stored. It is nearly identical to the Web Pages node in the Java Web Application project type discussed in the previous chapter. You can add JSP, HTML, CSS, images, and so on to this node.

One difference is that in the Visual Web Application project's Web Pages node, you can right-click any JSP file and select Set As Start Page. This option specifies that the file you clicked will be the default page displayed when the web application runs. The start page in the Web Pages node is denoted with a small green triangle next to the filename.

You can add new file types to this section by right-clicking the Web Pages node and selecting New ➤ File/Folder. In the New File wizard, select Visual Web from the categories section in the left pane. The list of available file types will then appear in the right pane of the window. For a visual web application, the following file types are available:

- Page

- Page Fragment

- JSP

- Servlet

- Filter

- Web Application Listener

- Tag Library Descriptor

- Tag File

- Tag Handler

- HTML

- XHTML

- Redirect HTML

After you click the Finish button to complete the wizard, the new file will be added under the Web Pages node and open in the IDE.

You should be aware of the differences in Page, Page Fragment, and JSP file types. A Page file type is a JSP page, but it is marked with a special icon and file type so that the VWP knows to open it in the Visual Designer. The JSP file type is intended for use with standard HTML and JSP content as described in the previous chapter. Even if you copied the JSP source content from a Page file type into a JSP file type, the VWP will still treat the JSP file type as a standard JSP file.

The Page Fragment file type is the same as the Page file type. However, the Page Fragment file type can be included inside a Page file type. In JSP code, you can use a special `include` directive to include the content of one JSP file inside another JSP. Many programmers use this approach when designing sites. If a site has a common page header, footer, or navigation menu, then each section can be contained in a JSP page and included into any page that needs to display that content. This way, the code for those sections is located in one place, making maintenance significantly easier. Page and Page Fragment file types are no different. They allow you to encapsulate commonly used sections into reusable pieces.

Themes

The Themes node contains the themes that you can use with your project. Themes are a collection of look-and-feel configurations that can be applied to a Visual Web Application project. They are made up of properties files, JavaScript files, CSS files, and images. Any component that appears in the Palette window under the Basic, Composite, and Layout sections uses themes.

In a JSF 1.2 and Java EE 5 Visual Web Application project, there is only one default theme: Web UI Default Theme. A small arrow next to the filename indicates that it has been applied to the project.

The VWP allows you to add your own themes and apply them to your project. The "Using VWP Themes" section later in this chapter covers how to customize a theme, install it, and apply it to your project.

Page Navigation

The Page Navigation node holds the VWP's tool for visually mapping the flow between pages. This is one of my favorite tools within the VWP, as it allows intuitive easy-to-use page navigation definition and management.

The Page Navigation tool allows you to drag-and-drop links between pages. As you create navigation links between pages, the VWP automatically generates content for the JSF framework's main configuration file, `faces-config.xml`. The "Using the Page Navigation Tool" section later in this chapter covers this tool in detail.

Managed Beans

The Managed Beans node contains the various JavaBeans that your Visual Web Application project manages. This file is automatically generated and updated as you work within the VWP, so it is highly recommended that you do *not* make any changes to it.

Application Bean, Request Bean, and Session Bean

The Application Bean, Request Bean, and Session Bean nodes represent the application scope JavaBean, request scope JavaBean, and session scope JavaBean, respectively. You can add properties, classes, and data that should be stored in each of these scopes of the project.

You can expand each of these nodes to see the child nodes Fields, Constructors, Methods, and Bean Patterns. You can right-click each of these subnodes to add a new element of the specified type to the corresponding class.

If you want to directly edit the class, double-click the appropriate Bean node in the Projects window. The corresponding ApplicationBean1.java, RequestBean1.java, or SessionBean1.java file will open in the Source Editor window.

Configuration Files

The Configuration Files node does not represent an actual folder in the project structure. The items that appear under this node are categorized as items that you would normally need access to when making configuration changes to the application. It also contains the deployment descriptor for the web application.

The Configuration Files node contains the web.xml, faces-config.xml, and other project configuration files. These are the same files that appear under the WEB-INF directory in the Web Pages node.

Note The files under the Configuration Files node are not copies of the files under other nodes. They simply represent an alternative method for viewing and accessing them. If you find it confusing, you don't even need to use the Configuration Files node.

Server Resources

The Server Resources node is where various types of resource are located. If you define a Java Database Connectivity (JDBC) resource, JDBC connection pool, Java Message Service (JMS) resource, persistence resource, JavaMail resource, and so on, they will be listed under this node. This is handy, since it gives you quick access to related resources.

Any items under the Server Resources node will appear under the Setup directory in the Files window.

Source Packages and Test Packages

The Source Packages node is where you define the Java source code to be used in your application. Here, you can add and maintain the package statements you would normally use, such as com.mycompany.projectname. Adding packages is extremely easy. Right-click the Source Packages node and select New ➤ Java Package. In the New Java Package window, you can specify the name of the new package, such as com.yourcompany.product. After you click the Finish button, the new package name is added under Source Packages in the Projects window.

The Test Packages node is nearly identical to the Source Packages node. However, the Test Packages node specifies the package structure for your application's test classes and JUnit tests.

If you were to execute the project tests by selecting Run ➤ Test *MyProjectName*, the classes in the Test Packages node would be executed.

Libraries and Test Libraries

The Libraries node is for defining class libraries that your application will use. If you need to use nonstandard libraries or classes from an external project, you can define them here. To add a JAR file to the libraries for your project, right-click the Libraries node and select Add JAR/Folder.

Similar to the Libraries node, the Test Libraries node contains class files or JAR files that your project test classes need to reference. You can add files to your test libraries by right-clicking the Test Libraries node and selecting Add JAR/Folder. The JAR file for JUnit exists by default in the Test Libraries section.

Component Libraries

The Component Libraries node is used to add new component libraries to the project. A component library, such as BluePrints AJAX Components, can be imported into NetBeans using the Component Library Manager.

You can access the manager by selecting Tools ➤ Component Library Manager. Once you have imported component libraries using the manager, they will be available to be added to a specific project.

To add a new component library to the project, right-click the Component Libraries node and select Add Component Library. The list of eligible libraries will appear, and you can add them to the project.

Importing and adding a component library to a NetBeans project will be covered in the "Working with Ajax-Enabled Components" section later in this chapter.

Data Source References

The Data Source References node contains a list of data sources configured for the Visual Web Application project. If you bind a database table to a component, then you instruct the VWP to reference the associated data source.

This node is useful because it displays all the database-related connections that are used by your Visual Web Application project. You do not have to go searching through your project code and configuration to discern which data sources you are using.

If you open a VWP project that has incorrect or missing data sources, you can use the Data Source References node to resolve or correct the missing data source. To do so, right-click the Data Source References node and select Resolve Data Source(s) from the context menu. See Chapter 18 for details on adding database connections.

Setting Project Properties

You can set properties for your Visual Web Application project by right-clicking the project name and selecting Properties. The Project Properties window lists several nodes in the left pane. Click each node to see the associated properties in the right pane. Many of these properties are similar to those available for other types of Java projects.

Of particular interest are the Packaging properties. Click the Packaging node to see the properties related to WAR files, as shown in Figure 5-5. The WAR file properties affect the packaging of the visual web application and which files are included. The WAR Content section lists each library in the project, along with its path in the WAR file where it will appear. If you want to package and deploy additional libraries or JAR files with the WAR file, such as JDBC drivers for a specific database, you can add them to the list.

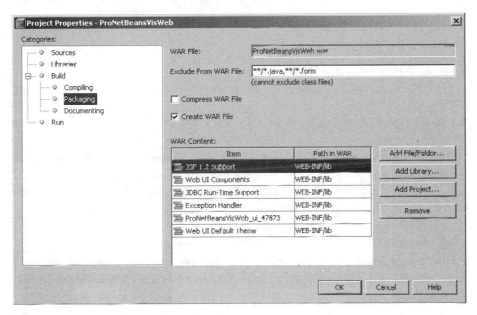

Figure 5-5. *The WAR file properties in the Project Properties window*

To add a JAR file or library to the WAR Content grid, click the Add File/Folder button or the Add Library button, and select the JAR file or library you want to include. Once it has been added to the WAR content grid, you will notice that the Path in WAR field for the newly added JAR file or library is blank. You must double-click inside the cell in the grid and type in the path, such as WEB-INF/lib. Click the OK button in the Project Properties dialog box to confirm the new property.

Navigating the Visual Web Application Project Layout

In the NetBeans IDE, you'll use a variety of windows while working on your Visual Web Application project. Each window has a specific purpose, some specifically for the VWP. Several of the most commonly used windows are described in the following sections.

Visual Designer Window

The Visual Designer window is where you'll perform the majority of the work for your Visual Web Application project. The Visual Designer is the WYSIWYG interface for working with JSF in NetBeans, as shown in Figure 5-6.

The Visual Designer window contains a white design surface with a dotted grid. You can drag-and-drop components onto this surface and arrange them any way you desire.

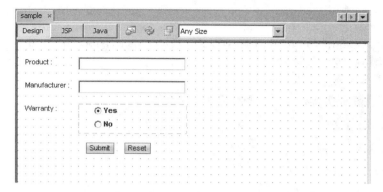

Figure 5-6. *The Visual Designer window*

At the top-left of the Visual Designer window are three view buttons: Design, JSP, and Java. The Design view, which appears by default, shows the visual design surface (Figure 5-6). The JSP view shows the source code of the JSP page, and the Java view shows the Java source code for the backing bean that matches the JSP page.

Note Throughout the rest of this chapter, I will refer to the Page file type as a *JSP page* or *JSP file*. The Page file type represents a JSF-aware JSP page that is specially recognized in the Visual Designer. Technically, you can add a non-JSF JSP page, but for the purposes of this chapter, I'll use the term *JSP* to refer to a JSF-aware JSP file.

To the right of the view buttons are several icons that provide access to common functions, as described in Table 5-1.

Table 5-1. *Toolbar Icons in the Visual Designer*

Icon	Function	Description
	Preview in Browser	Allows you to generate an HTML view of the JSP page currently open in the Visual Designer window. It will then open in the default browser.
	Refresh	Refreshes the page and components in case they are not displaying correctly.
	Show Virtual Forms	Displays any virtual forms that have been configured in the JSP file and outlines the components that are associated with each virtual form.

The drop-down list on the right of the Visual Designer toolbar is the Target Browser property. It specifies a screen resolution size for the web page you are developing. If you set it to the smallest size, 640x480 (600x300 page), and open a JSP page in the Visual Designer, you will notice the page visually denotes the shape and size.

Outline Window

The Outline window displays a listing of the objects in your visual web application. If you are viewing a JSP file in the Visual Designer window, the page name will appear as the top-level node in the Outline window, as shown in Figure 5-7.

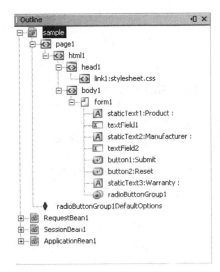

Figure 5-7. *The page node in the Outline window*

You can expand the page node and view the components that are part of the page. In Figure 5-7, you can see that the body node contains several child nodes, including a Form component, Static Text and Text Field components, and several other form-related components. This list of components represents the visual JSF elements that appear in Figure 5-6. You can right-click any of the components listed in the Outline window and manage them using the various context menu options.

The Outline window also displays nodes for the request bean, session bean, and application bean. These nodes are identical to the Request Bean, Session Bean, and Application Bean nodes that appear in the Projects window for a Visual Web Application project. You can double-click each of the nodes in the Outline window to open the corresponding source code in the Source Editor window.

If the Outline window is not displayed in the NetBeans IDE, you can open it by selecting Window ➤ Outline or by using the shortcut Ctrl+Alt+O.

Palette Window

The Palette window displays components specific to the file opened in the IDE. If you open a JSP file, the Palette window will display the JSF components you will use in the Visual Designer. You can click a component in the Palette window and drag-and-drop it into the JSP file open in the Visual Designer. The components available for Visual Web Application projects are covered in the "Working with JSF Components" section later in this chapter.

If the Palette window is not displayed, you can open it by selecting Window ➤ Palette.

Properties Window

The Properties window shows context-sensitive properties and values. As you select various elements in the NetBeans IDE, the associated properties are displayed in the Properties window. If you select an element or node in the Projects window, Outline window, or Visual Designer window, its properties are listed in the Properties window.

If the Properties window is not visible in the IDE, you can open in by selecting Window ➤ Properties or by using the keyboard shortcut Ctrl+Shift+7.

Dynamic Help Window

The Dynamic Help window displays specific help topics based on which element is selected in the various Visual Web Application project areas. If you select a component in the Palette window, a node in the Projects window, or any component in a JSP page, the Dynamic Help window will list the topic. Double-click the topic listed in the Help window to open the NetBeans Help and display the related help text.

You can open the Dynamic Help window by selecting Window ➤ Dynamic Help or by using the keyboard shortcut Ctrl+Alt+H.

Building a Project

During the development of your application, you may want to test compile the entire source code of your application. You may also want to create a distributable WAR file so that you can deploy the application to an external server. In NetBeans, you can choose to compile and build an entire web application without having to deploy it to an application server.

Building an application in NetBeans is quite simple. Just select Build ➤ Build Main Project. This assumes the project you want to build is set to the main project. If it is not, you can set it to the main project by right-clicking the project name in the Projects window and choosing Set Main Project. You can also right-click a project name and choose Build Project from the context menu if you want to build a specific project.

Once you have started the project build process, the Output window should appear. You will see a number of lines scroll through the Output window. The output lines are caused by the actions that are taking place in the background based on the project's build configuration (in other words, the project's Ant build file). Choosing the Build menu option actually activates an Ant target for the current project. For more details on how NetBeans projects are structured and integration with Ant, see Chapter 14.

The basics of what happened during the build are abstracted away for the most part. You should see a "Build Successful" message as one of the last lines in the Output window. This tells you that the Java source files compiled correctly and the web application was packaged as specified in the project properties. If you selected the Create WAR File property in the Project Properties window, the build process will generate a WAR file in the `dist` directory. You can review the project files and folders in the Files window.

Assuming the application compiled and was built correctly, you can now copy the WAR file to a J2EE server and run your application.

Cleaning and Building a Project

You may also choose the Build ➤ Clean and Build Main Project menu option. This does the same set of tasks as the Build option, with one difference: all content inside the `build` directory in the NetBeans project structure is deleted. This ensures that there are no class files or other resource files present.

After deleting the content of the `build` directory, the project is then recompiled into the `build` directory. This is sometimes necessary if you have made numerous code changes after you've built an application and want to feel confident that the compiled code is using the most current version of the source files. This also comes in handy after updating your application from a source code repository like CVS.

■Caution In NetBeans, you may occasionally have a problem cleaning and building a running web application. If JAR files in the `WEB-INF/lib` directory are in use by the application server, they often cannot be deleted by the clean operation. You need to go to the Runtime window and stop the running application server before initiating the Clean and Build operation.

Compiling JSP Files

For Visual Web Application projects, you may also want to make sure that all the JSP files are compiled during the project build operation. This is a configurable option that is disabled by default. It is highly recommended that you enable it, since it will let you know if your JSP files will compile correctly. To enable this property, do the following:

1. Right-click the project name in the Projects window and select Properties.

2. Under the Build category, choose Compiling.

3. Select the check box next to the Test Compile All JSP files During Builds field.

4. Click the OK button.

The next time you build your project, you should notice some additional text in the Output window under the heading `compile-jsps`. With each project build, all the JSP files will be compiled.

Running a Project

A large part of developing Visual Web Application projects is being able to test and run them in an application server. During the regular course of development, most programmers will run a JSP page dozens of times to make sure it functions as expected.

When you choose to run a web application, it is first built, packaged, and deployed. If the associated Java application server is not started, NetBeans attempts to start and deploy the application to it. NetBeans uses the project's Ant build file to compile, package, and run the application files.

To run the web application, select Run ➤ Run Main Project, or press F6. The Output window will appear. As the various steps in the build configuration progress, you will notice a separate tab for the run operation open in the Output window.

The various build steps will execute: compiling any Java source files, compiling JSP files, copying files to the project build directory, and so on. Before the application actually runs, you will notice the application files are packaged into a distribution file. For a Visual Web Application project, a WAR file is created, as discussed earlier in this chapter.

After the run and run-deploy steps in the build process execute, the target application server will be started. Additional tabs will open in the Output window for the application server.

After the application server has started, NetBeans should open the default web browser and display the application. For a Visual Web Application project, one JSP page is specified as the start page, and that page will open in the web browser.

Using VWP Themes

The available VWP themes are listed under the Themes node in the Projects window for a project. Themes are made up of JavaScript files, properties files, CSS files, message files, and images. As noted earlier in the chapter, the components in the Basic, Composite, and Layout sections of the Palette window use themes. Other components, such as those in the Standard section of the Palette window, do not use themes.

For a Visual Web Application project that is configured to use Java EE 5 and JSF 1.2, only one theme is available by default: Web UI Default Theme. However, you can import themes into NetBeans and apply them to your projects. If you are not sure how to create a theme, you can start with the default theme, modify it as you see fit, and import it as a new theme.

Customizing Themes

Since a theme is just a set of files packaged as a JAR file, you can locate the JAR file and extract its contents. Then you can modify the theme files to customize the theme.

Extracting Theme Files

The default theme JAR file is located at `<netbeans-install-dir>/modules/etc/` `webui-jsf-suntheme.jar`. Copy the JAR file to an empty folder and extract the contents. The root contents of the JAR file are the standard `META-INF` directory and a `com` directory that denotes the first portion of the package hierarchy in which the theme files are located.

Open each directory under `com` until you have located the directories in `com/sun/webui/` `jsf/suntheme`. This directory contains the following subdirectories:

- `css`

- `images`

- `javascript`

- `messages`

- `properties`

- `templates`

Each of the subdirectories contains a set of files that directly influence the behavior or look and feel of the theme. You can navigate to the files in each directory, make changes to them, and repackage the JAR file, thereby creating a customized theme.

Altering the Theme's CSS Files

The CSS files for the theme are located in the css directory of the theme package structure. You can edit each of these files to change the CSS properties that are applied to specific components in a Visual Web Application project.

The main CSS file is named css_master.css. Its contents are as follows:

```
@import url(layout.css);
@import url(typography.css);
@import url(colorAndMedia.css);
@import url("table2.css");
@import url("commontaskssection.css");
@import url("progressBar.css");
```

The css_master.css file contains nothing except import directives that instruct the web application to import the CSS properties from other files. You can open each CSS file and edit the properties.

Altering the Theme's Image Files

The images directory in the theme package structure contains numerous subdirectories. Each of these holds different image files used by the theme, which can be replaced with whatever custom images you want.

For example, the table directory contains images that are used by the JSF Table component, such as buttons, spacers, and icons. If you have created custom versions of these images, you can simply overwrite the existing files so the new images appear in the theme. If you add new image files, you need to make a change in the theme properties file, as described in the "Altering the Theme's Properties" section, coming up shortly.

Altering the Theme's JavaScript Files

The theme package structure also contains a javascript directory. In it are numerous .js files that contain the various JavaScript functions used by the widgets and components in the VWP.

If you need to alter the JavaScript behavior of one of the components, you can locate its code in one of these files. I recommend against changing any of the JavaScript code in these files unless you know exactly what you are doing, because any changes you make can have unknown side effects. If you need to make changes, a best practice is to make only one change at a time and test it. This reduces the risk of producing hard-to-fix bugs in the JavaScript.

■**Tip** One of the nice things about the JavaScript code that appears in the theme `.js` files is that it is clear, well written, and reasonably well documented. All too often, tools generate obtuse or obfuscated code with little or no documentation. If you need to use the JavaScript capabilities exhibited by a particular component, you can locate the associated JavaScript code and reuse it. The well-written code and the in-line documentation should make it relatively easy to understand and import into your own custom JavaScript.

Altering the Theme's Messages

One of my favorite theme customizations is to change the theme messages. These are words or phrases that appear in the various components used by the Visual Web Application project.

The theme package structure contains a `messages` folder, which has several `.properties` files in it. The `messages.properties` file contains the default messages, regardless of which locale is specified. There is also an identical file named `messages_en.properties`, which contains the specific messages for the English language. If you want to localize the messages that appear in the components in your project, you need to create a separate `.properties` file for the desired locale.

The messages in these `.properties` files are in *name=value* format. By changing the value, you can customize the text of the words that appear in various places in a component.

As an example, let's modify the messages for the JSF Add Remove component.

1. Right-click the Web Pages node in the Projects window and select New ➤ File/Folder.

2. Select the Visual Web category and the Page file type, and then click the Next button.

3. Name the file and choose a folder location in the project. Then click the Finish button.

4. In the Composite section of the Palette window, locate the Add Remove component. Drag-and-drop the Add Remove component to the JSP file to add it to the page.

5. Select the Add Remove component in the Visual Designer window.

6. Open the Properties window by selecting Window ➤ Properties.

7. Select the check boxes for the following properties:

   - `labelOnTop`

   - `moveButtons`

   - `selectAll`

   - `availableItemsLabel`

   - `selectedItemsLabel`

8. Click OK in the Properties window. The Add Remove component will display most of the message-related fields, as shown in Figure 5-8.

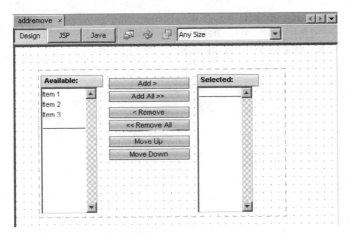

Figure 5-8. *The Add Remove component in the Visual Designer window*

9. Navigate to the theme messages folder, expand it, and open the messages_en.properties file. You will see a section for the Add Remove component. The list of messages appears as follows:

```
AddRemove.add=Add >
AddRemove.addVertical=Add
AddRemove.addAll=Add All >>
AddRemove.addAllVertical=Add All
AddRemove.remove- < Remove
AddRemove.removeVertical=Remove
AddRemove.removeAll= << Remove All
AddRemove.removeAllVertical=Remove All
AddRemove.moveUp=Move Up
AddRemove.moveDown=Move Down
AddRemove.available=Available:
AddRemove.selected=Selected:
```

10. Modify some of the fields to the following (slightly ridiculous) messages:

```
AddRemove.add=Add It >
AddRemove.addVertical=Add It
AddRemove.addAll=Add It All >>
AddRemove.addAllVertical=Add It All
AddRemove.remove= < Get Rid O' It
AddRemove.removeVertical=Get Rid O' It
AddRemove.removeAll= << Remove It All
AddRemove.removeAllVertical=Remove It All
AddRemove.moveUp=Move It Up
AddRemove.moveDown=Move It Down
AddRemove.available=Whatcha Got:
AddRemove.selected=Whatcha Picked:
```

11. Save the modified file.

After you package the theme files, import the theme JAR, and apply the theme, as described in the "Importing the Modified Theme" section, the Add Remove component should display some slightly different messages, as shown in Figure 5-9.

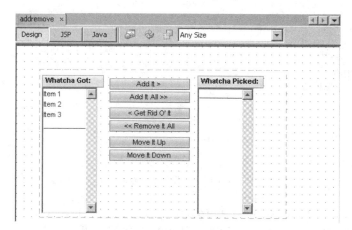

Figure 5-9. *The updated Add Remove component in the Visual Designer window*

Altering the Theme's Properties

The theme package structure's `properties` directory includes several `.properties` files that contain various *name=value* property settings. These properties associate certain theme elements with specific tag names so that the theme code can correctly reference them.

For instance, as mentioned earlier, the images associated with a theme can be overwritten with custom buttons and icons. You can also add new images and have them used by the theme. To use a new image file in place of an existing one, you need to modify the `images.properties` file in the `properties` directory. In this file, the *name=value* properties define the path to specific images as well as height, width, and alt text for many of the images. You can alter these properties for a specific image to set the values for your new image.

Altering the Theme's Templates

In the theme package structure's `templates` directory are several HTML files that define HTML templates used by the theme. The templates that are included with the default theme deal mostly with progress bars and tables. You can edit the text of each template and save the changes.

Importing the Modified Theme

After you have created a custom theme, to use it, you must package and import it into NetBeans. You can do so using the Library Manager, but you must first create a JAR file for the theme. You can use the JDK's `jar` tool or if you're lazy (like me), you can use your system's zip utility. Here are the steps:

1. Start in the original directory that contains the com and META-INF directories. Select both of them and add them to a new zip file named pronetbeans-theme.jar (or whatever you choose to name the JAR file).

2. Open NetBeans and select Tools ➤ Library Manager. The Library Manager window will display the various libraries that have been configured in NetBeans. The left side of the window contains a list of the different libraries organized by categories.

3. In the list of libraries, select the Theme Libraries category and click the New Library button.

4. In the New Library dialog box, enter a name for your library and click the OK button. The new library will be added to the list of libraries on the left side of the window.

5. With the new library selected, make sure the Classpath tab is selected, and click the Add JAR/Folder button on the right.

6. Using the Browse JAR/Folder dialog box, locate the JAR file for the new theme you created and click the Add JAR/Folder button. The path to the JAR file will be displayed for your theme library, as shown in Figure 5-10.

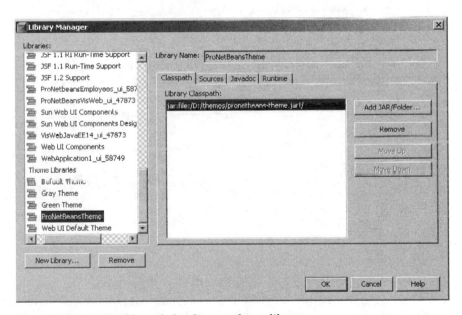

Figure 5-10. *The JAR file path for the new theme library*

7. Click the OK button to close the Library Manager. The new theme is now available for use in a Visual Web Application project.

In the Projects window, expand the plus icon next to the Themes node. You will see a node for your newly created theme. To apply your theme, right-click the theme name and select Set As Current Theme. NetBeans will process the change for a short period and then display an information message stating that the active theme has changed. It also mentions that for the changes to fully take effect, you may need to stop the application server, clean and build the project, and start the server before the theme is applied.

Using the Page Navigation Tool

The Page Navigation tool is one of those technologies that really surprise you with how well they work. When I first started working with the VWP and read about the Page Navigation tool, I was excited, but skeptical. It seemed too good to be true. After minutes of playing around and testing it, I realized it not only worked, but it worked well.

Defining Navigation Rules

The Page Navigation window is essentially a front-end for the `faces-config.xml` file. For those of you familiar with the format of the file, the actions you perform in the visual part of the Page Navigation window are translated into navigation rules in the `faces-config.xml` file. Here is an example of a `faces-config.xml` file:

```
<?xml version="1.0" encoding="UTF-8"?>
<faces-config version="1.2" xmlns="http://java.sun.com/xml/ns/javaee" ➥
            xmlns:xsi="http://www.w3.org/2001/XMLSchema-instance" ➥
            xsi:schemaLocation="http://java.sun.com/xml/ns/javaee ➥
            http://java.sun.com/xml/ns/javaee/web-facesconfig_1_2.xsd">

    <navigation-rule>
        <from-view-id>/addUsers.jsp</from-view-id>
        <navigation-case>
            <from-outcome>success</from-outcome>
            <to-view-id>/results.jsp</to-view-id>
        </navigation-case>
    </navigation-rule>
</faces-config>
```

The `faces-config.xml` file contains navigation rules that define the starting view, specified by the `from-view-id` tag. Each navigation result can also contain one or more cases that determine the destination view based on an outcome. In the preceding example, if the `addUsers.jsp` view returns an outcome of `success`, then the JSF controller routes page flow to the `results.jsp` view.

If you are confused by the format of the tags in the `faces-config.xml` file, or simply don't like to work with it, you can use the Page Navigation window to set up your page navigation.

Using the Page Navigation Window

To open the Page Navigation window, double-click the Page Navigation node under a Visual Web Application project in the Projects window. The Page Navigation window has a blank white background and dotted grid lines. If you have any JSP pages in your project, they are displayed in the Page Navigation window as icons.

Let's add several pages, configure some components, and create links to demonstrate using the Page Navigation tool.

1. Within your Visual Web Application project in the Projects window, double-click the Page Navigation node to open the Page Navigation window.

2. Right-click in a blank spot in the Page Navigation window and select Add Page. You can also press the shortcut Ctrl+A.

3. In the Select Page Name dialog box, enter menu as the name for your new page. You do not need to enter a file extension of .jsp, as it is assumed. A new file icon labeled menu.jsp is added to the Page Navigation window, as shown in Figure 5-11. The menu.jsp file is also added in the Projects window under the Web Pages node. It is the same as if you had right-clicked the Web Pages node, selected New ➤ File/Folder, and added the menu.jsp file.

Figure 5-11. *The menu.jsp file icon in the Page Navigation window*

4. Double-click the menu.jsp icon in the Page Navigation window. The corresponding file will open in the Visual Designer window.

5. From the Palette window, drag-and-drop three Button components and one Hyperlink component onto the menu.jsp file in the Visual Designer window.

6. Set the component properties as follows:

   - Select the first Button component. Set its id property to btnProducts and the text property to Products.

   - Select the second Button component. Set its id property to btnServices and the text property to Services.

   - Select the third Button component. Set its id property to btnAboutUs and the text property to About Us.

   - Select the Hyperlink component. Set its id property to lnkSiteMap and the text property to Site Map.

7. Save the changes by pressing Ctrl+S.

8. In the Page Navigation window, right-click in an empty space window and select Add Page.

9. Add four new pages named products, services, aboutus, and sitemap.

10. Arrange the four pages you just created in a vertical column on the right side of the Page Navigation window. Put the menu page on the left side of the window.

11. Click the menu page. The icon will expand and display a list of the Button and Hyperlink components contained within it. Next to each component name is a small blue icon.

12. Click and hold the small blue icon next to the btnProducts item. Then drag the cursor onto the products page and release the mouse button. An orange line now connects the two pages, as shown in Figure 5-12.

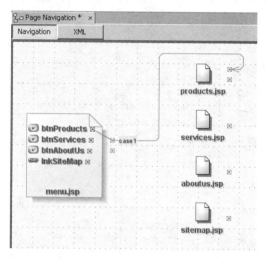

Figure 5-12. *The menu and products pages linked together in the Page Navigation window*

13. You have just created a JSF navigation rule in the faces-config.xml file. Click the XML tab along the top of the window to toggle to the faces-config.xml file. You will see the new navigation rule:

```
<navigation-rule>
    <from-view-id>/menu.jsp</from-view-id>
    <navigation-case>
        <from-outcome>case1</from-outcome>
        <to-view-id>/products.jsp</to-view-id>
    </navigation-case>
</navigation-rule>
```

14. The rule basically states that once the btnProducts button is clicked, if the button's action method in the backing bean returns the value case1, then the page flow will be directed to the products.jsp page. To verify this, click the menu.jsp icon in the Page Navigation window, and then double-click the btnProducts line. The menu.jsp file will open to the Java tab of the Visual Designer window. The cursor will also be placed inside the btnProducts_action method so that you can alter the code if necessary. Notice that the return outcome is already set to case1, as shown in this code snippet:

```
public String btnProducts_action() {
    // TODO: Process the action. Return value is a navigation
    // case name where null will return to the same page.

    return "case1";
}
```

15. Use the Page Navigation window to link the other components in the menu.jsp file to the other pages you've created:

- Connect the btnServices Button component to the services.jsp page.

- Connect the btnAboutUs Button component to the aboutus.jsp page.

- Connect the lnkSiteMap Hyperlink component to the sitemap.jsp page.

The resulting layout of the files in the Page Navigation window should look something like Figure 5-13.

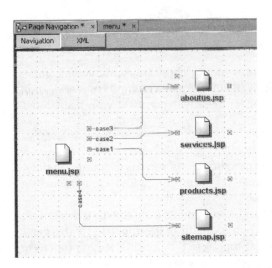

Figure 5-13. *The linked files in the Page Navigation window*

If your page links do not look like the ones in Figure 5-13, you can adjust them. You can click and drag the page icons up and down in the window so that they are ordered in any fashion you desire.

You can also move the little orange anchors that appear next to the icons and that connect the arrows. To do so, press and hold down the Ctrl key, and click one of the anchors. They should all turn red and allow you to move one anchor at a time to the top, bottom, left, or right of the page icon. After you are satisfied with the anchor's position, release the Ctrl key and click in a blank spot in the Visual Designer window. The link lines will be reorganized based on your modifications.

Working with JSF Components

The JSF components in the NetBeans VWP provide an amazing array of features and flexibility. The VWP abstracts away many of the mundane technical details of JSF, so that you can focus on making your application work.

The JSF components are a combination of HTML tags and JSTL tags that have properties, trigger events, and the ability to bind to data. In many cases, you can add a component to a JSP page, configure its properties, and bind it to a database table, field, or Java object without having to write a single line of code.

Like other NetBeans components, the JSF components are available in the Palette window, primarily from three sections:

- The Basic section contains components for text, form elements, hyperlinks, images, and calendars. The components all share a similar look and feel due to the theme that has been applied to the project.

- The Layout section contains components such as forms, page separators, tabs, grid panels, and layout panels. These elements are typically used for page layout and grouping of items.

- The Composite section contains only a few components. These are combination components that provide nicely wrapped functionality that represent commonly used widgets in a web application. Much of the programming for these widgets has already been done.

Setting Component Properties

After you've added a component to your page, you can click it and view its properties in the Properties window. In the Properties window, you can set the attributes for a component exactly as if you were writing code, only it's easier.

For example, Figure 5-14 shows a page with some components from the Basic section of the Palette window. If you click one of the Text Field components in the upper-left of this page, you can edit its properties. Suppose that you set the id property to txtName, the columns property to 16, the text property to John, and the maxLength field to 100. You also enabled the required check box. You could then view the corresponding JSP code for the component by clicking the JSP tab in the Visual Designer window. It would look like the following:

```
<webuijsf:textField binding="#{formComponents.txtName}"
                    columns="16"
                    id="txtName"
                    maxLength="100"
                    required="true"
                    style="left: 72px; top: 24px; position: absolute"
                    text="John" />
```

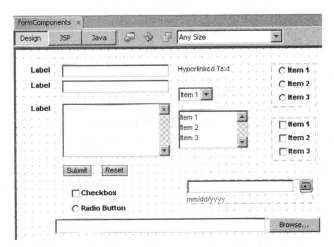

Figure 5-14. *Sample JSF components from the Basic section of the Palette window*

As you can see, the property settings in the Properties window are reflected in the code. Using the Properties window can often be faster than switching to the code view and trying to locate a specific line of code.

Setting Component Event Handlers

Most components have event handlers. There are client-side JavaScript behaviors that can be configured via the component properties in the Properties window. There are also server-side Java event handlers that are evoked when certain actions occur.

To set an event handler for a component, right-click it and select Edit Event Handler. This displays a submenu with a list of event handlers available for that specific type of component.

Let's return to the sample page in Figure 5-14. Suppose you want to set an event handler for when the value changes in the txtName Text Field component. Right-click that component and select Edit Event Handler ➤ processValueChange. The Java view of the Visual Designer window will open, displaying the source code for the JSP page's backing bean. The page should automatically scroll down to the txtName_processValueChange method. The method will be empty by default. You can use the ValueChangeEvent object passed in as a parameter to query the old and new value of the Text Field component whose value has changed. For example, you can retrieve the old and new values and output them to the standard output stream as in this code snippet:

```
public void txtName_processValueChange(ValueChangeEvent event) {

    Object objOld = event.getOldValue();
    Object objNew = event.getNewValue();

    if(objOld!=null) {
        System.out.println("Old=" + objOld.toString());
    }
    if(objNew!=null) {
        System.out.println("New=" + objNew.toString());
    }
}
```

If other components in the JSP page use event handlers, they will also be listed in the JSP page's backing bean source code. There is no guarantee that they will be placed sequentially in a file, so you may consider using the Navigator window (select Window ➤ Navigator or press Ctrl+7 to open this window) to view the list of methods in the file. Any event handlers will show up in the Navigator window, because they are implemented as Java methods.

Working with the Table Component

You will probably use the JSF Table component often in your Visual Web application projects. When you drag-and-drop the Table component from the Palette window into a JSP file in the Visual Designer, it has a basic table layout of three columns with column headers and five rows, as shown in Figure 5-15.

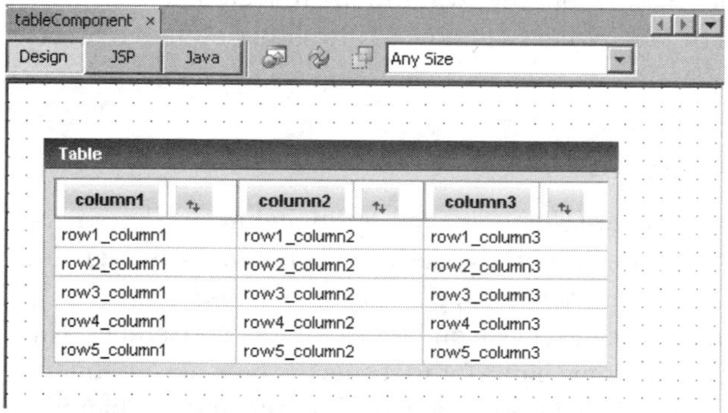

Figure 5-15. *A basic Table component in a JSP page*

Once you have added the table to the page, you can very quickly configure some advanced capabilities. You can access the advanced features and layout options of the table by right-clicking the component and selecting Table Layout. The Table Layout window will appear, as shown in Figure 5-16.

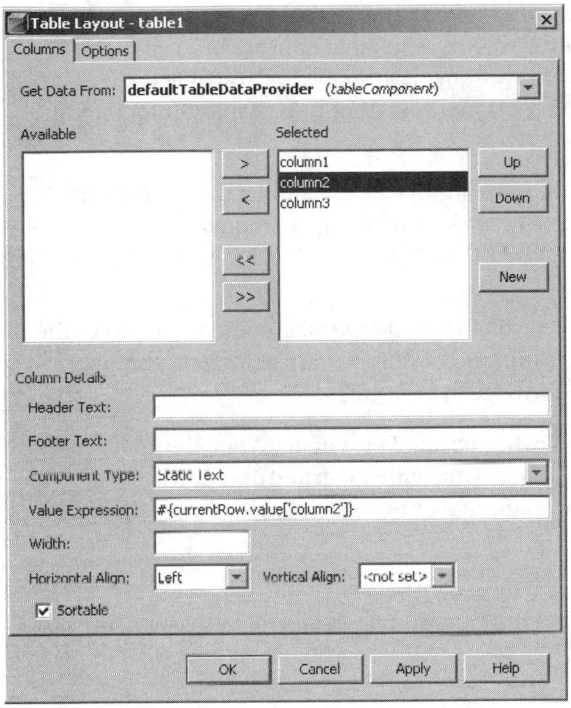

Figure 5-16. *The Columns tab in the Table Layout window*

Table Column Settings

The Columns tab of the Table Layout window contains the following fields and settings:

Get Data From: Specifies the data provider that populates the table, if you are using data binding. (Data binding is covered later in this chapter.)

Available and Selected: You can add items from the Available list into the Selected list. Once items appear in the Selected list, you can use the Up and Down buttons to reorder the columns as they appear in the table. You can also use the New button to create a new column in the table. As you select different columns in the Selected list, the fields in the Column Details area display the matching values.

Header Text: Specifies the name of the column header that will appear in the table. If you click any column in the Selected list, the Header Text field is initially blank.

Footer Text: Specifies the text that will appear in the footer row of the table. Like the Header Text field, this field is initially blank. Usually, you want the Header Text and Footer Text fields to have the same value.

Component Type: Specifies the kind of component that will display in the column in the table. By default, this field is set to Static Text. Any value that appears in a cell in the column will be rendered as plaintext. The drop-down list shows the available options, such as Static Text, Text Field, Text Area, Button, Hyperlink, Checkbox, Radio Button, Image, and so on.

Value Expression: Specifies the value that the column will display and primarily deals with data binding. I will discuss this field more in the section on data binding.

Width: Sets the pixel width of the column.

Horizontal Align and Vertical Align: Allow you to specify the alignment of the text in the table cell. These are basic presentation properties, but in certain situations, they can greatly affect how the data appears on the page in each cell.

Sortable: Allows the column to be sortable. It is selected by default. When the table appears in a web browser, the column will have a small icon with an up and down arrow next to the header. This icon allows you to sort the column in either ascending or descending order.

Table Option Settings

The second tab in the Table Layout window is the Options tab, as shown in Figure 5-17. This tab contains several table-level properties.

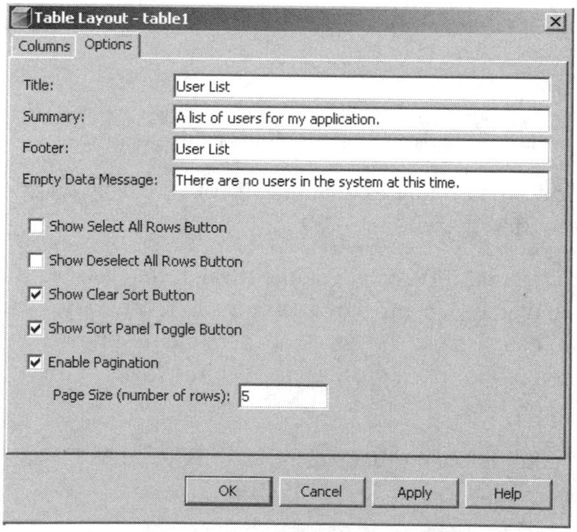

Figure 5-17. *The Options tab in the Table Layout window*

The Options tab of the Table Layout window contains the following fields and settings:

Title: The text in the Title field will appear in the title bar of the table.

Summary: This text does not display in the table; rather, it is read by Braille and media readers.

Footer: The text in this field appears beneath the last row of the table.

Empty Data Message: The text in this field appears if there are no records displayed in the table. This is mostly relevant when using data binding.

Show Select All Rows Button: If selected, the table will have an icon that allows you to select all the items in the table.

Show Deselect All Rows Button: If selected, the table will have an icon that allows you to deselect all the items in the table.

Show Clear Sort Button: If selected, an icon that will clear a sort will appear near the top of the table. If you have sorted any of the columns in the table, clicking the Clear Sort button will reset the table to the default sorting.

Show Sort Panel Toggle Button: If selected, you will have access to a convenient sorting utility from the table. The Sort Panel Toggle button is represented by an up and down arrow icon. When you click this button, the table header will expand and display the sorting utility, as shown in Figure 5-18. Here, you can select to sort the table by up to three columns. Sortable columns are available from the drop-down lists (sortable columns are those with their Sortable property set, which is an option on the Columns tab of the Table Layout window). After you click the OK button, the table will be reordered based on your settings.

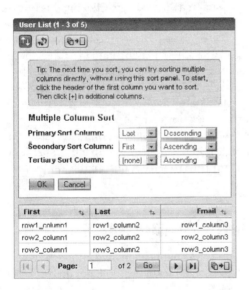

Figure 5-18. *The sorting utility for a Table component displayed in the browser*

Enable Pagination: If selected, adds a powerful set of pagination functions to the table (see Figure 5-19). The pagination icons appear along the bottom of the Table component in the Visual Designer window.

Page Size: If you check the Enable Pagination box, this field becomes active. Here, you can set the number of rows to appear on each page of the table.

If you enable pagination for your table, run the web application, and view the page, your table will include the pagination functions, as shown in Figure 5-19.

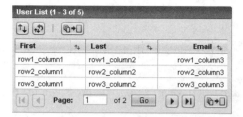

Figure 5-19. *The pagination icons along the bottom of the Table component*

The table displayed in the figure has a row along the bottom that contains the pagination icons. The leftmost buttons are the standard Go to First Page and Go to Previous Page functions. To the right of those buttons is a text label "Page:" followed by a text field with a number in it. You can enter a page number here and click the Go button to jump to that page. This means that if there are dozens of pages, you can jump to, say, page 14 without having to scroll through each one.

To the right of the page-jumping elements are buttons that represent the standard Go to Next Page and Go to Last Page functions. They may be disabled, depending on which page you are currently displaying. (Obviously, you cannot go the next or last page if you are already displaying the last page of records.)

The rightmost button has the function Show Data in a Single Page. Clicking this button refreshes the page with pagination disabled. This is handy when you want to display all the records on a single page and sort them.

It used to be common for programmers to worry about displaying data in a table and paginating the records. I've spoken to a good number of developers who laughed about the amount of time they wasted creating pagination features like next *N* records, last record, first record, and so on. As you've seen, in the NetBeans VWP, the Enable Pagination check box makes it all happen automatically. It's amazing what one little check box can do!

The Table component is an important element to any web application. Understanding how to use all its features will allow you to create high-impact applications. In the "Data Binding" section later in this chapter, I will discuss how to improve the usefulness of the Table component by binding it to a database table.

Working with Ajax-Enabled Components

If you haven't heard the buzzword *Ajax* by now, you've probably been living under a rock. Ajax is not a breakfast cereal or a cleaning product, but a packaged set of technologies that is currently redefining the paradigm of web development.

Ajax is an acronym that stands for Asynchronous JavaScript And XML. It represents two existing and proven technologies that have been around for years: JavaScript and XML. These technologies have been repackaged under the Ajax name and have much better cross-browser support than in the past. A growing number of frameworks are available for working with client-side Ajax, including Prototype, Dojo, Backbase, Atlas, and others. Server-side frameworks are also emerging for Ajax, such as the Google Web Toolkit (GWT).

Even though Ajax is a primarily a client-side technology, tools like the GWT provide Java-based APIs that, in turn, generate HTML and JavaScript that is Ajax-friendly. I couldn't possibly do justice to the GWT in this brief mention, but it is an impressive tool that every Java web programmer should download and try out. For more information about the GWT, check out its web site at http://code.google.com/webtoolkit.

The NetBeans VWP allows you to install a set of Ajax components from the Java BluePrints Solutions catalog. You can even create sample projects that use each component to review the code and see how it actually works. The first steps in using the Ajax components are downloading, installing, and importing the component library.

Installing the Ajax Components

To download the Ajax components, you must use the NetBeans Update Center. Open NetBeans and select Tools ➤ Update Center. In the Update Center window, scroll through the list to make sure the NetBeans Visual Web Pack Update Center is selected, and then click the Next button. NetBeans will connect to and query the Update Center, and then display the list of available modules. You should see a listing for BluePrints AJAX Components. Select the module and use the Update Center wizard to install it. (See Chapter 2 for details on using the NetBeans Update Center and installing modules.) You may be prompted to restart the IDE. Click the OK button and wait for NetBeans to restart.

To install the downloaded Ajax components, follow these steps:

1. Select Tools ➤ Component Library Manager. The Component Library Manager window will open, displaying the list of component libraries that have been installed in NetBeans. Unless you have previously installed component libraries, this list will be blank.

2. Click the Import button. The Import Component Library dialog box will open, as shown in Figure 5-20.

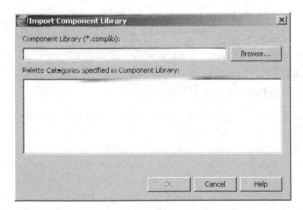

Figure 5-20. *The Import Component Library dialog box*

3. Click the Browse button and navigate your file system to locate the BluePrints AJAX Components library file named ui.complib that was downloaded and installed as part of the BluePrints AJAX Components module. The file browser should open to a display that lists the ui.complib file. If it does not, navigate to *<NetBeans-install-directory>/* rave2.0/sample, and you should see the file. Select this file.

4. You will see two Palette categories listed in the Import Component Library dialog box: BluePrints AJAX Components and BluePrints AJAX Support Beans. Click the OK button to import the component library. A small dialog box may appear with a progress indicator while the file is being imported, but that should disappear in a second or two.

The BluePrints AJAX Components library is now listed in the Component Library Manager window, as shown in Figure 5-21. Several nodes are listed under the BluePrints AJAX Components node. If you click each node, the right pane will display a file path to one or more JAR or zip files that make up the component library.

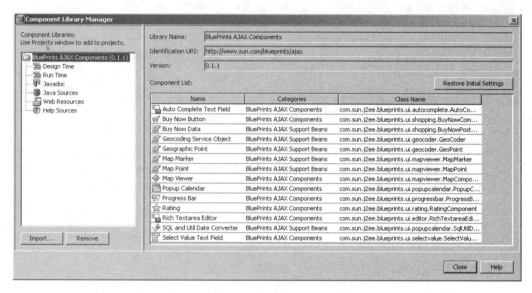

Figure 5-21. *The Component Library Manager with the BluePrints AJAX Components library*

Adding the Component Library to a Project

After you've imported the BluePrints AJAX Components, you need to manually add them to a Visual Web Application project before you can use them.

To add the components, right-click the Component Libraries node in the Projects window for a Visual Web Application project and select Add Component Library from the context menu. The Add Component Library dialog box lists the eligible component libraries. Select BluePrints AJAX Components from the list and click the Add Component Library button.

The component library will be added to the project under the Component Libraries node. The Ajax-enabled components are now available in the Palette window.

■**Caution** You must add the BluePrints AJAX Components to a project using the Component Libraries node before you can use them. A category listing for the component library may still appear in the Palette window, but none of the component icons will show up. Don't waste your time trying to figure out why they won't appear (like I did)!

Using the Ajax Components

The BluePrints AJAX Components are JSF components with asynchronous JavaScript built in. This in itself is not a big deal, but when you consider that you can drag-and-drop them into a JSP page in NetBeans, use the Visual Designer to arrange and position them, and use the Properties window to configure them, you should be starting to get excited!

One of the biggest benefits to using these components in a NetBeans Visual Web Application project is that they abstract away most of the details of working with Ajax. You also do not need to worry about many of the cross-platform, cross-browser coding issues you usually run into with JavaScript. Most, if not all, of the Ajax code is generated and managed by the component library.

The BluePrints AJAX Components library contains a short yet impressive list of components, as shown in Table 5-2. Several of these components will be described in more detail in the next sections.

Table 5-2. *The BluePrints AJAX Components*

Name	Description
Auto Complete Text Field	Provides "Google Suggest" capabilities. Text typed in a text box is sent asynchronously to the server to look up and return a matching list of values, which is displayed in a layer.
Buy Now Button	Provides a JSF wrapper for the PayPal BuyNow button.
Map Viewer	Provides mapping and lookup functionality using Google Maps.
Popup Calendar	Provides a pop-up Gregorian calendar for picking dates.
Progress Bar	Enables a progress bar for displaying activity of a lengthy process.
Rating	Displays a series of star images allowing you to select a rating.
Rich Textarea Editor	Provides a rich text area component with advanced text-editing capabilities.
Select Value Text Field	Provides Google Suggest capabilities similar to the Auto Complete Text Field, except that the results are displayed in a drop-down list.

Auto Complete Text Field Component

The Auto Complete Text Field component provides a capability similar to Google Suggest. As you type text into a text box, the system performs an asynchronous request behind the scenes to query the database. The text that was entered is used to query a set of data, perform a match, and return the results. The data results are returned to the component and displayed in a floating layer, as shown in Figure 5-22.

This type of component is great for web pages that contain numerous text fields, since it can save the user time. It can also help reduce data-entry errors for fields that contain names of businesses, organizations, or other text that could take several forms. For example, if an application requires you to enter the name of a college, you might enter Syracuse University, Syracuse Univ, Syracuse U, or SU. Each of these is correct, but they represent different entries in a database and could cause incorrect data to return from a query.

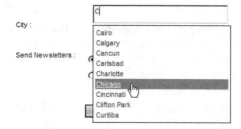

Figure 5-22. *A sample Auto Complete Text Field component*

Rating Component

If you have ever read a news article on MSNBC's web site, you have seen the Rating component. It allows you to mouse over a series of star-shaped images. As you mouse over a star, it becomes highlighted. If you click a particular star, you have applied a rating. This type of component uses Ajax; when you make your rating, the page refreshes, yet the rating value is sent to the MSNBC server behind the scenes.

The Rating component from the BluePrints AJAX Components library is nearly identical to those seen on popular news sites like MSNBC. However, the component allows you to customize numerous data and visual properties that affect how the component is rendered. For example, you can set the maximum number of stars (the maximum rating) that appear, show an icon labeled "No Comment" that allows the user to apply a zero rating, display the average rating that has been applied, and toggle between several modes. Figure 5-23 shows an example of a Rating component added to a page.

Figure 5-23. *The Rating component*

Rich Textarea Editor Component

The Rich Textarea Editor component is a JSF wrapper for the Dojo Rich Text Editor. It provides a nice, rich text widget that allows text formatting, coloring, and aligning, as shown in Figure 5-24.

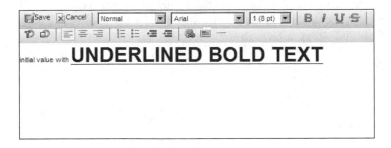

Figure 5-24. *The Rich Textarea Editor component displayed in a web browser*

You can edit text and use the component's processValueChange action method to read the old and new value in the text area. The value is returned as an HTML-formatted string. The value of the text displayed in Figure 5-24 is returned as the following code snippet:

```
initial value with <STRONG><U><FONT size=6> ➡
UNDERLINED BOLD TEXT</FONT></U></STRONG>
```

■**Caution** The Rich Textarea Editor component has some web browser support issues. I have used it with Internet Explorer 7 and Firefox 2. In both cases, I experienced rendering issues depending on where in the page I placed the component and the width I set for it. Be very careful with using this component and make sure you thoroughly test it in the target web browsers for your user base.

Data Binding

Data binding is an important feature provided by the VWP. It allows you to automatically associate data with components without having to write any code. You can bind a component to values in another component, a Java object, or a database table.

The really interesting aspect of data binding is that it can be performed via drag-and-drop in the NetBeans IDE. You can also change the data bindings at any time and use a powerful SQL editor to modify database-related bindings.

Binding to an Object

The NetBeans VWP allows you to bind components to a Java object. You can create properties in the RequestBean, SessionBean, or ApplicationBean and bind them to a component.

For example, suppose you wanted to display some application-scoped variables to the users of a web application. You can bind, or link, those application-scoped variables to specific components in a JSP file.

To see how this works, create a HomeOffice class with three encapsulated class members: location, manager, and numEmployees. Add the appropriate public getters and setters for each member variable. The code should look similar to the following:

```
public class HomeOffice {

    private String location;

    public String getLocation() {
        return this.location;
    }

    public void setLocation(String location) {
        this.location = location;
    }

    private String manager;

    public String getManager() {
        return this.manager;
    }

    public void setManager(String manager) {
        this.manager = manager;
    }

    private int numEmployees;

    public int getNumEmployees() {
        return this.numEmployees;
    }

    public void setNumEmployees(int numEmployees) {
        this.numEmployees = numEmployees;
    }

}
```

Next, create a member variable and associated getter and setter for the HomeOffice class in the ApplicationBean for your Visual Web Application project. The code added to the ApplicationBean class should look like this:

```
private HomeOffice homeOffice;

public HomeOffice getHomeOffice() {
    return this.homeOffice;
}
```

```
public void setHomeOffice(HomeOffice homeOffice) {
    this.homeOffice = homeOffice;
}
```

Finally, you can add several lines to the `ApplicationBean.init` method that will create an instance of the `HomeOffice` class, as follows:

```
private void _init() throws Exception {

    HomeOffice homeOff = new HomeOffice();
    homeOff.setLocation("Buffalo");
    homeOff.setManager("John Doe");
    homeOff.setNumEmployees(210);
    setHomeOffice(homeOff);
}
```

Next, you will need to create a new JSP file in your Visual Web Application project and add several components to it. Perform the following steps to create the JSP file for this example and bind some data:

1. Right-click the Web Pages node in the Projects window and select New ➤ File/Folder.

2. Select the Visual Web category and the Page file type, and then click the Next button.

3. Name the file and choose a folder location in the project. Then click the Finish button.

4. With the new file open in the Visual Designer window, add six Static Text components (by dragging them from the Palette window into the page's design area), as follows:

   • Set the first Static Text component's id property to `lblLocation` and the text property to `Office Location :`.

   • Place the second Static Text component beneath the first one. Set its id property to `lblManager` and the text property to `Manager :`.

   • Place the third Static Text component beneath the second one. Set its id property to `lblNumEmployees` and the text property to `# Employees :`.

   • Place the fourth Static Text component next to the `lblLocation` component. Set its id property to `txtLocation`.

   • Place the fifth Static Text component next to the `lblManager` component. Set its id property to `txtManager`.

   • Place the sixth Static Text component next to the `lblNumEmployees` component. Set its id property to `txtNumEmployees`.

   Next, you need to bind the Static Text components `txtLocation`, `txtManager`, and `txtNumEmployees` to the corresponding data elements in the `HomeOffice` class in the `ApplicationBean`.

5. Right-click the `txtLocation` component in the Visual Designer window (or in the Outline window) and select Bind to Data.

6. The Bind to Data window will appear. If it is not already selected, click the Bind to an Object tab.

7. In the Bind to Data window, the ApplicationBean1 node contains the HomeOffice class listing. Expand the homeOffice node to see the member variables that are part of the HomeOffice class.

8. To bind the txtLocation component to the corresponding application-level property, click the line property: location String, as shown in Figure 5-25. The Current Text property setting field at the top of the window should display #{ApplicationBean1. homeOffice.location}.

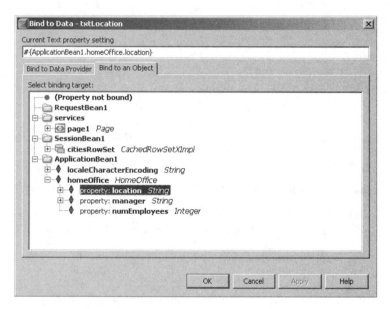

Figure 5-25. *The Bind to Data window*

9. Click the OK button to apply the binding. You will see that the txtLocation component displays the value abc. This indicates that it has been bound to string data.

10. Repeat steps 5 through 9 to bind the txtManager and txtNumEmployees components to their corresponding HomeOffice properties.

You now have a JSP page that displays six Static Text components: three bound and three unbound, as shown in Figure 5-26.

If you run the application and navigate to the JSP page, you should see the following:

```
Office Location : Buffalo
Manager : John Doe
# Employees : 210
```

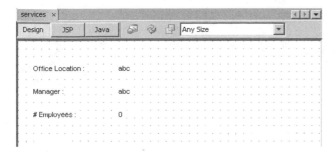

Figure 5-26. *The components after the data-binding operation*

Binding to a Database Table

The NetBeans VWP provides the ability to bind a database table to a JSF Table component. When you drag-and-drop the database table onto the component, the VWP generates code in the page's backing bean and the JSP file.

Binding the Data

To bind the data to the table, follow these steps:

1. Drag-and-drop a JSF Table component from the Palette window into a JSP page in the Visual Designer window. A table with three columns and several rows of filler data will be displayed, as shown in Figure 5-27. If you click the JSP tab in the Visual Designer window, you will see that the JSF tag `<webuijsf:table>` was added to the file. The `<webuijsf:table>` also contains the nested tags `<webuijsf:tableRowGroup>`, `<webuijsf:tableColumn>`, and `<webuijsf:staticText>`.

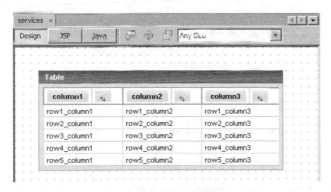

Figure 5-27. *A JSF Table component in the Visual Designer*

2. Now you need to connect to a database and bind data to the Table component. In the NetBeans Runtime window, expand the Database node to list the database connections you have defined. (If you have not defined a connection to a database, see Chapter 18 for instructions.) Expand the nodes in the Runtime window for the database connection you want to use until you locate a database table. For this example, I used an Oracle database table named CUST, which is defined as follows:

```
CREATE TABLE CUST
(
  LAST_NAME    VARCHAR2(50),
  FIRST_NAME   VARCHAR2(50),
  BUSINESS     VARCHAR2(200),
  JOBTITLE     VARCHAR2(100),
  ADDRESS1     VARCHAR2(100),
  ADDRESS2     VARCHAR2(100),
  CITY         VARCHAR2(100),
  STATE        VARCHAR2(20),
  ZIP          VARCHAR2(20),
  COUNTRY      VARCHAR2(100),
  CUST_ID      INTEGER
)
```

3. Click and drag the database table name in the Runtime window and drop it onto the JSF Table component. NetBeans will process for a moment, but will eventually refresh the JSF Table component in the Visual Designer.

The table will be reformatted to display all the columns from the database table. The column names will appear as the column headers in the table. The column values are represented as the various data-binding placeholders, such as abc for character fields and 1 for numeric fields.

If you look in the Outline window and expand the page node for the JSP file, you will see a node that defines an implementation of the CachedRowSetDataProvider class. The class name should start with the name of the database table you originally selected to bind and end with DataProvider.

The following code was also added to the JSP page's backing bean in the Managed Component Definition section near the top of the source file:

```
private CachedRowSetDataProvider custDataProvider = new ➥
CachedRowSetDataProvider();

public CachedRowSetDataProvider getCustDataProvider() {
    return custDataProvider;
}

public void setCustDataProvider(CachedRowSetDataProvider crsdp) {
    this.custDataProvider = crsdp;
}
```

The JSP page's backing bean must also specify the CachedRowSet that returns the data and add it to the CachedRowSetDataProvider class. The backing bean's init method contains the following line:

```
    custDataProvider.setCachedRowSet((javax.sql.rowset.CachedRowSet)➥
getValue("#{SessionBean1.custRowSet}"));
```

As you can see in this code snippet, a CachedRowSet was retrieved from the SessionBean1 object and set in the custDataProvider class (the CachedRowSetDataProvider).

When you bind the database table to the JSF Table component, the VWP generates an implementation of the CachedRowSet, which resides in SessionBean1. If you look in the Outline window under the SessionBean1 node, you will see the listing for the CachedRowSet. Its name starts with the name of the database table you selected for binding and ends with RowSet. You should also be able to see a short description of the SQL query that the CachedRowSet represents. This will be discussed in the "Working with the Visual Database Query Editor" section later in this chapter.

The SessionBean1 class defines the CachedRowSet as a member variable and creates the associated getter and setter methods. It also adds code to the init method that sets the CachedRowSet's data source name, table name, and SQL command. See the following code snippet.

```
private void _init() throws Exception {
    custRowSet.setDataSourceName("java:comp/env/jdbc/dataSource");
    custRowSet.setCommand("SELECT * FROM ITMSDB.CUST");
    custRowSet.setTableName("CUST");
}

private CachedRowSetXImpl custRowSet = new CachedRowSetXImpl();

public CachedRowSetXImpl getCustRowSet() {
    return custRowSet;
}

public void setCustRowSet(CachedRowSetXImpl crsxi) {
    this.custRowSet = crsxi;
}
```

The JSF Table component can then bind to the CachedRowSetDataProvider, which in turn retrieves the implementation of the CachedRowSet class (CachedRowSetXImpl) that retrieves the data from the database.

Customizing the Table

After the NetBeans VWP has added the appropriate objects and settings to the application code, you can customize the JSF Table component using the Table Layout window, as described in the "Working with the Table Component" section earlier in this chapter. Here, we'll look at the binding-related options.

In the Columns tab of the Table Layout window, notice that the database table fields are listed in the Selected box, as all the fields were originally added during the automatic data-binding process. You can remove fields from the list (and the data binding) by selecting the field name in the Selected list and clicking the < button. The field you selected will be removed from the Selected list and appear in the Available list. When you click the OK button, the table will appear in the Visual Designer window without that column.

For example, to format the table that I bound to the CUST database table (shown in the previous section), I used the < button to remove all the fields from the Selected list, except for LAST_NAME, FIRST_NAME, BUSINESS, JOBTITLE, and CITY, as shown in Figure 5-28. Then I clicked each field in the Selected list and changed the Header Text field to an easier to read value: Last Name, First Name, Job Title, and so on.

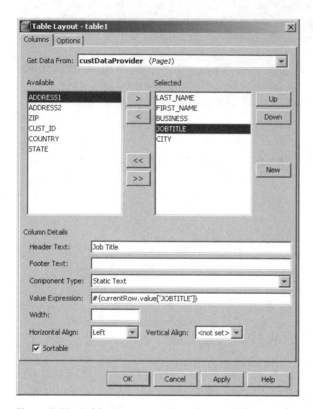

Figure 5-28. *Table Layout options for a Table component bound to a database table*

Then I clicked the Options tab in the Table Layout window. In the Title field, I entered the text List of Customers. This title will display along the header of the table. I activated pagination by selecting the Enable Pagination check box, and then I set the Page Size field to 4. (Normally, you would want between 20 to 50 records on a page, but that depends on the data, your application, and the software requirements.) Then I clicked the OK button, and the JSF Table component refreshed and appeared in its modified format.

If you want to view the JSP page in a browser and test it, you first need to set it as the start page, so it loads in the browser (assuming you haven't set up any page navigation). To do this, right-click the page in the Projects window and select Set As Start Page. A green arrow will appear next to the page name, denoting it as the start page.

Next, run the application by selecting Run ➤ Run Main Project (or press F6). After your application builds, the page will load in the browser. My sample table looks like Figure 5-29.

List of Customers				
Last Name	First Name	Business	Job Title	City
Doe	John	Microsoft	Programmer	Seattle
Smith	Bob	Sun Microsystems	Program Manager	San Francisco
Gonzalez	Pietro	Acme Widgets	Vice President	New York
Smith	Karen	New York Times	Senior Editor	New York
Philippe	Pierre	Acme Widgets	Software Architect	New York
Johnson	David	Acme Widgets	Technical Writer	New York
Lincoln	John	Microsoft	Financial Analyst	Seattle
Sully	Kathlene	Sun Microsystems	Vice President	San Francisco

Figure 5-29. *A data-bound JSF Table component displayed in a web browser*

Binding to a Drop-Down List

You can bind a database table to a JSF Drop Down List component using the NetBeans VWP. This is useful in that you can bind a list of cities, states, customers, businesses, and so on to a drop-down list without having to write any code.

Countless times in the past, I've written Java code to query a database, retrieve results, iterate through a resultset, and generate an HTML drop-down list like the following code snippet:

```
<select name="selCustomerNames" size="1">
  <option value="1">Smith, John</option>
  <option value="2">Jones, Daniel</option>
  <option value="3">Lincoln, Eric</option>
  <option value="4">Cristal, Henry</option>
  <option value="5">Aaronson, Elizabeth</option>
</select>
```

The name of each customer is displayed in the drop-down list, and the value is passed behind the scenes when the form is submitted. If you were using data binding with a drop-down list like this, you would need the flexibility to handle the situation where one database field is bound to the value attribute of the option tag and another database field is bound to the text value that appears between the <option> and </option> tags. The NetBeans VWP provides the means to handle this exact scenario.

To bind the data to a drop-down list, follow these steps:

1. Add a Drop Down List component to a JSP page in the Visual Designer window.

2. Drag a database table from the Runtime window onto the component to bind them. For this example, I created a table to represent a list of countries. The database table DDL is as follows:

```
CREATE TABLE COUNTRIES
(
  ID    NUMBER,
  NAME  VARCHAR2(100)
)
```

The COUNTRIES.ID field contains sequential values such as 1, 2, 3, and so on to represent the primary key of each country name. The COUNTRIES.NAME field lists sample countries, such as United States, Brazil, Canada, Spain, and so on.

3. Right-click the Drop Down List component and select Bind to Data.

4. In the Bind to Data window, select the Bind to Data Provider tab. The tab is divided into two sections: Value Field and Display Field, as shown in Figure 5-30.

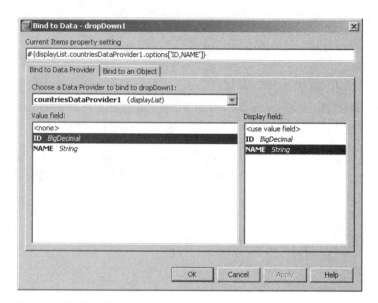

Figure 5-30. *The Bind to Data window for a JSF Drop Down List component*

5. The Value Field list on the left represents the value attribute of the HTML option tag. The Display Field list on the right represents the display text that appears between the <option> and </option> tags for a <select> element. Select the appropriate fields to bind to the value attribute and display field. For example, I selected the COUNTRIES.ID field to bind to the value attribute and the COUNTRIES.NAME field to bind to the display field.

6. Click the OK button, and the database table will be correctly bound to the JSF Drop Down List component.

Working with the Visual Database Query Editor

When you bind a JSF component to a database table, a CachedRowSet object maintains a SQL command that selects fields from a database table. You can use a SQL query-editing tool, called the Visual Database Query Editor, to manipulate the SQL query that was automatically created during the binding.

To open a query in the query editor, locate the CachedRowSet in the Outline window. You can double-click the name or right-click and select Edit SQL Statement. The Visual Database Query Editor window opens and displays the SQL statement, as shown in Figure 5-31. If you have ever used the SQL tools in the Microsoft SQL Server Enterprise Manager, this tool should look familiar.

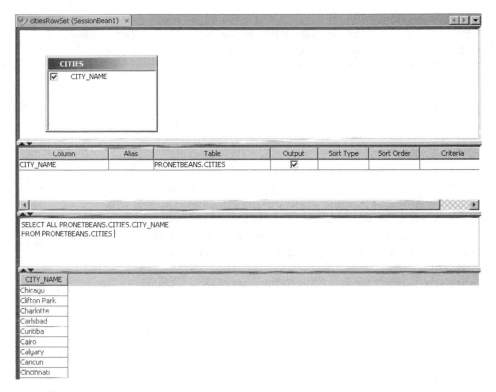

Figure 5-31. *The Visual Database Query Editor*

In the Visual Database Query Editor, you can select which columns you want to include in the query, set the sort order for each column, manually edit the SQL, and view the results of the query. This tool allows you to completely customize the SQL and the associated data in the CachedRowSet that is bound to a JSF component.

The editor window has four sections. The top section shows which tables are currently included in the query. You can right-click anywhere in the top section and select Add Table from the context menu. The Select Table(s) to Add dialog box lists the SQL tables available based on the defined database connection. You can select one or more tables and click the OK button. The tables will then appear in the top section of the query editor.

The second section allows you to perform several convenient actions:

- You can assign database table columns with aliases using the Alias column.

- You can also determine if columns should be included in the SELECT clause of the SQL statement by selecting or unselecting the check box in the Output column.

- In the Sort Type column, you can specify if the table field will be sorted in ascending or descending order.

- The Sort Order column allows you to specify in which order the table field will be sorted.

- The Criteria column allows you to specify a value (depending on the column's data type) to use in a SQL WHERE clause. For example, if you specified a value of LIKE 'New%' in the Criteria column for the CITY column, then the SQL would contain something similar to WHERE CITY LIKE 'New%'.

The third section contains the raw SQL text, which you can manually alter. If you modify any fields in the top two sections, you will see the changes to the SQL displayed here.

If you right-click in the window and select Run Query, any results that match the SQL query will be displayed in the bottom section.

Summary

This chapter covered the NetBeans VWP, beginning with how to install it and configure its options. Then we ran through the process of creating a Visual Web Application project, reviewing the project structure, and setting project properties. The VWP uses several standard NetBeans windows and tools, including the Palette, Properties, and Outline windows. The VWP also introduces the Visual Designer window and the Visual Database Query Editor.

You also saw how to customize a theme, import it into NetBeans, and apply it to a Visual Web Application project. Next, we reviewed the Page Navigation tool. You can use this powerful tool to drag-and-drop links between JSP pages and create JSF navigation rules in the faces-config.xml file.

After that, you learned how to use the JSF and Ajax components. These give you powerful features without requiring code.

Finally, we explored the NetBeans VWP data-binding capabilities. With these, you can automatically connect JSF components to database tables by simply dragging-and-dropping items. You can easily configure the bound data using the various properties and windows that NetBeans provides.

The NetBeans VWP offers an amazing set of rapid application development tools. The VWP allows you to create a project, add several components to a page, bind them to database tables, and execute a fully functioning application—all without writing a single line of code!

■ ■ ■

CHAPTER 6

Creating Java Enterprise Projects

Enterprise Java covers several diverse topics like JSF, JSP, Servlets, JMS, and EJBs. An EJB is a server-side Java class that contains business logic. The EJB does not need to provide an implementation of various features like security and transactional control. The EJB container that runs the application typically provides those features. NetBeans 5.5 supports the EJB 3.0 standard.

You can use NetBeans to manage your enterprise projects. The IDE provides various tools and wizards for writing enterprise-related code.

This chapter covers the different types of enterprise projects available in NetBeans, the different types of beans you can create, and using the Java Persistence API. NetBeans provides several excellent wizards and tools for generating Java Persistence API code.

Creating an Enterprise Application

The NetBeans Enterprise Application project is a compilation of web applications and EJB modules that are deployed as a Java EE application. Basically, this type of project simply wraps an enterprise application's components. It contains several configuration files, but no source code. When the project is packaged, it is bundled into an .ear file. You can then deploy it to a Java EE application server.

Note The examples in this chapter use Java EE 5 and the Sun Java System Application Server. Substitute your Java EE version and server as appropriate.

Creating an Enterprise Application Project

You can create a new Enterprise Application project manually or from existing sources.

Starting a New Enterprise Application Project

To create a new Enterprise Application project, follow these steps:

1. Select File ➤ New Project from the main menu.

2. In the New Project window, select Enterprise from the categories section on the left and Enterprise Application from the list of project types on the right. Click the Next button to proceed.

3. In the Name and Location window, shown in Figure 6-1, enter a project name and location.

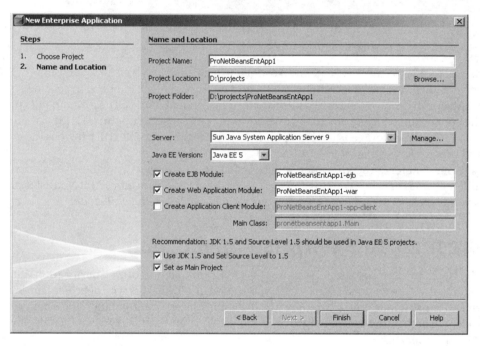

Figure 6-1. *Name and Location properties for a new Enterprise Application project*

4. Select the Sun Java System Application Server from the Server drop-down list, and then choose Java EE 5 as the Java EE version.

5. Select the modules you would like to create. The Create EJB Module and Create Web Application Module check boxes are selected by default, with names that correspond to each module (in the formats <Project-Name>-ejb and <Project-Name>-war). If you select the Create Application Client Module check box, the wizard will also create an application that has full access to the enterprise application server and can access web services and remote EJB modules. If you choose to create an Application Client module, you will be prompted to enter the package hierarchy and name of the Main class for the module.

6. Since you selected Java EE 5 for the Java EE Version field, make sure the Use JDK 1.5 and Set Source Level to 1.5 check box is selected.

7. Specify whether the enterprise application should be set as the main project in NetBeans.

8. Click Finish to complete the New Enterprise Application wizard.

The project is generated and displayed in the Projects window. The supporting module projects, EJB and WAR, that you specified in the wizard are also generated and appear in the Projects window, as shown in Figure 6-2.

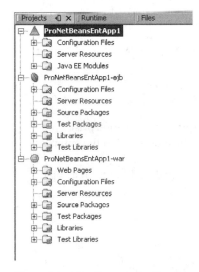

Figure 6-2. *The Enterprise Application and supporting module projects*

Creating an Enterprise Application Project with Existing Sources

In addition to creating an Enterprise Application project manually, you can also create one using existing sources, as follows:

1. Select File ➤ New Project from the main menu.

2. In the New Project window, select Enterprise from the categories section on the left and Enterprise Application with Existing Sources from the list of project types on the right. Click the Next button to proceed.

3. In the Name and Location window, select the location for the existing source code. Fill in the Project Name and Project Folder fields for the new project. Select the Sun Java System Application Server from the Server drop-down list, and then choose Java EE 5 as the Java EE version. Click the Next button to proceed.

4. In the Application Modules, you will see any modules that are part of the existing project sources. If you leave the modules on the list, they will be added to the new project. If you want to remove a module from the list, select it and click the Remove button. If you want to add other modules, click the Add button. After the list of modules is complete, click the Finish button.

The project is generated and displayed in the Projects window.

Navigating the Enterprise Application Project Structure

In the Projects window, you can see that an Enterprise Application project consists of three nodes (see Figure 6-2):

- Configuration Files

- Server Resources

- Java EE Modules

Note that the project does not contain any source code. It contains only various configuration and resource files, as well as references to the supporting EJB and WAR projects that contain the application code.

Configuration Files

The Configuration Files node contains the deployment descriptors for the enterprise application. The first file, `application.xml`, contains settings that define the modules that the enterprise application uses.

If you open the `application.xml` file in the Source Editor immediately after creating the project, you will see the following:

```
<display-name>ProNetBeansEntApp1</display-name>
    <module>
        <web>
            <web-uri>ProNetBeansEntApp1-war.war</web-uri>
            <context-root>/ProNetBeansEntApp1-war</context-root>
        </web>
    </module>
    <module>
        <ejb>ProNetBeansEntApp1-ejb.jar</ejb>
    </module>
```

The `application.xml` file defines the display name for the enterprise application, as well as two `<module>` tags: `<web>` and `<ejb>`. The `<web>` tag defines the WAR module that is associated with the enterprise application, and the `<ejb>` tag defines the EJB module.

The second file that appears under the Configuration Files node is `sun-application.xml`. This is an application deployment file similar to `application.xml`, but specific to the application server that the enterprise application defined as its target. In this case, the target application server is the Sun Java System Application Server.

You have two methods for editing the `sun-application.xml` file:

- You can edit the XML by right-clicking the file, selecting Edit, and modifying the XML code in the Source Editor.

- You can simply open the file (double-click it or right-click it and select Open), and it will open in the `sun-application.xml` Visual Editor.

This Visual Editor allows you to edit the XML file using several property fields and wizards. It is specific to the sun-application.xml file. Click the EAR node in the right pane of the editor to see several fields in the right pane. If the Pass By Reference field is set to true, the application's EJB modules use pass-by-reference parameter passing. If the field is set to false, the application's EJB modules use pass-by-value parameter passing. Optionally, you can use the Realm field to specify the name of a security realm that processes the application's authentication requests.

You can also use the sun-application.xml Visual Editor to assign principals and groups to security roles that are defined in your application.xml file. If you define a security role in the application.xml file and save the changes, the security role will appear in the sun-application.xml Visual Editor. You can define the security role in the application.xml file like this:

```
<security-role>
    <description>Managers in the ABC Division</description>
    <role-name>managers</role-name>
</security-role>
```

Then when you open the Visual Editor window, you will see the managers role listed as a node in the left pane. Click that node to display the list of principals and groups, as shown in Figure 6-3. The Principals Assigned to This Role grid displays the list of principal names and classes. You can add to this list by clicking the Add Principal button. In the Add Principal dialog box, fill in the Principal Name and Class fields. As you might expect, the Edit Principal button lets you to edit the field values for a principal, and the Remove Principal button lets you delete one. The bottom section of the Visual Editor displays the Groups Assigned to This Role grid, which contains a list of group names that are associated with the currently selected security role. You can use the Add, Edit, and Remove Group buttons to modify the list of groups.

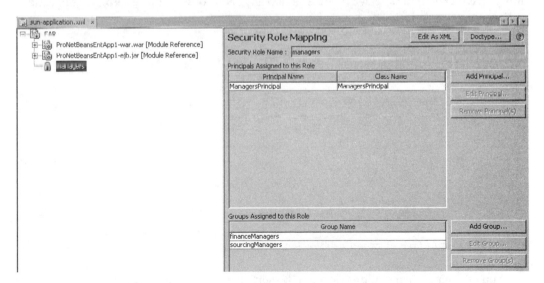

Figure 6-3. *The sun-application.xml Visual Editor*

After you've set up your principals and groups, click the Edit As XML button to view the XML that was created:

```
<sun-application>
    <security-role-mapping>
        <role-name>managers</role-name>
        <principal-name class-name="ManagersPrincipal">
            ManagersPrincipal
        </principal-name>
        <group-name>financeManagers</group-name>
        <group-name>sourcingManagers</group-name>
    </security-role-mapping>
</sun-application>
```

Server Resources

As with other types of NetBeans projects, the Server Resources node contains various resource files. You can add a JDBC connection pool, JDBC resource, JMS resource, and so on.

Using the New File wizard, you can create a resource and set its properties. The resource is then registered with the application server when the application deploys (assuming you are deploying to the Sun Java System Application Server).

Java EE Modules

The Java EE Modules node contains a list of the Java EE modules that have been associated with the Enterprise Application project.

To associate a new Java EE module with the project, right-click the node and select Add Java EE Module. The Add Java EE Module dialog box, shown in Figure 6-4, lists only modules that are open in the NetBeans Projects window. Click the name of the module you want to add, and then click OK. If the selected module has already been added to the Enterprise Application project, the OK button will be disabled.

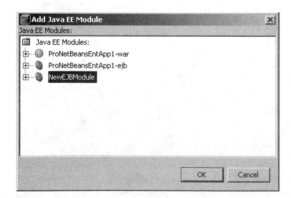

Figure 6-4. *The Add Java EE Module dialog box*

You can remove a module association by right-clicking the module name under the Java EE Modules node and selecting Remove from the context menu. You can also right-click the module name and select Open Project, which causes the module project to open in NetBeans (if it is not already open).

Creating an EJB Module

An EJB Module project contains the various beans that perform the work in a Java Enterprise Application. You can add session or message-driven beans to an EJB Module project, verify the module, deploy it to an application server, or add the EJB module to an Enterprise Application project or Enterprise Application Client project.

Creating an EJB Module Project

Like Enterprise Application projects, EJB Module projects can be created either manually or from existing sources.

Starting a New EJB Module Project

To create a new EJB Module project, follow these steps:

1. Select File ➤ New Project from the main menu.

2. In the New Project window, select Enterprise from the categories section on the left and EJB Module from the list of project types on the right. Click the Next button to proceed.

3. In the Name and Location window, shown in Figure 6-5, enter a project name and location.

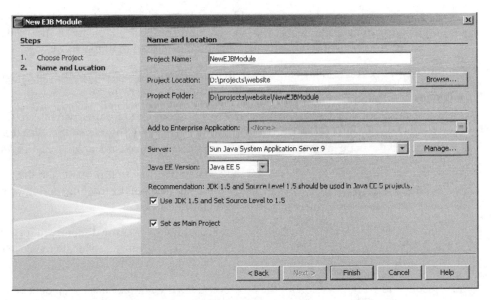

Figure 6-5. *The Name and Location window for adding an EJB Module project*

4. The Add to Enterprise Application field is enabled if one or more Enterprise Application projects are open in NetBeans. You can select one of the available items from the drop-down list to specify that the EJB module should be added to that project.

5. Specify the server and Java EE version in the corresponding fields (Sun Java System Application Server and Java EE 5 for the examples in this chapter).

6. Since you selected Java EE 5, make sure the Use JDK 1.5 and Set Source Level to 1.5 check box is selected.

7. Specify whether the EJB module should be set as the main project in NetBeans.

8. Click the Finish button to complete the process and create the project.

Creating an EJB Module from Existing Sources

In addition to creating an EJB Module project manually, you can also create one using existing sources, as follows:

1. Select File ➤ New Project from the main menu.

2. In the New Project window, select Enterprise from the categories section on the left and EJB Module with Existing Sources from the list of project types on the right. Click the Next button to proceed.

3. In the Name and Location window, select the location for the existing source code.

4. Fill in the Project Name and Project Folder fields for the new project.

5. The Add to Enterprise Application field is enabled if one or more Enterprise Application projects are open in NetBeans. You can select one of the available items from the drop-down list to specify that the EJB module should be added to that project.

6. Specify the server and Java EE version in the corresponding fields (Sun Java System Application Server and Java EE 5 for the examples in this chapter).

7. Click the Next button to move to the Existing Sources and Libraries window. In this window, you specify several directory paths in the existing sources so that the code and related files can be imported correctly into the new project, as shown in Figure 6-6.

8. Specify the configuration files folder path. Using the Browse button next to the Configuration Files Folder field, you can navigate the directory of the existing module to select the correct location.

9. Specify the libraries path. In the Libraries Folder field, enter the directory that contains the existing project's JAR files. You can click the Browse button to locate the correct directory.

10. Specify the source location for the project code in the Source Package Folders field. You can use the Add Folder button to select the src/java directory under the project structure.

11. Specify the test package location in the Test Package Folders field. You can click the Add Folder button to select the test directory in the project structure.

12. To complete the new project creation process, click the Finish button.

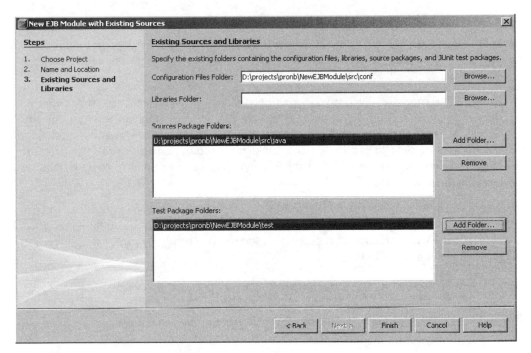

Figure 6-6. *The Existing Sources and Libraries window*

The existing project code is imported and added to the new project. The new project is then opened in NetBeans and listed in the Projects window.

Navigating the EJB Module Project Structure

As shown earlier in Figure 6-2, an EJB Module project consists of six nodes:

Configuration Files: Contains the manifest file. If the project contains non-EJB 3.0 code, this directory will contain the deployment descriptors.

Server Resources: Contains various resource files such as JDBC resources, JDBC connection pools, JMS resources, and so on.

Source Packages: The standard NetBeans source directory for the application code.

Test Packages: The standard NetBeans source directory for application test code.

Libraries: The standard NetBeans node for adding dependent libraries and JAR files to the project.

Test Libraries: The standard NetBeans node for adding test dependent libraries and JAR files to the project.

Working with Session Beans

Session beans service a user session for a specific period of time. They represent interactions between client applications and the EJB code that implement specific tasks. Session beans can be of two types:

Stateful: This type of session bean performs interactions with clients that need state persisted between requests. The various methods in a stateful session bean can add to or modify the session that exists between the bean and the client. For example, an online computer customization tool allows a customer to make repeated modifications to a product. In between requests, the changes that are made are persisted in the session in the EJB container running the application.

Stateless: This type of session bean represents a direct request between the client and the bean. It does not save state between requests. A stateless session bean often represents a set of procedures or steps that are completed and return a result. A simple, straightforward task is executed and data is returned.

The NetBeans IDE provides several wizards for creating and working with session beans.

Creating a New Session Bean

To create a new session bean, follow these steps:

1. Open an EJB Module project, right-click the project name, and select New ➤ File/Folder.

2. In the New File window, select Enterprise in the left pane and Session Bean in the right pane. Then click the Next button.

3. In the Name and Location window, enter a value for the EJB Name field, as shown in Figure 6-7. The Project field displays the name of the project where you started the session bean creation.

4. The Location field is set to Source Packages by default. If you have several source package folders specified for the project, you can add the session bean to any of them.

5. You can specify the Java package hierarchy in the Package field.

6. The Session Type field allows you to select either Stateful or Stateless to determine the type of session bean that is being created.

7. The Create Interface field determines which Java Interfaces are created and used by the session bean. A remote interface enables the session bean to be used by remote clients. A local interface allows the session bean to be used only by a client in the same JVM.

8. Click the Finish button to complete the code-creation process.

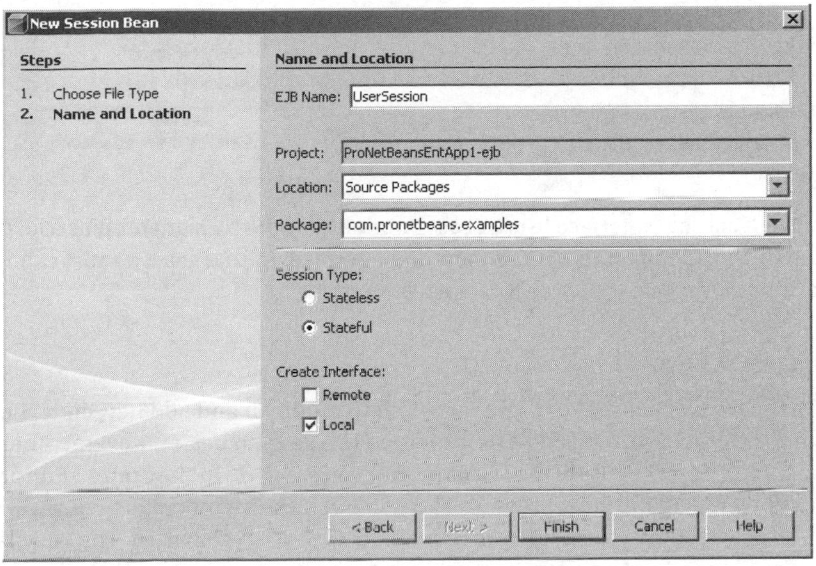

Figure 6-7. *Name and Location window in New Session Bean wizard*

After the wizard executes, the session bean is generated and opened in the Source Editor. For the sample session bean shown in Figure 6-7, the resulting code looks like this:

```
import javax.ejb.Stateful;
@Stateful
public class UserSessionBean ➡
implements com.pronetbeans.examples.UserSessionLocal
{

    /** Creates a new instance of UserSessionBean */
    public UserSessionBean() {
    }


}
```

The UserSessionBean class uses a @Stateful annotation to indicate the stateful type of the session bean. It also implements the UserSessionLocal interface, which indicates the session bean's access type is local.

The code for the matching business interface is also generated, as follows:

```
import javax.ejb.Local;
/**
*     This is the business interface for UserSession enterprise bean.
 */
```

```
@Local
public interface UserSessionLocal {
    boolean isValidUser(String sUsername);
    boolean isValidAdmin(String sUsername);
    void sendForgotPassword(String sUsername);
}
```

The UserSessionLocal interface lists a @Local annotation that designates it as a local interface. A session bean can implement more than one interface. In that case, it must explicitly
declare the annotations @Local or @Remote for each interface.

Modifying a Session Bean

Once a session bean has been created, you may wish to modify it and add new code. Besides
manually typing the code, you can add a new method to a session bean in several other ways.

One way is to right-click inside the session bean source code in the Source Editor and
select EJB Methods ➤ Add Business Method. The Add Business Method dialog box will open.
Fill in the Name field and select a value from the Return Type drop-down list. You can also type
the name of a Java object or primitive type directly into the Return Type field. The Use In Interface section has the Local check box field selected, since NetBeans knows you triggered the
wizard from a local interface.

You can use the Add Business Method dialog box to define a parameter for the new method so
that it can perform some work. To add a new parameter, click the Add button. The Enter Method
Parameter dialog box appears and prompts you to fill out the Type and Name fields. Enter the
desired values, and then click the OK button. Figure 6-8 shows an example of a completed
Add Business Method dialog box for an isValidUser method with a String parameter named
sUsername. Click the OK button to proceed. The new method is added to the UserSession bean:

```
public boolean isValidUser(String sUsername) {
    //TODO implement isValidUser
    return false;
}
```

An empty definition is also added to the UserSessionLocal interface:

```
boolean isValidUser(String sUsername);
```

You can also add a method to a session bean by copying and pasting an existing method.
For example, suppose that while you are working in the UserSession bean, you decide to add a
new business method. Instead of using a wizard to create it, you can copy and paste the existing
isValidUser method directly into the same source file and rename the copy isValidAdmin. You
can quickly and easily add the definition for this new method to the UserSessionLocal interface
by right-clicking the name of the new method and selecting EJB Methods ➤ Add to Local Interface. It may seem like nothing happened, but a new line is added in the interface:

```
boolean isValidAdmin(String sUsername);
```

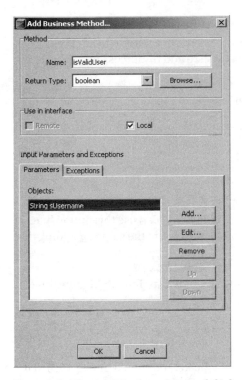

Figure 6-8. *The Add Business Method dialog box*

You can also add a method from the UserSession bean to the UserSessionLocal interface by using the NetBeans suggestion feature in the Source Editor. If you click anywhere in the line of the method name, the suggestion glyph icon (a light bulb) will appear, as shown in Figure 6-9. Click it or press Alt+Enter, and you will see the suggestion "Add to Local Interface" in a tooltip. Click the suggestion or press Enter, and the new method definition will be added to the interface. (See Chapter 9 for more information about the suggestion glyphs in the Source Editor.)

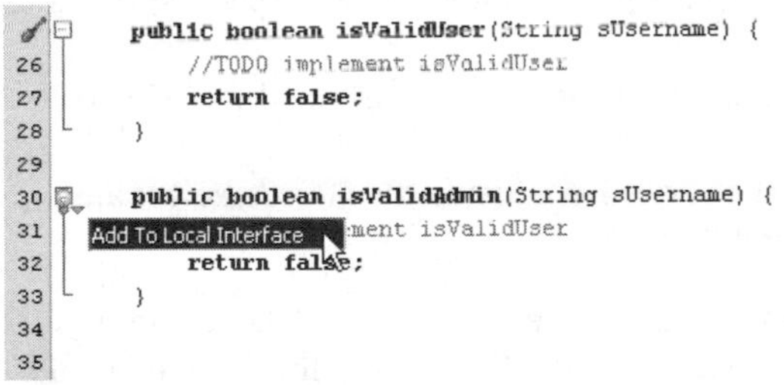

```
    public boolean isValidUser(String sUsername) {
26          //TODO implement isValidUser
27          return false;
28      }
29
30      public boolean isValidAdmin(String sUsername) {
31  Add To Local Interface    ment isValidUser
32          return false;
33      }
34
35
```

Figure 6-9. *The Source Editor suggestion to "Add to Local Interface"*

Adding Enterprise Resources to a Session Bean

NetBeans provides wizards for adding enterprise resource items to a session bean. In the Source Editor, right-click the session bean to which you wish to add resources and select Enterprise Resources. You will see four options:

Call Enterprise Bean: Generates code that references a bean's local or remote interface.

Use Database: Generates code that creates a reference to data source or uses an existing service locator class.

Send JMS Message: Generates code that sends a JMS message to a bean.

Send E-mail: Generates a resource reference to a `javax.mail.Session` class.

As an example, let's look at the Send E-mail option. Before you can use this option, you need to create a JavaMail resource in the EJB Module project. Here are the steps for adding the JavaMail resource to the project:

1. Right-click the Server Resource node in the Projects window for the EJB Module project and select New ➤ File/Folder.

2. In the New File window, select Sun Resources from the list of categories in the left pane and JavaMail Resource in the right pane. Click the Next button to continue.

3. The General Attributes–JavaMail Session window appears. You should modify the JNDI Name field to be specific to your application. Instead of `mail/mySession`, name it something like `mail/pnbSession`, as shown in Figure 6-10, or `mail/NetBeansEmailSession`. Also enter the standard email-based properties you might need in an application to send an email: Mail Host, Default User, Default Return Address, Description, and so on. The fields in the Advanced section are already filled out with suggested values. Once you have entered the appropriate values, click the Finish button to complete the New JavaMail Resource wizard.

A new resource file is now added under the Server Resources tab in the Projects window for the EJB Module project. If you named the resource (in the JNDI Name field) `mail/pnbSession`, the resource file is named `mail_pnbSession.sun-resource`.

Now that the JavaMail resource has been added, you can add the resource to the session bean:

1. With the session bean class open, right-click anywhere inside the Source Editor and select Enterprise Resources ➤ Send E-mail.

2. The Specify Mail Resource dialog box appears. Enter the name of the JNDI resource you previously created, such as `mail/pnbSession`. Select the Generate Inline Lookup Code option. Click the OK button to finish the process.

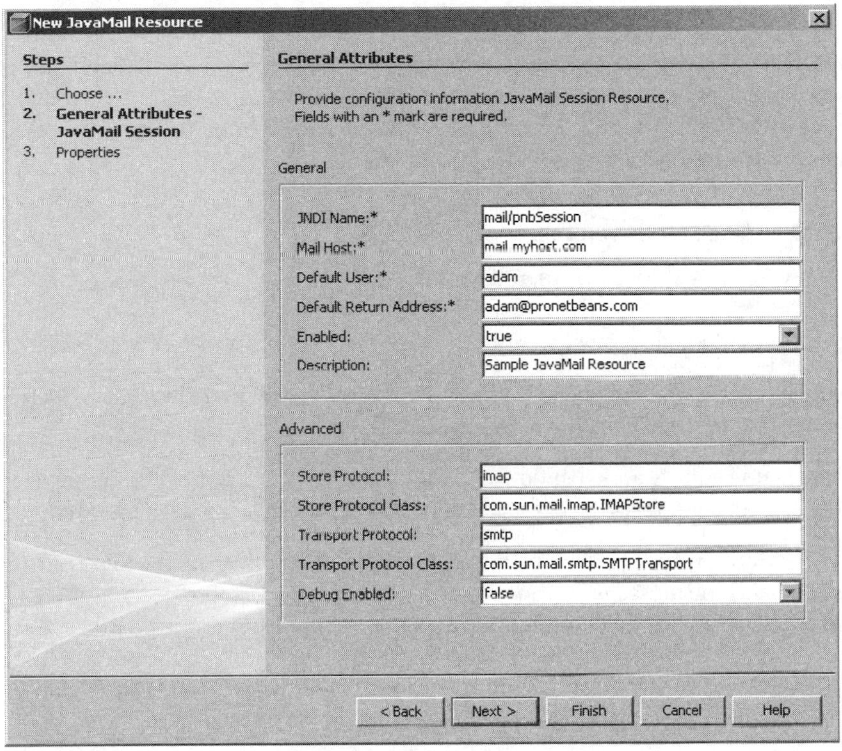

Figure 6-10. *Adding the JavaMail resource to the EJB Module project*

The session bean class now contains several imports from the javax.mail package as well as some new code. First, a class member was added for the JavaMail session. The Session class was marked with a @Resource annotation, and the name attribute specifies the JNDI name for the JavaMail resource you previously created.

```
@Resource(name = "mail/pnbSession")
private Session mailpnbSession;
```

The session bean also now contains a new private method, as follows:

```
private void sendMail(String email, String subject, String body) ➥
throws NamingException, MessagingException {
    MimeMessage message = new MimeMessage(mailpnbSession);
    message.setSubject(subject);
    message.setRecipients(RecipientType.TO, InternetAddress.parse(email, false));
    message.setText(body);
    Transport.send(message);
}
```

The sendMail method encapsulates the logic for sending an email. You can only call it internally within the class, since it has an access level of private.

Working with Message-Driven Beans

The second type of EJB you can create in NetBeans is called a message-driven bean. This type of EJB is often used for receiving asynchronous messages (for example, systems that listen for incoming messages like customer orders, data requests, and so on). Message-driven beans typically use a message delivery system such as the JMS.

Creating a New Message-Driven Bean

To create a new message-driven bean, follow these steps:

1. Open an EJB Module project, right-click the project name, and select New ➤ File/Folder.

2. In the New File window, select Enterprise in the left pane and Message-Driven Bean in the right pane. Then click the Next button.

3. In the Name and Location window, enter the name of the class, select a package location (Source Packages, Test Packages, and so on), and specify a package hierarchy.

4. The Destination Type field is specific to message-driven beans. This tells the EJB server how to send the message. If you select Queue, as in the example in Figure 6-11, the message-driven bean will have an activation configuration property that specifies the javax.jms.Queue interface. If you select Topic, the bean will reference the javax.jms.Topic interface.

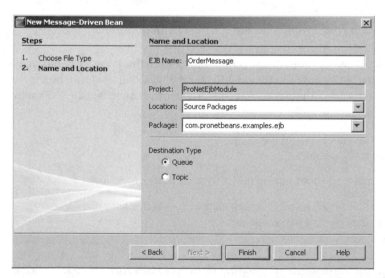

Figure 6-11. *The Name and Location window for a message-driven bean*

5. Click the Finish button to complete the wizard.

The new class that is generated is similar to the following:

```
@MessageDriven(mappedName = "jms/OrderMessage", activationConfig = {
        @ActivationConfigProperty(propertyName = "acknowledgeMode", ➥
propertyValue = "Auto-acknowledge"),
        @ActivationConfigProperty(propertyName = "destinationType", ➥
propertyValue = "javax.jms.Queue")
    })
public class OrderMessage implements MessageListener {
    public OrderMessage() {
    }

    public void onMessage(Message message) {
    }
}
```

Notice the annotations that appear at the top of the file. If you are familiar with EJBs, this should look similar to code you may have written in your own projects. The @MessageDriven annotation defines the class as a message-driven bean and also declares several other properties, such as mappedName and activationConfig.

In this code, the OrderMessage class implements the javax.jms.MessageListener interface, which defines the basic behavior for a message-driven bean. The code also contains an onMessage(Message message) method. This is the method that is executed when the message-driven bean receives an asynchronous message. Since the operation is asynchronous, the onMessage method has void as a return type.

You need to add code to the onMessage method to make the bean actually handle requests. Message-driven beans can handle different kinds of messages. If you have a bean that will be receiving different types of messages, you might want to implement code such as the following:

```
public void onMessage(Message message) {
    // check type of javax.jms.Message
    if(message instanceof TextMessage) {
        try {
            TextMessage txtMsg = (TextMessage)message;
            System.out.println("Message is = " + txtMsg.getText());

        } catch (JMSException ex) {
            ex.printStackTrace();
        }

    } else if (message instanceof ObjectMessage) {
        // do something
    } else if (message instanceof StreamMessage) {
        // do something
    } else if (message instanceof MapMessage) {
        // do something
    } else if (message instanceof BytesMessage) {
        // do something
```

```
        } else {
            // unknown type
        }
    }
}
```

In this `onMessage` method, the `message` parameter is checked for the message type. If the `message` parameter is an instance of `TextMessage`, the method casts the object to a new `TextMessage` instance and calls the `getText` method to retrieve the text of the message.

Once the message-driven bean has been created and given basic functionality, you can continue to use NetBeans to modify, compile, test, and deploy it.

Modifying a Message-Driven Bean

NetBeans provides several convenient features for working with and modifying message-driven beans. NetBeans allows you to work with the EJB annotations using code completion.

Using code completion for EJB annotations is the same as working with any other Java source code. If you defined the annotation `@Resource`, you can use code completion to fill in the attribute names. After typing the annotation name and an opening parenthesis, press Ctrl+spacebar to activate the code completion. The code completion box will pop up with a short list of available attributes for the `@Resource` annotation. Select one from the list and enter a value, such as `name = "jdbc/PNBDataSource"`. You can define additional attributes by typing a comma after the attribute value and pressing Ctrl+spacebar to activate the code completion box, as shown in Figure 6-12. (For details on using code completion, see Chapter 10.)

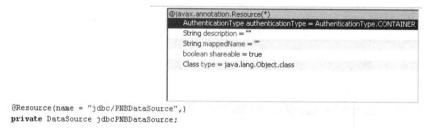

Figure 6-12. *Using code completion with EJB annotations*

Adding Enterprise Resources to a Message-Driven Bean

As for session beans, NetBeans provides several wizards for adding enterprise resources to a bean. As an example, here is how to add a database resource:

1. With the message-driven bean class open, right-click inside the Source Editor and select Enterprise Resources ➤ Use Database.

2. The Choose Database dialog box will appear. Select a value from the Data Source drop-down list, as shown in Figure 6-13. This field lists the data sources that have been previously configured in NetBeans. (As described in Chapter 18, you can define new database connections under the Databases node in the Runtime window.) If you do not have a data source defined for the database connection you intend to use, select New Data Source in the Data Source drop-down field. The Create Data Source dialog box will appear, allowing you to select a database connection and assign it a JNDI name.

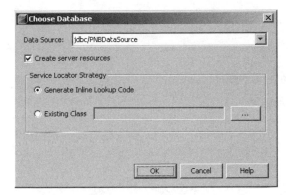

Figure 6-13. *The Choose Database dialog box*

3. If you are deploying the EJB module to the Sun Java System Application Server, leaving the Create Server Resources check box selected will cause a database connection pool resource to be created.

4. The Service Locator Strategy choices allow you to specify if NetBeans should generate the data source lookup directly in the message-driven bean or if it should use an existing class. In this example, Generate Inline Lookup Code is selected. The next example describes using the Existing Class option.

5. Click the OK button to finish.

The sample `OrderMessage` bean now contains the following code:

```
@Resource(name = "jdbc/PNBDataSource")
private DataSource jdbcPNBDataSource;
```

You can then modify the `onMessage` method to process the `TextMessage` instance using the `DataSource` object declared with the `@Resource` annotation. The following code snippet uses the `DataSource` instance `jdbcPNBDataSource` to retrieve a database connection. Then the code simply uses standard JDBC classes to define a `PreparedStatement`, set the parameter to the text of the message, and execute the SQL.

```
if(message instanceof TextMessage) {
    java.sql.Connection conn = null;
    PreparedStatement pstmt = null;
    String sSql = "INSERT INTO MESSAGES VALUES(?)";

    try {
        TextMessage txtMsg = (TextMessage)message;
        System.out.println("Message is = " + txtMsg.getText());

        conn = jdbcPNBDataSource.getConnection();
        pstmt = conn.prepareStatement(sSql);
        pstmt.setString(1,txtMsg.getText());
        pstmt.execute();
```

```
    } catch (Exception e) {
        e.printStackTrace();
    } finally {
        try {
            if(conn!=null && !conn.isClosed()) {
                conn.close();
            }
        } catch (SQLException ex) {
            ex.printStackTrace();
        }
    }
}
```

The database code here is quite standard, but the nice thing is that you don't have to write any DataSource object creation or implementation code. The EJB container handles the creation of the object through the standard EJB injection process.

In the Choose Database dialog box (Figure 6-13), you can also specify that the database lookup operation use an existing class, such as a service locator. You can create the service locator as follows:

1. Right-click the EJB project name and select New ➤ File/Folder.

2. In the New File window, select Enterprise from the left pane and Service Locator from the right pane. Click the Next button to continue.

3. In the Name and Location window, enter the name of the service locator such as PnbServiceLocator. Select a location, such as Source Packages, and specify a Java package hierarchy. Click the Finish button to generate the service locator.

At this point, the sample OrderMessage bean includes the following inline lookup code, generated in the previous set of steps (when Generate Inline Lookup Code was selected):

```
@Resource(name = "jdbc/PNBDataSource")
private DataSource jdbcPNBDataSource;
```

You would need to remove this code. Otherwise, the Choose Database dialog box would not allow you to add a new call.

After you've created the service locator (and removed any existing inline lookup code in the bean code), you can add the reference to the service locator:

1. Right-click inside the Source Editor window and select Enterprise Resources ➤ Use Database.

2. In the Choose Database dialog box, fill out the fields as before, but select the Existing radio button. Enter the name of the service locator that you created. Then click the OK button.

The bean should now contain a private member variable for your service locator, as well as several lookup methods.

```
private com.pronetbeans.examples.ejb.PnbServiceLocator serviceLocator;
private com.pronetbeans.examples.ejb.PnbServiceLocator getServiceLocator() {
    if (serviceLocator == null) {
    serviceLocator = new com.pronetbeans.examples.ejb.PnbServiceLocator();
    }
    return serviceLocator;
}

private DataSource getJdbcPNBDataSource() throws NamingException {
    return (DataSource) ➥
getServiceLocator().getDataSource("java:comp/env/jdbc/PNBDataSource");
}
```

Now all you need to do is to modify the code in the OrderMessage.onMessage method that retrieves the database connection. Change the following code:

```
conn = jdbcPNBDataSource.getConnection();
```

to this code:

```
conn = getJdbcPNBDataSource().getConnection();
```

The modified code now retrieves the service locator, PnbServiceLocator, and using it, retrieves the named data source. Other beans that need database access can then use the same service locator class.

Creating an Enterprise Application Client

The Enterprise Application Client project is a compilation of web applications and EJB modules that are deployed as a Java EE application. Basically, this type of project wraps together various enterprise application components. It can contain configuration files, resources, and source code, and is packaged and deployed to an application server. Its primary benefit is that it can use server resources specific to enterprise applications such as security roles, groups, and so on.

To create a new Enterprise Application Client project in NetBeans, follow these steps:

1. Select File ➤ New Project from the main menu.

2. In the New Project window, select Enterprise from the categories section on the left and Enterprise Application Client from the list of project types on the right. Click the Next button to proceed.

3. In the Name and Location window, enter a project name and location.

4. If any Enterprise Application projects are open in the Projects window, the Add to Enterprise Application drop-down list will be active. You can then select an available Enterprise Application project with which to associate the client project.

5. Specify the server and Java EE version in the corresponding fields (Sun Java System Application Server and Java EE 5 for the examples in this chapter).

6. Specify the package structure and name of the Main class.

7. Since you selected Java EE 5, make sure the Use JDK 1.5 and Set Source Level to 1.5 check box is selected.

8. Choose whether the project should be set to the main project in NetBeans.

9. Click Finish to complete the wizard.

The project is generated and displayed in the Projects window. The Main class should open in the Source Editor.

As with other enterprise projects, you can also create an Enterprise Application Client project from existing sources, as follows:

1. Select File ➤ New Project from the main menu.

2. In the New Project window, select Enterprise from the categories section on the left and Enterprise Application Client with Existing Sources from the list of project types on the right. Click the Next button to proceed.

3. Fill out the Name and Location window, as described in the previous set of steps, and then click the Next button.

4. In the Existing Sources window, specify the configuration files folder path. Using the Browse button next to the Configuration Files Folder field, you can navigate the directory of the existing source code to select the correct location.

5. In the Libraries Folder field, select the directory that contains the existing project's JAR files.

6. For the Source Package Folders field, you can use the Add Folder button to select the src/java directory under the project structure.

7. For the Test Package Folders field, you can specify the test directory in the project structure using the Add Folder button.

8. After you have set the directory paths and folders to the correct values, click the Finish button.

The existing project code is imported and added to the new project. The new project is then opened in NetBeans and listed in the Projects window.

Verifying an Enterprise Project

The NetBeans Verifier tool allows you to verify the correctness of a Java EE module. It analyzes the dependencies declared in the deployment descriptor and determines if there are any issues that may cause the application to fail after it has been deployed.

To verify an enterprise project, right-click the project name in the Projects window and select Verify Project. The Output window will display several actions that take place, such as compiling and building the project modules. The Verifier tool will open in a window and display the results of the project verification, as shown in Figure 6-14.

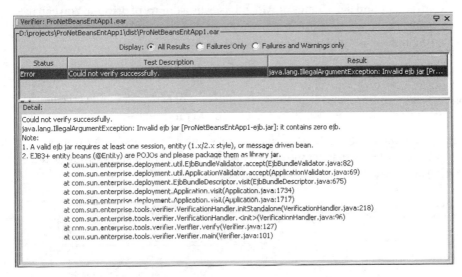

Figure 6-14. *The enteprise project Verifier tool*

If you attempt to verify a new Enterprise Application project or EJB Module project, you will receive a failure notice. An item should appear in the Verifier tool that lists a status of "Error" with a test description and result. If you select the line item in the grid, the detail result appears in the bottom portion of the window. The error states that the project is invalid since it does not contain at least one session, entity, or message-driven bean.

Along the top of the Verifier tool are several Display options. The default setting of All Results displays all line items with statuses of Pass, Not Applicable, Error, and so on. The other two options for the field allow you to display only the errors or the errors and warnings.

Working with Persistence

Prior to the EJB 3.0 specification, using Java persistence techniques in an enterprise application was moderately complex and heavyweight. The Java community tried to mitigate these issues with lightweight frameworks like Hibernate. When the EJB 3.0 specification was finalized, the Java Persistence API (JPA) was defined along with it.

The JPA defines a mechanism for using lightweight persistent objects that can be retrieved, inserted, updated, or deleted in a database. One of the best benefits of using the JPA is that you do not need an EJB module or enterprise project. Since the JPA uses Java 5 annotations to define object-relational mapping properties, you can use it in any Java project.

NetBeans provides full support for the Java 5 annotations and the JPA. It also provides several very useful wizards for creating persistence classes. You can create an entity class that represents data from a database table. You can also use NetBeans to generate a set of web pages that use the persistence entity classes in an application.

The first step to working with persistence in NetBeans is to create a new persistence unit.

Creating a Persistence Unit

The *persistence unit* defines how an application that uses the JPA saves its data. It defines a data source, type of transaction, and persistence provider (basically a library of drivers). You can use NetBeans to create a new persistence unit in almost any kind of Java project.

To create a new persistence unit, follow these steps:

1. Right-click a project in the Projects window and select New ➤ File/Folder.

2. In the New File window, select Persistence from the list of categories and Persistence Unit from the list of file types. Click the Next button to proceed.

3. In the Provider and Database window, specify the name of the persistence unit, as shown in Figure 6-15. By default, the Persistence Unit Name field shows a suggested value of PU appended to the name of the project.

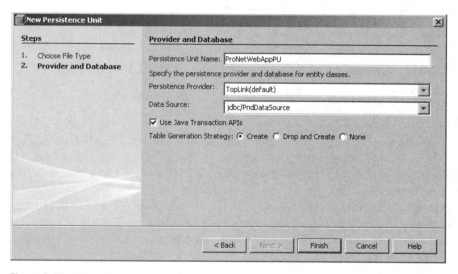

Figure 6-15. *Creating a new persistence unit*

4. Select a persistence provider. The Persistence Provider drop-down list shows various providers. The TopLink provider is selected by default, but you can select another listed provider or define a new provider.

5. Specify the data source that will be used. The Data Source drop-down list allows you to select a data source that you have previously defined in NetBeans to be used by the persistence unit. You can also create a new data source by selecting New Data Source from the Data Source drop-down list. The Create Data Source dialog box that appears prompts you to enter the name of the new data source and to select an existing database connection. (See Chapter 18 for details on adding database connections.)

6. If the Use Java Transaction APIs check box is selected, the data source needs to support the Java Transaction APIs.

7. The Table Generation Strategy selection specifies if tables associated with entity classes will be created, dropped and created, or not created at all.

8. Click the Finish button to create the persistence unit.

The persistence.xml file is created under the Configuration Files node in the Projects window and opened in the persistence.xml Visual Editor.

Understanding the persistence.xml File

The persistence.xml file that appears under the Configuration Files node contains the persistence configuration data you specified in the New File wizard when you created the persistence unit. The persistence.xml Visual Editor allows you to modify the fields in the persistence.xml file without having to manually edit XML content, as shown in Figure 6-16.

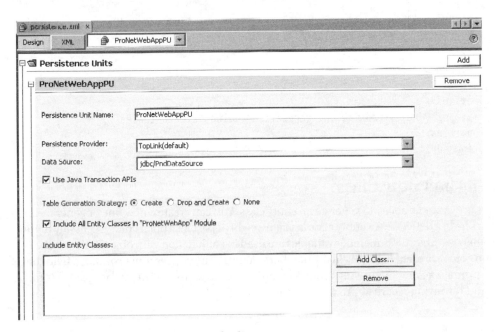

Figure 6-16. *The persistence.xml Visual Editor*

The persistence.xml Visual Editor allows you to select many of the same fields that appeared in the Provider and Database window of the New Persistence Unit wizard (Figure 6-15). You can modify the name of the persistence unit, change the persistence provider, and select a different data source. You can also change your selections for the Use Java Transaction APIs and Table Generation Strategy fields.

The lower half of the persistence.xml Visual Editor contains a check box named Include All Entity Classes in "*AppName*" Module. If this option is checked, all the entity classes in your project are included in the persistence unit. If it is not checked, you must use the Include Entity Classes field below it to specify specific entity classes.

Notice the minus icon next to the persistence unit name at the top of the editor window. This icon represents a section collapse feature similar to code folding. If you click the minus icon, the entire section for the persistence unit is hidden and the icon turns into a plus icon. If you click the plus icon, the persistence unit fields are displayed once again.

The upper-right corner of the editor contains Add and Remove buttons. The Remove button allows you to remove the persistence unit definition from the persistence.xml file. It should come as no surprise that the Add button allows you to create a new persistence unit to be added to the persistence.xml file. You can add as many persistence units as you like, but each one must have a distinct name.

By default, the persistence.xml Visual Editor displays in Design view, as shown in Figure 6-16. You can also view the XML content of the persistence.xml file by clicking the XML button along the top of the window.

If the editor window is closed, you can right-click the file in the Projects window and select Edit. The XML content of the file will be displayed in the Source Editor, as shown here:

```
<persistence-unit name="ProNetWebAppPU" transaction-type="JTA">
    <provider>
        oracle.toplink.essentials.ejb.cmp3.EntityManagerFactoryProvider
    </provider>
    <jta-data-source>
        jdbc/PndDataSource
    </jta-data-source>
    <properties>
        <property name="toplink.ddl-generation" value="create-tables"/>
    </properties>
</persistence-unit>
```

Creating an Entity Class

NetBeans provides the ability to generate an entity class. You can create a new one or generate an entity class from a database. An entity class is a lightweight persistence object that essentially represents a database table. Class member variables are used in conjunction with object/relational annotations to represent the fields in the database table. Entity classes must contain a field that acts as a primary key for identifying unique records. They also use an EntityManager class for storing and retrieving records from the database table.

Creating a New Entity Class

To create a new entity class using the New File wizard, follow these steps:

1. Right-click the name of a project in the Projects window and select New ➤ File/Folder.

2. In the New File window, select Persistence from the list of categories on the left and Entity Class from the list of file types on the right. Click the Next button to proceed.

3. In the Name and Location window, specify the filename, location, and package hierarchy, as shown in Figure 6-17.

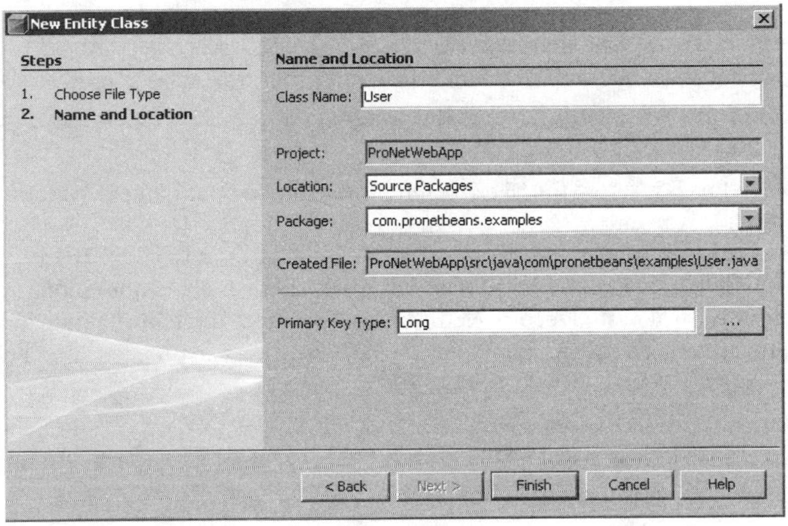

Figure 6-17. *The Name and Location window for a new entity class*

4. The last field in the window, Primary Key Type, allows you to specify the Java data type that the primary key field is represented by. Every entity must specify an @ID annotation that identifies the member variable that represents the entity's primary key in the matching database table. The Primary Key Type field in the Name and Location window simply presents the data type of that member variable. Leave the default value, Long, unless your database table's primary key is a character-based column; in which case, specify a value of String. If you need to, you can click the ellipsis button next to this field to browse the classes available in the project and/or IDE.

5. Click the Finish button to generate the entity class.

The entity class will then open in the Source Editor.

The sample entity class created in Figure 6-17 is named User. The class has the following source code:

```
@Entity
public class User implements Serializable {

    @Id
    @GeneratedValue(strategy = GenerationType.AUTO)
    private Long id;

    public Long getId() {
        return this.id;
    }

    public void setId(Long id) {
        this.id = id;
    }
}
```

■**Note** In the entity class code here, I removed several items for brevity, such as the constructor, the Javadoc comments, and several overridden methods. I left the important items in the snippet.

Notice that NetBeans inserted the @Entity annotation for the class name declaration. This specifies that the class is an entity.

The User class contains one member variable by default, private Long id. The id variable is annotated with the @Id tag and the @GeneratedValue tag. These are the annotations specific to the primary key for the persisted record. NetBeans also generates matching getter and setter methods so that you can set and retrieve the value of id. You can then proceed to add class members to the entity.

Creating Entity Classes from a Database

One of the nice features that NetBeans provides when working with entity classes is the ability to generate one or more entity classes from a database. You can create a database connection, assign it to a data source, and generate dozens of entity classes based on the database. You can perform all these actions without writing a single line of code!

To create one or more entity classes from a database, follow these steps:

1. Right-click the name of the project in the Projects window and select New ➤ File/Folder.

2. In the New File window, select Persistence from the list of categories on the left and Entity Classes from Database from the list of file types on the right. Click the Next button to proceed.

3. The Database Tables window appears, as shown in Figure 6-18. Select a data source (the database that contains the tables you want to view) from the top drop-down list. In the Available Tables list, NetBeans will display the tables available in the specified database.

4. If you added a Database Schema file to your project, the Database Schema field will be enabled. This field allows you to create one or more entity classes based on the schema defined in the file, as opposed to having to connect to an actual database to generate the entity class.

■**Tip** If you plan to use a database in any NetBeans project, I highly recommend saving the schema in your project. It is especially useful if you are working in a location without an Internet connection to the desired database (like on a long plane flight). You can learn more about creating database schema files in Chapter 18.

---

5. In the Available Tables list, select one or more items and use the Add or Add All button to move the tables to the Selected Tables list.

6. After you have included the correct tables, click the Next button to proceed.

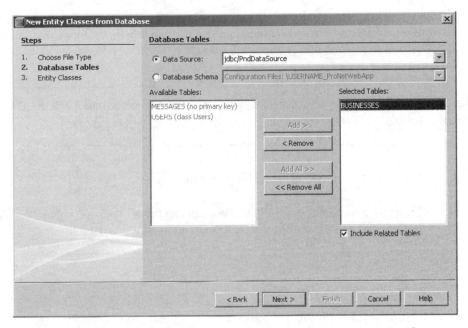

Figure 6-18. *The Database Tables window in the New Entity Classes from Database wizard*

7. In the Entity Classes window, you will see a list of each database table you previously selected and the suggested class name that will be created for the matching entity, as shown in Figure 6-19. You can specify the source location and Java package hierarchy for the generated entity classes.

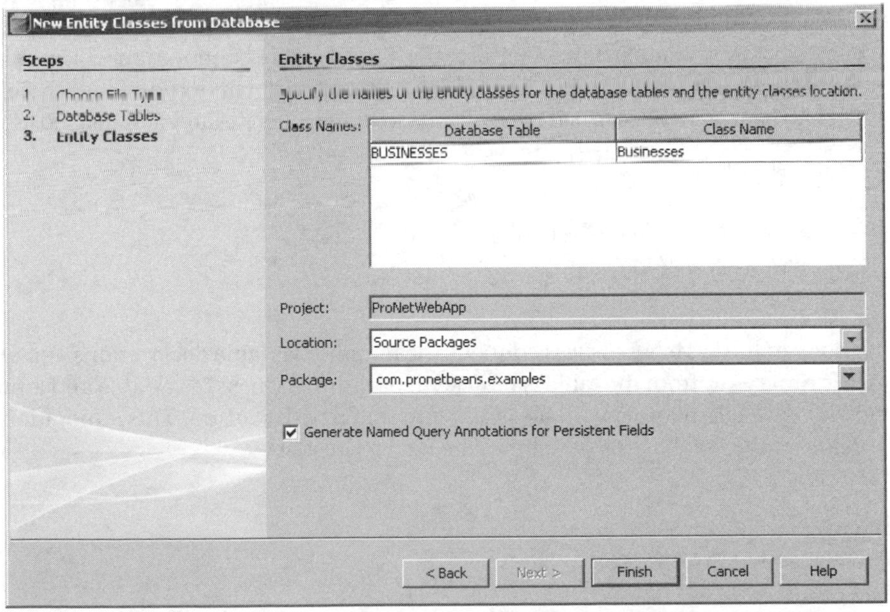

Figure 6-19. *The Entity Classes window in the New Entity Classes from Database wizard*

8. If the Generate Named Query Annotations for Persistent Fields check box is selected, NetBeans will generate special annotations that define a Java Persistence Query Language (JPQL) query for each field in the entity class.

■**Tip** JPQL can be used to query entities stored in a database. For more information about JPQL, see Chapter 27 of the Java EE 5 tutorial at `http://java.sun.com/javaee/5/docs/tutorial/doc/`.

---

9. Click the Finish button to generate the new entity classes.

Once NetBeans creates the new entity classes, you can review the code it generated. For the entity class created in the example, the class declaration contains the following:

```
@Entity
@Table(name = "BUSINESSES")
@NamedQueries( {
        @NamedQuery(name = "Businesses.findByBusinessId", ➡
query = "SELECT b FROM Businesses b WHERE b.businessId = :businessId"),
        @NamedQuery(name = "Businesses.findByBusinessName", ➡
query = "SELECT b FROM Businesses b WHERE b.businessName = :businessName")
    })

public class Businesses implements Serializable {
```

The class contains the standard `@Entity` annotation that declares this is an entity class. It also contains the `@Table` annotation that associates this entity with the matching database table. If you selected the Generate Named Query Annotations for Persistent Fields check box in the New Entity Classes from Database wizard, the `@NamedQueries` annotation will appear, as shown in the preceding code snippet. There is one `@NamedQuery` annotation for each field that appears in the database table. The `Businesses` database table in this example is defined as follows:

```
CREATE TABLE BUSINESSES
(
"BUSINESS_ID" NUMERIC(5) not null primary key,
"BUSINESS_NAME" VARCHAR(100)
)
```

The body of the `Businesses` class contains the member variable declarations and annotations. The primary key from the table is represented by the `businessId` variable and annotated with the `@Id` tag. Each member variable is also annotated with `@Column`. This annotation specifies the name of the database table column the field represents.

```
@Id
@Column(name = "BUSINESS_ID", nullable = false)
private BigDecimal businessId;

@Column(name = "BUSINESS_NAME")
private String businessName;
```

The remainder of the Businesses class contains the getters and setters for the class member variables, as well as the overridden hashCode, equals, and toString methods.

Creating JSF Pages from an Entity Class

People who know me would probably comment that I use the word *cool* too often. I normally try to reserve it for things that really are fascinating or amazing, particularly for new technologies. As of NetBeans 5.5, you can use the New File wizard to generate an entire CRUD application without writing a single line of code. To me, that's both amazing and cool!

CRUD is an acronym for Create, Read, Update, and Delete. These are the main functions that are frequently requested by customers when working with a table of data. The data may appear in a table in a report or populate items in a drop-down list. Regardless of its use, customers frequently want the ability to read the items in a table, modify individual records, add new records to it, and delete records from it. This defines a typical CRUD application.

In NetBeans, you can use JSF and entity classes to create a full-featured CRUD application. At the time of this writing, you can use this capability only in a Web Application project that has added JSF framework support. Here are the steps:

1. In a Web Application project, right-click the project name and select New ➤ File/Folder.

2. In the New File window, select Persistence from the list of categories and JSF Pages from Entity Class from the list of file types. Click the Next button to proceed.

3. The Entity Classes window displays a list of entity classes in the project (those flagged with the @Entity annotation). Select a class from the Available Entity Classes list and click the Add button to move it to the Selected Entity Classes list on the right. Click the Next button to continue.

4. The Generated JSF Pages and Classes window allows you to specify the folder in the web application where the new JSF files will be created. If you intend to create a CRUD tool for additional classes, I recommend putting each set of CRUD files in a separate folder using the JSF Pages Folder field. Finally, you can specify values for the Location and Package fields. Click the Finish button to complete the process.

As the wizard generates the new files, several things occur. Two new Java source files are created in the package you specified in the wizard:

BusinessesController: A class that defines the EntityManager and EntityManagerFactory classes needed to access the persisted data. It also defines the methods used to create, edit, and delete the persisted records in the database.

BusinessesConverter: A class that converts the business entity's ID field to different object types.

Also generated are four JSP files that contain JSF tags and references to the entity classes:

List.jsp: A JSP page that displays a list of all records in the entity's matching database table.

Detail.jsp: A JSP drill-down page that allows you to view all fields for the record.

New.jsp: A JSP page that contains a form that allows you to add a new record to the table.

Edit.jsp: A JSP page that contains a form that allows you to edit the record's fields.

Finally, since the Web Application project uses the JSF framework, the faces-config.xml file is modified to define the new beans and the navigation rules between the JSP pages.

The best way to see how the application works is to run it. Press F6 to execute the application or select Run ➤ Run Main Project. The Web Application project's default page, index.jsp, appears. This page has a link labeled List of Businesses. Click this link to see the List.jsp file, as shown in Figure 6-20.

Listing Businessess

New Businesses
Back to index
Item 1..9 of 9

BusinessId	BusinessName		
1	Acme Widgets, Inc.	Destroy	Edit
2	Sun Microsystems	Destroy	Edit
3	Red Hat	Destroy	Edit
4	JBoss	Destroy	Edit
5	Google	Destroy	Edit
6	Honeywell	Destroy	Edit
7	General Electric	Destroy	Edit
8	General Motors	Destroy	Edit
9	Ford	Destroy	Edit

Figure 6-20. *The List.jsp file*

The List.jsp page displays all the records in the database table. The BusinessId column is hyperlinked to the Detail.jsp page that displays all the fields in the entity class. So, if you decide to remove fields from the List.jsp page display, you will still be able to click the hyperlinked BusinessId column and drill down to view all the record's fields.

For each record, the List.jsp page contains Destroy and Edit links. Clicking the Destroy link will remove the corresponding record from the database table. Clicking the Edit link takes you to the Edit.jsp page, where each field is editable in a form.

■**Tip** You can edit the JSP page to change the name of the Destroy link to Delete, Remove, or whatever makes the most sense to you.

Clicking the New Businesses link at the top of the List.jsp page takes you to a form in the Add.jsp page, where you can add a new record to the database. The form on the Add.jsp page specifies an action of businesses.create. To trace where this form goes, you should first note that the faces-config.xml defines the BusinessesController class with the following XML code:

```
<managed-bean>
    <managed-bean-name>businesses</managed-bean-name>
    <managed-bean-class>
        com.pronetbeans.examples.BusinessesController
    </managed-bean-class>
    <managed-bean-scope>session</managed-bean-scope>
</managed-bean>
```

The BusinessesController class is defined as a managed bean with the name businesses. A managed bean is a JavaBean component that can be instantiated and called automatically in the value expression of a JSF tag. This allows the commandLink tags action attribute to refer to the create method in the BusinessesController class like this: #{businesses.create}.

The businessesId and businessesName fields are populated into the Businesses class, which is in turn passed to the setBusinesses method of the BusinessesController class. The BusinessesController.create method is defined as follows:

```
public String create() {
    EntityManager em = getEntityManager();
    try {
            utx.begin();
            em.persist(businesses);
            utx.commit();
            addSuccessMessage("Businesses was successfully created.");
    } catch (Exception ex) {
            try {
                addErrorMessage(ex.getLocalizedMessage());
                utx.rollback();
            } catch (Exception e) {
                addErrorMessage(e.getLocalizedMessage());
            }
    } finally {
            em.close();
    }
    return "businesses_list";
}
```

The utx variable refers to the UserTransaction class defined as a class member annotated with @Resource:

```
@Resource
private UserTransaction utx;
```

The create method uses the UserTransaction class to begin a transaction, calls the EntityManager.persist method to store the new instance of the Businesses class, and finally commits the transaction.

You can follow the same process to understand how the list, edit, and destroy portions of this CRUD application work. As I mentioned earlier, there is a lot of functionality automatically created for you without you having to write a single line of code. Once the set of files is generated, you have complete control to edit them however you wish.

Summary

This chapter covered the different types of Java enterprise projects that you can create in NetBeans. It reviewed the steps involved in creating the various types of projects and generating EJBs to give the projects functionality.

The EJB Module project was discussed in depth. You learned how to create session and message-driven beans, modify them, and use the various NetBeans wizards for generating content.

Finally, we covered how to work with persistence in your NetBeans projects. You can use JPA to create objects and persist them in a relational database. NetBeans also provides some excellent wizards for generating entity classes from a database and for creating a set of JSP pages that implement a CRUD application.

■■■

CHAPTER 7

Creating Web Service Projects: JAX-WS, SOA, and BPEL

The concept of software as a service is not new. People in the IT community have been discussing it for years. A related idea in software architecture, *modularization*, involves making portions of software separate and loosely coupled. Web services provide this loose coupling by separating software components.

Many of the tools that implement the alphabet soup of web service technologies are difficult to work with and have a steep learning curve. The NetBeans IDE and the Enterprise Pack attempt to supply simple solutions to working with these technologies. Together, they provide the support for the latest web service specifications, such as Java EE 5 and the Java API for XML Web Services (JAX-WS). These tools allow you to use Java EE 5 and annotations for quickly and easily defining web service servers and clients.

The Enterprise Pack also provides support for service-oriented architecture (SOA) tools like the Business Process Execution Language (BPEL) and its supporting features. You can use visual tools to design a business process, invoke web services, and test the entire process. These tools let you construct what is known as a composite application made up of various logical processes and web services. This helps enforce the modularization that web services aim to provide and allows you to quickly and easily interact with them.

Installing the Enterprise Pack

To use the XML, SOA, and BPEL tools available in NetBeans, you must download and install NetBeans Enterprise Pack 5.5. The installation process varies depending on whether you want to install the bundled application server, use a preinstalled application server, or skip the application server configuration. The Sun Java System Application Server (SJSAS) 9 is bundled with the Enterprise Pack.

Using the Bundled Application Server

To install the Enterprise Pack and the application server bundled with it, follow these steps:

1. Go to http://www.netbeans.org/products/enterprise/ and download the Enterprise Pack.

2. Once you have downloaded the Enterprise Pack, run the executable.

3. Accept the license, and then click the Next button.

4. Specify the NetBeans IDE installation directory, and then click the Next button.

5. In the next window, choose the components of the Enterprise Pack to install. Your choices are BPEL, XML, and Secure Web Services, as shown in Figure 7-1. All the components are selected by default. I recommend leaving them selected, because you can always disable them in the Module Manager (as described in Chapter 2) if you choose not to use them. Click Next to continue.

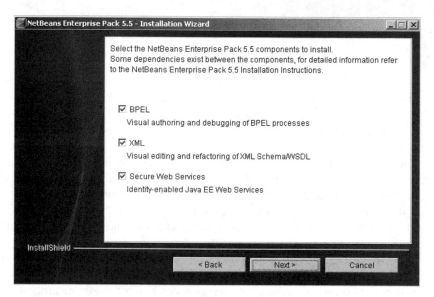

Figure 7-1. *Options for installing NetBeans Enterprise Pack 5.5*

6. The next window in the Enterprise Pack Installation wizard involves installing an application server. Choose to install the bundled application server, and then click the Next button.

7. Specify the application server installation directory. A default directory is specified, but you can select another directory. Click the Next button to continue.

8. The Installation wizard will briefly search for a list of compatible JDKs. You will then be prompted to specify which of the installed JDKs you want the application server to use. SJSAS 9, which is bundled with the Enterprise Pack, requires Java 5 or higher to work. Once you have selected the desired JDK, click the Next button.

9. The Installation wizard will next attempt to create a domain for the server to run, which requires an administrator username and password. You can leave the default values: admin for the Username field and adminadmin for the Password field. (To enter your own values, you must first disable the Use Default Username and Password check box.) Click the Next button to proceed.

10. In the next window, you can specify several port values. You can also set the Admin Port, Http Port, and Https Port fields, which specify the ports that the application server will listen on for specific types of requests. If you run more than one Java application server on the same machine, you should most likely change the port numbers, since ports such as 8080 are common across different servers. After specifying the desired port numbers, click the Next button.

11. The next window enables you to review your installation choices. If you specified to include all the modules available in the Enterprise Pack installation, you should see the following list of features displayed:

   - NetBeans Enterprise Pack 5.5

   - BPEL

   - XML

   - Secure Web Services

   - Sun Java System Application Server Platform Edition 9 UR1

   - Project Open ESB Starter Kit

   - Sun Java System Access Manager 7.1

   - Policy Agent 2.2 for Web Services

12. To complete the installation, click the Install button. Once the installation process executes and finishes, you can click the Finish button to close the wizard. The Enterprise Pack is now ready to use within the NetBeans IDE.

Using a Preinstalled Application Server

If you already have SJSAS running on your machine, you can configure the Enterprise Pack to use it. To do so, follow these steps:

1. Follow steps 1 through 5 of the preceding section to download the Enterprise Pack, start the installation, and choose the components to install.

2. In the window for configuring an application server, select the Use a Preinstalled Application Server option, and then click the Next button.

3. The Installation wizard searches briefly for a list of compatible application servers and prompts you to select one. If it cannot locate a server, you must specify the directory where one is located. Once you have specified a valid directory, click the Next button.

4. Enter values for the Username and Password fields. This username and password are for the application server's default domain. Click the Next button to continue.

5. The Installation wizard will start the application server and attempt to validate the values you supplied for the username and password. Assuming it validates correctly, you will see a final verification window that lists the features that will be installed. If you accepted the default to install all the components, NetBeans Enterprise Pack 5.5, BPEL, XML, and Secure Web Services will be listed.

6. To complete the Installation, click the Install button. Once the installation process executes and finishes, click the Finish button to close the wizard. The NetBeans Enterprise Pack is now ready to use within the NetBeans IDE.

Skipping Application Server Installation

When you get to the Installation wizard window for installing an application server (step 5 in the previous instructions for using the bundled application server), a third option is to skip installing the application server. You can select this option only if you choose to not install the BPEL and Secure Web Services components of the Enterprise Pack. In this case, you will immediately see a verification window that lists only the NetBeans Enterprise Pack 5.5 and the XML modules. From that window, you can choose to complete the installation.

Creating Web Services

One of my first experiences with web services was several years ago. As a beginner, I started using the several Apache libraries for working with XML and web services. These were a little unwieldy and took quite some time to learn considering the numerous acronyms, specifications, and implementations to sift through. Eventually, I began to comprehend the technology, and I found I could do some interesting web service calls via the Simple Object Access Protocol (SOAP).

SOAP provided some nifty capabilities, particularly RPC-type calls via HTTP that communicated on the standard port 80. This allowed web services to bypass many corporate firewalls and also added some flexibility in the web services paradigm, laying the groundwork for web applications to evolve into SOAs.

Up to this point, working with the various web service technologies was a little difficult. When Sun introduced the Java EE 5 platform, it included JAX-WS, a new API combined with annotations that greatly simplified the process of working with web services. This XML-based document approach is similar to SOAP and replaces the XML-RPC type of web services that existed in the past.

NetBeans 5.5 provides several convenient tools for creating web services using JAX-WS. These tools can help you quickly create web service servers and clients, as well as get rid of much of the boilerplate code you typically write.

In NetBeans, you can specify several different web service file types using the New File wizard:

Web Service: Creates an empty web service that is part of an EJB or web container that is called by a client application.

Web Service Client: Specifies the client application that calls a web service.

Web Service from WSDL: Generates a web service based on a Web Services Description Language (WSDL) file. A WSDL file is an XML-based file that describes a web service as defined by the W3C specification. It acts like an interface to the web service by describing its network bindings, protocol, and messages.

WSDL: Creates an empty WSDL file that describes a web service using XML.

Logical Handler: Creates a Java class that allows you to perform preprocessing and post-processing of web service messages.

Message Handler: Creates a Java class that allows you to perform preprocessing and post-processing of web service messages and affects the body and header of the message. This file type is typically used for security and/or logging purposes.

These file types can be employed in several different types of NetBeans projects. The following examples use a Web Application project type for the web service and a Java Application project type for the client.

Creating a Web Service

Let's say you wanted to create a web service in a Web Application project that allowed client applications to retrieve customer information. Define a simple Customer class like the following:

```java
package com.pronetbeans.examples.services;

public class Customer {

    public Customer() {}

    private long Id;
    private String FirstName;
    private String LastName;

    public long getId() {
        return Id;
    }

    public void setId(long Id) {
        this.Id = Id;
    }

    public String getFirstName() {
        return FirstName;
    }

    public void setFirstName(String FirstName) {
        this.FirstName = FirstName;
    }
```

```
    public String getLastName() {
        return LastName;
    }

    public void setLastName(String LastName) {
        this.LastName = LastName;
    }
}
```

The Customer class contains three member variables. The Id variable represents the number used to uniquely identify a customer in a database system. The FirstName and LastName variables define the customer's name. I've used a simple example for demonstration purposes. Obviously, a Java class that represents a real customer would have numerous fields for items like billing address, shipping address, phone numbers, payment details, and so on.

Tip You don't have to actually type all the getter and setter methods in the example. You can highlight the three member variables, right-click in the Source Editor window, and select Refactor ➤ Encapsulate Fields, which will generate the getter and setter methods for you. See Chapter 11 for details on refactoring.

In this example, the Customer class will be populated with data and sent to the client applications that execute the web service. To create the web service, follow these steps:

1. Right-click the project name in the Projects window and select New ➤ File/Folder.

2. In the New File wizard, select Web Services from the list of categories in the left pane and Web Service from the list of file types in the right pane. Then click the Next button to continue.

3. In the Name and Location window, shown in Figure 7-2, specify a value for the Web Service Name field, such as CustomerInfo. This is the name that client applications will use to call the web service, so you should try to make it a meaningful one. You can also specify the Location and Package fields in this window.

4. Choose how your web service is generated by selecting either the Create an Empty Web Service option or the Delegate to Existing Session Enterprise Bean option. Specify an EJB if necessary. Then click Finish.

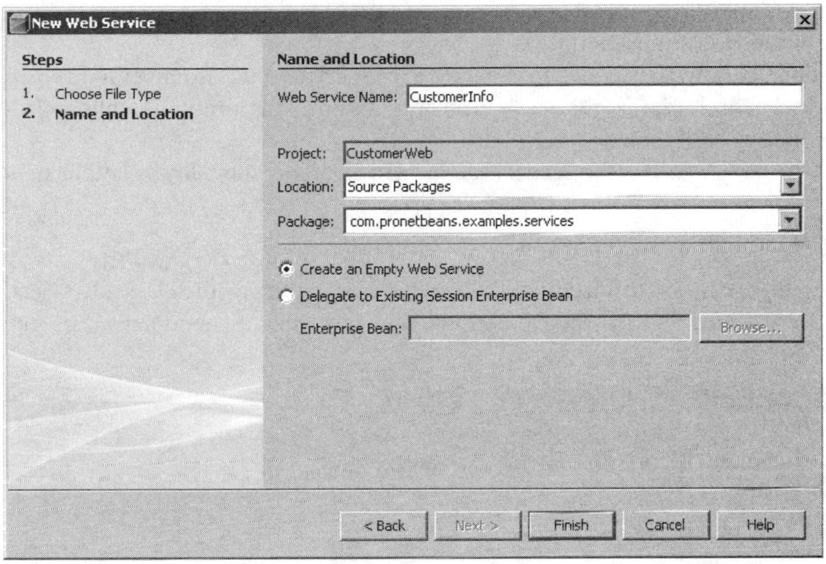

Figure 7-2. *Adding a web service in the Name and Location window*

The Create an Empty Web Service option will simply generate a skeleton web service class with no code or operations. More often than not, you will choose this default option. If you leave it selected and click the Finish button, the following web service class will be generated (the package and import statements are not included):

```
@WebService()
public class CustomerInfo {

}
```

The Delegate to Existing Session Enterprise Bean option allows you expose an EJB as a web service. When you click the Browse button to select an EJB, a dialog box will display a list of any enterprise modules or projects currently open in the Projects window. Once you have selected an EJB from this dialog box, you can click Finish to complete the new file creation process. The new web service class is created with the following code:

```
@WebService
public class CustomerInfoImpl {

    @EJB
    private com.pronetbeans.examples.NewSessionLocal newSessionBean;

}
```

In this example, `NewSessionLocal` class is the EJB selected to expose as a web service. It is marked with the `@EJB` annotation.

Regardless of how you choose to generate a web service, you should end up with a class that is marked with the `javax.jws.WebService` annotation. This annotation allows JAX-WS to handle the Java class like a web service.

Once you have created a web service, you need to give it functionality by adding operations.

Adding an Operation to a Web Service

You can add an operation to a web service by right-clicking inside the class and selecting Web Service ➤ Add Operation. The Add Operation dialog box will appear, as shown in Figure 7-3.

Figure 7-3. *The Add Operation dialog box for a web service*

Nothing in the Add Operation dialog box should look particularly foreign. This dialog box essentially allows you to add a Java method with a name, parameters, return type, and exceptions.

The name of the operation is what the client calls. The Return Type field denotes the type of value that is returned to the client. The field contains a drop-down list of suggested values, such as `long`, `String`, `int`, and so on. You can choose one of these values or type directly in the field. If the return type is not listed, you can click the Browse button to open the Browse Class dialog box. This dialog box allows you to type a partial or complete name of a Java class and view the matching results. For example, if you search on the value `Cust`, the `Customer` class created in the previous example will appear in the results.

You can then choose to add an input parameter to the operation. The bottom half of the Add Operation dialog box allows you to add, edit, and remove parameters. Each parameter has a type and a name associated with it. You can also order the parameters in the operation using the Up and Down buttons in the dialog box.

As you can see in Figure 7-3, I have specified a name of getCustomerById, a return type of com.pronetbeans.examples.services.Customer, and a single parameter of long lngCustomerId. Once the fields are properly set, click the OK button to create the operation.

The code that is generated will look similar to the following:

```
@WebMethod
public Customer getCustomerById(@WebParam(name = "custId") int custId) {
        // TODO implement operation
        return null;
}
```

In the preceding code, you can see that the method is marked with the @WebMethod annotation. The matching import statement for the @WebMethod annotation is also added to the class as import javax.jws.WebMethod;. This annotation identifies the method as a web operation that should be exposed through the web service. The input parameter is also marked with an annotation named @WebParam, which contains a name attribute that explicitly defines the name of the parameter. You can learn more about this class (and all the annotation classes) by reviewing the Java EE 5 Javadoc available at http://java.sun.com.

The body of the method is empty, but you can quickly add content to make the web service functional. In the following code, I have defined and instantiated an instance of the Customer class. I then perform an if-else check on the input parameter to see whether it matches a certain value. If it matches either of two values, I populate the Customer object with fake data to be returned to the calling client application. This is to simulate a query to a data source. If the custId parameter does not match either of the two hard-coded values, the Customer object is populated with meaningless values and returned.

```
@WebMethod
public Customer getCustomerById(@WebParam(name = "custId") int custId) {

    Customer cust = new Customer();

    if(custId==1234567890) {
            cust.setId(1234567890);
            cust.setFirstName("Adam");
            cust.setLastName("Myatt");
    } else if(custId==123) {
            cust.setId(123);
            cust.setFirstName("John");
            cust.setLastName("Doe");
    } else {
            cust.setId(-1);
            cust.setFirstName("");
            cust.setLastName("");
    }
    return cust;
}
```

The web service operation I defined here will accept a customer identification number as a parameter, retrieve the customer data from a data source, and return a `Customer` class filled with customer data.

Yes, Virginia, there is a Santa Claus! With a few quick clicks, you have a real working web service in NetBeans using Java EE 5 and JAX-WS.

Testing the Web Service

The SJSAS comes with a web service testing application, which you can use to test your web service without having to write a client application. To test the web service, follow these steps:

1. Press F6 or select Run ➤ Run Main Project. Once the project runs and deploys, the application server will automatically start.

2. Expand the Web Services node in the Projects window, right-click the web service, and select Test Web Service.

3. Once the application has opened in the browser, you will see the web service testing page for the specific service you are testing. In this example, the `CustomerInfo` web service is exposed and available to be tested using a simple HTML form, as shown in Figure 7-4. The text field represents the input parameter for the web service method. For this example, enter the value 1234567890 in the input field. Then click the getCustomerById button to submit the value.

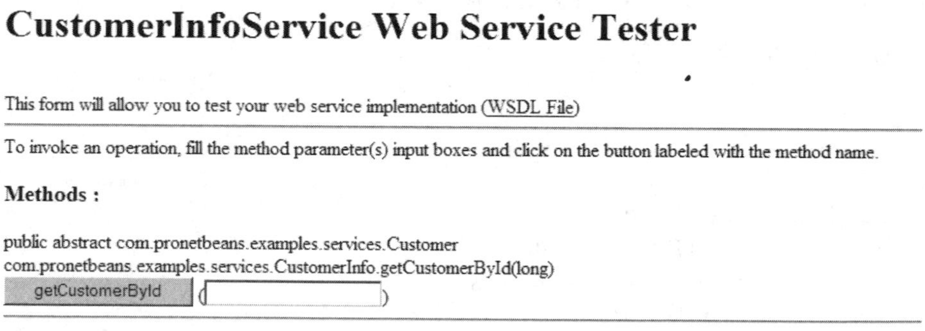

CustomerInfoService Web Service Tester

This form will allow you to test your web service implementation (WSDL File)

To invoke an operation, fill the method parameter(s) input boxes and click on the button labeled with the method name.

Methods :

public abstract com.pronetbeans.examples.services.Customer
com.pronetbeans.examples.services.CustomerInfo.getCustomerById(long)

| getCustomerById | ([   ]) |

Figure 7-4. *The SJSAS web service testing application*

The testing application returns a `Customer` object filled with data as specified in the definition of the `getCustomerById` method. The results page will display the SOAP request XML:

```
<?xml version="1.0" encoding="UTF-8"?>
<soapenv:Envelope xmlns:soapenv=http://schemas.xmlsoap.org/soap/envelope/ ➥
xmlns:xsd=http://www.w3.org/2001/XMLSchema ➥
xmlns:ns1="http://services.examples.pronetbeans.com/">
```

```
<soapenv:Body>
    <ns1:getCustomerById>
        <lngCustomerId>1234567890</lngCustomerId>
    </ns1:getCustomerById>
</soapenv:Body>
</soapenv:Envelope>
```

This SOAP envelope defines the body of the request, the function name getCustomerById, and the input parameter lngCustomerId. The value that was specified in the web service testing application is listed between the opening and closing tags that define the lngCustomerId parameter.

The application also displays the SOAP response XML:

```
<?xml version="1.0" encoding="UTF-8"?>
<soapenv:Envelope xmlns:soapenv="http://schemas.xmlsoap.org/soap/envelope/" ➥
xmlns:xsd="http://www.w3.org/2001/XMLSchema" ➥
xmlns:ns1="http://services.examples.pronetbeans.com/">
    <soapenv:Body>
        <ns1:getCustomerByIdResponse>
            <return>
                <firstName>Adam</firstName>
                <id>123456/890</id>
                <lastName>Myatt</lastName>
            </return>
        </ns1:getCustomerByIdResponse>
    </soapenv:Body>
</soapenv:Envelope>
```

The data returned in the SOAP response shows that the web service actually functioned correctly and returned the correct values for the id, firstName, and lastName fields.

Creating a Web Service Client

A web service client represents the application code that executes a web service. It can be created as part of a Web Application project or a standard Java Application project. This allows you to call a web service from almost any type of Java application.

For the purposes of this chapter, I will show you how to create a new web service client in a Java Application project. To create the project and the web service client, follow these steps:

1. Select File ➤ New Project from the main menu.

2. In the New Project window, select General from the list of categories on the left and Java Application from the list of available project types on the right, and then click the Next button.

3. In the Name and Location window, name the project, select a project location, and specify the name and package of the Main class for the application. Click the Finish button to generate the project.

4. In the Projects window, right-click the project name and select New ➤ File/Folder.

5. In the New File wizard, select Web Services from the list of Categories in the left pane and Web Service Client from the list of file types in the right pane. Then click the Next button.

6. In the WSDL and Client Location window, shown in Figure 7-5, first specify the WSDL file. Your choices are Project, Local File, or WSDL URL. If you select Local File, you can browse to and select a WSDL file on the local file system. If you select the WSDL URL field, you must enter a complete URL to the WSDL file, such as http://www.myhost.com/ webapp/mywebService?wsdl. For this example, select the Project radio button, and then click the Browse button. In the Browse Web Services dialog box, expand the project name node, select the web service, and click the OK button.

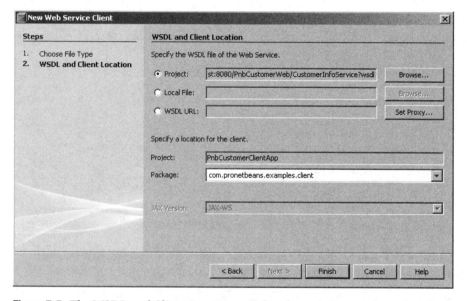

Figure 7-5. *The WSDL and Client Location window for creating a web service client*

7. Specify the Java package hierarchy for the web service client.

8. Click the Finish button to complete the process.

As NetBeans generates the web service client, you will see a progress bar and a status message indicating it is importing the WSDL file. After the web service client is generated, a new node named Web Service References appears under the project name in the Projects window. The WSDL file is located under the Web Service References node. Double-click the WSDL file node (CustomerInfoService in this example), to open the WSDL file in the Source Editor window. The following is a snippet of XML from the WSDL file:

```
<message name="getCustomerById">
  <part name="parameters" element="tns:getCustomerById"/>
</message>
<message name="getCustomerByIdResponse">
  <part name="parameters" element="tns:getCustomerByIdResponse"/>
</message>
<portType name="CustomerInfo">
  <operation name="getCustomerById">
    <input message="tns:getCustomerById"/>
    <output message="tns:getCustomerByIdResponse"/>
  </operation>
</portType>
<binding name="CustomerInfoPortBinding" type="tns:CustomerInfo">
  <soap:binding transport="http://schemas.xmlsoap.org/soap/http" style="document"/>
  <operation name="getCustomerById">
    <soap:operation soapAction=""/>
    <input>
      <soap:body use="literal"/>
    </input>
    <output>
      <soap:body use="literal"/>
    </output>
  </operation>
</binding>
```

Calling the Web Service

The WSDL file defines several configuration options for the service and allows web service clients to interact with the service via the defined port, binding, and message. The WSDL file allows you to use JAX-WS and the NetBeans web services tools to easily create Java code that calls the web service, as follows:

1. Open the Main class that was generated during the project creation process. You will see that the main method is empty.

2. Right-click anywhere inside the main method and select Web Service Client Resources ➤ Call Web Service Operation. The Select Operation to Invoke dialog box will appear, as shown in Figure 7-6.

3. Expand each node in the Select Operation to Invoke window until you can see the getCustomerById web service.

4. Click the web service name, and then click the OK button. NetBeans will generate code to call the web service inside the main method.

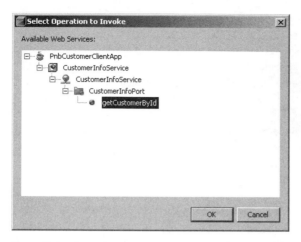

Figure 7-6. *The Select Operation to Invoke dialog box*

For this chapter's example, the following template code is generated:

```
public static void main(String[] args) {
    try { // Call Web Service Operation
        com.pronetbeans.examples.client.CustomerInfoService service = new ➥
com.pronetbeans.examples.client.CustomerInfoService();
        com.pronetbeans.examples.client.CustomerInfo port = ➥
service.getCustomerInfoPort();
        // TODO initialize WS operation arguments here
        long lngCustomerId = 0;
        // TODO process result here
        com.pronetbeans.examples.client.Customer result = ➥
port.getCustomerById(lngCustomerId);
        System.out.println("Result = "+result);
    } catch (Exception ex) {
        // TODO handle custom exceptions here
    }
}
```

The first two lines in the `try` block define and instantiate instances of the
`CustomerInfoService` and `CustomerInfo` classes. Creating these instances initializes the web
service for execution. The preceding code then calls the `getCustomerById` method, passing in
the `lngCustomerId` parameter. You can specify a value for the `lngCustomerId` field other than the
default value of 0 that is listed. The `getCustomerById` method returns a `Customer` instance,
which can then be used to retrieve the desired values.

You can modify the `main` methods as follows:

```
public static void main(String[] args) {
    try {
        CustomerInfoService service = new CustomerInfoService();
        CustomerInfo port = service.getCustomerInfoPort();

        long lngCustomerId = 1234567890;

        Customer result = port.getCustomerById(lngCustomerId);

        System.out.println(" Cust Id = " + result.getId());
        System.out.println(" First   = " + result.getFirstName());
        System.out.println(" Last    = " + result.getLastName());

    } catch (Exception ex) {
        ex.printStackTrace();
    }
}
```

You can remove the fully qualified package names for the classes and add the necessary imports by selecting Source ➤ Fix Imports (or use the shortcut Alt+Shift+F).

The modified main method also contains a value for the lngCustomerId field, which is passed to the getCustomerById method, which calls the web service on the remote server. Once the Customer object is returned, you can call the getter methods to retrieve the values that were passed along by the web service.

Running the Web Service Client

To run the web service client, you can simply press F6 to run the project assuming you used the Main class that was specified during the project creation process. If you added the web service code to a different class, select Run ➤ Run File ➤ Run "<*YourFile*.java>" to execute that specific class.

Once the Main class runs, the web service client is invoked and passes the request to the remote web service via the SOAP request. It then receives the SOAP response via the XML and translates the returned values into the Customer object. (The SOAP request and response are described in the earlier section about testing a web service.)

Testing the Web Service Client

To fully understand what is taking place between the web service client and the web service, you can use a network-monitoring program such as Ethereal to monitor the TCP/IP traffic that is exchanged between the client and server. You can also use the HTTP Monitor built in to the NetBeans IDE, as described in Chapter 4, but there are certain nonparameterized pieces of data that do not display in the HTTP Monitor.

Using a network-monitoring program allows you to view the protocols, IP address, and entire set of data exchanged between the client and server. You can start by following these steps:

1. Activate your network monitor to track the incoming and outbound data.

2. Make sure that the web service has been deployed to a running Java application server.

3. Open the client application and run it. The Main class should execute, call the web service client, and retrieve data from the remote web service.

4. Disable your network monitoring program and view the accumulated data.

In the results, you should be able to see that the application performed an HTTP GET on the WSDL file:

```
GET /PnbCustomerWeb/CustomerInfoService?WSDL HTTP/1.1
```

The contents of the WSDL file are returned from the server to the client. The web service client then performs an HTTP POST operation and passes the request as follows:

```
POST /PnbCustomerWeb/CustomerInfoService HTTP/1.1
Content-Length: 302
SOAPAction: ""
Content-Type: text/xml; charset=utf-8
Accept: text/xml, application/xop+xml, text/html, image/gif, ➥
  image/jpeg, *; q=.2, */*; q=.2
User-Agent: Java/1.5.0_10
Host: localhost:8080
Connection: keep-alive

<?xml version="1.0" ?>
<soapenv:Envelope xmlns:soapenv=http://schemas.xmlsoap.org/soap/envelope/ ➥
xmlns:xsd="http://www.w3.org/2001/XMLSchema" ➥
xmlns:ns1="http://examples.pronetbeans.com/">
<soapenv:Body>
<ns1:getCustomerById>
<id>123456</id>
</ns1:getCustomerById>
</soapenv:Body>
</soapenv:Envelope>
```

The SOAP response that appears as part of the server response will look similar to this:

```
X-Powered-By: Servlet/2.5
Content-Type: text/xml;charset=utf-8
Content-Length: 364
Date: Wed, 13 Dec 2006 19:00:51 GMT
Server: Sun Java System Application Server Platform Edition 9.0_01
```

```
<?xml version="1.0" ?>
<soapenv:Envelope xmlns:soapenv=http://schemas.xmlsoap.org/soap/envelope/ ➡
xmlns:xsd="http://www.w3.org/2001/XMLSchema"  ➡
xmlns:ns1="http://examples.pronetbeans.com/">
<soapenv:Body>
<ns1:getCustomerByIdResponse>
<return>
<first>Adam</first>
<id>123456</id>
<last>Myatt</last>
</return>
</ns1:getCustomerByIdResponse>
</soapenv:Body>
</soapenv:Envelope>
```

You can see that the SOAP XML passed back and forth between the client and server is nearly identical to the SOAP XML you saw when testing the web service using the web testing application.

■**Note** In the preceding examples, I've formatted the XML on multiple lines and added spaces to make it easier to read. In the actual GET and POST HTTP operations, the XML is typically sent in one long string, without spaces to minimize the number of characters that are transmitted.

Once your web service client's code has finished running, look at the Output window. As expected, the Customer logging text should appear as shown here:

```
Customer
   Id       = 123456
   First   = Adam
   Last    = Myatt
```

Creating a Web Service from a WSDL File

NetBeans also provides a wizard for generating a new web service based on an existing WSDL file. If you want to import an existing WSDL file, or create a new one manually in an application and then model a web service from it, you can do so using the New File wizard.

To create a new web service from a WSDL file, follow these steps:

1. Right-click the project name in the Projects window and select New ➤ File/Folder.

2. Select Web Services from the list of categories in the left pane and Web Service From WSDL from the list of file types in the right pane. Click the Next button to proceed.

3. In the Name and Location window, specify the web service name as well as values for the Location and Package fields, as shown in Figure 7-7.

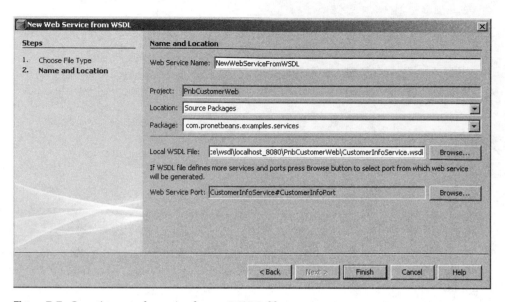

Figure 7-7. *Creating a web service from a WSDL file*

4. Click the upper Browse button to locate the local WSDL file. The dialog box allows you to browse your entire file system, not just WSDL files in open projects. Once you have located the WSDL file you want to use, click the Open button and review the settings in the Name and Location window.

5. If the WSDL file defines multiple services and ports, click the Browse button next to the Web Service Port field to specify the port you wish to use.

6. Click the Finish button to complete the process. NetBeans will generate the web service and list it in the Projects window under the Web Services node. The Java source file that represents the web service should also open in the Source Editor.

Creating a Message Handler

A message handler is a Java class that can typically access the header and body blocks of a SOAP message in a web service or client.

Generating a New Message Handler

To create a message handler, follow these steps:

1. Right-click the project name in the Projects window and select New ➤ File/Folder.

2. In the New File window, select Web Services from the categories list in the left pane and Message Handler from the file types list in the right pane. Click the Next button to proceed.

3. In the Name and Location window, you need to specify values only for the Message Handler Name, Location, and Package fields. After completing these fields, click the Finish button to generate the new handler class.

The skeleton code for the message handler that is generated will look similar to the following:

```
public class PnbMessageHandler implements SOAPHandler<SOAPMessageContext>{

    public boolean handleMessage(SOAPMessageContext messageContext) {
        SOAPMessage msg = messageContext.getMessage();
        return true;
    }

    public Set<QName> getHeaders() {
        return Collections.EMPTY SET;
    }

    public boolean handleFault(SOAPMessageContext messageContext) {
        return true;
    }

    public void close(MessageContext context) {
    }
}
```

In the preceding code, the handleMessage method is processed for all incoming and outgoing messages. You can use the SOAPMessage object to gain access to various bits and pieces of information for each message that passes into and out of the web service (for example, if you wanted to log a specific header for each request).

Adding the Message Handler to a Web Service

To configure the web service to use the new handler, you must add it to the service, as follows:

1. Under the web application's Web Services node, right-click the web service name and select Configure Handlers.

2. The Configure Message Handlers dialog box will appear. Click the Add button to open the Add Message Handler Class dialog box, as shown in Figure 7-8.

3. Expand the Source Packages node and select the message handler class. Then click the OK button.

4. The class you selected will now appear in the Handler Classes list in the Configure Message Handlers dialog box. Click the OK button to complete the process.

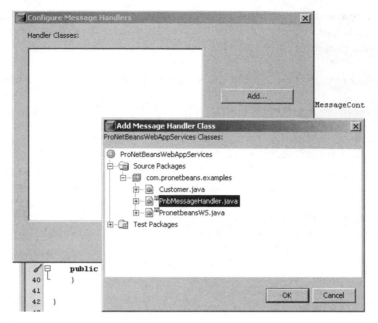

Figure 7-8. *The Add Message Handler Class dialog box*

A new file named `CustomerInfo_handler.xml` is created and added to the package where the Message Handler class exists. Its content defines the basic handler chain for the web service and lists the name and class for each handler that is configured for a web service.

```xml
<?xml version="1.0" encoding="UTF-8"?>
<handler-chains xmlns="http://java.sun.com/xml/ns/javaee">
  <handler-chain>
    <handler>
      <handler-name>
          com.pronetbeans.examples.PnbMessageHandler
      </handler-name>
      <handler-class>
          com.pronetbeans.examples.PnbMessageHandler
      </handler-class>
    </handler>
  </handler-chain>
</handler-chains>
```

The web service class itself is also modified to reference the handler chain:

```java
@WebService()
@HandlerChain(name = "CustomerInfo_handlerChain",
                      file = "CustomerInfo_handler.xml")

public class CustomerInfo {
    // class content removed
}
```

Now, when you build, deploy, and execute the web service, the message handler class is invoked.

Creating a Logical Handler

A logical handler is a Java class that can handle blocks of a SOAP message in a web service or client for the purposes of reading or modifying the message to augment its processing. Typical uses for a logical handler in a web service are logging and security.

To create a logical handler, follow these steps:

1. Right-click the project name in the Projects window and select New ➤ File/Folder.

2. In the New File wizard, select Web Services from the categories list in the left pane and Logical Handler from the file types list in the right pane. Click the Next button to proceed.

3. In the Name and Location window, you need to specify values only for the Logical Handler Name, Location, and Package fields. Once you have specified the values, click the Finish button to generate the new handler class.

The skeleton code for the logical handler that is generated will look similar to the following:

```
public class PnbLogicalHandler implements LogicalHandler<LogicalMessageContext> {

    public boolean handleMessage(LogicalMessageContext messageContext) {
        LogicalMessage msg = messageContext.getMessage();
        return true;
    }

    public boolean handleFault(LogicalMessageContext messageContext) {
        return true;
    }

    public void close(MessageContext context) {
    }
}
```

As with a message handler, the `handleMessage` method of a logical handler is executed for each incoming and outgoing message. You can use the `LogicalMessage` object to gain access to the internals of the SOAP message.

Working with SOA and BPEL

The NetBeans Enterprise Pack provides a variety of tools for working with SOA and BPEL applications. You can use tools to create and manage a WSDL file, create and modify a BPEL process, define a Composite project, and execute and test a business process.

Creating a BPEL Module Project

A BPEL Module project contains the design logic for a business process. You can visually define a flow of data, perform various conditional branches and checks, and invoke web services, depending on the desired functionality of your business process.

To create the BPEL Module project, follow these steps:

1. Select File ➤ New Project from the main menu.

2. In the New Project window, select Service Oriented Architecture from the list of categories in the left pane and BPEL Module from the list of projects in the right pane. Then click the Next button.

3. In the Name and Location window, enter the name for the BPEL Module project, and then click the Finish button.

The BPEL Module project will be generated and listed in the Projects window. It contains a single subnode called Process Files, which is where the BPEL processes and WSDL files are created. You can add the BPEL process files directly to this node.

Creating the BPEL Process File

The BPEL process file is what allows you to define an actual business process in a visual representation. To create a BPEL process, follow these steps:

1. Right-click the Process Files folder under the BPEL Module project name in the Projects window and select New ➤ File/Folder.

2. In the New File window, select Service Oriented Architecture from the categories listed in the left pane and BPEL Process from the file types listed in the right pane. Click the Next button to continue.

3. In the Name and Location window, as shown in Figure 7-9, enter the filename for the new BPEL process and select a folder. The default folder that is suggested for use is the src directory in the project.

4. Enter a value for the Target Namespace field. This field specifies the XML namespace for the BPEL process that aligns with the targetNamespace attribute in the XML definition.

5. Click the Finish button to complete the process.

The BPEL process file will be generated and listed under the Process Files node in the Projects window.

The BPEL process file will also open in the BPEL Design window in the center of the IDE. An empty BPEL process will be displayed in the window. It contains a Process Start point, an empty Sequence component (represented by a rectangle), and a Process End point, as shown in Figure 7-10.

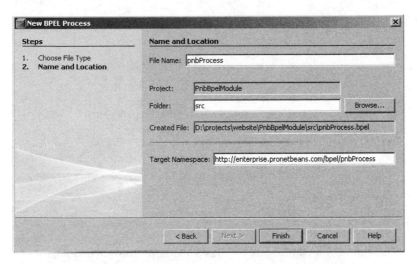

Figure 7-9. *The Name and Location window for creating a BPEL process*

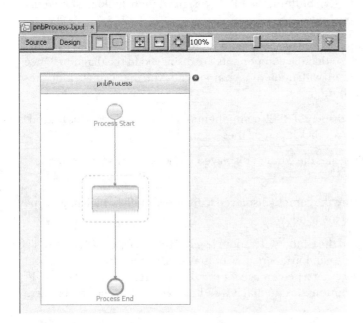

Figure 7-10. *A BPEL process displayed in the BPEL Design window*

Navigating the BPEL Design Window

The BPEL Design window, which currently shows the empty BPEL process, offers two views for working with the business process: Source and Design. The Design button is selected by default. Click the Source button to see the mostly empty XML code that defines the current process:

```xml
<?xml version="1.0" encoding="UTF-8"?>
<process
    name="pnbProcess"
    targetNamespace="http://enterprise.pronetbeans.com/bpel/pnbProcess"
    xmlns="http://schemas.xmlsoap.org/ws/2004/03/business-process/"
    xmlns:xsd="http://www.w3.org/2001/XMLSchema"
    xmlns:bpws="http://schemas.xmlsoap.org/ws/2004/03/business-process/"
    xmlns:wsdlNS="http://enterprise.pronetbeans.com/bpel/pnbProcess">

    <sequence>
        <empty/>
    </sequence>

</process>
```

Once you have visually created the BPEL process, this XML definition will include the detailed XML code. As you make changes in the Design view, NetBeans updates the XML code.

Along with the Source and Design buttons, the BPEL Design window toolbar, shown in Figure 7-11, includes the following buttons:

Show Partner Links: Toggles the display of BPEL components called Partner Links. This button is selected by default so that the components are displayed in the diagram. Once you have created a large diagram with numerous components, you may want to hide these components by clicking the button.

Show Sequences: Toggles the display of BPEL components called Sequences. This button is selected by default, and you can click it to hide these components.

Fit Diagram: Automatically scales the content displayed in the window so it fits in one window.

Fit Width: Automatically scales the content displayed to fit horizontally, which may or may not add a vertical scrollbar to the window.

Zoom: Displays the content in the window at a zoom level of 100%. Depending on the size of the content displayed in the window, there may or may not be horizontal and vertical scrollbars. You can manually enter a percentage for the zoom level in the small text field displayed to the right of the button. Next to that is a sliding bar you can click and drag to set the zoom level.

Validate XML: Allows you to validate XML.

Figure 7-11. *The BPEL Design window toolbar*

The Validate XML feature is available for most XML files. For BPEL process files, it validates the content to ensure it follows the defined XSD and rules. If you click the Validate XML button without adding any content to the newly created BPEL process, the Output window will open and display an error message:

```
XML validation started.
D:/projects/website/PnbBpelModule/src/pnbProcess.bpel:2,0
To be instantiated, an executable business process must contain at least
one <receive> or <pick> activity annotated with a createInstance="yes" attribute.

1 Error(s),  0 Warning(s).
XML validation finished
```

The BPEL process displayed in the BPEL Design window also denotes the error with a red circled *X* in the upper-right corner of the Process component. If you click the red circle, you will see a small dialog box that lists any errors for the BPEL process, as shown in Figure 7-12.

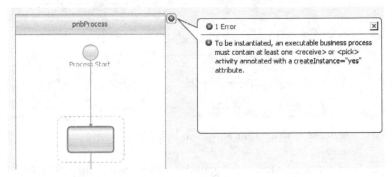

Figure 7-12. *The error dialog box in the BPEL Design window*

Creating the WSDL File

A BPEL process uses web services and WSDL files to define a link into and out of the business process. You can use NetBeans to create and manage a WSDL file that describes that interaction. Once the WSDL file has been created, you can add it to the business process and associate it with the various component operations in the process.

To create a WSDL file in the BPEL Module project, follow these steps:

1. Right-click the Process File node in the Projects window for the BPEL Module project and select New ➤ WSDL Document.

2. The Name and Location window will appear, because you already selected to create a WSDL document. Define the filename and the target namespace, and click the Finish button to proceed to the Abstract Configuration window.

3. In the Abstract Configuration window, shown in Figure 7-13, specify a value for the Port Type Name and Operation Name fields. The port type defines one or more operations for a web service. The operation name defines the initial web service function you want to create in the WSDL file.

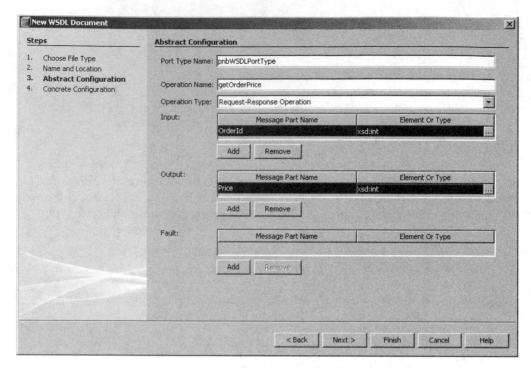

Figure 7-13. *Creating a WSDL file in the Abstract Configuration window*

4. The Operation Type field defines the functioning of the web service in the WSDL file. The drop-down lists offers four choices:

- *Request-Response Operation:* The web service will receive a value and send a response. This is most commonly used in services that receive an input parameter, perform a lookup or calculation, and return a result to the calling client. Possible uses for this type of service include an authentication or authorization service, a product order querying system, or a financial calculation service.

- *One-Way Operation:* The web service operation will only receive an input message and will not send any output. This type of operation could be useful when creating a logging application that can be called by other services.

- *Solicit-Response Operation:* The web service operation sends an output message to another service and waits to receive the reply. This type of service might be used with a process that monitors a local resource waiting for a condition to be true. If the condition occurs, it activates and notifies another service and waits for a response.

- *Notification Response:* The web service operation sends an output message only and does not wait for a response.

5. The remainder of the Abstract Configuration window prompts to specify the input and output parameters for the operation. Depending on the value for the Operation Type field, these input and/or output sections may or may not be filled out. To add an input or output parameter, click the Add button that appears under each section. A new line will be added to the grid in the specific section and allow you to type directly in the column fields. You can also optionally add any faults (errors) that occur in the process. Once you have specified the input, output, and fault parameters, click the Next button.

6. In the Concrete Configuration window, shown in Figure 7-14, specify the binding name. The binding name defines the binding type and subtype for the web service.

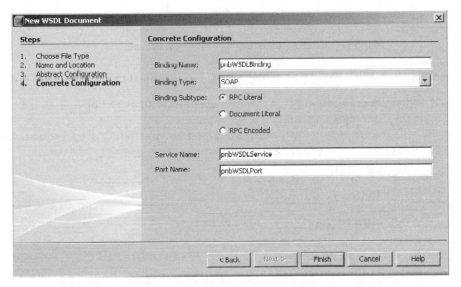

Figure 7-14. *The Concrete Configuration window when creating a WSDL file*

7. The only available value for the Binding Type field is SOAP.

8. Choose a value for the Binding Subtype field. The binding subtype defines how the binding will be translated into a SOAP message. You have three choices:

   - *RPC Literal*: The SOAP binding will be defined as `<soap:binding style="rpc"` ➡ `transport="http://schemas.xmlsoap.org/soap/http"/>`.

   - *Document Literal*: The SOAP binding will be defined as `<soap:binding style=` ➡ `"document" transport="http://schemas.xmlsoap.org/soap/http"/>`.

   - *RPC Encoded*: The SOAP binding will be defined as `<soap:binding style="rpc"` ➡ `transport="http://schemas.xmlsoap.org/soap/http"/>`.

9. Set the values for the Service Name and Port Name fields. These names affect how the web service is called, so you should specify something meaningful.

10. Once you have finished specifying the values for the WSDL file, click the Finish button to complete the process.

The WSDL file will be generated and listed under the Process Files node in the Projects window. The WSDL file is also opened in the WSDL Editor.

The WSDL XML will define the SOAP binding according to your selection for the binding subtype. If you chose RPC literal (the default), the SOAP binding will appear as follows:

```
<operation name="getOrderPrice">
  <soap:operation/>
  <input name="input1">
    <soap:body use="literal"
                namespace="http://j2ee.netbeans.org/wsdl/pnbWSDL"/>
  </input>
  <output name="output1">
    <soap:body use="literal"
                namespace="http://j2ee.netbeans.org/wsdl/pnbWSDL"/>
  </output>
</operation>
```

Notice that the `<soap:body>` tag has an attribute of use with a value of literal, based on the selection in the Concrete Configuration window (Figure 7-14).

If you selected Document Literal for the binding subtype, the SOAP operation defined following the SOAP binding will appear as follows:

```
<operation name=" getOrderPrice">
  <soap:operation/>
  <input name="input1">
      <soap:body use="literal"/>
  </input>
  <output name="output1">
      <soap:body use="literal"/>
  </output>
</operation>
```

If you selected RPC Encoded for the binding subtype, the SOAP operation is defined as follows:

```
<operation name=" getOrderPrice">
  <soap:operation/>
  <output name="output1">
    <soap:body use="encoded"
          encodingStyle=http://schemas.xmlsoap.org/soap/encoding/
          namespace="http://j2ee.netbeans.org/wsdl/wsdl232232323"/>
  </output>
</operation>
```

Navigating the WSDL Editor

As the name implies, the WSDL Editor allows you to edit a WSDL file. It has three main views: Tree, Source, and Column. Since the WSDL file contains metadata that describes the web service and how to access it, you should be familiar with creating and modifying WSDL files.

The WSDL Editor displays the Tree view, a parent-child node view of the XML elements in a WSDL file, by default. (You can also toggle Tree view off and on by clicking the Tree icon in the toolbar, to the right of the WSDL button.) As you can see in Figure 7-15, it is intended to provide a simple view of the data in the file.

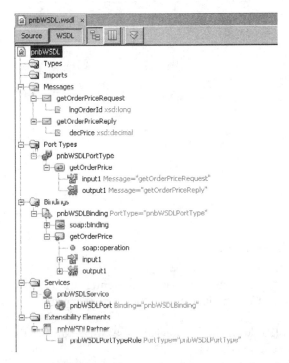

Figure 7-15. *The Tree view of a WSDL file in the WSDL Editor*

For each of the nodes that appear in the Tree view of the WSDL Editor, you can access specific sets of actions by right-clicking the nodes. You can right-click most nodes and select Go to Source, which toggles the WSDL Editor to the Source view and places the cursor in the section of XML that corresponds to the node you selected. This is useful if the WSDL file is quite long and you do not want to search through numerous lines of XML for a specific element.

You can also modify the WSDL file by adding new elements to it. In several sections, you can right-click a node and select Add ➤ *Element*, where *Element* is a context-sensitive element that can be added to the node. Using the context menus, you can add additional services, port names, bindings, operations, input/output parameters, and so on. All of this can be done without having to write any XML code.

The WSDL Editor also offers the Column view, which can be accessed by clicking the Column icon in the editor's toolbar. This is a great way to work with XML-based data, such as a WSDL file, because it gives you a left-to-right view of the parent-child relationships, as shown in Figure 7-16. If you select an element that contains a subnode (or child), a new column appears to the right of the current column and displays the child nodes. This provides a type of navigation that is similar to the standard Tree view but can be easier for some people to follow.

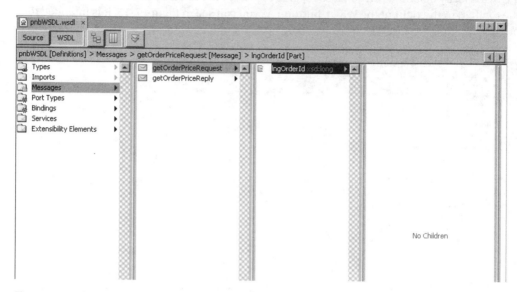

Figure 7-16. *Column view of a WSDL file in the WSDL Editor*

The Column view of the WSDL file provides the same sort of context menu features that are available in the Tree view. You can right-click any node to access the context-specific settings and options for it.

Now that you've seen how to create a WSDL file and how to navigate the WSDL Editor, let's get back to the BPEL process we created earlier and add to it.

Working with the BPEL Designer and the BPEL Mapper

The pnbProcess BPEL process you created in the section "Creating the BPEL Process File" is relatively blank, as shown earlier in Figure 7-10. You need to add functionality to it.

You can add BPEL components to the BPEL process in the BPEL Design window by dragging and dropping them from the Palette window. The Palette window contains components specific to web services and BPEL, as described in Table 7-1. (You can open the Palette window by selecting Window ➤ Palette or pressing Ctrl+Shift+8.)

Table 7-1. *The BPEL and Web Service Components in the Palette Window*

Category	Component	Description
Web Service	Invoke	Sends a message to a partner web service defined by a Partner Link.
Web Service	Receive	Waits for an incoming message from a web service defined by a Partner Link that was originally initiated by the Invoke component.
Web Service	Reply	Sends a message to a web service defined by a Partner Link in reply to a message that came in through the Receive component.
Web Service	Partner Link	Defines a web service that will interact with the BPEL process.
Basic Activities	Assign	Copies data between different variables and allows you to assign new data type values to variables.
Basic Activities	Empty	Represents an empty activity that does nothing. You can use this component if your BPEL process needs to ignore certain outcomes or paths.
Basic Activities	Wait	Causes the BPEL process to pause for a specified amount of time using various criteria.
Basic Activities	Throw	Generates an error or exception from within a BPEL process.
Basic Activities	Exit	Halts the flow of a BPEL process.
Structured Activities	If	Represents a conditional process that allows you to determine separate paths of execution for a BPEL process.
Structured Activities	While	Repeats a branch in the process as long as a condition continues to succeed.
Structured Activities	Repeat Until	Repeats a branch in the process as long as a condition continues to succeed after each loop iteration.
Structured Activities	For Each	Repeats a branch inside a Scope component as defined by specific criteria.
Structured Activities	Pick	Executes an activity after an event has occurred.
Structured Activities	Flow	Allows a BPEL process to perform multiple actions in parallel sequence.
Structured Activities	Sequence	Defines a group of activities that are executed in a sequential order.
Structured Activities	Scope	Defines an activity with an individual scope that contains its own internal local variables, links, and errors.

To have a BPEL process receive a message, perform a conditional check, and send a reply, you need to configure the conditional check in the If component. You do this through the BPEL Mapper window, which allows you to visually construct logical expressions, assign values to input and output parameters, and create logical checks of data, as shown in Figure 7-17.

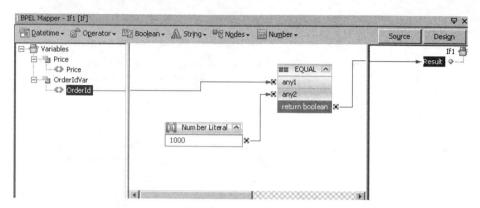

Figure 7-17. *The BPEL Mapper window*

When the If component is selected in the BPEL process, the BPEL Mapper window will display the list of variables in the left pane and a result node in the right pane, allowing you to map a true or false Boolean condition to it. The toolbar along the top of the BPEL Mapper contains several drop-down menus that allow you to choose from specific categories of components, such as date and time elements, Boolean elements, operators (addition, subtraction, multiplication), and so on.

Once you have reviewed the web services and BPEL components that are available, you can begin to add them to your BPEL process. The following sections walk you through creating a sample BPEL process.

Adding a Partner Link Component

To be able to interact with a web service, a BPEL process needs to have a Partner Link component:

1. Select the Partner Link component in the Palette window and drag it to a blank spot on the BPEL process canvas in the BPEL Design window. (You can also click a WSDL file in the Projects window and drag-and-drop it onto the BPEL process canvas.) Once the Partner Link component has been added, the Partner Link Property Editor window will open, as shown in Figure 7-18.

2. In the Partner Link Property Editor, specify a value for the Name field and select a WSDL file to which to apply the Partner Link.

3. Choose to use an existing partner link type or create a new partner link type. The partner link type is defined in the WSDL and specifies interaction rules.

4. Click the OK button. A square representing the Partner Link is added to the BPEL process.

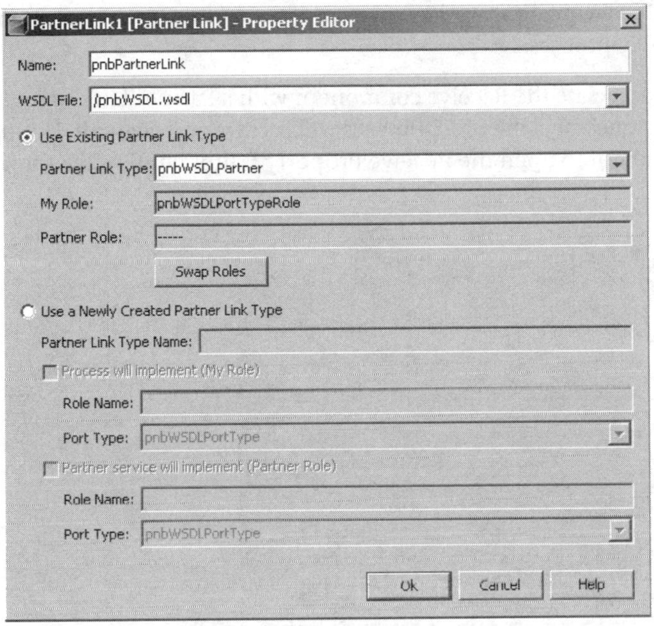

Figure 7-18. *The Partner Link Property Editor*

Adding a Receive Component

The next task in this example is to add a Receive component to the BPEL process:

1. Click the Receive component in the Palette window and drag it over the Process Start circle.

2. While still holding down the mouse, move the component straight down until you see a small dotted circle light up, as shown in Figure 7-19 (it will appear orange on your screen).

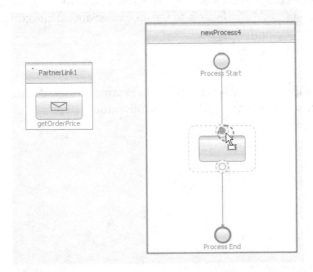

Figure 7-19. *Adding a Receive component to the BPEL process*

3. Once the circle is filled with orange, release the mouse, and the Receive component will be added to the BPEL process.

4. Next, you want to associate the Receive component with a Partner Link so that when a web service sends a message, the BPEL Process will receive and act on it. Double-click the Receive component to open the Receive Property Editor window, as shown in Figure 7-20.

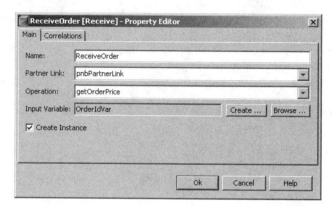

Figure 7-20. *The Receive Property Editor*

5. In the Receive Property Editor window, specify the name of the Receive component as it will appear in the BPEL process, define which Partner Link the component will receive a message from, and specify the web service operation that will send the Receive component a message.

6. In the Input Variable field, create or use an existing local variable to store the message received from the web service via the Partner Link.

7. Click the OK button. The Receive component will be configured to receive a message from the Partner Link. You should also be able to see an orange dotted line connecting the Partner Link and Receive components.

Adding a Reply Component

Next, you will add the Reply component, which responds to the Partner Link with a message allowing the calling web service to retrieve a value. To do so, follow these steps:

1. Select the Reply component in the Palette window and drag it over the Receive component in the BPEL process.

2. While holding down the mouse button, move the mouse straight down until the orange dotted circle target below the Receive component becomes filled in. This indicates you are over a target location where you can drop the component.

3. Release the mouse button to add the Reply component to the BPEL process.

4. Double-click the Reply component to open the Reply Property Editor window, as shown in Figure 7-21.

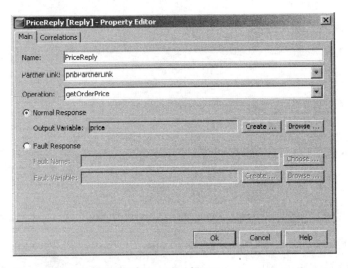

Figure 7-21. *The Reply Property Editor*

5. In the Reply Property Editor window, specify the name of the Reply component as it will appear in the BPEL process. Also specify to which partner link and operation the component will send a reply.

6. In the Output Variable field, create a new variable or specify an existing variable that will hold the reply message to be transmitted back to the Partner Link.

7. Click the OK button to proceed.

At this point, the BPEL process should contain a Partner Link, a Receive component, and a Reply component, as shown in Figure 7-22. The remaining steps you will perform determine how the input variable is checked, what conditions apply, and how the output variable is set.

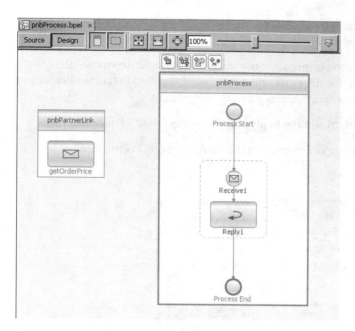

Figure 7-22. *The BPEL process containing Partner Link, Receive, and Reply components*

Adding an If Component

Next, to add a conditional check to the BPEL process, do the following:

1. Click the If component in the Palette window and drag it over the BPEL process.

2. Move the mouse directly below the Receive component and drop the If component into the circle target below the Receive component. Now you need to configure the If component using the BPEL Mapper.

3. Open the BPEL Mapper window by selecting Window ➤ BPEL Mapper or pressing Ctrl+Shift+9.

4. To configure the If component to check an input variable and return true if a certain condition is met, click Operator in the BPEL Mapper window menu bar and select EQUAL. The EQUAL element appears in the center section of the BPEL Mapper. It contains two lines with variables any1 and any2, and a third line labeled return Boolean.

5. Select Number ➤ Number Literal. This adds a single-line element labeled Number Literal. Double-click the empty line and enter a value, such as 1000.

6. In the left pane, expand the Variables node until you find the OrderId variable.

7. Drag the OrderId variable to the right and drop it onto the any1 line of the EQUAL element. A line connecting the two elements will appear.

8. Click and drag a line between the Number Literal element connecting it to the any2 line of the EQUAL element.

9. Click and drag a line between the return Boolean line of the EQUAL element and the Result node in the right pane of the BPEL Mapper window. The final result should look similar to Figure 7-17 (shown earlier).

Adding an Assign Component

Continue with the following steps to add an Assign component and finish creating the sample BPEL process:

1. Drag an Assign component from the Palette window onto the BPEL process in the BPEL Design window.

2. Click the Assign component in the BPEL process and open the BPEL Mapper window (select Window ➤ BPEL Mapper or press Ctrl+Shift+9).

3. Add a Number Literal element by selecting Number ➤ Number Literal.

4. Once the Number Literal element is displayed in the center pane of the BPEL Mapper window, double-click it and enter a number, such as 123456789.

5. Click and drag a line from the Number Literal element over to the Price variable in the right pane of the BPEL Mapper window, as shown in Figure 7-23.

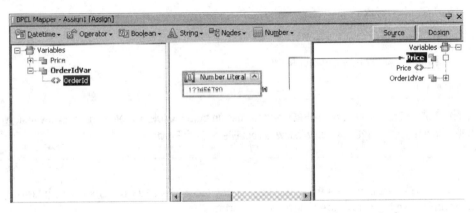

Figure 7-23. *Configuring the Assign component in the BPEL Mapper window*

Reviewing the Completed BPEL Process

The finished BPEL process should look similar to Figure 7-24 and perform the following steps:

- The BPEL process receives a message from a web service and assigns it to the OrderId variable.

- The process compares the OrderId variable to a numeric value of 1000. If the variable is equal to 1000, the If condition succeeds and activates the Assign component.

- The Assign component will assign the value of 123456789 to the Price variable.

- The If component finishes and hands off control to the Reply component.

- The Reply component passes the Price variable back as a response to the Partner Link web service.

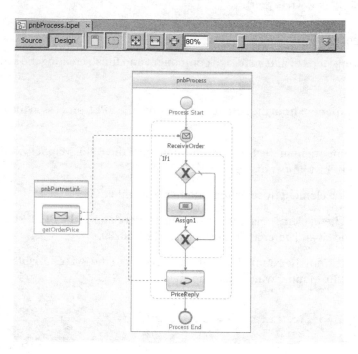

Figure 7-24. *The completed BPEL process*

■**Tip** You can print a copy of the BPEL process design from the IDE. To see a print preview first, with the BPEL file open in the BPEL Design window, select File ➤ Print Preview.

Once the BPEL process is complete, you need to add it to a Composite Application project to actually use it, as described in the next section.

Creating a Composite Application

A Composite Application project is deployed to a Java Business Integration (JBI) server. The SJSAS used throughout this book fully supports JBI server functionality. You can add a JBI module to it to execute your business application (also known as a BPEL module).

Creating a Composite Application Project

To create a new Composite Application project, perform the following steps:

1. Select File ➤ New Project from the main menu.

2. In the New Project window, select Service Oriented Architecture from the categories section on the left and Composite Application from the list of projects on the right. Click the Next button.

3. In the Name and Location window, enter a project name and location.

4. Click the Finish button to generate the Composite Application project.

Setting Composite Application Project Properties

You can review and configure several project properties that affect the Composite Application project. To access the properties, right-click the project name and select Properties from the context menu.

In the Project Properties window, you will see several nodes in the left pane. If you select a node, the related properties appear in the right pane of the window. The different nodes and their properties are as follows:

General: Displays properties such as Service Assembly Alias, Service Assembly Description, Service Unit Alias, and Service Unit Description.

Packaging Project: Displays properties that define the target components and service assembly artifacts for the Composite Application project, as shown in Figure 7-25. Also allows you to specify the JBI filename, which is typically a JAR file that is deployed to the target application server.

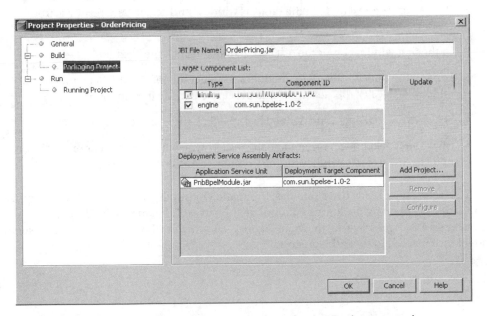

Figure 7-25. *The Composite Application project's Packaging Project properties*

Running Project: Displays a drop-down list of available application servers that support JBI functionality.

Adding a JBI Module

To enable the Composite Application project to use the BPEL Module project created in the previous section, you need to add a JBI module by following these steps:

1. Right-click the JBI Modules node in the Projects window and select Add JBI Module.

2. In the Select Project dialog box, locate and select a BPEL Module project, and then click the Add Project JAR Files button. The JAR file for the BPEL Module project will appear under the JBI Modules node.

3. Once the JBI module has been added to the Composite Application project, deploy it to the JBI application server by right-clicking the project name and selecting Deploy Project.

■**Note** You must first start the target application server before you can deploy the Composite Application project.

Testing the Composite Application and BPEL Process

NetBeans composite applications allow you to write test cases similar to JUnit tests. You can generate a test case that exercises a web service that, in turn, runs the BPEL process.

To create a new test case for your Composite Application project, do the following:

1. Right-click the Test node in the Projects window and select New Test Case from the context menu. The New Test Case wizard will appear.

2. In the first window, enter the test case name and click the Next button.

3. Expand the node for the BPEL module and select the WSDL file that contains the operation to test. Click the Next button to proceed to the next window.

4. Select the actual operation defined by the WSDL file you previously selected.

5. Click the Finish button to generate the test. The new test will appear under the Test node in the Projects window for the Composite Application project.

The new test contains two subnodes: Input and Output. If you double-click the Input node, a file will open in the Source Editor named Input.xml. It contains XML content that represents a SOAP message, as shown in Figure 7-26, which will be passed to the web service and, in turn, passed to the BPEL process.

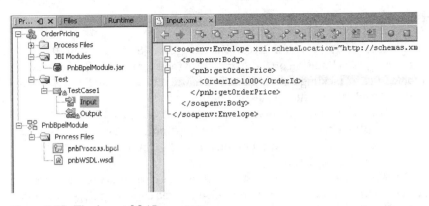

Figure 7-26. *The input SOAP message*

To customize the input passed to the web service, you can change the text inside the ⟨OrderId⟩ and ⟨/OrderId⟩ tags. This is the value assigned to the OrderId variables received by the Receive component in the BPEL process. Once you have configured the Input node text, you can execute the test in one of two ways:

- Right-click the project name and select Test Project or press Alt+F6 to execute all of the tests in a project. For this example, this executes the single test contained under the Test node in the Composite Application project.

- To execute a specific test, right-click the test and select Run Test from the context menu.

Once your test runs, it will load the results into the Output node and the matching Output.xml. Figure 7-27 shows the output SOAP message that results, which contains the value 123456789 in this example.

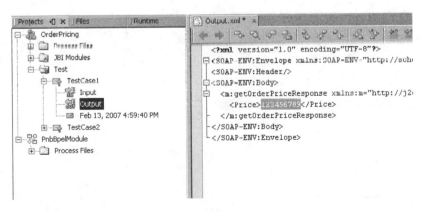

Figure 7-27. *The output SOAP message*

Summary

In this chapter, we discussed working with web services using JAX-WS, SOA, and BPEL. The NetBeans IDE and Enterprise Pack add-on provide a variety of tools for making it easier to work with these technologies. Before tackling web services, you learned how to install the NetBeans Enterprise Pack and explored some of the installation options available.

The chapter moved on to creating web services using JAX-WS and Java EE 5 annotations, adding an operation, and testing it. Creating a web service is extremely easy in NetBeans, and you can use the available wizards to generate operations. The SJSAS provides a web testing application that you can use test a web service.

As you learned, NetBeans also allows you to create a web service client that executes a remote web service, and you have the option to create empty skeleton web services and generate web services from a WSDL file. You can also create message and logical handlers that allow you to read and modify the header and body of a SOAP message.

You also learned how to model a business process using BPEL visual design tools. You can add a variety of BPEL components onto a canvas and use a visual mapping tool to create logical expressions. The BPEL process can interact with web services using components called Partner Links, which allow a web service to pass in and retrieve variables from a business process. You can then add the BPEL module to a composite application, which can be deployed and tested on a JBI application server.

CHAPTER 8

■ ■ ■

Creating UML Projects

Many programmers agree that modeling can help in planning and designing software. You need to be able to document the design of your program. You may also want to model customer use cases for people who will interact with a system, model a sequence of messages in a communication protocol, or model the possible states that a system can have. Performing this type of design work well in advance of your project implementation can save a lot of time and money. Having an object-based road map can also help ensure your software systems are better designed and easier to maintain.

The Unified Modeling Language (UML) is a general specification language that is used for modeling objects and relationships. You can use UML to model almost any process in life, but it is particularly useful in mapping out software designs. Using UML concepts, you can create different types of diagrams, such as class, deployment, use case, sequence, and collaboration diagrams.

The Object Management Group (OMG) is the international not-for-profit consortium that defines several standards, including the one for UML. The OMG was formed by companies such as Sun Microsystems, Hewlett-Packard, and IBM, but is open to any organization. The current specification for UML is version 2.0.

Although it is an industry best practice to fully model software systems, some shops simply do not have the resources, budget, or time to complete this necessary step. NetBeans offers a solution.

As of NetBeans 5.5, you can use a set of UML tools that are directly integrated with the Java IDE. The tool suite is contained in a module that you can download through the NetBeans Update Center.

Setting UML Options

Once you have downloaded and installed the UML module from the NetBeans Update Center Beta (as described in Chapter 2), you can set several options. These options allow some simple control over the features the UML module provides.

To set UML options, select Tools ➤ Options. In the left pane of the Basic Options window, click the UML icon. A message appears in the right pane, indicating that you must access the options in the Advanced Options section. Click the Advanced Options button, and then click the plus sign next to the UML node in the left pane of the Advanced Options window. The entire list of UML options will appear, as shown in Figure 8-1.

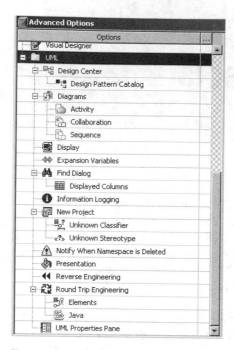

Figure 8-1. *The UML options in the Advanced Options window*

The options shown in Figure 8-1 allow you to set some properties that affect your interaction with the UML module. Some of the options affect the behavior of the system; others are merely for your convenience. The following sections describe some of the most often used properties in the New Project, Presentation, and Round Trip Engineering nodes.

New Project Properties

Clicking the New Project node in the UML Advanced Options window reveals the following properties in the right pane:

Create New Diagram: When you create a new UML project, you will be prompted to also create a new diagram. You can suppress the default behavior of always asking if you want to create a new diagram after generating a project. To disable the prompt, simply set the Create New Diagram property to No.

Default Diagram Name: Using this property, you can specify the value to always use when suggesting a name for a new diagram. If you use a standard naming convention for diagrams, you can specify it by changing this property to the desired value.

Default Element Name: When you add a new element to a UML project, it is typically named Unnamed until you specify a value. You can change this suggested name by customizing the Default Element Name property.

Presentation Properties

The Presentation properties allow you to control the look and feel of UML diagrams in NetBeans. Click the Presentation node to see the following properties:

Documentation Font: Use this property to set the font type and size for the text that appears in the UML Documentation window.

Grid Font: Use this property to set the font type and size for the text that appears in various grids, such as the Properties window.

Set Global Colors and Fonts: This is the most useful property under the Presentation node. It does not contain a single value, but allows you to set additional properties for the UML module through a custom editor.

To access the extra Presentation properties, click the ellipsis (three dots) button next to the Set Global Colors and Fonts property. A custom editor window will appear, as shown in Figure 8-2.

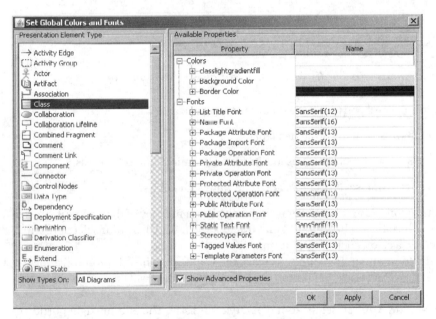

Figure 8-2. *Modifying global font and color properties for the UML module*

The property editor shown in Figure 8-2 allows you to set numerous presentation properties. The left side of the window lists the various presentation element types available in the system. The right side displays the properties available to be customized as you select an element in the left pane. The Show Types On drop-down list at the bottom of the left pane allows you to filter the list of element types. If you click the field and select a diagram type from the list, the Presentation Element Type list will display only properties for that diagram type. The Show Advanced Properties check box at the bottom of the right pane toggles on and off the display of properties designated as "advanced" in the right pane.

You can change any presentation property in the UML module using the custom editor. In the example in Figure 8-2, the element type Class was selected.

The properties are typically separated into categories of Colors and Fonts. For each color property, you can click the value to edit it. The property's value will then display a small ellipsis button. Click that button to display a standard color picker window, as shown in Figure 8-3.

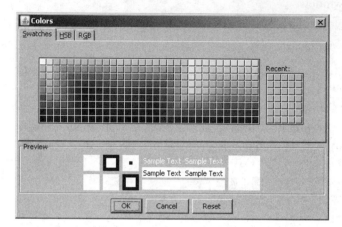

Figure 8-3. *The color picker window displayed when editing Presentation properties*

The color picker allows you to select a color in several ways:

- Select a color swatch on the Swatches tab.

- Click the HSB tab and specify values for the hue, saturation, and brightness.

- Click the RGB tab and set red, green, and blue values for colors.

The bottom section of the color picker window displays a preview of the different kinds of combinations of text color and background that would appear based on your selection. Once you have decided on a color, click the OK button.

To change the font settings for a property, click the value. An ellipsis button will appear next to the text of the value. Click that button, and the Font window will appear, as shown in Figure 8-4.

In the Font window, you can set the font type, style, and size. The bottom-right portion of the window contains a preview of how your font selections will appear. Once you have decided on a font setting, click the OK button to continue.

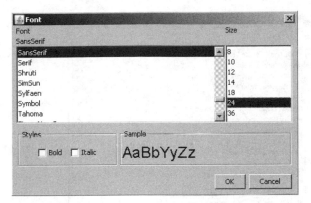

Figure 8-4. *The font editor window displayed when editing Presentation properties*

Round-Trip Engineering Properties

Round-trip engineering involves generating source code from models and vice versa. NetBeans allows you to set several types of properties that affect both the forward and reverse portions of the round-trip engineering process. Click the Round Trip Engineering node to see the following properties:

Replace Conflicting Elements: A new element from Java source code could have the same name as an element in the UML model, causing a conflict. This property controls whether the conflicting UML elements in the model are automatically replaced with the elements from the Java source code. This property is set to the value of Ask Me by default. It can also be set to Always or Never.

Save Project: This property determines if associated projects will be saved automatically before the reverse-engineering process occurs. If the property is set to the value Ask Me, NetBeans will prompt you prior to saving the projects during the reserve-engineering process. If you set the value to Always, the projects will be saved automatically.

The Round Trip Engineering node also has two child nodes that appear under it in the Advanced Options window:

Elements node: Click this node to set various preferences for determining which UML elements are transformed to Java code during the reverse-engineering process. Each element can have a value of Yes or No, which determines whether or not it is transformed.

Java node: Click this node to see the properties shown in Figure 8-5. These properties control Java-specific settings for UML models when they are reverse-engineered into Java code. Typically, I suggest leaving these properties set to the default values. However, the longer you work with the NetBeans UML module, the more comfortable you will become with it. You will have a better understanding of how to customize specific properties like those for Java round-trip engineering.

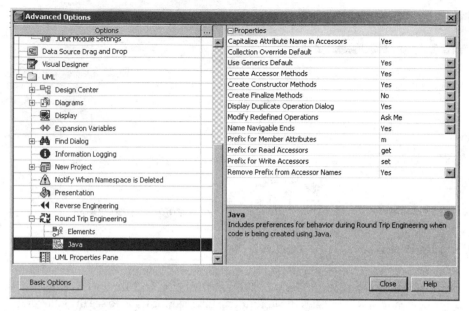

Figure 8-5. *Java properties for round-trip engineering in the Advanced Options window*

Navigating the UML Project Layout

The UML module provides content-specific options that appear in many of the standard NetBeans windows and menus. Before you create a UML project, you should become familiar with the associated windows and tools.

Palette Window

The NetBeans Palette window provides a panel of content-specific components that you can drag-and-drop into your project. When working with web application files, a specific set of HTML and JSP components is displayed in the Palette window. When working with visual web applications and JSF, another set of components appears. A separate set of components is available for UML projects. (Chapter 9 provides more information about working with the Palette window in general.)

UML projects can be composed of numerous types of diagrams. Each diagram has a specific set of UML components associated with it. If you create a use case diagram, select it in the Source Editor, and look at the Palette window, you will see components named Actor and Use Case. If you select a class diagram in the Source Editor, you will see a long list of class diagram components, as shown in Figure 8-6.

In the Palette window, component names like Class, Interface, Package, Enumeration, and Implementation should be familiar to Java programmers. However, you might not recognize names like Navigable Aggregation, Composition, and Association. Table 8-1 provides a brief description of some of the class diagram components.

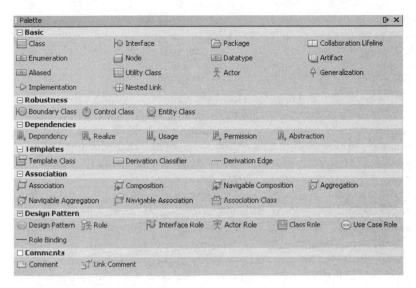

Figure 8-6. *The Palette window displaying class diagram components*

■Tip For more information about UML and its components, a good reference is *UML for Java Programmers* by Robert C. Martin (Prentice Hall, 2003).

Table 8-1. *Class Diagram Components*

Component	Description
Package	A group of Class elements
Interface	A type of class that contains only public operations
Class	An object that represents a Java class
Enumeration	A type of object for a list of named values
Implementation	A concrete implementation of an element
Generalization	A link between a class and a subclass
DataType	An object type that represents objects and primitive values
Actor	A person or role that represents a user in the system
Nested Link	A relationship between Class objects

UML Documentation Window

The UML Documentation window provides the ability to take notes on any UML element in a project. You can use this functionality to document the purpose of a diagram, explain a class, or explain the attributes and operations of an element.

The documentation you create for UML elements can be tied to the Javadoc for Java source code. If you reverse-engineer Java source code into a UML project, any Javadoc that exists will be visible in the UML Documentation window for each element. If you use a UML project to generate Java source code, any UML documentation you have will be inserted as Javadoc into the newly generated code.

If the Documentation window is not displayed in NetBeans, you can open it by selecting Window ➤ UML Modeling ➤ UML Documentation from the main menu. To document an element, select it in the Projects window or the Diagram Editor window. The UML Documentation window will display any existing documentation for the element. To add documentation, you can type directly in the UML Documentation window. It offers a basic WYSIWYG text editor, similar to popular word processing tools like Microsoft Word.

The toolbar along the top of the window provides some simple text-formatting capabilities. The icons allow you to create bold, underlined, and italicized text. You can also change the font type, align the text, and change the color. Place the mouse over each icon and view a tooltip that describes its function.

One of the features on the UML Documentation window that may not be obvious is the ability to edit the source code of the documentation that is displayed. For example, Figure 8-7 shows some HTML-based documentation that includes a table with several rows and columns. To see the source code for the content, open the NetBeans Properties window (select Window ➤ Properties or press Ctrl+Shift+7). In the Properties window, you will see a property named Documentation. To the right of the label is a brief line of text followed by an ellipsis button. Click that button to open a window displaying the source code for the content from the UML Documentation window, as shown in Figure 8-8. This window allows you to edit code and save it by clicking the OK button. This means you can copy and paste HTML code directly into this window.

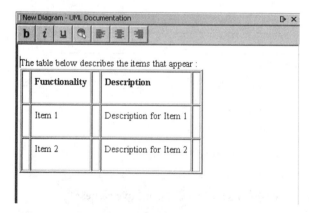

Figure 8-7. *The UML Documentation window*

You can also copy and paste the WYSIWYG content into the UML Documentation window. The content displayed in Figure 8-7 was copied from an HTML page displayed in a web browser and pasted into the UML Documentation window. However, I don't recommend this approach, because the HTML source code behind the scenes can often end up being quite messy.

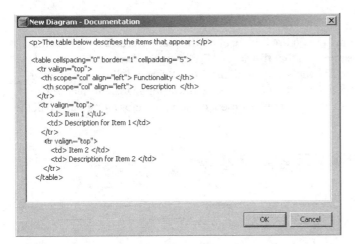

Figure 8-8. *Documentation source code for a UML element*

UML Properties Window

The UML Properties window is the regular NetBeans Properties window, but it displays UML-specific properties. As you select UML elements in the Projects window, Diagram Editor, or other locations throughout the NetBeans IDE, any existing properties are displayed in the Properties window.

You can edit the properties in a variety of ways. Some properties contain text values that you can click and edit; others are drop-down lists of values; and others have pop-up windows that allow you to edit them.

If the Properties window is not visible, you can open it by selecting Window ➤ Properties or pressing the shortcut Ctrl+Shift+7. As with any window in NetBeans, you can resize or move the Properties window to suit your own preferences.

UML Design Center Window

The UML Design Center window provides quick and convenient access to a catalog of professional design patterns. You can use this window to view and apply design patterns to your UML project. At the time of this writing, it includes patterns for EJB 1.1, EJB 2.0, and the traditional list of patterns from the Gang of Four.

Note The Gang of Four refers to Erich Gamma, Richard Helm, Ralph Johnson, and John Vlissides, who wrote *Design Patterns: Elements of Reusable Object-Oriented Software* (Addison-Wesley, 1995). The book is a difficult read even for experienced programmers, but it is one of the industry-leading books on the subject. For a phenomenal explanation of design patterns with examples in Java, I recommend *Head First Design Patterns* by Eric Freeman, Elisabeth Freeman, Kathy Sierra, and Bert Bates (O'Reilly, 2004).

Diagram Editor

The Diagram Editor window, shown in Figure 8-9, displays the elements and diagrams for a UML project. It appears in the same area that the Source Editor does when working with Java source code, but shows UML-specific tools and elements. The Diagram Editor is displayed when you double-click any diagram listed in the Projects window for a UML project. If you have more than one diagram open, the names will appear on separate tabs along the top of the Diagram Editor.

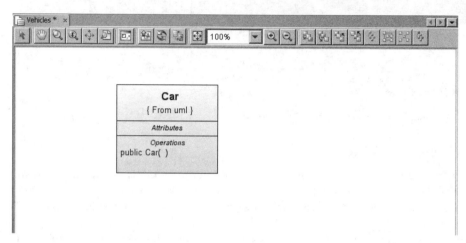

Figure 8-9. *The UML Diagram Editor*

The toolbar along the top of the Diagram Editor window offers a wide array of functionality, such as panning, zooming, arranging elements in the diagram, and exporting the diagram to an image. Table 8-2 lists the Diagram Editor toolbar icon functions.

Table 8-2. *UML Diagram Editor Toolbar Functions*

Icon	Function
	Select
	Pan
	Zoom with marquee
	Zoom interactively
	Navigate link

Table 8-2. *UML Diagram Editor Toolbar Functions*

Icon	Function
	Print preview the active diagram
	Overview window
	Export as image
	Diagram synchronization
	Relationship discovery
	Fit to window
	Zoom In
	Zoom out
	Move forward one position in the element ordering
	Move to front (to the very front of the ordering)
	Move backward one position in the element ordering
	Move to back (to the very back of the element ordering)
	Hierarchical layout
	Orthogonal layout
	Symmetric layout
	Incremental layout

Choosing a UML Project Type

NetBeans offers several different types of UML projects. The project types vary in how they are created and what you do with them, but overall, they are identical in that they are composed of elements and diagrams. Several different kinds of diagrams can be added to any project, regardless of type.

You can choose from three types of UML projects:

- Platform-Independent Model

- Java-Platform Model

- Reverse Engineer a Java Project

Note At the time of this writing, the UML module was classified as a beta release, so the project types are subject to change. Some of the UML documentation online discusses being able to import Rational Rose files, but that feature does not seem to be included with the current release. The only other third-party files you can import are Telelogic DOORS requirements files. You can do this in the UML Design Center, as discussed in the "Importing Requirements" section later in this chapter.

Creating a Platform-Independent Model Project

The Platform-Independent Model project provides the ability to work with UML diagrams in a non-Java environment. You cannot generate source code from any models with this type of project.

To create a Platform-Independent Model project, do the following:

1. Select File ➤ New Project from the main menu.

2. In the New Project wizard, select the UML category from the list on the left, select Platform-Independent Model from the list of projects on the right, and then click the Next button.

3. Fill in the Project Name and Project Location fields, and then click the Finish button.

4. The Create New Diagram window appears (unless you disabled it, as described earlier in this chapter), as shown in Figure 8-10. If you want to add a diagram to the newly created project, choose a diagram from the Diagram Type list. Then name the diagram using the Diagram Name field. Finally, select the namespace. Because you are creating a diagram at the same time as a new project, the only available namespace is the name of the project. When you are finished, click the Finish button to complete the process.

The UML project is created and listed in the Projects window. The UML project contains three child nodes named Model, Diagrams, and Imported Elements. If you created a diagram using the Create New Diagram wizard, it will be listed under the Diagrams node. The Model node contains the list of UML elements that currently exist in the project. The Imported Elements node will be empty by default, as you have not imported any elements into the new project.

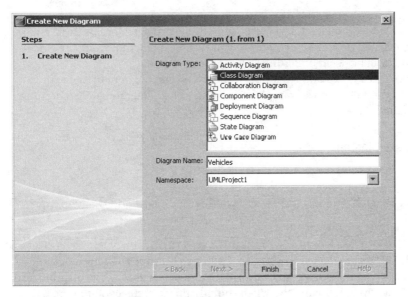

Figure 8-10. *Using the Create New Diagram wizard*

Creating a Java-Platform Model Project

The Java-Platform Model project provides the ability to work with UML diagrams in a Java environment. With this project type, your models can follow Java-based constraints and rules, such as inheritance, encapsulation, and so on. Your models can also be forward-engineered into Java source code.

Forward-engineering involves converting high-level abstractions of data or ideas into a concrete implementation in program source code. You can create a UML diagram of any number of objects that represent people, places, products, and so on. You can then define attributes and operations for these objects. The NetBeans UML module allows you to convert the models of the objects to Java classes, which, in turn, contain class members and methods.

To create a Java-Platform Model project, follow these steps:

1. Select File ➤ New Project from the main menu.

2. In the New Project wizard, select the UML category from the list on the left, select Java-Platform Model from the list of projects on the right, and then click the Next button.

3. Fill in the Project Name and Project Location fields, and then click the Finish button.

4. The Create New Diagram window appears (unless you disabled it, as described earlier in this chapter), as shown in Figure 8-10. If you want to add a diagram to the newly created project, choose a diagram from the Diagram Type list, name the diagram, and select the namespace (the name of the project). Click the Finish button to complete the process.

The UML project should be generated and listed in the Projects window. Similar to the Platform-Independent Model project, the Java-Platform Model project contains three child nodes: Model, Diagrams, and Imported Elements. If you created a diagram using the Create New Diagram wizard, it will be listed under the Diagrams node.

Once you have created a Java-Platform Model project, you can begin to model your software program. Let's go through a quick example of creating a class diagram and generating Java source code from the model.

Creating a Simple Class Diagram

To create a diagram that models Java classes, do the following:

1. Right-click the Diagrams node in the Project window and select Add Diagram from the context menu.

2. In the Create New Diagram wizard (see Figure 8-10), select a diagram type, enter a diagram name, and choose a namespace. Then click the Finish button. The new diagram is created and listed under the Diagrams node in the Projects window. The diagram also opens in the Diagram Editor window, which should appear in the center of the IDE.

3. Initially, the diagram displays a white background with no content, since you have not added any elements to it. To add elements to the new diagram, you use the UML Palette window. Open the Palette window by selecting Window ➤ Palette or using the shortcut Ctrl+Shift+8.

4. Locate the Class component in the Basic section in the Palette window. This component represents a Java class. Click the Class component and click anywhere inside the diagram in the Diagram Editor. The new Class object should be created.

5. Activate the diagram select functionality by clicking the Select icon in the Diagram Editor toolbar (see Table 8-2). This deactivates the Class component in the Palette window, so that additional mouse clicks in the diagram do not result in a new Class object being created.

6. Once the Class object had been added to the diagram, you can proceed to modify its properties. Double-click the Unnamed text in the object. The text should become highlighted and editable. Type a name for the class, such as Employee.

7. To add an attribute, right-click inside the Attributes section of the Class object and select Insert Attribute. You can also use the shortcut Alt+Shift+A.

8. A new line appears in the Attributes section: private int Unnamed. The Unnamed variable is highlighted, which allows you to type over it and change it. Enter a name, such as name, and then click outside the Class object so it loses focus in the diagram.

9. To add a new operation to the Class object, right-click inside the Operations section of the Class object and select Insert Operation. You can also use the shortcut Alt+Shift+O.

10. The initial text appears: public void Unnamed(). Again, type over Unnamed to give your method a name, such as getName.

You have now modeled a class, added an attribute, and added a single operation. Your class diagram should look like Figure 8-11. You can now save it, print it, export it to a JPEG file, or convert it into Java source code. Working with class diagrams will be discussed in more detail in the "Creating Class Diagrams" section later in this chapter. For now, let's generate some Java code from this diagram.

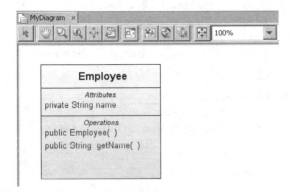

Figure 8-11. *The Employee Class element added to the class diagram*

Generating Java Code from UML

The ability to generate Java source code from UML models is part of software documentation and creation. You can model an entire application consisting of hundreds of Class objects without having to write any code. Once you are confident you have correctly modeled the program, you can generate the code. This saves you time and improves the accuracy of matching your models to your code.

In the NetBeans UML module, you can generate Java source code for any Java-Platform Model project, for a package of model elements, or for a single Class element in a diagram. Generating code is remarkably simple.

To generate Java source code for an entire Java-Platform Model project, follow these steps:

1. Right-click the UML project name in the Projects window and select Generate Code. The Generate Code dialog box will appear, as shown in Figure 8-12.

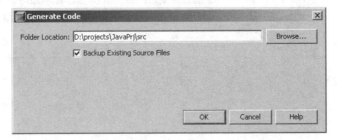

Figure 8-12. *The Generate Code window for a UML project*

2. In the Generate Code dialog box, enter a folder location. This folder will be where the newly created (or updated) Java source will be placed. If you have previously created a Java Application Library project to use for the Java source, you should navigate to the src directory in that project. If you configured your UML elements with package names, the correct package hierarchy will be created (or preserved if it already exists).

3. In the Generate Code dialog box, the Backup Existing Source Files check box is selected by default. Leave it checked to ensure that any existing Java source code that might be modified is saved in a backup file prior to being overwritten by anything created during the UML-to-Java forward-engineering process. For example, if a file were named MyFile.java, it would be saved as a backup named MyFile.java1.

4. Click the OK button to generate the source code.

If the NetBeans Output window is open, you should see the following lines of debugging text displayed as the Java source code is generated:

```
Begin processing Generate Code: 1 item

Code Generation selected options:
Source Folder Location D:\projects\JavaPrj\src

Processing element 1 of 1: Class Employee


==================================
Task Successful (total time: 3 seconds)
```

The Java source code that was generated should be viewable in the Java project. If you open the source code that matches the UML class object that you modeled, you will see the attribute and operation you created. The access-level and return types may not be correct. In the "Creating Class Diagrams" section later in the chapter, you will learn how to fully configure a UML Class object prior to generating code for it.

Caution If you plan to forward-engineer your model into a project that is configured with JDK 1.4, 1.3, or older, be careful about your use of generics or other Java constructs. When the NetBeans UML module generates the Java code, it creates exactly what the model says to create. If generics or some other unsupported language features are generated into a Java project, your code will not compile.

Reverse-Engineering a Java Project

The project type Reverse Engineer a Java Project is almost identical to the project type Java-Platform Model. The main difference is how it is created. A Java Application project with one or more Java source files is reverse-engineered into a set of UML models.

This type of project is useful for generating UML class diagrams for an existing base of Java code. More often than not, programmers are assigned to an existing project that does not have complete documentation or diagrams. They can use the NetBeans UML module to generate a set of UML models from the Java code.

The process of reverse-engineering begins with a Java Application project. Review the Java code in Listing 8-1, which describes the Vehicle abstract class. It contains four abstract methods that can be implemented by subclasses. Listing 8-2 describes the Truck class, and Listing 8-3 shows the Bus class. These two classes extend the Vehicle abstract class and implement its methods.

Listing 8-1. *The Vehicle Abstract Class*

```
public abstract class Vehicle {
    public abstract void start();
    public abstract void stop();
    public abstract void slowDown();
    public abstract void speedUp();
}
```

Listing 8-2. *The Truck Implementation Class*

```
public class Truck extends Vehicle{

    public void start() {
        System.out.println("Truck.start()");
    }

    public void stop() {
        System.out.println("Truck.stop()");
    }

    public void slowDown() {
        System.out.println("Truck.slowDown()");
    }

    public void speedUp() {
        System.out.println("Truck.speedUp()");
    }
}
```

Listing 8-3. *The Bus Implementation Class*

```java
public class Bus extends Vehicle {

    public void start() {
        System.out.println("Bus.start()");
    }

    public void stop() {
        System.out.println("Bus.stop()");
    }

    public void slowDown() {
        System.out.println("Bus.slowDown()");
    }

    public void speedUp() {
        System.out.println("Bus.speedUp()");
    }
}
```

If you needed to quickly understand these classes and their relationships, you could open and examine all three source code files. But a quicker way is to use NetBeans to reverse-engineer them into a UML diagram.

To reverse-engineer the code, right-click the name of the Java project in the Projects window. Select Reverse Engineer from the context menu, and the Reverse Engineer window will appear, as shown in Figure 8-13.

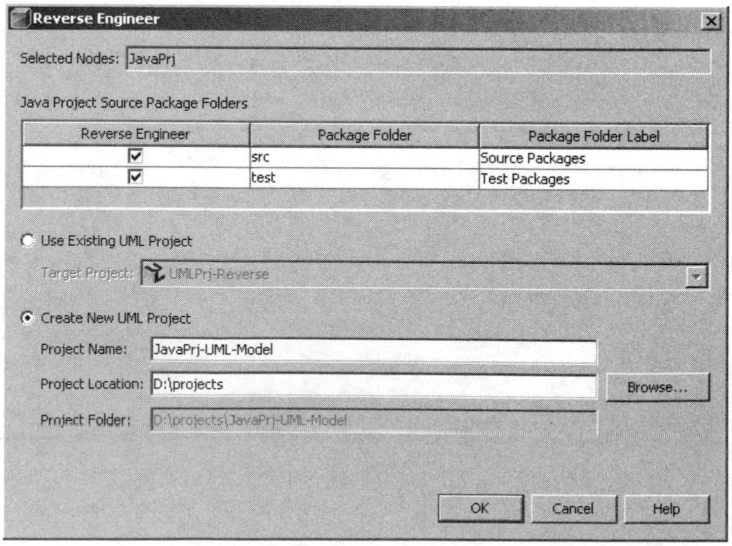

Figure 8-13. *The Reverse Engineer window*

The Selected Nodes field at the top of the window displays the name of the Java project that you are about to reverse-engineer. Below the project name is a grid of source and test packages from the Java project that will be reverse-engineered. The check boxes in the Reverse Engineer column are selected by default. If you unselect a check box, any code appearing under that node will not be reverse-engineered.

The bottom half of the Reverse Engineer window contains the choices for determining which UML project will contain the generated models:

Use Existing UML Project: If you select this option, the Target Project drop-down list becomes active. Recently opened UML projects or UML projects that are located in the same directory are *not* displayed in this list. It contains the name of any UML project that is currently open in the Projects window in NetBeans.

Create New UML Project: If you select this option, the Project Name and Project Location fields become active. You must enter a project name for the new UML project and select a root project location.

After you click the OK button in the Reverse Engineer window, the reverse-engineering process takes place. NetBeans will log various lines of text to the Output window, as follows:

```
Begin processing Reverse Engineering
Parsing 3 elements
Analyzing attributes & operations for 3 symbols
Resolving 2 attribute types
Integrating 3 elements
Building the query cache.
=================================
Task Successful (total time: 3 seconds)
```

The resultant output describes the operations that took place: three Java source code files were used to generate three model elements. If you expand the node for the UML project in the Projects window, you can view the generated model elements under the UML project's Model node.

To complete the process, you need to create a new class diagram and add the model elements to it. To add the class diagram, right-click the Diagrams node in the UML project and select Add Diagram. In the Create New Diagram wizard (see Figure 8-10), select Class Diagram as the diagram type, name the diagram, select the namespace, and click the Finish button. The new diagram will be added under the Diagrams node and open in the Diagram Editor.

Once the diagram is open, you can add the model elements to it. Locate the Vehicle, Bus, and Truck model elements under the Models node in the Projects window. Drag-and-drop each element onto the diagram. The associated object should appear, as shown in Figure 8-14. Once you have added the three elements, you can save the diagram.

In general, creating UML projects, models, and diagrams is quite an easy process. NetBeans provides a lot of convenient functionality and makes it available with only a few mouse clicks. Now that you have seen the basics of each type of UML project, we will further explore how to work with models and diagrams.

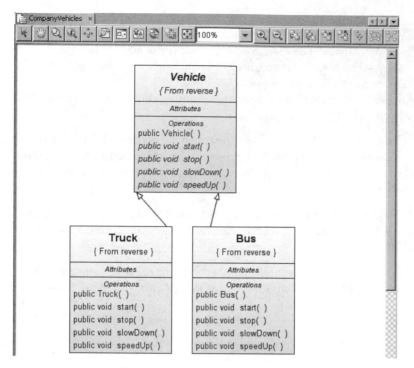

Figure 8-14. *The CompanyVehicle diagram with classes*

Working with Model Elements

The Model node beneath a UML project lists all the elements that exist in the UML project that can be added to a diagram. Model elements can be directly listed under this node or appear categorized under a Package element (similar to how Java source code is organized into Java packages). The list of child nodes under the Model node is initially empty, unless you reverse-engineered a Java project.

Note   Technically, all the diagrams in the UML project are also listed under the Model node, but you obviously cannot add them to diagrams.

Adding Model Elements

As you work with each of the diagram types, you can add model elements by dragging-and-dropping them from the Palette window into the diagram displayed in the Diagram Editor.

You can use also a wizard to add model elements to a UML project. Right-click the Model node for a UML project and select Add ➤ Element. The New Element wizard will appear, as shown in Figure 8-15.

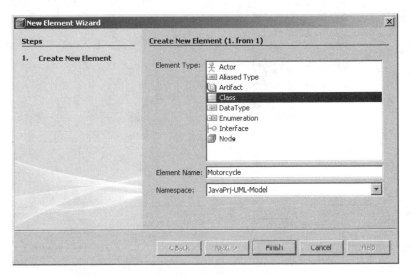

Figure 8-15. *The New Element wizard for a UML project*

The wizard prompts you to select the type of element you want to add to the project. The list contains only a small selection of elements, but they are typically the most commonly used elements. (If you need to add an element to the project that is not displayed, you can always use the Palette window to drag-and-drop the element into the diagram instead of using this wizard.) Next, name the element and select a namespace. After you click the Finish button, the new element will be added to the list of elements displayed under the Model node in the UML project.

Filtering Model Elements

NetBeans provides the ability to filter the display of different types of elements. For new UML projects, this isn't very useful. However, if you reverse-engineered a large Java project, dozens or hundreds of elements may be displayed under the Model node. For example, when a Java project is reverse-engineered, some of the elements added to the Model node are UML DataType elements. Any primitive variable or object that is a Java class member variable, passed in to a method, or returned from a method is considered a valid DataType element. Having the ability to temporarily hide the DataType elements can help save visual real estate in the Projects window when navigating the list of elements and make it easier to find other elements.

To filter the list of elements, right-click the Model node and select Filter. The Filter dialog box appears, as shown in Figure 8-16. The Filter dialog box contains two nodes: Model Elements and Diagrams. You can expand the nodes to locate the element or diagram type that you wish to hide. Uncheck the box next to an element to remove it from the display, and then click the OK button. The element will no longer be listed under the Model node in the Projects window. To redisplay the element or diagram type, open the Filter dialog box and check the item.

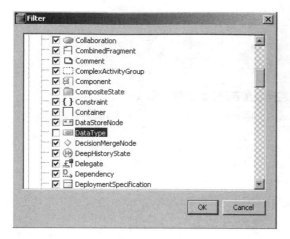

Figure 8-16. *Filtering out the DataType element*

Working with UML Diagrams

A UML diagram is essentially a pictorial drawing of a concept represented by structures or objects. The objects can have numerous shapes; contain internal metadata like attributes, properties, and operations; and possess relationships to other objects. In NetBeans, diagrams act as a canvas onto which you can draw model elements.

You can create a new diagram in several ways:

- After you initially create a new UML project, create a new diagram using the wizard that starts automatically.

- Right-click the Diagrams node in a UML project and select Add Diagram from the context menu.

- Select one or more model elements, right-click them, and select Create Diagram from Selected Elements from the context menu.

The NetBeans UML module offers eight different types of diagrams. Here, we'll focus on the class diagram, because it directly pertains to the subject of Java and UML. We'll also take a brief look at the activity diagram, to give you an idea of how to work with other types of diagrams.

Note The UML standard from OMG defines 13 types of diagrams. See `http://www.omg.org/gettingstarted/what_is_uml.htm#12DiagramTypes` for more information.

Creating Class Diagrams

The UML class diagram allows you to model the relationships and internal contents of Java classes. Using a class diagram, you can represent the Java concepts of abstract classes, interfaces, inheritance, class member variables, and methods.

The example in this section uses the classes presented in the "Reverse-Engineering a Java Project" section earlier in this chapter (in Listings 8-1, 8-2, and 8-3): an abstract class Vehicle, which has two concrete implementation classes named Bus and Truck. Each Java class that was reverse-engineered is logically represented by a Class element and is visually represented by a rectangle, as shown earlier in Figure 8-14. The Class element is divided into three basic sections:

- The top section of the Class element lists its name. If you double-click the name, it will become highlighted and editable. To change the name, simply type the new one and press the Enter key. If you decide to not change the name, press the Escape key, and any changes to the name will be undone.

- The middle section of the Class element lists its attributes. The attributes correspond to the class member variables in Java.

- The bottom section of the Class element lists its operations. The operations correspond to the class methods in Java.

Adding Attributes

The Vehicle, Truck, and Bus classes do not contain any class member variables, so the Class elements in the diagram in Figure 8-14 do not contain any attributes. However, let's say the requirements you used to originally write the code have changed. You now need to add an attribute that indicates whether a vehicle has completely stopped or if it's moving.

In Java, you might add a class member variable private boolean isMoving and provide a matching getter and setter. To add this specific attribute to the Vehicle class in the class diagram, perform the following steps:

1. In the Vehicle element in the diagram, right-click within the Attributes section and select Insert Attribute.

2. A line of text appears. Type the name of the new attribute, isMoving, and then press the Enter key.

3. Click the new attribute in the Class object and open the NetBeans Properties window.

4. Highlight the value next to the Type attribute displayed in the Properties window. Type **Boolean**, and then press the Enter key.

The Vehicle element in the diagram now contains the proper attribute. Notice that when you added the new attribute, it also generated two methods. The UML module created the matching getter getIsMoving and setter setIsMoving.

If you need to make modifications to the metadata for the attribute, click it in the diagram and open the Properties window. The Properties window displays the UML-specific attributes for each type of object that is currently selected, whether it is a UML project, a diagram, a model element, an element attribute, or an element operation.

Some of the most common attributes to change for a Class element include the name, type, visibility, documentation, and whether it is final or static. The Properties window provides a very convenient method for editing these types of attributes for elements. I highly recommend leaving the window displayed during all your UML-related work.

Adding Operations

In the previous section, you added a single attribute to the Vehicle element. NetBeans automatically created the matching getter and setter methods. If you need to create additional operations, you can do so in a manner similar to adding attributes.

To add a new operation to a Class element, follow these steps:

1. Right-click inside the Operations section of the element and select Insert Operation. You can also use the keyboard shortcut Alt+Shift+O.

2. A new line of text appears in the Operations section, defining the default operation `public void Unnamed()`. The operation name will initially be highlighted, allowing you to immediately type over and change it.

3. With the operation selected in the diagram, open the Properties window. It will display a list of properties for the operation. You can then edit these properties to modify the semantic representation of the operation. Change the Name property to `turn`. Then press the Enter key or click outside the property, and the operation changes in the diagram. You can also change the operation's return type by editing the Return Type property in the Properties window.

Adding Parameters to Operation

Now suppose that the `turn` operation needs an input value that tells the `Vehicle` class how many degrees it should turn. You need to modify the `turn` operation so it contains a parameter. To add this parameter to the operation, follow these steps:

1. Select the `turn` operation in the Vehicle element in your diagram.

2. In the Properties window, locate the Parameters property and click the ellipsis button next to the value `public int turn()`.

3. The Parameters window will appear. Here, you can add, edit, delete, and order the parameters for an operation. Click the Add Parameter button.

4. In the dialog box that appears, enter the name (`degrees` in this example) and type (`int` in this example) of the parameter. Click the OK button.

5. The parameter will appear in the Parameters list on the left side of the window, as shown in Figure 8-17. Once you have tweaked the parameter values to your liking, click the OK button. The new operation `public int turn(int degrees)` will be displayed in the Vehicle element in the diagram.

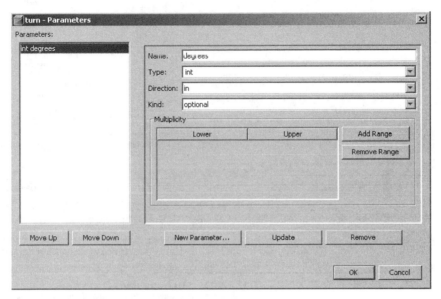

Figure 8-17. *The operation Parameters window*

Regenerating the Source Code

Now that you have made some modifications to your UML diagram, you can regenerate the matching Java source code. This helps keep your model in sync with your software application. It also helps programmers that are relatively new to UML to understand how various UML properties affect Java code.

To generate the Java source code for the Vehicle abstract class, right-click the Class element and select Generate Code. In the Generate Code dialog box, select the source folder location for the code that will be generated and click the OK button.

Once the code has been generated, you can right-click the Class element in the diagram and select Navigate to Source from the context menu. The matching Java source code will then open in a Source Editor window. The updated Vehicle class should look like Listing 8-4.

Listing 8-4. *The Modified Vehicle Abstract Class*

```java
public abstract class Vehicle {
    private boolean isMoving;

    public boolean getIsMoving() {
        return isMoving;
    }
}
```

```java
    public void setIsMoving(boolean val) {
        this.isMoving = val;
    }

    public int turn(int degrees) {
        return 0;
    }

    public abstract void start();
    public abstract void stop();
    public abstract void slowDown();
    public abstract void speedUp();
}
```

Creating Activity Diagrams

A UML activity diagram is primarily used to model a business process. This is the diagram type
you should use if you are trying to capture the business logic of a single use case or transaction.
The NetBeans UML module provides the typical UML elements for working with this type of
diagram.

As an example, let's create a diagram for an activity that you may find familiar. Occasionally,
a customer will experience an issue with a particular piece of software. If you're the software
developer who supports that software, chances are you will somehow get notified. The customer
might decide to send you an email about the problem, particularly if it is an unimportant
problem with a short description. He also might choose to call you on the phone if the problem
is more difficult to describe. If you're truly unlucky, he might walk into your office unannounced to
discuss the issue in person. This is not a serious example of a UML activity diagram, but it serves
to demonstrate how to construct one.

Follow these steps to create a new activity diagram:

1. In the Create New Diagram wizard, select the Activity Diagram type, name the diagram
   `MyActDiagram`, select a namespace, and click the Finish button. The blank canvas of the
   diagram appears in the Diagram Editor.

2. Locate the Partition element in the Palette window and add one to the diagram. Initially, it
   looks like a rectangle with two text headings. The Partition element can be subdivided
   into multiple rows or columns, so you can segment various activities performed by different people.

3. You'll have two areas for various activities: one for the customer and one for the programmer. Divide the Partition element by right-clicking it in the diagram and selecting
   Partitions ➤ Add Partition Column to the Right.

4. The Partition element will change into a two-column table with header text across the top and header text for each column. Double-click the text of each header and type in a new name for each. Name the overall Partition element **Customer Issue Reporting**. Name the column on the left **Customer** and the column on the right **Programmer**.

5. Locate the Invocation element in the Palette window and add five of them to the diagram. An Invocation element is a basic activity that is performed during the process. It can represent a digital or physical activity and be connected to other activities.

6. To add text to an Invocation element, double-click it and type the desired text. For this example, the Customer column of the Partition element has four Invocation elements, with the text **Determines an issue needs to be reported**, **Sends email**, **Calls on phone**, and **Walks on down**. The Programmer column contains one Invocation element, with the text **Goes out to lunch**. The resulting diagram should look similar to Figure 8-18.

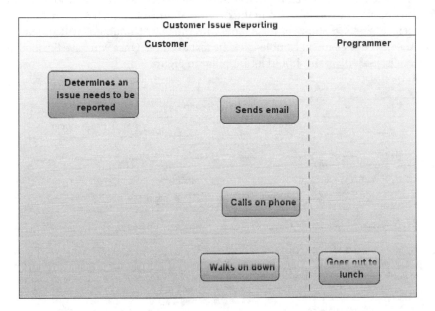

Figure 8-18. *The activity diagram with two partition columns and five invocations*

7. To define the beginning of the activity process flow, in the Palette window, click the Initial Node element. Then click in the diagram to the left of the first Customer Invocation element to place the Initial Node element there. Right-click to deselect the Add Element tool.

8. To define the end of the activity process flow, in the Palette window, click the Activity Final Node element and add it to the diagram above the Programmer Invocation element. The element is represented by a large red circle and indicates this is the proverbial end of the line for this set of activities.

9. Before the customer can report the issue, he needs to decide how he will report it. Locate the Decision element in the Control section of the Palette window and add it to the diagram between the four Customer Invocation elements.

10. Now you need to connect all the elements (basically playing a game of connect-the-dots). Click the Activity Edge element in the Palette window. Connect the Initial Node element to the first Invocation element in the Customer column. Then connect the first Invocation element with the Decision element. In turn, connect the Decision element to the remaining three Invocation elements in the Customer column.

11. Use an Activity Edge element to connect the customer "Walks on down" Invocation element to the programmer "Goes out to lunch" Invocation element. Then connect the "Goes out to lunch" Invocation element with the Activity Final Node element.

12. Label the Activity Edge elements that come out of the Decision element so that the criteria for the decision are understood in the diagram. Right-click each Activity Edge element and select Labels ➤ Show Name. A label with the text "Unnamed" will appear next to the Activity Edge element. Double-click the text to edit it. Once you have finished adding the labels, your diagram should look similar to Figure 8-19.

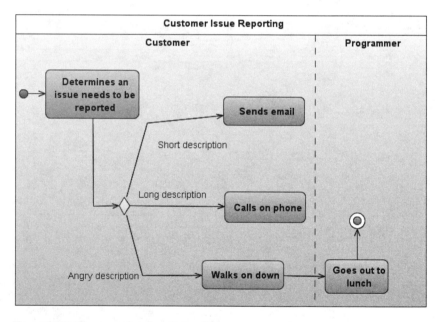

Figure 8-19. *The completed activity diagram*

Exporting Diagrams

One of the key tenets of software programming is writing good documentation. Part of that process involves capturing the models and diagrams of your software in your organization's standards documents. This is obviously quite difficult to do if you have no means of importing your design diagrams into your documentation.

Like many popular UML tools, the NetBeans UML module allows you to export a diagram in a variety of image formats, such as JPEG, SVG, and PNG. You can access this functionality by clicking the Export As Image icon in the Diagram Editor toolbar (see Table 8-2) or by using the keyboard shortcut Ctrl+Shift+X. This brings up the Export As Image dialog box, as shown in Figure 8-20.

In the dialog box, select the type of image you want to export as well as the filename. Depending on your type selection, additional fields will become active. In the Image Characteristics section, you can set the image quality using the slider. The Size section includes options for setting the size of the image. Once you have set the fields, click the OK button. The diagram will be exported to the specified location and filename.

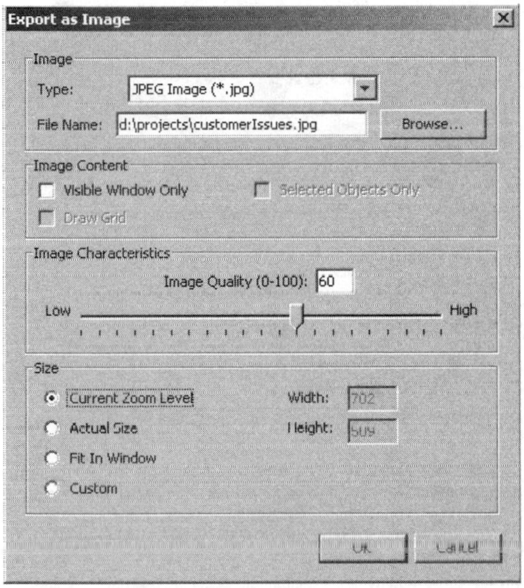

Figure 8-20. *The Export As Image dialog box*

Working with Diagram Layouts

The UML module offers various layout options for your UML diagrams. As you add model elements and notations to a diagram, you need to be able to easily position them on the screen and navigate them.

As you add elements to a diagram, you can click, hold, and drag them in any direction. If you drag an element off the edge of the screen, scrollbars appear and the window expands and moves in the same direction. As your UML diagram expands to larger than a single window, you can use the various NetBeans UML tools to help navigate.

Using Automatic Layouts

The UML module allows you to apply a predefined layout to your diagrams to arrange them automatically. These predefined layouts reorder the elements based on specific rules and logic. The four layout icons on the Diagram Editor toolbar provide quick access to this feature. You can also use keyboard shortcuts to access the layouts, as shown in Table 8-3.

Table 8-3. *UML Layout Shortcuts*

Layout	Shortcut	Description
Hierarchical	Ctrl+Shift+H	A configurable hierarchy pattern
Orthogonal	Ctrl+Shift+B	A configurable rectangular pattern
Symmetric	Ctrl+Shift+Y	A symmetric pattern centered on a single element
Incremental	Ctrl+Shift+I	A pattern that uses the existing layout and reorders the elements to be closer together

Suppose you start with the layout shown in Figure 8-21. If you apply the Symmetric layout to the class diagram, the diagram will be rearranged as shown in Figure 8-22. Notice how the elements are now arranged around the package element in the center.

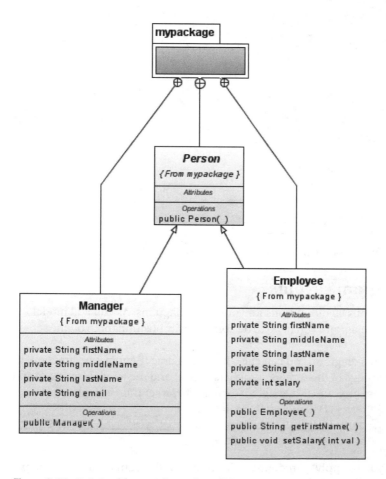

Figure 8-21. *Original layout for a class diagram*

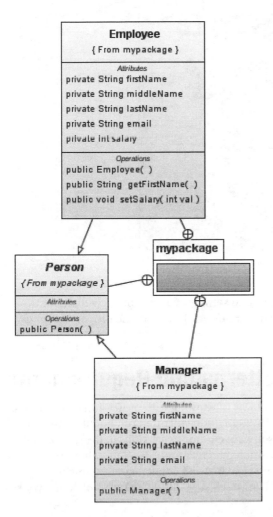

Figure 8-22. *The Symmetric layout applied to the class diagram*

Setting Layout Properties

The different layouts have sets of properties that you can configure. You can modify various layout properties, apply them to the current layout, or apply a new layout using the modified properties.

To access the layout properties, right-click the diagram canvas and select Layout ➤ Properties. The Layout Properties window will appear, as shown in Figure 8-23. The Layout Properties window allows you to set properties for the different layout types as well as specify several general UML layout options. You can specify whether constant or proportional margin spacing is used, whether components and disconnected nodes are detected, and the overall spacing between nodes and edges.

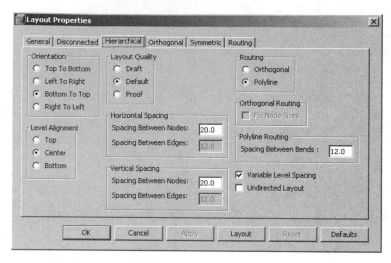

Figure 8-23. *The Layout Properties window*

Once you have set the properties to the desired settings, you can preview them for the currently displayed diagram by clicking the Layout button. To accept the property settings, click the OK button.

Working with Design Patterns and Requirements

The NetBeans UML module provides the capability of working with professional Java design patterns. When working with object-oriented systems, you will often run into the same or similar design over and over. Every piece of software contains variations in the design, but many programs are written to solve the same problems. Over time, developers have recognized these patterns, modeled them, and made them available as a catalog for everyone to reuse.

The NetBeans UML module allows you to apply existing design patterns or create your own patterns.

Viewing Design Patterns

To view the catalog of design patterns available in the NetBeans UML module, select Window ➤ UML Modeling ➤ Design Center. You can also use the keyboard shortcut Ctrl+Shift+C. The UML Design Center window will open and can be docked almost anywhere inside the IDE.

You can explore the various design patterns in the UML Design Center by expanding the nodes. The first set of patterns is the EJB 1.1 patterns. This set includes BeanManaged, ContainerManaged, StatefulSession, and StatelessSession from the EJB 1.1 Specification. The second set, EJB 2.0 is essentially the same as the EJB 1.1 pattern set, except for the addition of the MessageDriven pattern. The last set is named the GoF Design Patterns. This node contains several top-level categories of patterns. If you expand the node for each category, you will see numerous pattern names.

You can view the elements under each pattern and open the pattern's diagram in the Diagram Editor. As you select a pattern, it displays some documentation in the UML Documentation window. In Figure 8-24, I have repositioned the UML Design Center and UML Documentation windows to be side by side. The Factory Method pattern is selected in the UML Design Center window, and a description of the pattern is displayed in the UML Documentation window. This is convenient way to quickly read about the purpose of each pattern. You can then expand the pattern node and view the model for the pattern.

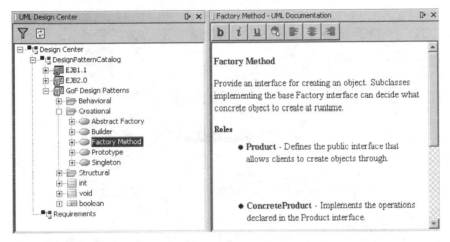

Figure 8-24. *The UML Design Center window and the UML Documentation window*

Applying a Pattern

If you decide you would like to apply one of the design patterns to your UML project model, you can do so directly from the UML Design Center. Follow these steps:

1. Open the Design Center window by selecting Window ➤ UML Modeling ➤ Design Center.

2. Right-click the name of the pattern you want to apply and select Apply Design Pattern from the context menu.

3. The Apply Design Pattern wizard will open with an introductory message displayed. Click the Next button to continue.

4. In the Pattern Selection step of the wizard, the Project and Design Pattern fields are disabled because you have already chosen the type of design pattern to apply. Click the Next button to continue.

5. In the Target Scope step, you can enter a namespace that will apply to the design pattern or leave the field blank. Once you have made your selection, click the Next button to continue.

6. The Choosing Participant step appears, as shown in Figure 8-25. The left column contains the roles in the design pattern. These are the placeholder objects that make up the actual design. The right column contains the suggested names of the participants. For each item in the Participants column, you can click the suggested name and type in a new one. You can also view a drop-down list of possible values. This list of values contains the various model elements that exist in the UML project currently open in NetBeans. If you choose these elements as participants, they will be overwritten. After you have selected the correct participant for each role, click the Next button to continue.

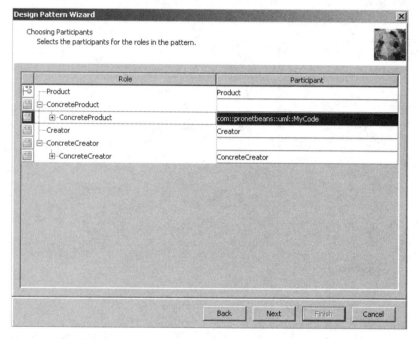

Figure 8-25. *The Choosing Participants step in the Apply Design Pattern wizard*

7. The Options step contains a single check box and text field. If you check the box, it directs the wizard to create a new class diagram and prompts you for a diagram name. After you have entered the name of the class diagram, click the Next button to proceed.

8. The final window contains a short summary of your selections. To complete the wizard, click the Finish button.

9. NetBeans will process for a moment and display the Select Methods to Redefine window if you chose existing elements as participants, as shown in Figure 8-26. You can review each class and method and select whether it will be redefined. After clicking the OK button, the process of applying the design pattern will be complete. If you chose to generate a diagram, it will open in the Diagram Editor for your review.

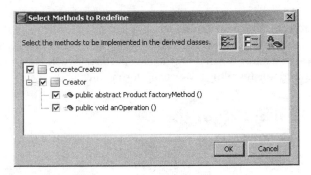

Figure 8-26. *Redefining operations*

Creating Design Patterns

The UML Design Center allows you to create design patterns from scratch or from an existing UML project. This means that you can create your own software design patterns and catalog them for future use.

Adding a UML Project As a Pattern

To add an existing UML project as a design pattern, follow these steps:

1. Open the Design Center window by selecting Window ➤ UML Modeling ➤ Design Center.

2. Right-click the top level Design Center node and select Insert ➤ Insert Project into Workspace.

3. A file system browser window appears, prompting you to locate and select a modeling project file (.etd). Look in the directory for the UML project you wish to add and locate the modeling project file. Select the file and click the Open button. The project will be added under the Design Center node.

After you've added the pattern, you can treat it like a regular design pattern and apply it to another UML project if you wish.

Generating a New Pattern

You can also generate a new UML design pattern without having an existing UML project, as follows:

1. Open the Design Center window by selecting Window ➤ UML Modeling ➤ Design Center.

2. Right-click the DesignPatternCatalog node and select New ➤ Project.

3. The Create Design Center Project dialog box will appear, as shown in Figure 8-27. Specify a value for the Project Name field and select a Project Location. This type of project is different from regular NetBeans projects because it belongs in the design catalog. NetBeans suggests a default location for the new pattern, which I recommend using. Click the OK button to finish adding the new pattern project.

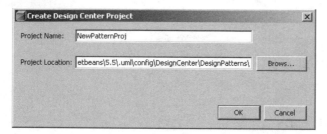

Figure 8-27. *The Create Design Center Project dialog box*

The new pattern will be added under the Design Center node. You can now right-click the pattern name and use the Add submenu to create new packages and diagrams. Once you have added a diagram, you can right-click the diagram name under the pattern node and use the Add submenu to create elements, attributes, and operations.

Importing Requirements

The UML Design Center window contains one node other than the Design Pattern node. The Requirements node allows you to import different types of requirements files via XML files or Telelogic DOORS files. This is beneficial since you can import requirements from a third-party tool into NetBeans, which, in turn, allows you to generate a UML module and Java code.

To import a requirements file into the Design Center, follow these steps:

1. Open the Design Center window by selecting Window ➤ UML Modeling ➤ Design Center.

2. Right-click the Requirements node and select Add Requirements Source.

3. The Requirements Provider dialog box will open. Use the Providers drop-down list to select either XML Requirements Source or DOORS Requirements Provider. Then click the OK button.

4. You will be prompted to locate, select, and open the corresponding requirements file.

The imported content will be listed under the Requirements node, allowing you to drag-and-drop the items onto model elements as needed.

Generating Model Reports

The NetBeans UML module provides the ability to generate model reports. These are HTML-based reports that are very similar to Javadoc documentation. They provide an insightful and convenient look into a UML project, especially if the project contains several diagrams.

To generate a report, right-click the UML project name in the Projects window and select Generate Model Report. The Output window will open and display the UML Report Log. A report directory is added to the project root (visible in the Files window for the UML project). Additionally, a web browser will open with the default report file index.html displayed.

The UML Report Log displays output text like the following during the generation of the report.

```
generating report for UMLPrj to D:\projects\ch\UMLPrj\report
generating summary files
processed 60 elements 1 diagrams
Report Successful (total time: 1 seconds)
```

The model report displays in the All Elements view by default, as shown in Figure 8-28. The upper-left section contains the package names and the link to switch between the All Elements view and the All Diagrams view. If you click one of the hyperlinked package names, it will change the content in the lower-left section of the report. The lower-left section displays the list of elements filtered by what you select in the upper-left section.

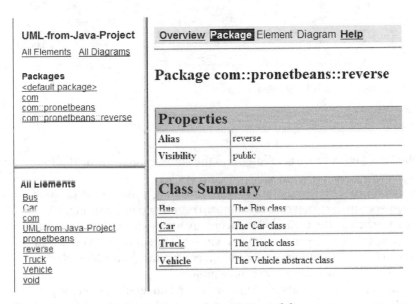

Figure 8-28. *The All Elements view of the UML model report*

Once you know which element to want to view, you can click the hyperlinked name in the lower-left section of the report. This will display the Element view that lists the element name, package, known associations, and enclosing diagrams. Similar to Javadoc for a class, the Element page view contains sections for the Properties, Attributes, Constructors, and Operations.

You can switch the model report to the All Diagrams view. In the upper-left corner of the report window, click the All Diagrams hyperlink. The lower-left section will refresh and display the list of diagrams in the project. If you click the name of a diagram, it will refresh the right pane of the report and display the diagram you selected, as shown in Figure 8-29.

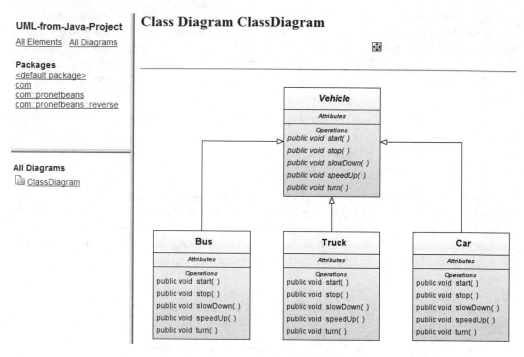

UML-from-Java-Project

All Elements   All Diagrams

Packages
<default package>
com
com::pronetbeans
com::pronetbeans::reverse

All Diagrams
ClassDiagram

Class Diagram ClassDiagram

Figure 8-29. *The All Diagrams view of a UML model report*

Summary

This chapter described the NetBeans UML module and the various tools it provides for programmers and designers.

You learned about the various configuration options for setting presentation properties, specifying Java code generation parameters, and setting up round-trip engineering.

Next, you read an overview of the UML project layout, including the various tools and windows. Then you learned how to create the different kinds of UML projects. You saw that you are able to work with UML in a platform-independent environment, in a Java-platform environment, and by reverse-engineering a Java source project.

We then talked about the numerous ways you can represent actions and structures in pictorial diagrams. We explored how you can use object representations, add attributes and operations, and document what is created. You also learned how to apply various layout styles to diagrams.

The UML module provides a UML Design Center, and you saw how to work with professional design patterns and create your own. Finally, you learned how to generate reports on elements and diagrams.

PART 2

The NetBeans Coding Experience

CHAPTER 9

The Source Editor

The Source Editor is arguably one of the most important areas of NetBeans. It is where developers write new code, rework existing code, refine their documentation, and perform many other tasks.

The NetBeans Source Editor is not only a mechanism for writing text, but also a full-featured environment designed to assist you. It aims to provide every possible convenience, including abbreviations for faster coding, automatic code completion, navigation and documentation aids, and more.

This chapter provides an overview of the core features of the Source Editor. Some of the features, such as code completion, are explained in more detail in upcoming chapters. This chapter is intended to serve as a quick introduction.

Arranging and Navigating Files

When you open a source code file, it appears in the Source Editor. Even though one file is displayed at a time by default, you can view files in alternate ways.

Having two different files displayed at the same time can be convenient if you are writing code in one file that is based on another file or uses a similar algorithm. You can place files side by side so that they are displayed on the left and right or the top and bottom.

You can also view the same file in multiple windows at the same time. To do so, you need to clone the document window by right-clicking the tab of the document and selecting Clone Document from the context menu. A new tab will appear along the top of the window displaying the original file you cloned.

To arrange the files, click and drag around the tab of one file within the Source Editor window. As you move the mouse around the window, you will notice an orange outline. When you release the mouse, the file will embed itself in the area that was defined by the outline.

Open several files in NetBeans and start experimenting with file layouts. You can even arrange a single source file to be displayed in four quadrants, as shown in Figure 9-1. (Exactly why you would do so is beyond me, but it's possible.)

If multiple source files are open with only one displayed, you can easily navigate among them. You can do so without using a mouse. To switch between the tabs, press and hold down the Ctrl key. Then press the Tab key. You will see a small pop-up window displaying the list of currently opened files. Each time you press Tab, you toggle between the files. Press Ctrl+Shift+Tab to navigate the list of files in reverse order. Once you have selected the file you wish to view, release the Ctrl key.

Figure 9-1. *Splitting the editor window to view a file in four quadrants*

Accessing Source Editor Options

The Source Editor menu and toolbar provide links to the most commonly used pieces of functionality that you will need as you are coding. NetBeans also provides keyboard shortcuts for frequently used options.

The Source Editor Context Menu

To activate the context menu in the Source Editor, right-click anywhere in the window. The menu that appears offers numerous options. Many of them are also available in the main menu structure in NetBeans, but if invoked here, they can be context-sensitive to the file, section, line, or even word highlighted.

Additional items appear on the context menu when you right-click inside a file in the Source Editor. These options will be covered in later chapters on the related topic.

Here, we'll look at the first two items: Go To and Select In. The Go To option has its own submenu, listing Source, Declaration, Super Implementation, Test, Line, and Class, as shown in Figure 9-2. These submenu options are also available from the main Navigate menu in NetBeans.

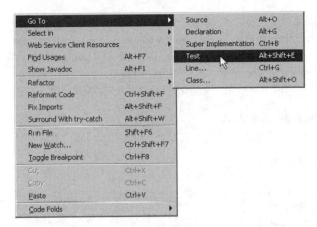

Figure 9-2. *The Source Editor context menu and Go To submenu*

Go To Source

The Go To Source menu option allows you to open the source code for an element. You can do this either by highlighting the name or by placing the cursor inside the name of the element for which you wish to view the source code.

For example, suppose you are not familiar with the java.lang.System class and want to discover how the internal code works. You have this code:

```
System.out.println("How does this thing work?");
```

You can right-click anywhere inside the System class name and select Go To ➤ Source. You can also use the keyboard shortcut Alt+O. The source file for the System class will open as a separate tab in the Source Editor.

Tip If the status bar along the bottom of the NetBeans IDE states that the source for the class cannot be found, you need to locate the source for the platform or library you are using. Many open source projects, such as projects from SourceForge.net or the Apache Software Foundation, provide downloadable bundles of source code. Use the Library Manager or Java Platform Manager to link the source code bundle to the appropriate set of APIs. The managers are accessible from the NetBeans Tools menu.

If you right-clicked the name of a method, the source file will open and scroll to the specified method. This is extremely useful since you don't have to spend time scrolling through the file.

Overall, I like to think of the Go To Source option as a convenience for a programmer who is curious about how code works. Using this submenu option, you can quickly drill down through classes and methods, opening the source code for each element you want to investigate. This functionality can help you to quickly learn how a third-party API works.

Go To Declaration

The Go To Declaration submenu option allows you to jump directly to where a method or field is defined in the code. By right-clicking the element and selecting Go To ➤ Declaration, or pressing Alt+G, you can jump to the line where the element is defined. This can be convenient if you need to jump to an element and see the details about the data type, access modifier, and so on.

For example, suppose you have the following class:

```
public class EmailClient {
public static String smtp = "mail.mydomain.com";

    public static void main(String[] args) {
        System.out.println("Hello World!");
        System.out.println("SMTP = " + smtp);
    }
}
```

This EmailClient class has a class member variable named smtp. This variable is then logged to the standard output stream inside the main method. If the EmailClient class were hundreds of lines of code long, you would not want to have to scroll through the entire class to find the definition of the smtp member. By right-clicking the smtp variable in the System.out. println("SMTP = " + smtp); line and selecting Go To ➤ Declaration, you immediately jump to the second line where the smtp variable is declared.

Go To Super Implementation

The Go To Super Implementation submenu option allows you to jump directly to the declaration of the super interface for a class. By right-clicking the class, method, or field and selecting Go To ➤ Super Implementation, or pressing Ctrl+B, you can jump to the line where the element is defined in the super interface. What exactly does this mean?

Suppose you define a class interface named MyInterface and a class that implements the interface named MyImpl:

```
public interface MyInterface {

    public void doSomething();
}


public class MyImpl implements MyInterface {

    public void doSomething() {
        System.out.println("MyImpl.doSomething");
    }
}
```

The MyImpl class implements the MyInterface interface and provides a simple implementation of the doSomething method. If you choose Go To ➤ Super Implementation after selecting the MyImpl.doSomething method, the Source Editor will open the MyInterface file. The cursor in the file will start at the MyInterface.doSomething definition, since MyInterface is the super implementation in this case.

Next consider the following similar code:

```
public interface MySuperInterface {
    public void doSomething();
}

public interface MyInterface extends MySuperInterface {

    public void doSomething();
}


public class MyImpl implements MyInterface{

    public void doSomething() {
        System.out.println("MyImpl.doSomething");
    }
}
```

In this code, MyImpl implements MyInterface, which in turn extends MySuperInterface. Thus, MySuperInterface.doSomething becomes the super implementation for MyImpl.doSomething.

Go To Test

The Go To Test submenu option allows you to jump directly to the corresponding JUnit test for a class. When you right-click inside the Source Editor window for a class and select Go To ➤ Test, the corresponding test class opens. You can also use the shortcut Alt+Shift+E to open the test class.

If you have the cursor inside a method for which a corresponding test method exists, then the test method is selected when the test class opens. Otherwise, the test class opens without a particular area initially selected.

Go To Line

The Go To Line submenu option is a great navigation tool. As the name suggests, it allows you to quickly jump directly to a specific line in the code.

When you right-click in an open file in the Source Editor and select Go To ➤ Line, or press Ctrl+G, the Go To Line dialog box opens, as shown in Figure 9-3.

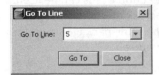

Figure 9-3. *The Go To Line dialog box*

When you're working with large classes, and need to jump back and forth between several sections, this option can save you a lot of scrolling. If you need to debug a class after reviewing an error stack trace, then you already know the line number, and the Go To Line option will let you jump directly to it.

Go To Class

The Go To Class submenu option allows you to search for and jump to a Java class. Right-click in any piece of code open in the Source Editor and select Go To ➤ Class, or press Alt+Shift+O, to open the Go To Class dialog box, as shown in Figure 9-4.

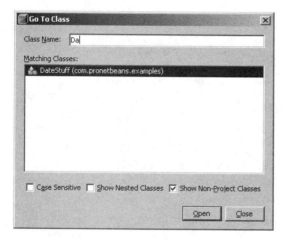

Figure 9-4. *The Go To Class dialog box*

In the Go To Class dialog box, you can type a few characters in the Class Name field. If any classes in your project match, they will appear in the middle section. You can modify this class matching by using the check boxes at the bottom of the dialog box: Case Sensitive, Show Nested Classes, and Show Non-Project Classes.

Checked by default, the Show Non-Project Classes option can be useful in filtering out matching classes that appear in the JDK or in any third-party libraries you have associated with the project. In Figure 9-4, the letters *Da* appear in the Class Name field, and the DateStuff class is the only one that matched. If you were to uncheck the Show Non-Project Classes check box, the list of matching classes would be quite long.

Select In

The Select In option on the Source Editor context menu will cause the file to be displayed and highlighted in the Projects or Files windows, depending on your selections. This can be useful if you have multiple projects and/or source files open and you lose track of where you opened the file. It can also be a convenient way to access other classes in the same package structure without having to click the nodes and drill down through the files yourself.

The Source Editor Toolbar

The Source Editor toolbar, shown in Figure 9-5, provides links to useful code editing and navigation tools. The functionality available from the toolbar is also spread across several of the main menus, but the icons provide quicker access. Here, we'll look at the functions provided by each section of the toolbar (the sections are divided by the vertical gray separator).

Figure 9-5. *The Source Editor toolbar*

■**Note** The exact arrangement of the icons on Source Editor toolbar is subject to change based on ongoing development work and improvements in each edition of NetBeans. However, the core features should stay the same between versions.

Navigating the Jump List

The first two icons allow you to navigate the jump list. The jump list is sort of like an Internet browser's history. In a browser, you can click Back and Forward to navigate between pages. In the Source Editor, you can click Back and Forward to navigate between locations in code where you have opened source code or made changes. If you are in a page of source code and use the Go To Source option to open the code of another class, the Back icon becomes active. You can then click it to return to your original location.

■**Tip** Combined with the Go To Line option, the Back and Forward icons are very convenient tools if you are trying to debug code after reading an error stack trace. You can locate the line in the first class, drill down to the offending line in the next class using Go To Source, and navigate your way back to where you started by clicking the Back icon.

Finding Text

The next section of icons in the Source Editor toolbar deals with finding text. From left to right, the icons are Find Previous Occurrence, Find Selection, Find Next Occurrence, and Toggle Highlight Search.

  The text selection icons allow you to highlight one or more characters and locate all occurrences of that text in the open file. You can also place the cursor anywhere in or next to a class name, method, or variable and use the Find Selection icon to highlight the occurrences. Use the Previous and Next Occurrence icons to navigate back and forth between the different occurrences. The Toggle Highlight Search icon allows you to turn off the highlighted search term so that each occurrence is not marked in the source code.

Navigating Bookmarks

The third section in the Source Editor toolbar contains three icons: Toggle Bookmark, Next Bookmark, and Previous Bookmark. Bookmarks are useful if you want to flag a line of code and come back to it later. By using the Toggle Bookmark icon, you can enable or disable bookmarks in your code. Using the Next and Previous Bookmark icons, you can scroll through all the bookmarks you have set to quickly navigate and view what you wanted to remember.

Matching Words

The fourth section on the Source Editor toolbar is for use with the Match Word feature. This is one of those nifty features that you should train your brain to try to remember, along with code completion, code templates, and so on.

The Match Word feature allows you to use the icons or keyboard shortcuts to add the previous or next "word" after the cursor. For example, suppose you are appending values to a `java.lang.String` like this:

```
String myVeryLongStringName = null;
MyVeryLongStringName = myVeryLongStringName + " add this text";
```

After typing the equal sign in the second line, you could click the Previous Matching Word icon, or press Ctrl+K. Since the element `myVeryLongStringName` was the last word typed, it immediately appears after the cursor. If you pressed Ctrl+K again, `null` would appear in place of `myVeryLongStringName`.

You can also highlight a word anywhere in the code and use the Next and Previous Matching Word icons to alter it and literally scroll through each and every word in the file.

Shifting Lines

The fifth section on the Source Editor toolbar deals with shifting lines. These two icons allow you to shift one or more lines of code to indent or unindent them.

■**Tip** You can set the number of spaces the line or lines are shifted in the Options ➤ Editor section, on the Indentation tab. See the "Indenting Code" section later in this chapter for more information about indenting code in NetBeans.

This feature comes in handy if you copy and paste in blocks of code and want to adjust the indentation. You can make the indentation line up with the rest of the file without having to format the entire source file.

To shift lines left, you can use the shortcut Ctrl+D. To shift lines right, you can use the shortcut Ctrl+T.

Working with Macros

The sixth section on the Source Editor toolbar is for working with macros. Using these two icons, you can start and stop recording macros. See the "Creating and Running Macros" section later in this chapter for details about recording macros.

Commenting Code

The seventh and final section of the Source Editor toolbar deals with commenting code. No Java IDE can be called a Java IDE unless it provides this basic piece of functionality.

When you are writing code, you will want to comment out a line or block of code without having to manually add the comment characters. The Comment icon allows you to automatically comment out the line that is currently active in the Source Editor window. If multiple lines are highlighted, they are all commented out. You can also access this feature by using the shortcut Ctrl+Shift+T.

Obviously, the Uncomment icon performs the opposite action. Lines that were commented out can be quickly and easily uncommented using the Uncomment icon or by pressing Ctrl+Shift+D.

Source Editor Keyboard Shortcuts

Many menu options have keyboard shortcuts, which appear next to the options in the menus. Table 9-1 lists some of the most commonly used keyboard shortcuts you might need while working with source code or in the Source Editor.

Table 9-1. *Keyboard Shortcuts Specific to the Source Editor*

Shortcut	Option
Ctrl+– (minus)	Collapse Fold
Ctrl+ + (plus)	Expand Fold
Ctrl+Shift+– (minus)	Collapse All Folds
Ctrl+Shift++ (plus)	Expand All Folds
Alt+O	Go To Source
Alt+G	Go To Declaration
Ctrl+B	Go To Super Implementation
Alt+Shift+E	Go To Test
Ctrl+G	Go To Line
Alt+Shift+O	Go To Class
Ctrl+Shift+F	Reformat Code
F9	Compile File
F11	Build Main Project
Shift+F6	Run File

Table 9-1. *Keyboard Shortcuts Specific to the Source Editor (Continued)*

Shortcut	Option
F6	Run Main Project
Ctrl+D	Shift Left
Ctrl+T	Shift Right
Ctrl+Shift+T	Comment Code
Ctrl+Shift+D	Uncomment Code

Using File Templates

A file template is a file prepopulated with elements and metadata that are standard in a particular type of file. Templates are useful for many reasons. The first and obvious reason is that they save you from having to type the same text over and over each time you create a file. Saving time often translates into increased productivity (or at least freeing up some time to make another run to the soda machine). The second and most valuable reason is standardization.

NetBeans comes with file templates for the standard file types. For example, suppose you want to add an HTML file to your project. Right-click the project name and select New ➤ File/Folder. In the New File window, choose the Web category and select the file type HTML. Click the Next button, name the file, and click Finish. The created file should look like the following:

```
<!DOCTYPE HTML PUBLIC "-//W3C//DTD HTML 4.01 Transitional//EN">
<html>
  <head>
    <title></title>
  </head>
  <body>

  </body>
</html>
```

This is a generic interpretation of the basic elements in an HTML file that you would need. However, there is nothing custom or specific in the file template based on the filename, the project, the current date and time, and so on.

Next, use the New File wizard to create a Java Class file type. Name the file MyClassFromTemplate and place it in the com.pronetbeans.examples package, as shown in Figure 9-6. After you click the Finish button, the class is created and added to your project.

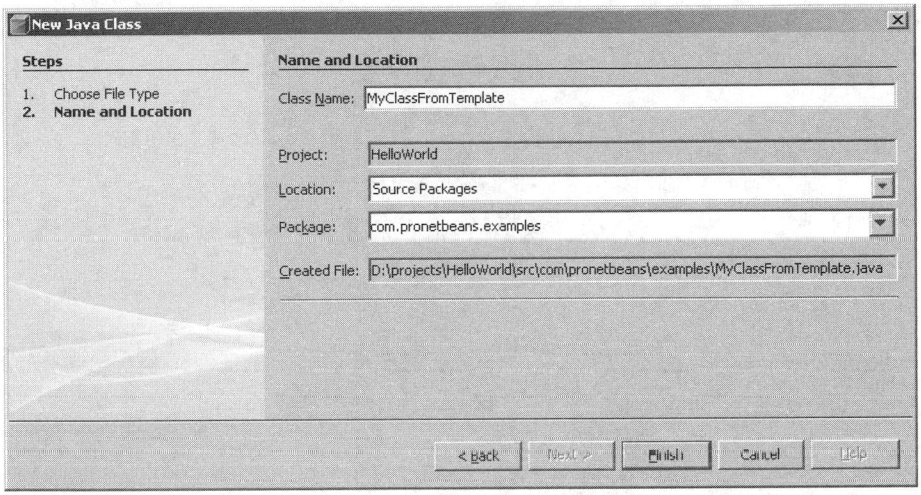

Figure 9-6. *Creating a new Java class file*

When I open the class, I see the following code:

```
package com.pronetbeans.examples;

/**
 *
 * @author Adam Myatt
 */
public class MyClassFromTemplate {

    /** Creates a new instance of MyClassFromTemplate */
    public MyClassFromTemplate() {
    }

}
```

The NetBeans Java Class template has special markers for the name of the author, the name of the class, and the name of the constructor to be inserted when the new file is generated.

The NetBeans templates can be opened, manipulated directly in NetBeans, and customized to suit your needs.

Working with Templates

To work with file templates, select Tools ➤ Template Manager. Using the Template Manager, you can add, view, and delete file templates. As shown in Figure 9-7, templates are arranged in folders, which represent the categories that appear in the New File wizard.

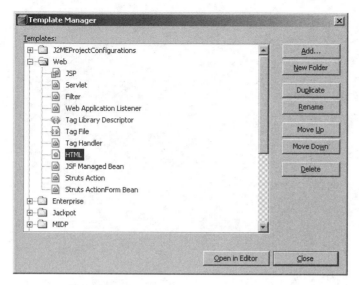

Figure 9-7. *The Template Manager*

To view a template, select an item and click the Open in Editor button. For example, select HTML under the Web folder. The template that opens should look exactly like the empty HTML file you created previously. There's little or no magic here.

Next, in the Java Classes folder, select the Java Class template and click the Open in Editor button. Notice that the template file that opens does *not* look exactly like the `MyClassFromTemplate` class you previously created. The template looks like the following:

```
/*
 * __NAME__.java
 *
 * Created on __DATE__, __TIME__
 *
 * To change this template, choose Tools | Template Manager
 * and open the template in the editor.
 */

package Templates.Classes;

/**
 *
 * @author __USER__
 */
public class Class {

    /** Creates a new instance of __NAME__ */
    public Class() {
    }
}
```

Notice the special NAME, DATE, TIME, and USER tags. These are replaced by the New File wizard when the actual file is created, based on the system values in the IDE and the values entered into the wizard. The Templates.Classes text is replaced with the package name of the class you create, and the name Class is replaced with the actual name you specified.

If you make any changes to a template file and then save the file, they will be present in the generated file of that type the next time one is created.

Adding and Creating Templates

Many web developers maintain a large web site where pages have different content but follow a standard layout. Why create a file and copy and paste the different elements you need into it? Why save a copy of an existing file and try to remove all the information you don't need from it? Create a custom template that is specific to your needs and avoid such hassles.

To add a new file template into NetBeans, click the Add button in the Template Manager. In the file system browser that opens, navigate to the template you previously created. If you had a category selected when you chose to add the template, it will be created inside that category. Otherwise, it will be added to the bottom of the list of category folders. You can then drag-and-drop it into the appropriate category folder.

If you want to create a file template inside NetBeans, you need to start with a file. The file can be of any type, such as HTML, Java, XML, and so on. In the Projects or Files window, right-click the file and select Save As Template from the context menu. The Save As Template dialog box will appear, as shown in Figure 9-8. Select the appropriate template category folder, and then click the OK button. The new template will then be available in the New File wizard.

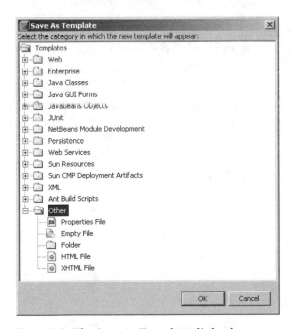

Figure 9-8. *The Save As Template dialog box*

Tip When you make changes to the default templates or create your own, they are stored on the file system at `<user-directory>` `.netbeans\###\config\Templates`, where ### is the version number of your installation. If you have created a lot of templates, I recommend periodically backing up this templates folder, in case your user directory is ever corrupted (which happens occasionally on Windows).

Working in the Source Editor

Since the Source Editor is arguably one of the most important components of NetBeans, you should be familiar with it and its related tools. Some of the best tools available in the Source Editor are the subtle helpers that make your day-to-day coding easier.

Identifying Errors

Chapter 3 included a brief section on syntax and error highlighting. I introduced this as possibly one of the most important features of any Java IDE tool. That statement still stands. Knowing that syntax errors exist immediately after you type a line of code is extremely helpful.

I can still remember my early days of Java programming, when I would type a lot of code and finally get around to compiling. There would always be several dozen errors, which were mostly syntax-related, since I didn't remember the exact case of certain methods or forgot the semicolon at the end of a line.

When many programmers get inspired and literally fly through code, they don't want to stop and compile every few lines. This leads to long error lists when they finally do compile. Having a visual means of immediately identifying errors can be quite an asset.

NetBeans provides a great feature set for identifying errors in code.

Error Highlighting

You've already seen the NetBeans highlighting feature. If you type a line of code that is syntactically incorrect, a wavy red line appears under it, as shown in Figure 9-9. In this example, the semicolon at the end of the line was omitted.

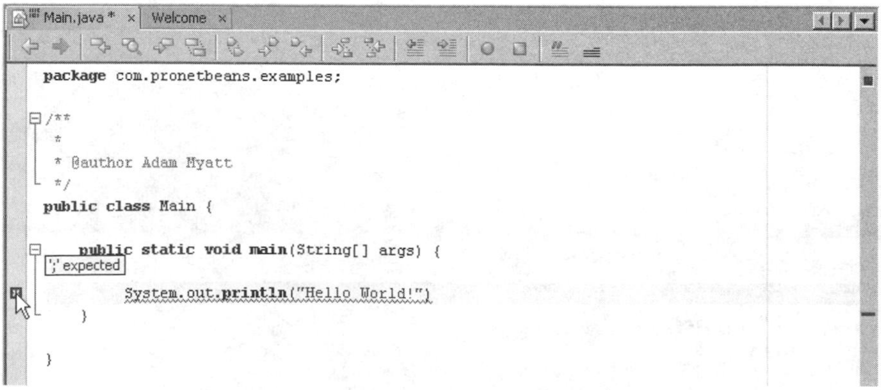

Figure 9-9. *Error highlighting in the Source Editor*

In Figure 9-9, also notice the error glyph icon in the left margin of the Source Editor. Error glyph icons help to make an issue with code stand out visually to the programmer. You can mouse over the icon to see a description of the issue, as shown in Figure 9-9. Annotation glyph icons also appear to denote warnings, suggestions, breakpoints, bookmarks, and so on. You can make some changes to these annotations through the Fonts & Colors section of the Basic Options window, as described in Chapter 2.

The error stripe is the other important feature when identifying errors in code. This is the gray vertical bar along the right side of the window, which you can also see in Figure 9-9. This bar represents the entire file, regardless of length. As the file grows longer and longer, this bar remains the same length. As errors appear in the code and the glyph margin, they also appear in the error stripe bar. If you mouse over the small red rectangle that appears in the error stripe to signify an error, it will display the exact error message, just as when you mouse over the error glyph icon in the left margin. If you click the red rectangle in the error stripe, you will go directly to the line of code that is causing the problem. This is an important feature, since you may have hundreds of lines of code and don't want to have to scroll through all of it just to find the one error that is being highlighted.

Suggestion Glyphs

If you made an error that NetBeans thinks it can help you fix, a suggestion glyph icon will appear in the glyph margin. For example, suppose your code calls a method of an object that does not exist. A suggestion glyph icon will appear. If you click the suggestion glyph icon, you will see the suggestion to create the method in the class to make the code valid (or at least compile). In the example in Figure 9-10, clicking the suggestion glyph icon revealed the following suggestion, shown in blue highlighted text: "Create method doSomething() in com.pronetbeans. examples.Main." You can also force the suggestion to appear by clicking anywhere on the line and pressing Alt+Enter.

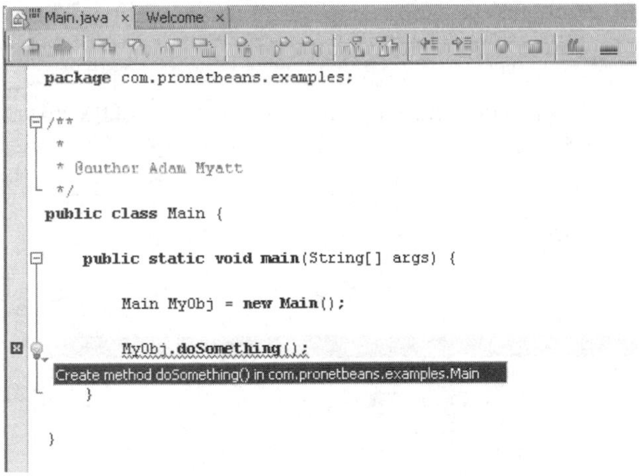

Figure 9-10. *Suggestion glyph icon in the glyph margin and the suggested fix*

If you click the highlighted text or press the Enter key, NetBeans will implement the suggestion, and the suggestion glyph icon will disappear. In the example, the following code would be added to the class:

```
private void doSomething() {
    throw new UnsupportedOperationException("Not yet implemented");
}
```

As you can see, NetBeans added a `private` method `doSomething` that throws an `UnsupportedOperationException` if executed. This allows your code to compile, but it will throw the exception if you execute the method without fully implementing it. The access modifier `private` is how NetBeans makes sure additional classes don't call the method until you explicitly make the decision to change it to `public`, `protected`, or `default`.

The following are some additional reasons you might see suggestion glyph icons:

- If you need to surround a block with `try` and `catch` statements

- If you use a class without first importing it or its package

- If you type a local variable in a method's `return` statement without first having created the variable

- If you define and reference a variable without first initializing it with a value

For the complete list of situations where NetBeans displays the suggestion glyph icon, see the NetBeans help page. Select Help ➤ Help Contents and search the index for the word "suggestions."

Output Window

Another error-related feature is the NetBeans Output window. When code is built or executed, the output from the standard out and error streams is displayed in the Output window. If there is a compilation error, the standard error stream that is displayed in the Output window will be linked directly to the source code.

For example, in the following code, the semicolon is missing from the end of one of the lines:

```
public class Main {

    public static void main(String[] args) {

        Main MyObj = new Main()
        MyObj.doSomething();
    }
}
```

When this code is compiled, the Output window will display that a semicolon is expected and the line where the issue occurred. The line is also linked to the matching line in the source code, as shown in Figure 9-11.

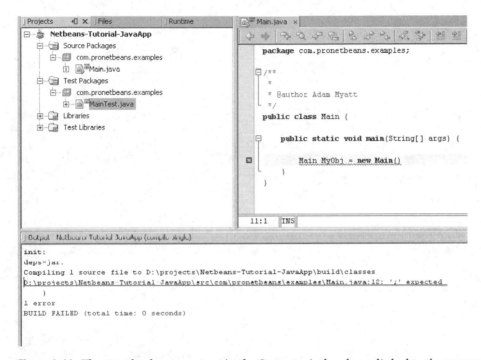

Figure 9-11. *The standard error output in the Output window hyperlinked to the source code*

Clicking the hyperlinked error message opens the matching code in the Source Editor, scrolled to the line where the error occurred. This can be a very useful feature if you are compiling an entire package or project and numerous errors occur in the Output window. Not only do you see the errors, but NetBeans intelligently links them directly to the source code to save you time.

Indenting Code

Few programmers would say that indenting code doesn't matter. Formatting your code and properly indenting each line makes it more readable and easier to maintain. When code contains numerous nested blocks, it can sometimes be difficult to know where one if or else statement begins and another ends. Many programmers have played the "count the curly brackets" game to understand how some legacy code works. Look at the following code:

```
public class BadClass {

public BadClass() {

int x = 0;
int y = 1;
int z = 2;
int outputNum = 0;

if(x < y) {
System.out.println("X is less than Y");
if(x==0) {
outputNum = 9;
}
else if(x==1) {
x+=463;
}
else if(x==2) {
x+=x;
}
}
else if(x<z) {
z+=y;
}
}
}
```

At first glance (and maybe even second glance), it is not easily discernable which else-if blocks are nested inside which if blocks.

Good programming practice is to indent the code using spaces and tabs. Following some sort of standard indentation scheme is also important, so indentation is consistent across multiple files. NetBeans helps enforce this best practice.

NetBeans uses a standard indentation scheme. You can create code and have NetBeans enforce good indentation. If you are dealing with a file created outside NetBeans, you can reformat it to use the correct indentation following the NetBeans standard.

To apply the formatting, select Source ➤ Reformat Code, or press Ctrl+Shift+F. After reformatting with indentation, the previous BadClass example looks like Figure 9-12. Notice that each nested block is properly indented. Each if, else-if, and else is easier to read, and you can quickly identify the start and end of the blocks. Note that each block is indented a set number of spaces. This is a property that can be configured.

To set indentation properties, select Tools ➤ Options. In the Basic Options window, select Editor from the list on the left, and then click the Indentation tab, as shown in Figure 9-13. You can set the Number of Spaces per Indent value, which affects how far each line or block is indented. By default, it is set to 4. You can change this to whatever value you want. If multiple developers work on the same project, I recommend making sure the value is the same for every member of the team.

```
public class BadClass {

    public BadClass() {

        int x = 0;
        int y = 1;
        int z = 2;
        int outputNum = 0;

        if(x < y) {
            System.out.println("X is less than Y");
            if(x==0) {
                outputNum = 9;
            } else if(x==1) {
                x+=463;
            } else if(x==2) {
                x+=x;
            }
        } else if(x<z) {
            z+=y;
        }
    }
}
```

Figure 9-12. *The reformatted BadClass example with indentation applied*

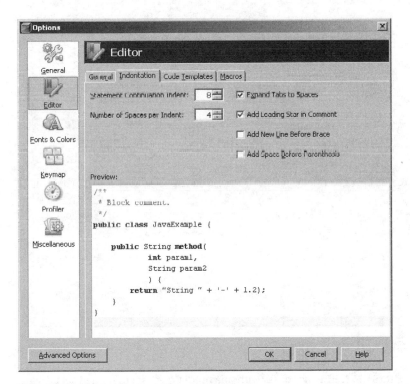

Figure 9-13. *Setting indentation properties*

Creating and Running Macros

A macro is a set of automated keystrokes or behaviors that can be repeated as needed. If you find yourself performing similar and repetitive actions, you might want to consider creating macros. Macros provide you with the ability to automate numerous steps that can be triggered with a simple keyboard shortcut. They can be recorded or created manually.

Using the Macro Editor

You can use the Macro Editor to work with macros created in NetBeans. To open the Macro Editor, select Tools ➤ Options. Select the Editor icon from the list on the left and click the Macros tab. The Macro Editor displays a list of the existing macros (name and shortcut). When you click the macro name, the corresponding macro code is displayed at the bottom of the tab, as shown in Figure 9-14.

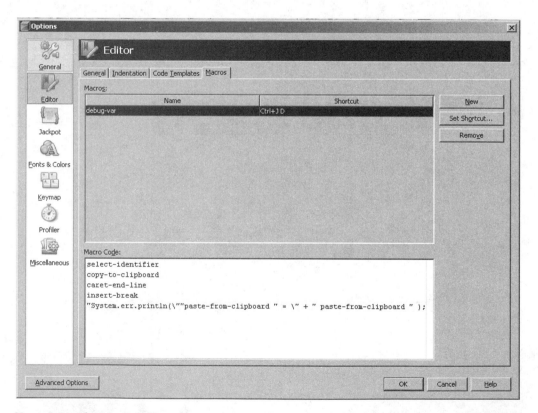

Figure 9-14. *The Macro Editor*

As you can see in Figure 9-14, NetBeans comes with one predefined macro named debug-var. This macro adds an output statement for an identifier. The following is the code for the debug-var macro:

```
select-identifier
copy-to-clipboard
caret-end-line
insert-break
"System.err.println(\""paste-from-clipboard " = \" + " paste-from-clipboard " );
```

The code includes individual macro actions that are performed during execution of the macro. It is easy to understand most of the action names. (See Table 9-2 for a list of some of the more common actions and a brief description of what they do.) Here's what the debug-var macro does:

- Selects the current identifier
- Copies it to the clipboard
- Moves the caret (the cursor) to the end of the line
- Adds a line break
- Types the characters System.err.print("
- Pastes the text from the clipboard
- Types the characters = " +
- Pastes the text from the clipboard
- Types the characters);.

Suppose you had the code String FirstName = "Adam";. Place the cursor inside the FirstName variable and activate the debug-var macro by pressing Ctrl+J, D. The code created would look like the following:

```
String FirstName = "Adam";
System.err.println("FirstName = " + FirstName);
```

Writing or Recording a Macro

You can create your own macros manually by clicking the New button in the Macro Editor (see Figure 9-14). You'll be prompted to name the macro. You can then assign a shortcut using the Set Shortcut button and type in the macro code. If this manual process does not appeal to you, record your macros instead.

When you record a macro, you tell NetBeans to "watch" the set of steps you are about to perform. To begin recording, click the Start Recording button in the Source Editor toolbar, or press Ctrl+J, S. Then perform the steps you want to automate. NetBeans writes down, or records, the names of the actions you use. When you're finished, tell NetBeans to stop recording by clicking the End Recording button on the Source Editor toolbar or by pressing Ctrl+J, E. You will be prompted to name the macro and set its shortcut. That set of steps—the macro—can then be replayed by using your assigned shortcut.

After you have created a macro, you can edit the code for the macro at any time through the Macro Editor. This is a great feature when working with macros. You can record a long series of steps, and then manually edit and tweak them as necessary.

Table 9-2 lists some macro actions you might use. You can experiment and discover all the actions that are available by recording a macro and clicking every button and menu item possible to see what the macro records.

Table 9-2. *Some Macro Actions in NetBeans*

Macro Action	Description
select-identifier	Select the identifier the cursor is currently on.
select-word	Select the word the cursor is currently on.
caret-forward	Move the cursor forward one space.
caret-backward	Move the cursor backward one space.
caret-end-line	Move the cursor to the end of the current line.
insert-break	Insert a line break after the current line.
bookmark-toggle	Toggle a bookmark on or off for the current line.
bookmark-next	Jump to the next bookmark.
bookmark-previous	Jump to the previous bookmark.
comment	Comment the current line or selection of code.
uncomment	Uncomment the current line or selection of code.
format	Cause the current source code file to be reformatted.
shift-line-right	Shift the current line or selection right by the default number of spaces.
shift-line-left	Shift the current line or selection left by the default number of spaces.
word-match-prev	Insert the previous matching word.
word-match-next	Insert the next matching word.
paste-from-clipboard	Paste the text from the clipboard.
copy-to-clipboard	Copy the currently selected text to the clipboard.
cut-to-clipboard	Cut and copy the currently selected text to the clipboard.
fix-imports	Run the Fix Imports refactoring.
try-catch	Surround the current selection or line with a try-catch statement.
collapse-fold	Collapse the code fold for the current block.
expand-fold	Expand the code fold for the current block.
collapse-all-folds	Collapse all the code folds in the file.
expand-all-folds	Expand all the code folds in the file.

Using the Component Palette

The component palette, or Palette window, is essentially a fancy toolbar that allows you quick access to language elements. To open the Palette window, select Window ➤ Palette or press Ctrl+Shift+8. Based on the type of file you have open in the Source Editor, the Palette window will display custom elements and tags.

Adding JSP and HTML Components

When you open a JSP or an HTML file in the Source Editor, the Palette window displays elements related to that content, as shown in Figure 9-15. You can drag these HTML and JSP elements from the Palette window into the currently open file.

Figure 9-15. *The Palette window with HTML components*

NetBeans does not have a WYSIWYG HTML/JSP editor like Dreamweaver or FrontPage. However, it does provide some nice features that save you time coding HTML.

Suppose that you need to add an HTML link to a URL. Click and drag the Link component from the Palette window into the open source file. As you move the mouse, the cursor follows inside the file. When the cursor is in the correct line and column where you want the `<a href>` tag to appear, release the mouse button. The Insert Link dialog box will open, as shown in Figure 9-16.

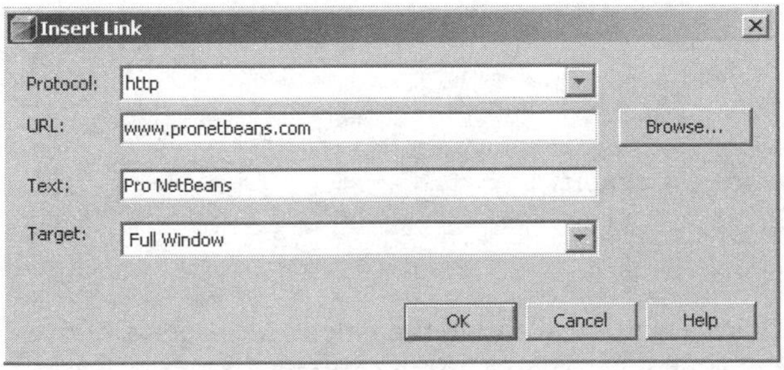

Figure 9-16. *The Insert Link dialog box*

Using this dialog box, you can set several parameters about the link without having to write the code for them. The most convenient is the ability to set the Target field. The Target drop-down list contains the values Same Frame, New Window, Parent Frame, and Full Window. These values are easier to work with than the HTML attributes values they represent.

If you try to add several additional elements from the Palette window, you will see that NetBeans prompts you with an element-specific wizard in an attempt to save you coding and configuration. These prompts are nice in that you don't need to remember the exact syntax of each tag's attributes.

Adding Swing Components

Another area where the Palette window comes in extremely handy is when working with Java Swing. If you are designing a Swing class that will contain Swing elements, having a palette with the available elements is almost mandatory.

For example, if you added a new class of type `JFrame Form`, the Palette window would contain Swing elements, as shown in Figure 9-17.

Figure 9-17. *The Palette window with Swing components*

Using the Palette Manager

You can configure some aspects of the Palette window through the Palette Manager. Choose Tools ➤ Palette Manager and select the type of palette you want to configure. Figure 9-18 shows the Palette Manager that appears when you choose the HTML/JSP palette.

Figure 9-18. *The Palette Manager window for the HTML/JSP palette*

Using the Palette Manager, you can show and hide the different sections and elements that appear in the Palette window. You can also sort and order the elements to be arranged and displayed as you see fit.

To hide an element, simply uncheck the check box next to the name of the element. To show the element again, just check the box.

A limited set of features is available in the Palette Manager. The only other features that might not be obvious are those available when you right-click a palette category or element name. On the context menu that appears, you can sort the element in each category or sort the categories.

You can also create a new category by clicking the New Category button. You can name the category, and then copy and paste existing elements from the Palette window into that category. You cannot manually add new elements to the Palette window.

After you've used the Palette window for a while, it will become an integral part of your development process. It offers quick access to commonly used pieces of functionality in a drag-and-drop manner. As NetBeans evolves, expect more and more features to be available on the Palette window for each file type.

Summary

In this chapter, you learned a lot about working in the NetBeans Source Editor. Many topics were covered, but with a strong focus on how specific features relate to coding, code navigation, and automating development.

You saw that source file windows can be arranged in a variety of ways, allowing for several viewing options (left and right, top and bottom, and so on). We also reviewed the Source Editor context menu options, toolbar, and keyboard shortcuts.

This chapter also covered file templates. You can provide any type of dynamic page structure or layout and save it as a template. Then, in the New File wizard in NetBeans, you can select this template file to be added to your project. This helps with standardization and saves time.

Next, we reviewed some important Source Editor features for working with code:

Syntax and error highlighting: NetBeans provides several methods for identifying problems in code, navigating around files to locate errors, and offering suggestions for fixing the errors.

Code indentation: Developers need to format code in a readable manner so that it is easy to maintain and understand. NetBeans attempts to enforce this best practice by automatically indenting various blocks as you type lines of code. You can reformat code at any time to conform to the indentation standards.

Macros: A time-saving feature, macros can be used in conjunction with code completion and code templates (covered in Chapter 10) to save you time and keystrokes. You can record sequences of actions and play them back using keyboard shortcuts.

Palette window: This component palette lets you drag-and-drop context-specific elements into your source code. It also provides various wizards to assist you in adding the code without having to remember all the attribute names or syntax.

Many of the features discussed in this chapter, and in NetBeans as a whole, relate to saving you time as a developer. Learning all the ins and outs of these features can take a little time but, in the end, your time investment pays off dramatically by making you more productive.

■ ■ ■

CHAPTER 10

Code Completion and Templates

This chapter covers two time-saving features that NetBeans provides for programmers: code completion and code templates. Code completion allows you to enter the name of a class, interface, package, field, or method without having to type the entire name. A code template is a block of text or code that can be automatically inserted into your file by typing only a few characters.

Code Completion

As you type in the NetBeans Source Editor, a pop-up window—also known as the code completion box—appears, showing a context-sensitive list of possibilities. As you type additional characters, the list is further filtered to display only those items that match what you have typed. This saves time and makes coding easier, since you don't have to remember the exact case-sensitive name of every construct in Java.

■**Note** The NetBeans code completion feature is active by default, but it can be disabled through the Basic Options window. See the "Configuring Code Completion" section later in this chapter for details.

Working with the Code Completion Box

If you type a period and pause for a moment, the code completion box should appear. (The amount of time it takes for the code completion to appear after typing a period is configurable, as described in the "Configuring Code Completion" section later in this chapter.) However, even if you have not typed a single character, you can press Ctrl+spacebar to bring up the code completion box. It will display the classes, methods, and packages that are available, as well as the variables that are in scope.

Classes and items displayed in the code completion list are assembled from the JDK, any Java projects that are currently open in NetBeans, and any additional libraries defined in the Library Manager. To add libraries, select Tools ➤ Library Manager and click the New Library button.

You can use various keyboard shortcuts to work with the code completion box, as listed in Table 10-1.

Table 10-1. *Keystrokes Affecting Code Completion*

Keystroke	Action
Ctrl+spacebar	Forces the code completion box to appear
Enter	Inserts the selected item into your code
Escape	Closes the code completion box and cancels any text insertions
Tab	Filters items displayed in the list based on the longest common string
Alt+O	Opens the source file the insertion point is on
Alt+G	Navigates to the variable declaration the insertion point is on
Alt+F1	Opens the Javadoc for the item the insertion point is on
Page-Up	Scrolls up through the list of items
Page-Down	Scrolls down through the list of items
Home	Scrolls to the first item in the list
End	Scrolls to the last item in the list

An icon may appear next to some of the elements listed in the code completion box. The icon denotes the access level, such as public, protected, private, and default. See Table 10-2 for a list of some of these icons and the elements they represent.

Table 10-2. *Access Level Icons for Classes, Interfaces, Initializers, Fields, and Methods*

Icon	Access Level
	Java class or inner class
	Java interface or inner interface
	Constructor with protected access
	Non-static private field

Table 10-2. *Access Level Icons for Classes, Interfaces, Initializers, Fields, and Methods*

Icon	Access Level
	Non-static field with default access
	Non-static field with protected access
	Non-static public field
	Static private field
	Static field with default access
	Static field with protected access
	Static public field
	Non-static private method
	Non-static method with default access
	Non-static method with protected access
	Non-static public method
	Static private method
	Static method with default access
	Static method with protected access
	Static public method

Configuring Code Completion

In NetBeans, the code completion feature can be enabled or disabled. You can also configure several additional parameters related to code completion for the IDE.

Basic Options

To see the code completion configuration options, select Tools ➤ Options ➤ Editor. The Code Completion section is in the lower half of the General tab, as shown in Figure 10-1.

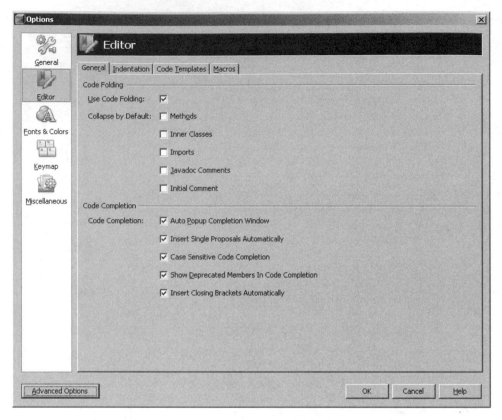

Figure 10-1. *Code completion settings*

The Code Completion section has five check boxes:

Auto Popup Completion Window: If you turn off this option, the code completion window will not pop up while you are typing. You can still open it by pressing Ctrl+spacebar.

Insert Single Proposals Automatically: When this option is selected, the code completion box will not appear when there is only one possible completion for the current expression. Instead, the completion will be inserted automatically. One example of this option would be typing the text System.current and pressing the Enter key (you need to pause for half a second or so after typing the period). The text System.currentTimeMillis(); will appear in the Source Editor window.

Case Sensitive Code Completion: As the name suggests, this option filters items from the code completion box based on the case of the character typed. Thus, typing String.C results in the suggestion of String.CASE_INSENSITIVE_ORDER. Items such as String. copyValueOf are filtered out of the list. This feature is most useful when working with custom-created classes. If your custom class has similarly named members and methods, you will find the case-sensitive filter helpful.

Show Deprecated Members in Code Completion: If you turn off this option, deprecated class elements are filtered out of the items displayed in the code completion box. If it's checked, deprecated items are displayed, but they have a line drawn through the name. In Figure 10-2, the code completion options for the `java.lang.System` class are displayed. Notice that the `runFinalizersOnExit(boolean b)` method has a line drawn through it. This method is deprecated in the version of the JDK I use with NetBeans, but if you have an older version, it may not be deprecated.

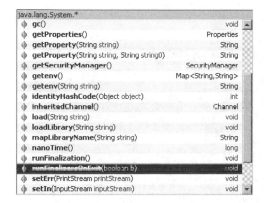

Figure 10-2. *Code completion window for the java.lang.System class showing a deprecated element*

Insert Closing Brackets Automatically: With this feature enabled, the Source Editor generates the closing parenthesis, bracket, brace, or quotation mark after you type the first one. Many Java IDE tools have similar functionality, but too often, the autocompletion feature gets in the way. However, NetBeans handles generating closing elements very nicely, allowing you to type right over them and not inserting duplicate closing characters.

Advanced Options

To change additional code completion properties, click the Advanced Options button in the Options window. This changes the display and lists a variety of options in the left pane. Navigate the tree structure by drilling down to Editing ➤ Editor Settings ➤ Java Editor. In the right pane, a list of properties and expert options are displayed, as shown in Figure 10-3.

The Auto Popup Completion Window check box allows you to disable/enable the code completion window. This has the same effect as the Auto Popup Completion Window check box in the Basic Options window.

The Delay of Completion Window Auto Popup property is set to 250 by default. This value represents the time in milliseconds it takes for the code completion window to appear. A lot of developers change this value to 1000 (for 1 second).

The Code Completion Natural Sort check box, if enabled, sorts the results in the code completion box in natural order. If it's unchecked, the uppercase items are listed before the lowercase ones.

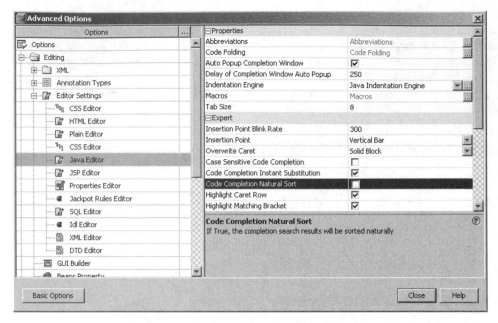

Figure 10-3. *The Java Editor properties in the Advanced Options window*

Using Code Completion

Code completion is useful in many scenarios in Java coding. I've been coding Java for more than a few years, and I still cannot remember the name of every class, method, member, and exception that exists in the language. Code completion saves you the time of having to look up the Java API Javadocs whenever you need a reminder of the methods of a class or the package structure of a set of APIs.

In the following sections, we'll look at several specific areas where you can use code completion.

Packages (Imports)

When working with packages, you sometimes have long combinations of text that define your class hierarchy. Many companies use package statements like this:

```
com.mycompany.mydivision.myorganization.thisproduct.database;
com.mycompany.mydivision.myorganization.thisproduct.model;
com.mycompany.mydivision.myorganization.thisproduct.view;
```

or like this:

```
com.mycompany.product.client;
com.mycompany.product.server;
com.mycompany.product.server.threads;
com.mycompany.product.server.db;
```

Package names are not difficult to paste into your source code editor, but they can be annoying to try to remember. That's where code completion becomes useful.

Open any Java source file in the NetBeans Source Editor and try typing an `import` statement. After the first package element, press the period key. The code completion box should appear, listing the next available package names. Depending on the package, the code completion box may contain classes and package names. Figure 10-4 shows an example of importing the `java.util` package.

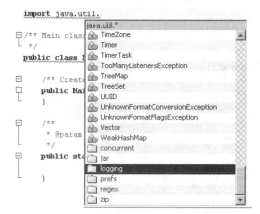

Figure 10-4. *The code completion listing for the java.util package*

Methods

The most frequent use of code completion is with methods. Whether you are trying to reference static or non-static methods, the code completion box will try to assist you. One intelligent feature NetBeans provides is static method code completion.

In the Source Editor, type `String` and press the period key. The code completion box will appear with a list of suggestions. An interesting thing to note is that since you typed the name of a class, the items in the code completion box are only the static members and methods of the `String` class, as shown in Figure 10-5.

```
package com.mycompany.projectname;
                    java.lang.String.*
                  class                                 Class
import java.  CASE_INSENSITIVE_ORDER      Comparator<String>
              copyValueOf(char[] c)                     String
]/** Main cl  copyValueOf(char[] c, int i, int i0)      String
- */          format(String string, Object[]... object)   String
public class  format(Locale locale, String string, Object[]... object)  String
              valueOf(Object object)                    String
]    /** Cre  valueOf(boolean b)                        String
]    public   valueOf(char c)                           String
-    }        valueOf(char[] c)                          String
              valueOf(double d)                         String
]    /**      valueOf(float f)                          String
     * @par   valueOf(int i)                            String
-    */       valueOf(long l)                           String
]    public   valueOf(char[] c, int i, int i0)          String
        String.
```

Figure 10-5. *Static elements of the String class display in the code completion box*

Let's look at an example of including both static and non-static items. Enter the following code in the Source Editor:

```
String MyString = "some string";
```

On the second line of your code, type the MyString variable name and press the period key. The list that appears in the code completion box contains *both* static and non-static items, as shown in Figure 10-6.

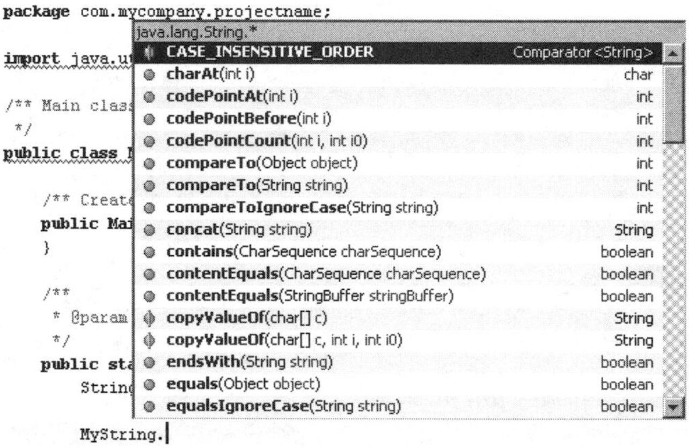

Figure 10-6. *Static and non-static elements of the String class*

Class Members

The code completion box can also display class members. If you take a look at the java.sql. ResultSet interface, you will see that it contains a number of static integers such as TYPE_ SCROLL_SENSITIVE, CONCUR_READ_ONLY, and FETCH_FORWARD. These fields are mostly used when creating a java.sql.Statement object and specifying various parameters for the database operation you are about to perform.

For example, suppose you are typing this code:

```
Statement stmt = con.createStatement(
            ResultSet.TYPE_SCROLL_SENSITIVE,
            ResultSet.CONCUR_UPDATABLE);
```

Once you type the ResultSet class name and press the period key, you will see the static members of the class, as shown in Figure 10-7.

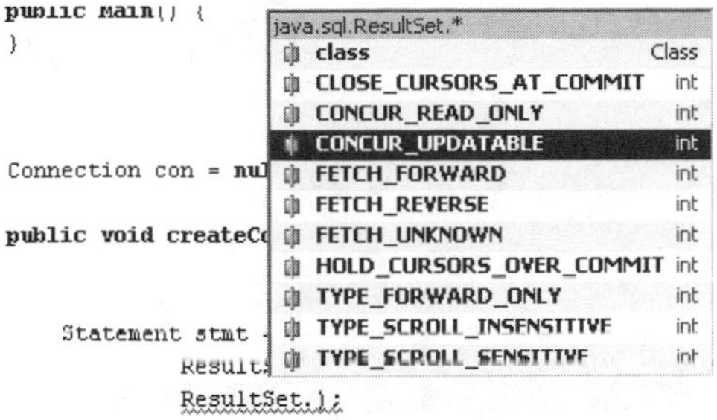

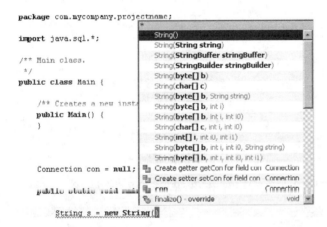

Figure 10-7. *Static elements of the java.sql.ResultSet class in the code completion box*

Constructors

Code completion can also be used when creating an instance of an object and selecting which constructor you need to use. For example, Figure 10-8 shows the code completion box for java.lang.String, which has numerous constructors.

Figure 10-8. *Constructors for java.lang.String displayed in the code completion box*

The code completion box will not automatically appear for constructors. In the example, after typing the opening parenthesis for the String constructor, you need to press Ctrl+spacebar to force the code completion box to appear.

super and this

You can use code completion immediately after super and this. Using code completion referencing the this object is most useful if you are creating getter and setter methods and need to have quick access to class member variables. This is especially true if you have dozens of class member variables and you have scrolled down through the file.

For example, consider the following code:

```
public class MyMain {

    private String firstName;

    public void setFirstName(String fname) {

    }
}
```

Inside the `setFirstName` method, if you were to type `this` and press the period key, the code completion box would appear, as shown in Figure 10-9. From this list, you could quickly select the `firstName` member variable without having to remember the exact syntax or retype the entire name.

Figure 10-9. *Locating the class member variable firstName in the code completion box*

The new Operator

You can also use code completion when constructing a new instance of an object in conjunction with the new operator. Type the code `Map myMap = new`, and then press Ctrl+spacebar to open the code completion box. You can start to type the name of the class you would like to create a new instance of, and the list will filter accordingly, as shown in Figure 10-10.

```
import java.util.*;

/**
 * MyMain class.
 */
public class MyMain {

    private String firs

    public void setFirs

        Map DataMap = new Hash
```

Hash*
HashAttributeSet (javax.print.attribute)
HashDocAttributeSet (javax.print.attribute)
HashMap (java.util)
HashPrintJobAttributeSet (javax.print.attribute)
HashPrintRequestAttributeSet (javax.print.attribute)
HashPrintServiceAttributeSet (javax.print.attribute)
HashSet (java.util)
Hashtable (com.sun.org.apache.xalan.internal.xsltc.runtime)
Hashtable (java.util)
Hashtree2Node (com.sun.org.apache.xml.internal.utils)

Figure 10-10. *Filtered list of classes in the code completion box*

Code Templates

Code templates are an interesting feature of several Java IDE tools. They allow you to automatically insert a block of text or code by typing just a few characters. At first, it can be annoying to attempt to remember the correct abbreviation for the code template you want. Over time, as you develop code in NetBeans, you will learn the abbreviations (at least, the important ones).

In addition to using the predefined code templates that come with NetBeans, you can create your own custom code templates.

Using Code Templates

Consider the following block of text in a Java source file:

```
System.out.println("print something to command line");
```

I can't even begin to count the number of times I have typed that statement or copied and pasted it repeatedly. Using the NetBeans code template and abbreviation functionality, you can simply type sout and press the spacebar. The sout text is expanded into this:

```
System.out.println("");
```

Notice that the cursor rests inside the quotation marks. Once the sout statement has been expanded, you can begin typing the text you want to appear on the standard output stream.

A similar abbreviation is available for the standard error stream. Typing serr and pressing the spacebar produces the following code:

```
System.err.println("");
```

The code template feature is nice to have for commonly used code phrases such as these. However, less useful abbreviations are available, such as pu, which expands to public, and re, which expands to return. Personally, if I need public in a block of code, it is usually faster for me to type the entire word than try to remember the exact abbreviation. Some people would argue that since the abbreviation is the first two characters of the word, it should be easy enough to remember. I prefer to save space in my brain for abbreviations that represent longer blocks of code. The following are some examples of truly useful code abbreviations that are predefined in NetBeans.

trycatch

Typing the abbreviation `trycatch` expands the text into the following:

```
try {

} catch (Exception e) {

}
```

The object type, `Exception`, is highlighted, so as soon as you start typing, you overwrite the text with the name of the intended exception (`NumberFormatException`, `NullPointerException`, and so on). Once you are finished typing the name of the desired exception, press the Enter key. The cursor will jump to the first line of the `try` block. This allows you to start typing the expression that should be protected in a `try-catch` block.

ifelse

Typing the abbreviation `ifelse` expands the text into the following:

```
if (condition)
{

}
else
{

}
```

The condition text that appears inside the `if` block is highlighted and overwritten as soon as you start typing. You can add any Boolean expression into this area and press the Enter key. The cursor should immediately jump to the first line of the `if` block.

fori

Typing the abbreviation `fori` expands the text into the following:

```
for (int i = 0; i < arr.length; i++)
{

}
```

The integer variable name is highlighted by default once this piece of code is expanded from its abbreviation. You can type any variable name you like, and it will be changed in all three places in the code where it appears. Before pressing the Enter key to jump to the first line of the `for` block, you can press the Tab key to jump to and highlight the `arr` variable, so you can change the name if desired.

Customizing Templates

The code template abbreviations described in the previous sections are only a small portion of what is available in NetBeans. The system provides a language-specific listing of code templates that can be completely customized. Additionally, you can add your own code templates.

Modifying Code Templates

To view the list of language-specific templates, select Tools ➤ Options ➤ Editor and click the Code Templates tab. From the Language drop-down list, select the programming or scripting language for the templates you wish to view. The Java language is selected by default. Scroll through the long list of templates, and you will see the abbreviations I mentioned in the previous sections, as shown in Figure 10-11.

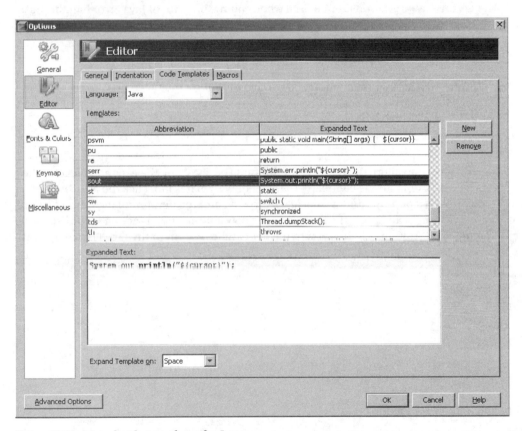

Figure 10-11. *List of code templates for Java*

Click any of the Java code template abbreviations in the list to see the expanded text in the text box at the bottom of the tab. The expanded text is what the abbreviation itself is actually expanded into once you press the spacebar after typing the abbreviation. For example, the following is the expanded text for the trycatch abbreviation:

```
try {
    ${cursor}
} catch (${Exception} e) {

}
```

Notice the text ${Exception} and ${cursor} that appears in the code template. The first piece, ${}, represents the variable that you want to possibly overwrite, and the text that appears within serves as a default value. The ${cursor} text is a marker for where the actual cursor will jump to once you press the Enter key, thereby "exiting" the abbreviation sequence. When you use the code template abbreviation in the Source Editor, you will not actually see the text ${cursor} in the code once the abbreviation has been expanded. It is only a behind-the-scenes marker.

The trycatch abbreviation is often used when coding, but a lot of Java error handling also uses the try-catch-finally form:

```
try {

} catch(Exception e) {

} finally {

}
```

You can create an alternate template for this quite easily. Copy the expanded text for the trycatch abbreviation into the clipboard. In the Code Templates tab, click the New button. NetBeans displays a pop-up window that allows you to enter the new template's abbreviation. Type trycatchfinally and press the Enter key. The new abbreviation is added to the list. Paste the expanded text from the clipboard into the field at the bottom of the tab. Then modify it as follows:

```
try {
    ${cursor}
} catch (${Exception} e) {

} finally {

}
```

Creating a Code Template

Using the common code templates can prove to be very useful. However, I use many of my own custom code templates, which save me a lot of time. Much of the code I find myself rewriting is database-related. Frequently, I write a method in a class that connects to a database, performs a SQL query, and iterates through the result to do something.

As an example, suppose that you need to write a method that takes a java.sql.Connection object and an int as input variables, queries the database to retrieve some values, and returns some formatted text. You might code the following:

```
public String dbLookup(Connection conn, int Pkey) {

}
```

If you were coding this by hand, you would need to define other `java.sql` class objects, define the SQL statement, write the `java.sql.ResultSet` iteration code, and add the error handling. In NetBeans, I solve this problem by defining a code template with the abbreviation of dblookupret. Notice the prefix of db to signify a database operation. I use a naming convention for my code templates. I add the db prefix to all my code templates that perform database operations, such as select, insert, update, delete, stored procedure execution, and so on.

The expanded text for dblookupret is shown in Listing 10-1.

Listing 10-1. *Expanded Code for the dblookupret Code Abbreviation*

```
PreparedStatement pstmt = null;
ResultSet rs = null;
StringBuffer sb = new StringBuffer();

try {
        pstmt = conn.prepareStatement("SELECT COL1, COL2, COL3 FROM"
                    + " SOMETABLE WHERE INDEXCOL=?");

        pstmt.setInt(1, iPkey);
        rs = pstmt.executeQuery();
        sb = new StringBuffer();

        while(rs.hasNext()) {

                String sCol1 = rs.getString("COL1");
                String sCol2 = rs.getString("COL2");
                String sCol3 = rs.getString("COL3");

                sb.append(sCol1).append(",");
                sb.append(sCol2).append(",");
                sb.append(sCol3).append(",");
        }
} catch(Exception e) {
        // Good error handling goes here
        e.printStackTrace();
} finally {
```

```
        try {
                if(rs!=null) {
                        rs.close();
                }
                if(pstmt!=null) {
                        pstmt.close();
                }
        } catch(Exception e) { }
    }

    return sb.toString();
```

This code is obviously not perfect, but you can tailor it to your needs. For brevity, I have left out issues like proper error handling and resource cleanup.

Setting up commonly used functions as code templates can save you a lot of time, as well as help to enforce consistent coding methodologies. They should never be used in place of a good library or set of reusable classes, but they can provide a convenient place to store your commonly used code or expressions.

Code templates can be used for more than Java. They can also be defined for JSP, CSS, DTD, XML, SQL, HTML, plain text, and properties. For example, it is sometimes useful to group together commonly used pieces of SQL, such as date formatting or certain kinds of string parsing and formatting functions.

In one of my recent projects, I needed to make frequent use of the Oracle date functions. Rather than having to always look up the functions and their specific usage scenarios, I defined one slightly long SQL SELECT statement as a code template and assigned it the abbreviation sqldates. The SQL statement used most of the Oracle date functions in different ways. This way, the majority of the functions I might need would be readily available as an abbreviation. This trick can obviously be applied to HTML, XML, and CSS as well.

Summary

In this chapter, we reviewed code completion and code templates. NetBeans provides a rather intuitive method for discovering class, method, and field names or syntax. It also attempts to give hints as to the access level of the items referenced in the code completion box.

As a NetBeans user, you can customize and create code templates for several languages. This saves you time because you don't need to retype frequently used code snippets. It can also save you the hassle of having to repeatedly look up the Javadoc or the exact code syntax of a method or function. I never used to use code templates, but after a while, I got tired of telling myself it really didn't take *that* long to look up the exact syntax of some SQL function or to retype some piece of Java code.

CHAPTER 11

■■■

Refactoring

Refactoring capabilities are very important when working in the software industry. Anyone who has ever had to overhaul an existing code base has run into issues with changing code. One of the most common examples is moving classes between packages and having to manually edit the package statements at the top of each file. Another example is wanting to delete an element in code (such as a class member, an old utility method, and so on) and not knowing if code in your application still uses that element.

Manually performing these types of operations can be time-consuming and error-prone. In the days before advanced development environments, programmers used simpler tools like basic text editors, vi, or Emacs. While some of these tools allow you to search, match, and replace text, they are not Java-aware and thus produce incorrect results.

With the advanced capabilities available in IDE tools like NetBeans, developers have tool sets for refactoring code. With access to parsed source files and near-real-time syntax validation, NetBeans can intelligently allow a developer to alter source code.

In this chapter, we'll review the NetBeans refactoring options.

Using NetBeans Refactoring Options

NetBeans provides many refactoring options on its Refactor menu:

- Move Class

- Rename

- Safely Delete

- Use Supertype Where Possible

- Move Inner to Outer Level

- Encapsulate Fields

- Pull Up

- Push Down

- Convert Anonymous to Inner

- Extract Method

- Extract Interface

- Extract Superclass

- Change Method Parameters

- Query and Refactor

When you execute a refactoring operation, a dialog box appears with options for the corresponding refactoring. All of them include a Preview All Changes check box, which is selected by default.

When it comes to refactoring, no tool is perfect, so I recommend always previewing changes before applying them. As shown in Figure 11-1, the preview window allows you to review each and every change that will be made to your code before it is applied.

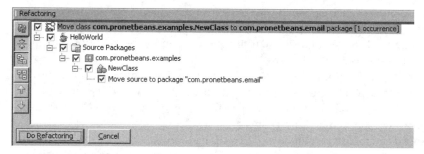

Figure 11-1. *Previewing changes for the Move Class refactoring*

The icons along the left side of the preview window let you work with the preview as follows:

- The top icon refreshes the refactoring changes listed in the window.

- The second icon collapses or expands the tree hierarchy of the changes. This can be very useful when the list of changes is long.

- The third icon displays the logical view of the refactoring actions that will be performed.

- The fourth icon displays the physical view of the refactoring actions that will be performed.

- The last two icons let you navigate up and down to each change.

As you navigate up and down the changes in the preview window, the source file opens in the Source Editor and highlights the line to be changed. This lets you examine each change if you are concerned about the validity of the refactoring. You can click the Do Refactoring button to apply the changes, or click Cancel if you don't want the changes to be made.

Now let's look at how each of the refactoring options works.

Move Class Refactoring

Moving a Java class from one package to another seems like a simple task at first glance. A developer can manually copy and paste a source file into the new directory, and then edit the package statement at the top of the file. However, if other classes import or reference that class, then the developer must also search through and modify those files as well.

In NetBeans, the Move Class refactoring does exactly as the name implies. It allows you to move a Java class to a different project, different package hierarchy, or between source and test packages. It also corrects the references to the moved class that exist in other classes.

To use the Move Class option, select a class, and then choose Refactor ➤ Move Class or use the keyboard shortcut Alt+Shift+V. You will see the Move Class dialog box, as shown in Figure 11-2. In the Move Class dialog box, you can choose to move the class to a different project, location, or package.

■**Tip** If you move one or more classes to the wrong package and apply the changes, don't panic. Most refactorings can be undone in NetBeans. From the main Refactoring menu just select the Undo option.

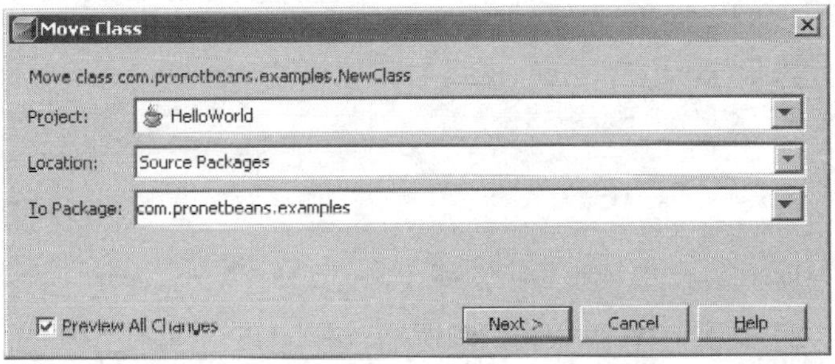

Figure 11-2. *The Move Class dialog box*

You can also activate the Move Class refactoring by dragging-and-dropping a class in the Projects window into a different location. The only difference in using the refactoring in this manner is that an additional option appears in the Move Class dialog box: Move Without Refactoring. If this option is checked, NetBeans moves the class without scanning additional classes to correct references to the moved class. You might want to use this option if you need to move a class out of a package temporarily, and move it back later. For example, while testing a package or running some analysis tool against a package, you may want to quickly exclude a class under development.

Rename Refactoring

The Rename refactoring can be used for two main purposes:

Renaming Java classes: Using the Rename refactoring will not only change the name of the class, but also any constructors, internal usages, and references to the renamed class by other classes. If you need to rename a Java class, this is definitely the way to do it.

Renaming entire package structures: This can be useful if a programmer named a package incorrectly or misspelled a word that appears in the package structure. Rather than having to manually make the corrections, the Rename option can correct the errors all at once across the entire project.

To rename a class or package, select it and choose Refactor ➤ Rename. Enter the new name in the Rename Refactoring dialog box. Figure 11-3 shows an example of the pending changes in the preview window for a Rename operation. In the example, the com.pronetbeans. examples package is being renamed to com.pronetbeans.examples2.

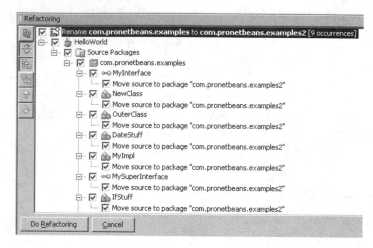

Figure 11-3. *The preview window for the Rename refactoring*

Safely Delete Refactoring

During the software development process, programmers frequently revisit previously written code. During that time, they review what was written and decide what can and cannot be cleaned up and removed. One common mistake is removing a class member variable that you think is not used, only to discover that it does indeed appear in your code, and now your class does not compile.

Using the Safely Delete refactoring, you can identify each usage of a class, method, or field in code before deleting it. This functionality can be invaluable, especially if you are removing a class method that may be used by multiple classes. For example, consider the following code fragment, which is a sample method that declares several method local variables and performs some nonsense operations.

```java
public void calc() {

    int y = 2;
    int x = 0;
    int z = 0;

    z = x + y;

    if(z>3) {
        System.out.println("Z was greater than 3");
    }
    else if(y==2){
        System.out.println("x = "  + x);
    }
}
```

During a review of this class, you decide to delete the variable x. You could visually scan the class to see if the x variable is being used anywhere. In this example, it is pretty easy to find x being output in the System.out.println statement. However, if this method were 100 lines long and contained multiple nested statements, spotting x would be much more difficult.

To execute the Safely Delete refactoring, highlight the variable you want to delete (x in the example) and select Safely Delete. In the Safely Delete dialog box, the Search in Comments check box makes sure that the element is also deleted in any Javadoc comments in which it may appear. The only other option is the standard Preview All Changes check box, allowing you to review each change before it is made.

If an element is not used anywhere in your code, it is safe to delete. However, if the element you are attempting to delete is used somewhere in your code, some additional steps may be necessary. After clicking the Next button in the initial Safely Delete dialog box, a list of errors and warnings will appear, as shown in Figure 11-4. As long as there are only warnings displayed, you can proceed with the refactoring.

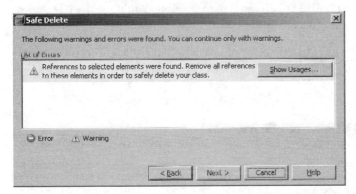

Figure 11-4. *List of errors and warnings for the Safely Delete refactoring*

If you see errors in the list, you'll need to do a bit of work. The Show Usages button is key to resolving any sections in your code that reference the variable being deleted. Click the Show Usages button to open the Usages window, as shown in Figure 11-5.

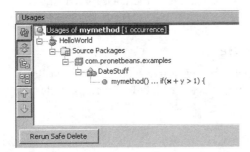

Figure 11-5. *Viewing usages of the element to delete*

The Usages window displays each usage of the element you are trying to delete. Click a usage in the window, and the exact line in the source code will open in the Source Editor window. After navigating to each usage and manually correcting the code to not use the variable being deleted, you can click the Rerun Safe Delete button.

The Safely Delete refactoring may seem like a waste of time in certain circumstances. For instance, you may not need to use it if you are deleting a local variable in a method that is five or ten lines long. It is most useful if you have a class member variable or method that is used across numerous classes. The Safely Delete option allows you to review each usage and make sure you do not delete the element until there are no more references to it.

Use Supertype Where Possible Refactoring

The Use Supertype Where Possible refactoring converts usage of a subclass to a superclass. Suppose you have the following code in a source file:

```
ArrayList myarray = new ArrayList();
```

If you want to convert it to use a specific superclass, double-click or highlight the object type ArrayList and select Refactor ➤ Use Supertype Where Possible. You'll see the Use Supertype dialog box, which allows you to select a superclass or interface, as shown in Figure 11-6.

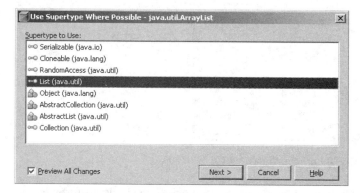

Figure 11-6. *The Use Supertype Where Possible dialog box for java.util.ArrayList*

Obviously, this is a ridiculously simple example, but it demonstrates the core functionality. This method can also be used in conjunction with the Extract Superclass refactoring, described later in this chapter.

Move Inner to Outer Level Refactoring

The Move Inner to Outer Level refactoring converts an inner class to a separate external class declared in its own file. Suppose you have the following code, in which the InnerClass class is declared inside the OuterClass class.

```
public class OuterClass {
    public class InnerClass {
        public void execute() {
            System.out.println("execute...");
        }
    }
}
```

To move the InnerClass class to its own source file, highlight the class name and select Refactor ➤ Move Inner to Outer Level. In the Move Inner to Outer Level dialog box, you can specify a new name for the class that is being moved, as shown in Figure 11-7. This can be convenient, especially since inner classes are often named to make sense within the context of the containing outer class. Optionally, you can select to declare a field for the current outer class and enter a name for that field.

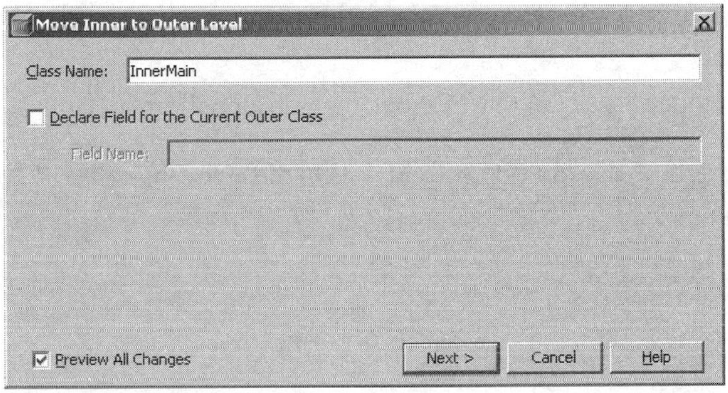

Figure 11-7. *The Move Inner to Outer Level dialog box*

If you apply the refactoring using the default settings, when you click the Next button, the code that results is as follows:

```
public class InnerClass {
    public void execute() {
        System.out.println("execute…");
    }
}
```

The InnerClass code is moved to its own individual source file of the same name in the same package as OuterClass.

If you select the Declare Field for the Current Outer Class option and name a variable, the refactored code looks like this:

```
public class InnerClass {

    private final OutClass myvar;

    public void execute(OuterClass newvar) {
        this.newvar = newvar;

        System.out.println("execute...");
    }
}
```

This option can be useful when separating the classes, especially if the InnerClass class used the members or methods of the OuterClass class.

Encapsulate Fields Refactoring

When writing applications, it is often useful to represent objects in the real world as classes with attributes. For example, you may choose to represent the fields for an employee as an Employee class with first name and last name public members:

```
public class Employee {
    public String FirstName;
    public String LastName;
}
```

Of course, you might also include address, phone number, organizational, and personal fields in the class.

Such an Employee class is quick and easy to work with, such as in the following code:

```
public class NewHire {
    public static void main(String[] args) {
        Employee newemp = new Employee();
        newemp.FirstName = args[0];
        newemp.LastName = args[1];
        saveEmployee(newemp);
    }
}
```

In the NewHire class, an instance of Employee is instantiated and the FirstName and LastName fields are set from the arguments passed on the command line. (Obviously, there are a lot of problems with the code in the NewHire class, such as no parameter or error checking, but here we are just focusing on the topic of encapsulation.)

As a programmer, you should be starting to realize this approach has some negative design features. For example, suppose your client has requested that the employee name be stored in the database with initial capital letters, such as John Smith. However, in the application, the values need to be processed in uppercase. You could rewrite the entire application to add the usage of String.toUpperCase() anywhere the Employee.FirstName and Employee.LastName fields are output or processed throughout the entire code base. You could also encapsulate the fields.

Encapsulation involves controlling access to a class member variable using getter and setter methods. The class member variable is set to private, so that no code outside the class can interact with it. The getter and setter methods are usually given a public accessor, so that any code can retrieve or set the value of the member variable.

In the following code, the Employee class has been modified to use getters and setters for the FirstName and LastName member variables.

```
public class Employee {
    private String FirstName;
    private String LastName;

    public void setFirstName(String FirstName) {
        this.FirstName = FirstName;
    }
```

```
    public String getFirstName() {
        return this.FirstName;
    }

    public void setLastName(String LastName) {
        this.LastName = LastName;
    }

    public String getLastName() {
        return this.LastName;
    }
}
```

You can also modify the code in the NewHire class to interact with the updated Employee class. The NewHire class must now use the getter and setter methods.

```
public class NewHire {
    public static void main(String[] args) {

        Employee newemp = new Employee();
        newemp.setFirstName(args[0]);
        newemp.setLastName(args[1]);

        saveEmployee(newemp);
    }
}
```

Using this type of design, you are in a better position to modify the code to handle special conditions. In the example, the code in the Employee class can be modified to convert the member variables to uppercase when they are set using Employee.setFirstName and Employee.setLastName.

```
public class Employee {
    private String FirstName;
    private String LastName;

    public void setFirstName(String FirstName) {
        if(FirstName!=null) {
            this.FirstName = FirstName.toUpperCase();
        } else {
            this.FirstName = null;
        }
    }

    public String getFirstName() {
        return this.FirstName;
    }
```

```
    public void setLastName(String LastName) {
        if(LastName!=null) {
            this.LastName = LastName.toUpperCase();
        } else {
            this.LastName = null;
        }
    }

    public String getLastName() {
        return this.LastName;
    }
}
```

Note It is usually preferable to perform any data conversion, checking, or modification in the setter method for a member variable, rather than in the getter method. If the data conversion is implemented in the getter, each time the data is retrieved, the data conversion will take place, thus slightly reducing performance.

Generally, it is a common best practice to never have a public member of a class for which you write other code to set or get the value. Arguably, the only exception to the rule is using static constants.

Now that you have read a quick review of a key object-oriented concept, we can discuss how NetBeans can assist in encapsulation. (I apologize to those of you groaning about now, but this is one of the most frequent mistakes I see programmers make, so it deserves some review.)

The Encapsulate Fields refactoring in NetBeans allows you to easily implement the design paradigm of encapsulation. It helps you to generate getter and setter methods for the members of a class to enforce good design.

Suppose you have the simple Employee class shown at the beginning of this section:

```
public class Employee {
    public String FirstName;
    public String LastName;
}
```

If you highlight the name of the class and select Refactor ➤ Encapsulate Fields, the Encapsulate Fields dialog box will list all the class fields, all selected by default. If you highlight specific class fields and select the Encapsulate Fields option, the dialog box will still display the entire list of fields in the class, but only the field or fields you highlighted will be selected by default. For example, if you highlighted the FirstName and LastName fields (the entire line for each field), the dialog box will list both the fields, as shown in Figure 11-8.

You can disable or enable creation of the getter and setter methods using the check boxes next to each one. In this dialog box, you can also manually alter the names of the getter and setter methods. The Fields' Visibility and Accessors' Visibility drop-down lists allow you to set the access level to the original fields (should be private) and to the getters and setters (should be public), respectively.

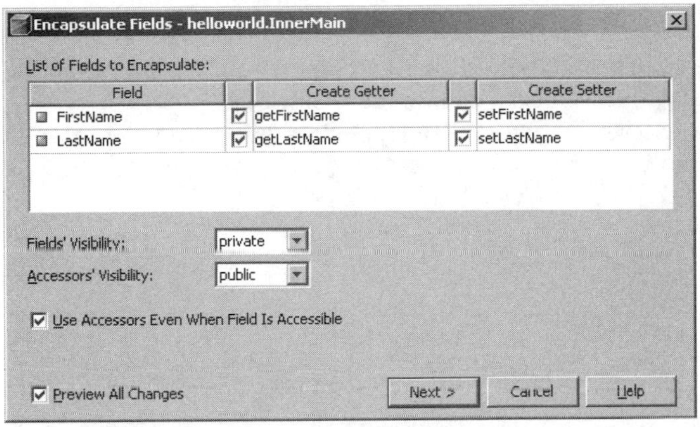

Figure 11-8. *The Encapsulate Fields dialog box*

In my opinion, the Use Accessors Even When Field is Accessible option should always remain checked. Then the refactoring procedure attempts to correct code in other classes that use the class member variables and convert it to use the accessors (getters and setters). The only time you might want to disable this option is when you set the Fields' Visibility option to anything other than private. The refactoring will then perform the Encapsulate Fields operation, but will not convert code to use the accessors.

Once the overall refactoring is complete, the Employee class should look like this:

```
public class Employee {
    private String FirstName;
    private String LastName;

    public String getFirstName()
    {
        return FirstName;
    }

    public void setFirstName(String FirstName)
    {
        this.FirstName = FirstName;
    }

    public String getLastName()
    {
        return LastName;
    }

    public void setLastName(String LastName)
    {
        this.LastName = LastName;
    }
}
```

Pull Up Refactoring

The Pull Up refactoring is useful when dealing with classes and superclasses. It allows you to move class members and methods from a subclass up into the superclass.

For example, suppose you have a Vehicle class and a Truck class that extends Vehicle:

```
public class Vehicle
{
    public void start()
    {
        // start the vehicle
    }
}

public class Truck extends Vehicle
{
    public void stop()
    {
        // stop the vehicle
    }
}
```

If you want to move the stop() method from the Truck subclass to the Vehicle superclass, select the stop() method and select Refactor ➤ Pull Up. In the Pull Up dialog box, select the destination supertype, the exact list of members to pull up, and whether or not to make them abstract, as shown in Figure 11-9.

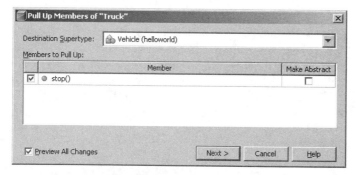

Figure 11-9. *The Pull Up dialog box*

Once the refactoring changes have been applied, the Truck and Vehicle classes look like this:

```
public class Vehicle
{
    public void start()
    {
        // start the vehicle
    }
```

```
    public void stop()
    {
        // stop the vehicle
    }
}

public class Truck extends Vehicle
{
}
```

Push Down Refactoring

The Push Down refactoring is exactly the opposite of the Pull Up refactoring. It pushes an inner class, field, or method in a superclass down into a subclass. For example, suppose that you added a lowerTailgate() method to the Vehicle class shown in the previous example:

```
public class Vehicle
{
    public void start()
    {
        // start the vehicle
    }

    public void stop()
    {
        // stop the vehicle
    }

    public void lowerTailgate()
    {
        // lower tailgate of vehicle
    }
}

public class Truck extends Vehicle
{
}
```

However, since many vehicles (such as cars, planes, and boats) do not have tailgates, you want to push the lowerTailgate() method down to the Truck subclass.

Select the lowerTailgate() method and choose Refactor ➤ Push Down. In the Push Down dialog box, select which class members you want to push down into the subclass, as shown in Figure 11-10. You can also choose whether you would like to keep them abstract if they already are abstract.

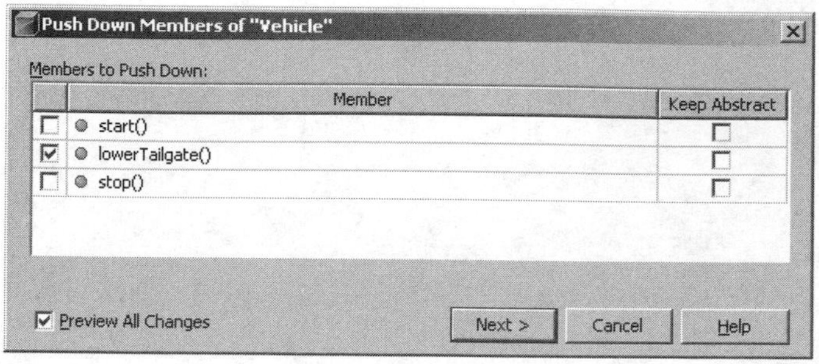

Figure 11-10. *The Push Down dialog box*

After you have applied the code changes, you can view the result. As expected, the `lowerTailgate()` method will now be in the `Truck` subclass.

```
public class Truck extends Vehicle
{
    public void lowerTailgate()
    {
        // do something
    }
}
```

If the superclass has multiple subclasses (which is usually the case), you could still perform a Push Down refactoring of a method from a particular class. For example, if you had a `Car` subclass that extended `Vehicle`, you could still push down a method from the `Vehicle` class. Suppose the `Truck`, `Car`, and `Vehicle` classes were defined as follows:

```
public class Vehicle
{
    public void changeTire()
    {
        // general method for changing tire
    }
}

public class Car extends Vehicle
{
    // car class
}

public class Truck extends Vehicle
{
    // truck class
}
```

The Truck class represents a large tractor-trailer. Changing a tire for this type of vehicle will most likely involve a different procedure than for a car. Thus, you might want to have the changeTire() method in the Car and Truck classes override the one in the Vehicle superclass. The changeTire() method in the Vehicle class should also be left as abstract (even though some vehicles, like boats, do not have tires that need changing).

In the Push Down dialog box, you need to select the check box to keep the changeTire() method abstract in the Vehicle class. Preview the changes to make sure the code is modified as you expect. In Figure 11-11, notice the third suggested operation is altering Vehicle.changeTire() to make it abstract. If the Keep Abstract option is not selected during the refactoring operation, then the line in the preview window would say "Remove changeTire() element." You could prevent it from being removed from the Vehicle class by unselecting the check box next to this option.

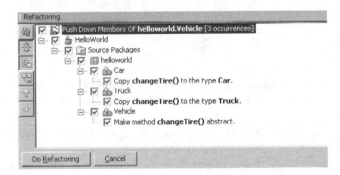

Figure 11-11. *Push Down refactoring with one superclass and two subclasses*

Convert Anonymous to Inner Refactoring

The Convert Anonymous to Inner refactoring is used to separate an anonymous inner class into an actual inner class. There are several varieties of anonymous inner classes:

- Inner class for defining and instantiating an instance of an unnamed subclass

- Inner class for defining and instantiating an anonymous implementation of an interface

- Anonymous inner class defined as an argument to a method

For this section, we will focus on the first type: unnamed subclasses. Suppose you have the following code:

```java
public class Item {
    public void assemble() {
        System.out.println("Item.assemble");
    }
}
```

```
public class Factory {
    public void makeStandardItem(int type) {
        if(type==0) {
            // make extremely unusual item .01% of the time
            Item myitem = new Item() {
                public void assemble() {
                    System.out.println("anonymous Item.assemble");
                }
            };
            myitem.assemble();
        } else {
            // make standard item 99.9% of the time
            Item myitem = new Item();
            myitem.assemble();
        }
    }
}
```

The code declares a class Item with a method named assemble(). The Factory class defines a variable myitem of type Item and instantiates an anonymous subclass of Item that overrides the assemble() method.

Why would you bother using an anonymous inner class instead of a normal inner or outer class? In this example, if the one-off case where the anonymous inner class is used were the only area it is needed, you might not want to create a separate class. However, if you find that you need the code in the anonymous subclass in multiple areas, you might want to convert it to an inner class.

To convert the code to an inner class, click anywhere inside the anonymous class or highlight the name of the Item class constructor in the following section of the code:

```
Item myitem = new Item() {
    public void assemble() {
        System.out.println("anonymous Item.assemble");
    }
};
```

Then select Refactor ➤ Convert Anonymous Class to Inner. In the Convert Anonymous Class to Inner dialog box, you'll see the default class name of NewClass, as shown in Figure 11-12. You can set the name of the new inner class that will be created, the access level, and whether it should be declared static. If the constructor for the anonymous class has any parameters, the dialog box will also list them.

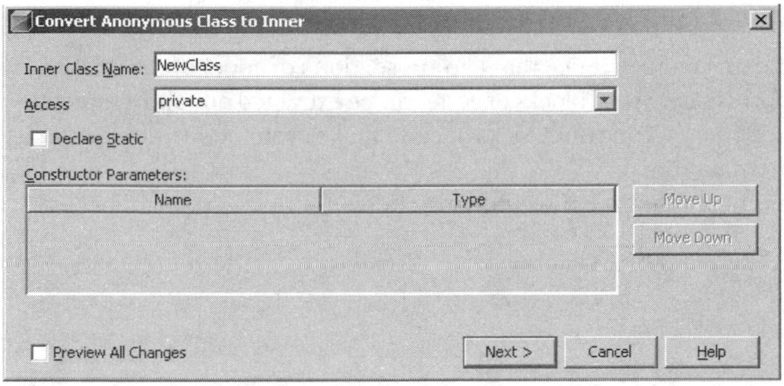

Figure 11-12. *The Convert Anonymous Class to Inner dialog box*

Suppose you named the new inner class StrangeItem. The refactored code would look like this:

```
private class StrangeItem extends Item {

    public void assemble() {
        System.out.println("anonymous item.assemble");
    }
}
```

This class would be declared inside the Factory class, since that is where the original anonymous inner class resides.

In the following code, notice that the creation of the anonymous inner class has been altered to create an instance of the new inner class.

```
public void makeStandardItem(int type) {
    if(type==0) {
        // make extremely unusual item .01% of the time
        Item myitem = new StrangeItem();
        myitem.assemble();
    } else {
        // make standard item 99.9% of the time
        Item myitem = new Item();
        myitem.assemble();
    }
}
```

The purpose of using this refactoring is to make your code more reusable and modular. Extracting the anonymous inner class into its own inner class helps improve many aspects of your code. It makes no sense to redefine the same anonymous inner class in multiple places in the Factory class, and the Convert Anonymous to Inner refactoring can help correct the situation.

Extract Method Refactoring

As you review code in a project, you may notice that certain sections of code, even small ones, contain similar looking blocks of code. These blocks of code can be extracted out into a separate method that can then be called. Separating out blocks of code makes your code more readable, more reusable, and easier to maintain.

As a simple example, suppose you have the following code:

```java
public void processArray(String[] names)
{
    for(int i=0;i < names.length; i++)
    {
        names[i] = names[i].toUpperCase();
    }
    // rest of method here
}
```

This block of code contains a loop that iterates through a String array and converts each String to uppercase. You might want to put this code into a separate method. The Extract Method refactoring can do this for you.

To activate the refactoring, highlight the code you want to convert to a method and select Refactor ➤ Extract Method. In this example, highlight the entire for loop in the processArray(String[]) method.

In the Extract Method dialog box, you can set the name of the new method, the access level, and whether it should be declared static, as shown in Figure 11-13. The refactoring is even smart enough to assume that a String array should be passed into the method and lists it as a parameter for the new method.

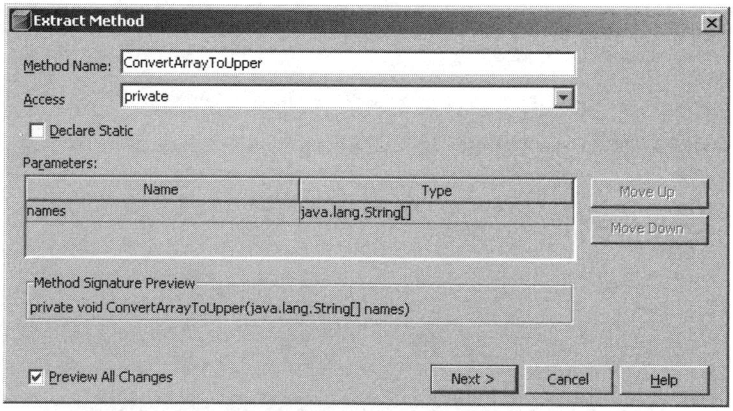

Figure 11-13. *The Extract Method dialog box*

After applying the refactoring, the resulting code has the loop split out:

```
public void processArray(String[] names)
{
    ConvertArrayToUpper(names);
    // other method code here
}

private void ConvertArrayToUpper(final String[] names)
{
    for(int i=0;i < names.length; i++)
    {
        names[i] = names[i].toUpperCase();
    }
}
```

You can see that not only has the selected code been extracted out into a separate method, but it was also replaced with the correct call to the new method with the correct parameter.

Extract Interface Refactoring

The Extract Interface refactoring allows you to select public non-static methods and move them into an interface. This can be useful as you attempt to make your code more reusable and easier to maintain.

For example, suppose that you want to extract two public non-static methods in the following Item class into an interface.

```
public class Item {
    public void assemble() {
        System.out.println("Item.assemble");
    }

    public void sell() {
        System.out.println("sell me");
    }
}
```

You can activate the refactoring by highlighting the class in the Projects window (or by simply having the class open in the Source Editor) and selecting Refactor ➤ Extract Interface.

As shown in Figure 11-14, the options for the Extract Interface refactoring are quite straightforward. You can specify the name of the new interface that will be created. You can also select exactly which methods you want to include in the interface.

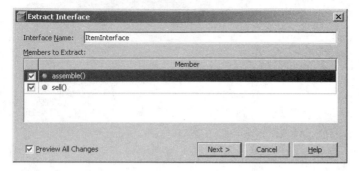

Figure 11-14. *The Extract Interface dialog box*

After applying the refactoring, the code for the interface looks like this:

```
public interface ItemInterface {
    void assemble();
    void sell();
}

public class Item implements ItemInterface {
    public void assemble() {
        System.out.println("Item.assemble");
    }

    public void sell() {
        System.out.println("sell me");
    }
}
```

The original Item class has been modified to implement the ItemInterface.

Extract Superclass Refactoring

The Extract Superclass refactoring is nearly identical to the Extract Interface refactoring. The only difference is that Extract Superclass pulls methods into a newly created superclass and extends the refactored class. Using the refactored code from the previous section as an example, you might want to modify the Item class to have a superclass.

```
public class Item implements ItemInterface {
    public void assemble() {
        System.out.println("Item.assemble");
    }

    public void sell() {
        System.out.println("sell me");
    }
}
```

Starting with the Item class selected, select Refactor ➤ Extract Superclass. As shown in Figure 11-15, the Extract Superclass dialog box allows you to set the name of the new super-class that will be created. You can select which members you wish to extract and place them in the superclass. Since the Item class implements the ItemInterface, you can decide if you want to extract the implements clause into the superclass. You can also select whether or not the methods that are extracted are made abstract in the superclass. Selecting this option inserts abstract methods into the superclass and leaves the concrete implementations in the Item subclass.

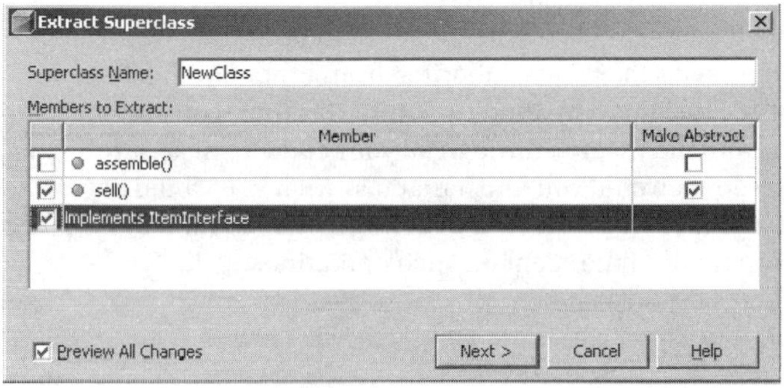

Figure 11-15. *The Extract Superclass dialog box*

For this example, select all the members for extraction. Then select the Make Abstract field only for the Item.sell() method. Preview the changes and apply the refactoring. The following code will be generated:

```java
public interface ItemInterface {
    void assemble();
    void sell();
}

public abstract class ItemSuperclass implements ItemInterface {

    public void assemble() {
        System.out.println("Item.assemble");
    }

    public abstract void sell();
}

public class Item extends ItemSuperclass {

    public void sell() {
        System.out.println("sell me");
    }
}
```

Now you have an Item class with a concrete implementation of the sell() method. It extends the ItemSuperclass. ItemSuperclass implements ItemInterface, and contains an abstract sell() method and a concrete implementation of the assemble() method. ItemInterface contains the definitions of the assemble() and sell() methods.

Using refactoring options like Extract Method, Extract Interface, and Extract Superclass, you can attempt to structure your code to take full advantage of good design principles. Ideally, for new code projects, you would design classes correctly and wouldn't need refactoring. However, many programmers take over projects that have been implemented poorly and need refactoring.

Change Method Parameters Refactoring

The Change Method Parameters refactoring is one of the most useful options in NetBeans. I have made extensive use of it on projects that I have inherited from other developers.

In the old days of development, changing a method signature was time-consuming. You would need to modify the method and then search through all your code to make sure all the references to it were updated. No sooner would you finish that task then you would decide to change the data types on the arguments or rearrange their ordering in the method. The Change Method Parameters refactoring can reduce time spent on such operations.

Suppose you had the following code:

```java
public class Item extends ItemSuperclass {

    public void sell() {
        System.out.println("sell me");

        System.out.println("Price(12345) : " + findPrice(12345));
    }

    public double findPrice(long itemNumber) {

        double price = 0.00;
        // look up itemNumber in database and set price variable
        return price;
    }
}
```

The Item class contains a findPrice(long) method. The method accepts an item number, looks it up in a database, and returns a price to the calling sell() method. If your client decided he wants to also be able to return the price and the currency in which it is specified, you would need to alter the findPrice(long) method.

Assume you need to add a String argument to the findPrice(long) method that allows you to specify the type of currency. Highlight the name of the method and select Refactor ➤ Change Method Parameters. In the Change Method Parameters dialog box, you can add and remove parameters to the method. You can also change the order of the parameters and specify the method's new access level.

■**Tip** You don't have to actually alter the parameters of a method to reorder them. You can use the Change Method Parameters refactoring just to reorder parameters—a task I find myself doing often when I am developing code.

To add the new parameter, click the Add button. A new line appears in the parameters grid. Change the name, type, and default value fields, as shown in Figure 11-16. Then click the Next button, preview the changes, and apply the refactoring.

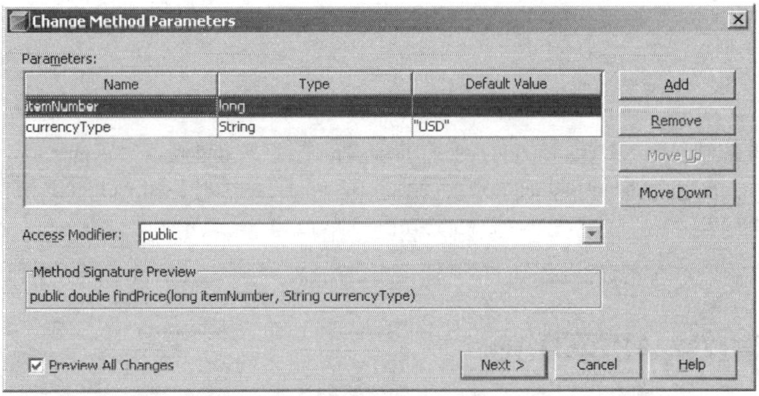

Figure 11-16. *The Change Method Parameters dialog box*

Your refactored code will look like this:

```
public class Item extends ItemSuperclass {

    public void sell() {
        System.out.println("sell me");

        System.out.println("Price(12345) : " + findPrice(12345, "USD"));
    }

    public double findPrice(long itemNumber, String currencyType) {

        double price = 0.00;
        // look up itemNumber in database and set price variable
        return price;
    }
}
```

Notice that the findPrice(long) method has been altered to include the new parameter. The sell() method has also been altered to call the modified method and pass it the default value of "USD", which was specified during the refactoring operation.

Refactoring Keyboard Shortcuts

At the time of this writing, NetBeans provides only three refactoring keyboard shortcuts, as listed in Table 11-1.

Table 11-1. *Refactoring Keyboard Shortcuts*

Option	Shortcut
Move Class	Alt+Shift+V
Rename	Alt+Shift+R
Extract Method	Ctrl+Shift+M

■**Tip** You can add your own shortcut for each refactoring option by selecting Tools ➤ Options ➤ Keymap ➤ Refactor. Make sure to explore the existing key mappings to get an idea of what is already used. NetBeans will prevent duplicates from being added.

Refactoring with Jackpot

The Jackpot project was announced by Sun at the JavaOne 2006 conference. For NetBeans 5.0 and 5.5, it is a separate module that needs to be installed. As of NetBeans 6.0, the Jackpot refactoring engine is more tightly integrated with the IDE.

Jackpot provides an impressive set of refactoring capabilities. It is not just a refactoring engine, but provides type-aware modeling, querying, and transformation of Java source files. Jackpot queries can run against large bases of Java source and intelligently manipulate elements, all while maintaining the original code formatting. While this sounds simple, it is actually quite an advanced set of capabilities that makes Jackpot unique. It does not simply use a parsed model of the data, but integrates tightly with the information provided by the Java compiler `javac`.

Adding a Jackpot Refactoring Query

The main way to interface with Jackpot is to write queries in the Jackpot rule language. Written by James Gosling, this rule language is similar to Java's regular expression library, but is type- and Java semantic-aware. Here is the general format of a Jackpot query:

```
pattern expression    =>    replacement expression :: guard/filter expression;
```

The pattern expression is the element or expression you want to attempt to replace. It should be no surprise that the replacement expression is what you want to replace it with. The guard expression is used to match the pattern expression and provide type-aware filtering of matched results. If the guard expression is satisfied, the pattern is substituted with the replacement expression.

You can also use meta-variables to provide wildcard matching in your query expression. A meta-variable is simply a regular Java identifier preceded by a $ character.

Another element of a Jackpot query is a meta-list. A meta-list is essentially the same as a meta-variable, but a meta-list starts and ends with the $ character. Meta-lists also allow more than one expression to be matched.

These topics can be a little confusing at first, but you can go online and read more about Jackpot at the official site, `http://jackpot.netbeans.org/`.

Let's start with a simple example. The following is an old piece of date formatting code I once found in an application:

```
Date objStartDate = new Date();
String sDate = objStartDate.toLocaleString();
System.out.println("Date is : " + sDate);
```

In this code fragment, the developer defined and instantiated an instance of the Date class. A String representation of the system local date was then retrieved and written to the standard output stream. The only problem with this code is that the toLocaleString() method is deprecated as of JDK 1.1. It has since been replaced by DateFormat.format(Date).

If you were a developer who was tasked with updating this entire project so it did not use deprecated elements, you could start by adding a Jackpot query through the Refactoring Manager. The Refactoring Manager is the main user interface for working with Jackpot query sets, or groups of related queries, as shown in Figure 11-17. You can open it by selecting Tools ➤ Refactoring Manager.

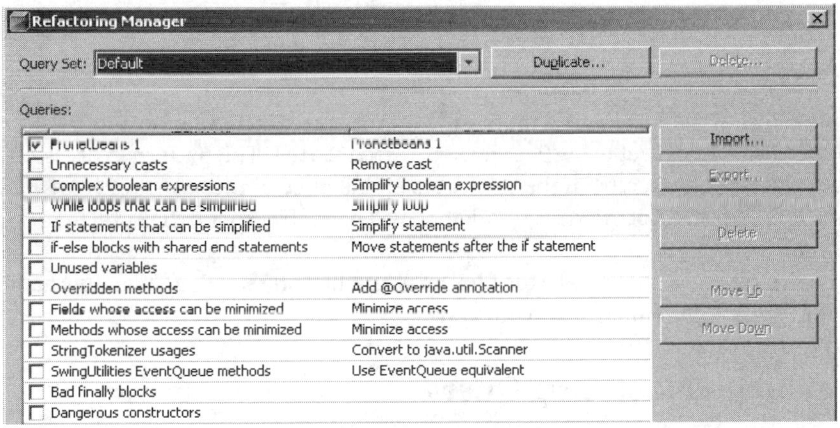

Figure 11-17. *The Jackpot Refactoring Manager*

Initially, Jackpot has two query sets: Default and Effective Java Items. Select a query set to see its queries listed in the Refactoring Manager.

You can create your own set of queries by clicking the Duplicate button next to the query set name and assigning a name to the new query set. Then you can add, edit, and delete queries in whatever manner you wish.

To add a new query, click the New Query button. Fill in the query name, refactoring name, and description, as shown in Figure 11-18.

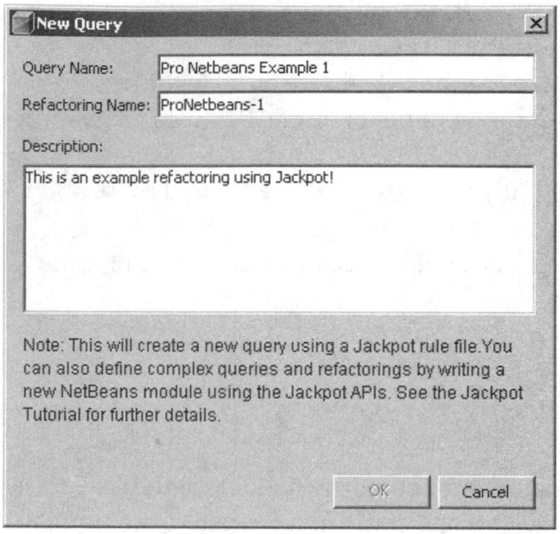

Figure 11-18. *The Jackpot New Query dialog box*

Once you click the OK button, the query name is added to the list in the Refactoring Manager. To actually add the query rule, highlight the query name and click the Edit Query button. At this point, a new code window will open in the Source Editor. The name of the file open in the Source Editor is the name you assigned in the New Query dialog box (Pro NetBeans Example 1 in the example in Figure 11-18), with the file extension of .rules (Pro NetBeans Example 1.rules).

Enter the query expression you would like the new query to contain, such as the following:

```
$object.toLocaleString() => java.text.DateFormat.format($object) :: ➡
$object instanceof java.util.Date;
```

This query rule replaces the deprecated method Date.toLocaleString() with a more correct way to format the Date object using DateFormat.format(Date). The pattern expression to search for is $object.toLocaleString. If the $object is an instance of the java.util.Date class, the fragments that use the toLocaleString() method will be replaced with the DateFormat.format(Date) method.

After you've entered the query rule, save the file and close the code window. You now have a valid Jackpot query that can be run against your code.

Running a Jackpot Refactoring Query

To use Jackpot refactoring, with a Java project open and selected, choose Refactoring ➤ Query and Refactor. In the Query and Refactor dialog box, you can choose to apply an entire query set or just a single query to the project code. Select the query and click the Query button.

Jackpot then runs the refactoring query against your code. If no results are found, a status message appears in the lower-left status bar. If the query matched code in your project, you'll see a list of pending changes. None of the refactorings are applied until you click the Do Refactoring button.

Click the Do Refactoring button to apply the changes. Once the refactoring has been executed, you can review the source code. The example shown at the beginning of this section would now look like this:

```
Date objStartDate = new Date();
String sDate = DateFormat.format(objStartDate);
System.out.println("Date is : " + sDate);
```

This is a very simple example. You can use Jackpot queries to refactor poorly designed code and help apply good design principles to your project.

As you become more experienced with Jackpot, you will find it easier to write query rules to scan for bad sections of code. The benefits of this refactoring capability are well worth the time you spend learning the Jackpot rule language and writing queries.

Summary

In this chapter, you saw the wide variety of refactoring options available in the NetBeans IDE. You can use them to rework existing code or to make your new coding smoother.

Some of these refactorings will obviously be used more often than others, but you should become familiar with when and how to use each one. Using these refactoring options when working with large code bases can be a lifesaver.

PART 3

NetBeans and Professional Software Development

CHAPTER 12

Generating and Accessing Javadoc

One of the most important aspects of writing code is documentation. Project documentation should not only cover system design, architecture, and logic, but also include details on how each class and method functions. The Java platform provides a very useful documentation tool called *Javadoc*.

The Javadoc tool scans source code and extracts special types of comments to create a bundle of HTML files. These files are linked together in a cross-referenced documentation web site commonly referred to by programmers as *Javadoc* or the *project Javadoc*. Developers traditionally generate this Javadoc bundle and store it with the rest of their project documentation.

Future project developers can then use the Javadoc as a quick reference for the functionality of the code. It is also useful to project architects and project managers who want a handle on what code does without having to read through the actual source.

This chapter describes the NetBeans features for creating and working with Javadoc.

Elements of Javadoc

Adding Javadoc comments to source code is extremely simple. You can use a variety of special documentation elements or tags that the Javadoc tool will recognize as having special meaning. During the generation of the HTML files, these special elements are formatted and marked for each Java member for which they are provided.

The following sections provide a quick overview of the main elements used in writing Javadoc. This is not a complete list, of course, but covers the elements you will probably use most often.

Class Description

The first Javadoc element that should be written for a class is the overall class description. The first sentence of this description should be as brief and direct as possible. The Javadoc tool will insert the first sentence from the class description into the index page for each package that lists the classes it contains.

The entire class description can be as brief or detailed as you feel is necessary. There are no rules or best practices regarding the length of class descriptions. You should attempt to describe the overall purpose and function of the class. Some programmers provide sample usage code in the class description that can serve as a type of user manual.

Here is an example of a class description in Javadoc:

```
package com.pronetbeans.chapters;

/**
 * Utility class for representing static constant color values.
 * The color constants used in this class are string representations
 * of HTML color codes.
 */
public class ColorConstants {
    // code for class here
}
```

Notice that the first line starts with the characters /**. This is how you flag a comment as a Javadoc comment, and not just as a regular comment. The last line ends with the characters */. The asterisks in between are optional as of Java 1.4, but are usually added to provide a consistent visual flow.

Class Tags

The following are some class tags commonly used in Javadoc:

@author: Specifies who wrote the class. Multiple @author tags are allowed. The text for the author of a class can be just a name or include an email address, web site URL, or other contact information. You can format the information that is displayed using the HTML <br> tag.

@version: Specifies the version of the class. Certain source code repositories allow you to use wildcard variables in this field, so that when the code is checked out, the actual version and date can be inserted in place of the wildcard variables.

@since: Specifies the version of the code in which this class was added. This can be useful if you are writing an actual API that others programmers will use. As your API evolves over time, it is important to note in which version a specific class was added.

@see: Allows you to include a reference to an element in the class or another Java class or package. You can link directly to a specific method or to a section in the Javadoc.

Note NetBeans does not include the @author and @version tags by default during the generation of a project's Javadoc. To include the tags, you need to edit the properties of a project. In the Project Properties window's Categories list, select the Documenting option. The check boxes for including the @author and @version tags are listed under the heading Document Additional Tags.

The following shows the class tags added to the sample Javadoc in the previous section:

```
package com.pronetbeans.chapters;

/**
 * Utility class for representing static constant color values.
 * The color constants used in this class are string representations
 * of HTML color codes.
 *
 * @author John Doe<br>john.doe@somesite.com<br>John Doe Consulting
 * @author Jane Doe
 * @version 1.45
 * @since 2.1.0
 * @see com.pronetbeans.chapters
 */
public class ColorConstants {
    // code for class here
}
```

Class Member Variables

Each member variable defined in a class should have a matching Javadoc statement. Public member variables usually represent some type of constant and thus should have a full description explaining how to use them. The following shows the ColorConstants class in an abbreviated form. Notice that each member variable has a description.

```
public class ColorConstants {

    /** The HTML code for the color blue. */
    public static final String BLUE = "#0000FF";

    /** The HTML code for the color red. */
    public static final String RED = "#FF0000";

}
```

Constructors

Javadoc descriptions can also be added for constructors. For constructors that have parameters, the description should include what effect the parameters might have on the state of the object as it is instantiated.

If a constructor has a parameter, you can use the @param Javadoc tag to describe it. The @param tag should be followed by a space, the name of the parameter, another space, and the description of the parameter, as in this example:

```
public class ColorConstants {

    /** Default constructor */
    public ColorContstants() {

    }

    /** This constructor allows the debug mode to be enabled or disabled.
     *
     * @param debug true if logging should be enabled, false otherwise.
     */
    public ColorConstants(boolean debug) {
        // do something with the debug variable
    }
}
```

Methods

Javadoc for class methods is probably the most common type of documentation you will write as a programmer. A method has a description just like a class, member variable, and a constructor. The first sentence of the description is listed in the method summary section.

Method Javadoc can also include tags for the method parameters, method return type, and any exceptions that the method may throw, as follows:

@param: Describes a method's parameter. The @param tag should be followed by a space, the name of the parameter, another space, and the description of the parameter. If there are multiple parameters in a method definition, use multiple @param tags.

@return: Documents the return type of a method. The @return tag is used to specify the description of the parameter being returned to the calling code. A method can have only one return parameter, so only one @return tag is valid. Methods with a return type of void do not need a @return tag.

@throws: Describes an exception thrown by a method. You must use one @throws tag per exception. This lets programmers know what type of exceptions to expect to have to handle in their code.

Here is an example of Javadoc for a method:

```
public class ColorConstants {

    /**
     * Retrieve a list of all color code constants.
     *
     * @param filter A filter value to retrieve color codes that match.
     * @return An ArrayList of the color code values.
     * @throws NullPointerException If the filter parameter is null.
     */
```

```
    public ArrayList listColorCodes(String filter)
        throws NullPointerException, NumberFormatException {

        // do something

    }
}
```

Creating Javadoc in NetBeans

In NetBeans, you can write Javadoc directly in a source file in the Source Editor window. One of the nice features that the editor provides is the ability for Javadoc comments to utilize code folding. Sections of Javadoc can be collapsed and expanded for ease of viewing.

■Tip Javadoc for certain classes can be quite long. Sometimes when you are developing, it can visually get in your way. You can fix this with the menu option View ➤ Code Folds ➤ Collapse All Javadoc. You can also set Javadoc to be collapsed by default by choosing Tools ➤ Options ➤ Editor and selecting the Javadoc Comments field.

Using the Auto Comment Tool

Rather than manually editing Javadoc in the Source Editor, you can use the NetBeans Auto Comment tool. As shown in Figure 12-1, this tool provides a GUI for editing Javadoc comments and tags. The Auto Comment tool not only allows you to add, edit, and remove tags, but it also helps you to identify code that does not contain Javadoc.

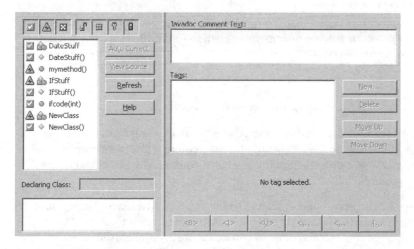

Figure 12-1. *The Auto Comment tool*

To open the Auto Comment tool, highlight a class or package and select Tools ➤ Auto Comment. You can also right-click a class or package and select Tools ➤ Auto Comment.

On the left side of the Auto Comment window is a list of the classes, methods, and other Java elements. Above the list is an icon bar with options for filtering the list. The first three icons filter for completeness of the element's Javadoc. Javadoc is considered complete if all the standard tags and descriptions have been added. Otherwise, it is considered partially complete. The other four icons filter the Java elements based on the access level of each element—public, package, protected, or private. Table 12-1 describes the filtering options.

Table 12-1. *Icons for Filtering Classes in the Auto Comment Tool*

Icon	Description
	Displays compliant class and members with full Javadoc. If the Auto Comment tool finds all the relevant tags for an element filled out, the Javadoc is considered complete for that element.
	Displays classes and members with partial or erroneous Javadoc. If the Auto Comment tool finds some tags filled out and others missing, the Javadoc is considering partially complete. For example, if a method has two parameters and only one @param tag is used, the Javadoc is considered partial.
	Indicates classes and members without any Javadoc. The Auto Comment tool will flag an element as having no Javadoc if no Javadoc tags are defined. This can help you quickly locate areas of your source code that have poor documentation and target them for improvement.
	Displays classes and members with a public access level. It is a best practice to always include detailed and complete Javadoc for any public class, member, or method.
	Displays classes and members with a package access level. Toggling this icon will display or hide Java elements with an access level of package.
	Displays classes and members with a protected access level. Elements with a protected access level are usually not included in Javadoc, but it is always important to write Javadoc for them anyway.
	Displays inner classes, class members, and class methods with a private access level. Displaying this level is used for documenting elements that will most likely not be included in the overall project Javadoc.

To the right of the list of Java elements are several useful buttons:

- The Auto Correct button will be active when you select an element from the list that has no Javadoc. Clicking the Auto Correct button for an element will add an empty description comment, as well as define the tags the element requires. The actual text in the tags is left blank for you to fill in.

- The View Source button allows you to select an element from the list and jump directly to where it is declared in the source code. This is useful if you want to manually edit the Javadoc or examine what a method does so you can write accurate Javadoc.

- The Refresh button will refresh the list of elements and their associated flags (complete, partial, or none), in case you changed Javadoc directly in the source.

The lower-left portion of the Auto Comment window is an informational area that tells you two important pieces of data: the first field is the declaring class in which the element you have selected belongs, and the second is exact details as to what is missing from the Javadoc for the element. Using this information, you can add the required Javadoc into the source using the Auto Comment tool.

The right side of the Auto Comment window is where you can enter the description for the Java element and add, edit, and remove Javadoc tags. The large text field labeled Javadoc Comment Text is where you enter the class or method description.

To add Javadoc using the Auto Comment tool, select a class or method that has partial or no Javadoc in the element list on the left. In the Tags section on the right, click the New button. If you selected a class, the list of tags available at the class level will appear, as shown in Figure 12-2. If you selected a method, you'll see the list of tags available at the method level, as shown in Figure 12-3.

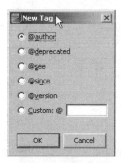

Figure 12-2. *List of Javadoc tags available at the class level in the Auto Comment tool*

Figure 12-3. *List of Javadoc tags available at the method level in the Auto Comment tool*

Select a tag and click the OK button. The tag is then added to the Tags list, and the lower-right portion of the Auto Comment tool is enabled. Here, you can edit the actual value of the tag using straight text or HTML. There are several convenience buttons at the bottom for adding markup to the tag text.

Editing the Javadoc tags for an element is quite simple. Select an element from the list on the left, select a tag from the Tags list on the right, and then edit the tag text in the bottom right. To delete a tag, just select it from the Tags list and click the Delete button.

The Move Up and Move Down buttons allow you to rearrange the order in which the tags appear. The general order of tags that most developers use is @param, @return, and @throws.

Overall, the Auto Comment tool included with NetBeans is very useful. It allows quick identification of Java elements with partial or no Javadoc. And it's easy to use this interface to add, edit, and delete Javadoc from your project source code.

Generating Project Javadoc

Once you have finished writing Javadoc comments in your source, you need to actually generate the HTML files. NetBeans makes this ridiculously easy to do. Simply select a project and choose Build ➤ Generate Javadoc for "*ProjectName*". You can also right-click a project in the Projects window and select Generate Javadoc for Project.

Once you have directed NetBeans to generate the files, the Output window appears, and you can watch the logging statements fly by as your project Javadoc is generated. After the process is complete, the project Javadoc homepage (typically index.html) should open in your Internet browser. If it does not open, in the Files window, locate the javadoc directory in the dist directory and open the index.html file.

Configuring Javadoc Properties

As you review the Javadoc that was generated for your project, you may notice several items you wish to change the next time you run the process. You can configure several Javadoc-related settings for the project in the Project Properties window. To access these properties, right-click the project name and select Properties. In the Categories list, select Documenting to see the options shown in Figure 12-4.

The Documenting properties allow you to decide which parts of the Javadoc you want to generate. You can also specify other items, such as the access levels to include, any special tags, or if there are special command options to pass to the actual javadoc tool during the file-generation process. If you do not want the Javadoc to open in an Internet browser after it is generated, deselect the Preview Generated Javadoc check box.

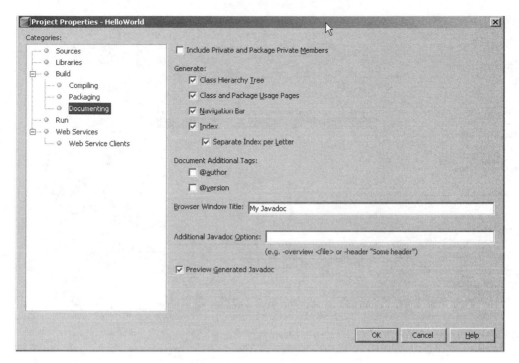

Figure 12-4. *The Javadoc properties for a project*

Accessing Javadoc

Along with tools for creating Javadoc for your projects, NetBeans provides several features to help you access existing Javadoc quickly and easily.

Attaching to Libraries and Platforms

If your project makes use of third-party libraries, you may want to consider attaching the associated Javadoc. Doing so allows you quick access to the documentation for that code and speeds up your development process.

Adding Libraries

NetBeans allows you to specify one or more JAR files as a library. Libraries are a good way to organize the third-party JAR files you want to use. You can define the binary class files that are executed, the matching source code, and the path to the Javadoc documentation.

To work with libraries, select Tools ➤ Library Manager. In the Library Manager, you can add new libraries, remove libraries, or modify existing libraries. The window has three tabs for managing a library, classpath, sources, and Javadoc. Each tab allows you to add a reference to one or more JAR or zip files for the class files, source code, or Javadoc. If the Javadoc resides in a directory, you can add a reference to that directory using the Javadoc tab, as shown in Figure 12-5.

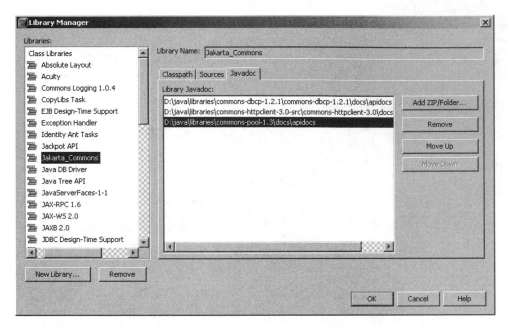

Figure 12-5. *The Javadoc tab in the Library Manager*

Adding Javadoc for Platforms

You can also add Javadoc for each Java platform that is defined in NetBeans. When you download and install a JDK, you should also make sure to download the source and the Javadoc. These can prove to be valuable resources, especially to novice programmers. Even pros can't remember every class and method usage in the entire Java platform. Having local access to the Javadoc for your JDK, as opposed to having to go online to look it up, can save valuable time.

In NetBeans, you can add the Javadoc to each platform by selecting Tools ➤ Java Platform Manager. In this window, you can view the default platform that NetBeans is configured with, as well as any additional platforms you may have installed.

For each platform, the window has three tabs: Classes, Sources, and Javadoc. The JAR files should have been added automatically when you originally added the new platform. You need to manually reference the sources and Javadoc on each tab, as shown in Figure 12-6.

Once you have added Javadoc to your libraries and Java platforms, you can view the context-sensitive Javadoc during coding.

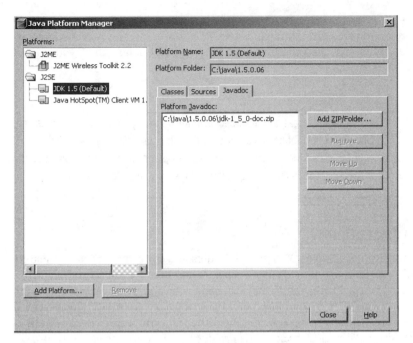

Figure 12-6. *Adding Javadoc in the Java Platform Manager*

Viewing Context-Sensitive Javadoc

During the code-editing process, you can view context-sensitive Javadoc. This allows you to quickly access documentation and usage information directly in the Source Editor window.

As you code, you may have already seen the first method of viewing Javadoc, if you have the code completion feature activated (see Chapter 10). When you type a period after a package or class name, the code completion box appears. For the Java element highlighted in the code completion box, an additional pop-up window also appears, displaying the Javadoc for the currently selected element. If you use the keyboard arrow keys to scroll up and down the list, the Javadoc window should update accordingly, as shown in Figure 12-7.

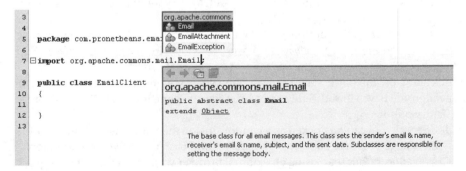

Figure 12-7. *Context-sensitive Javadoc during code completion*

You can also force the Javadoc window to appear. Highlight the class or package for which you wish to view Javadoc and press Ctrl+Shift+spacebar. The pop-up window will display the Javadoc for the selected item. This can sometimes prove faster than opening the Javadoc in a web browser.

■Tip You can also highlight or select an element and right-click. On the context menu that appears is an item called Show Javadoc. The Show Javadoc option will attempt to open the Javadoc page specific to the element you selected. If you have not attached the Javadoc to the library or platform the element belongs to, you will see the status message "Javadoc Not Found" at the bottom of the Source Editor window.

Searching Javadoc

The Javadoc Search tool, shown in Figure 12-8, provides quick and convenient access to search Javadoc registered with NetBeans. Any Javadoc that has been referenced for a library or platform can be searched and displayed using the tool. It can also display Javadoc that was generated for any open project.

If you are in the Source Editor writing code, highlight the term you wish to display in the Search tool and press Shift+F1. You can also access the Javadoc Search tool by selecting Tools ➤ Javadoc Index Search. The Javadoc Search tool will immediately open and display the search results for the selected text. I have personally found this to be one of the fastest and easiest methods for viewing Javadoc.

The Javadoc Search window is divided into two sections: searching and viewing. The top pane allows you to search for Javadoc elements based on partial name matching. In the example in Figure 12-8, I started off by typing Date in the search field. When you have finished entering the phrase you want to search for, press the Enter key or click the Find button next to the search field.

The tool scans all the known Javadoc and displays the results. If you select any result in the list, the matching Javadoc page is displayed in the lower pane. You can jump directly to the source code for an element by clicking the View Source button. You can also sort the search results by name, package, and type by clicking the corresponding buttons. There is also a button to toggle the display of the HTML viewer window (lower pane). Move your mouse over each button to see a tooltip describing its function.

In the HTML viewer pane at the bottom of the window, you can scroll up and down a page of Javadoc for the selected element, exactly as if you were viewing it in an external browser. You can also click the hyperlinks in the Javadoc, just like in an external browser.

The buttons along the top of the HTML viewer pane allow you to navigate back and forth through the Javadoc you have viewed. Similar to a browser, the pane has Back, Forward, Stop, Reload, and History buttons.

The Javadoc Search tool can be docked as a window inside the Source Editor section of NetBeans, just like a page of source code. It is often faster and easier to leave the Search tool open for viewing Javadoc, rather than using an external browser window. It can provide quick access to Javadoc for your associated libraries and source code.

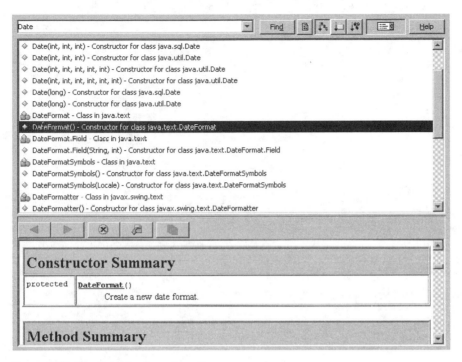

Figure 12-8. *The Javadoc Search tool*

Summary

This chapter provided a quick overview of the Javadoc-related features available in NetBeans. Writing Javadoc to go along with your code is a best practice for any new or seasoned developer to follow. NetBeans tries to make working with Javadoc simple by providing some helpful tools. These include the Auto Comment tool for adding, editing, and removing tags from your classes, and the Javadoc Search tool for querying all the Javadoc associated with your code and libraries.

As you saw in this chapter, there are many different tags that you can use in your Javadoc. The entire list can be quite complex, but many developers who first start out using Javadoc only need the basics. To learn more about Javadoc, visit `http://java.sun.com/j2se/javadoc`.

CHAPTER 13

■■■

Managing Version Control

An important aspect of software development is controlling your source code. In single and multideveloper projects, it is essential to ensure the longevity of your code by storing the files somewhere other than on the developers' computers. It is also important to be able to track versions of individual source files and be able to control changes.

Two popular version control systems are the Concurrent Versioning System (CVS) and Subversion. Out of the box, NetBeans provides full support for CVS. To use Subversion with NetBeans, you can download and install the Subversion module. This chapter covers working with CVS and Subversion.

Using CVS

CVS allows you to back up your project into a system that is external from your development machine. You can store files in CVS, have it manage individual unique versions of code, and retrieve those versions as you need them. A good CVS tool also allows you to perform comparisons between different versions of a file to see the changes. The NetBeans CVS module provides all of these capabilities.

■**Note** Obviously, you could be running a CVS server on your local machine, but it is a best practice, even for small programming shops, to have a separate computer running a source code repository. This increases the likelihood of your project code surviving a hardware crash or other problem.

When NetBeans is initially installed, support for CVS is activated by default. You should see the CVS menu on the NetBeans menu bar, as shown in Figure 13-1.

If you install other version control system modules, such as Subversion, the CVS module may be disabled. If the CVS module is disabled (and you are not using another version control system), you can use the Module Manager to enable it. Select Tools ➤ Module Manager. Under the Version Control node in the Module Manager, you will see a CVS Versioning System option. Put a check in the check box in the Active column to enable it, as shown in Figure 13-2. Once the module is activated, you will see the CVS main menu in the IDE.

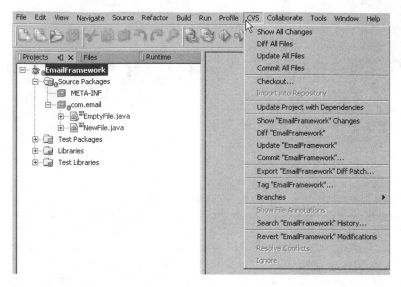

Figure 13-1. *The CVS main menu*

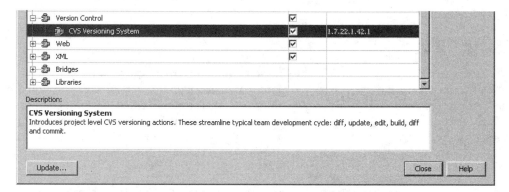

Figure 13-2. *Enabling the CVS Versioning System module in the Module Manager*

Configuring a Project to Use CVS

You can start using CVS in a NetBeans project in two main ways:

- Create a new project and import it into your CVS repository. This assumes there is no prior code stored for your module or project in the repository.

- Download the most recent copy of the source code from the repository (also referred to as "grabbing the latest version" or "checking out the latest version").

Importing a Project into the Repository

If you have a new or existing NetBeans project, you can easily import it into the repository. To begin, right-click the project in the Projects window and select CVS ➤ Import into Repository. You will see the first step of the Import Project Options window, CVS Root, as shown in Figure 13-3.

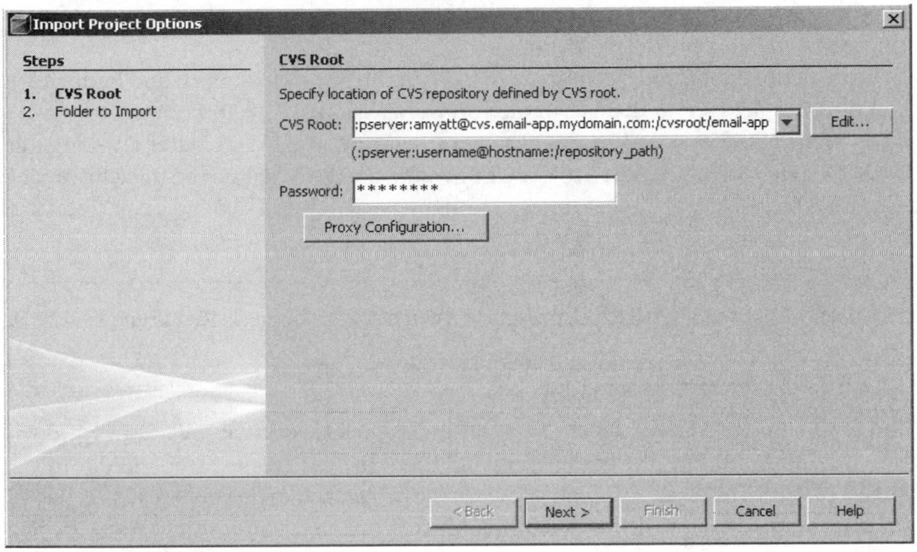

Figure 13-3. *The CVS Root window*

The first field requests the CVS root string. If you are unfamiliar with setting the CVS root, you can click the Edit button next to the field to use the Edit CVS Root dialog box to enter the string, as shown in Figure 13-4. If you are relatively new to CVS, using the Edit CVS Root dialog box can help you avoid making syntax errors in the CVS root string.

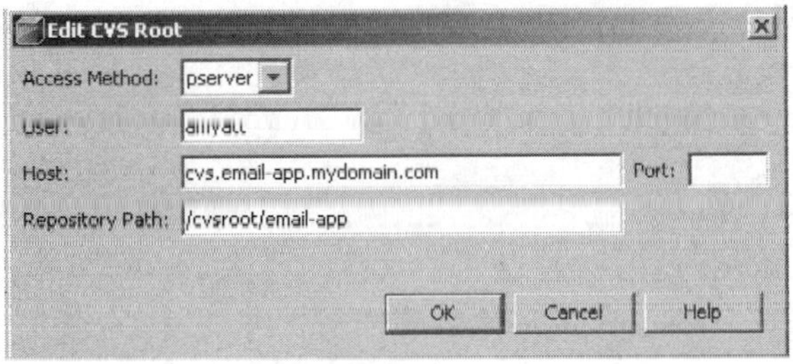

Figure 13-4. *The Edit CVS Root dialog box*

In the Edit CVS Root dialog box, select a method from the Access Method drop-down list. You have four choices:

- pserver allows you to connect to a remote server with a username and password.

- ext is similar to pserver, except it uses Secure Shell (SSH).

- As the name implies, local allows you to connect to a source code repository running locally on your machine.

- fork is just an alternate version of local.

In most environments, you would use pserver unless you are concerned about the source code traveling across the network as plaintext.

In the Edit CVS Root dialog box, you also need to fill in the User, Host, Port, and Repository Path fields. In the User field, enter the username you were assigned in your code repository. The Repository Path value is normally in the format of /cvsroot/myproject. After entering the values, click OK to return to the Import Project Options window, where your string will appear in the CVS Root field.

Tip If your CVS repository is configured to use the standard port of 2401, you can leave the Port field blank.

Once you have configured the correct CVS root string, click Next in the CVS Root window. NetBeans will attempt to validate the connection and then display the next step, Folder to Import, as shown in Figure 13-5. In this window, specify the project folder on your local machine to import. It should be already set to the project root folder of your NetBeans project. You can also specify the repository folder. This is the name the module will be placed under in the CVS repository. When you are finished, click the Finish button.

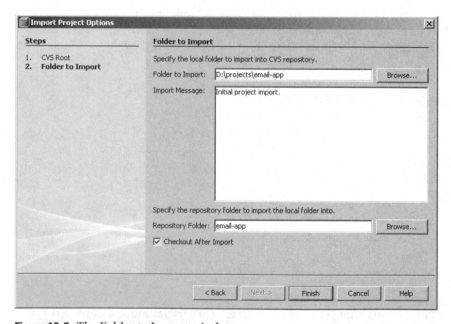

Figure 13-5. *The Folder to Import window*

Checking Out Code from the Repository

For an existing project, you may need to check out the code from the repository. This assumes that the code you have in your repository is structured in a NetBeans project hierarchy.

To check out an existing project, select CVS ➤ Checkout. In the first window that appears, specify the CVS root string, as discussed in the previous section, and then click the Next button.

In the Module to Checkout window, you need to specify several properties. The module is the actual code from the repository you want to download. If you know the name of the module, you can type it directly in the Module field. Alternatively, click the Browse button next to the Module field to browse the repository and select the module from a list, as shown in Figure 13-6. In the Browse CVS Module dialog box, you can drill down through the nodes to find the module under the root (/cvsroot/email-framework in the example shown in Figure 13-6). You can have multiple modules defined under the root. Select the one you want and click the OK button.

Figure 13-6. *The Browse CVS Module dialog box*

You can also choose to check out code using a CVS branch or tag, if they are used in your repository. Click the Browse button next to the Branch field to open the Browse Tags dialog box, as shown in Figure 13-7. If there is no specific branch or tag to use, click the HEAD node, and then click the OK button.

Figure 13-7. *The Browse Tags dialog box*

In the Module to Checkout window, you also need to specify the local folder where the code will be copied. I usually use a standard location, such as a folder named `projects`, to store all my code. Your team or organization may have a standard directory structure, so be sure to pick the correct location. Click the Finish button after you have set the properties. The checkout operation will proceed.

When the checkout operation is finished, you will see a dialog box stating that the checkout is complete and asking if you want to open the project or close the window. If you click the Open Project button, the dialog box will close, and the project will now be listed in the Projects window.

Performing Common CVS Operations

You can perform many types of operations when working with a source code repository— adding code, updating, checking differences between two versions, tagging, branching, and searching. Sometimes the terms can be a little confusing. Learning the version control system features can take a little patience and experimentation.

Showing Changes

When working with CVS, you need to know when files have changed, when files have been added to the project, and when they have been deleted.

When a source file is checked out of CVS and edited, the filename appears in blue in the interface. This flags the file as having been changed. You will also see a blue cylinder icon next to the name of the source package and project name in the Projects window, as shown earlier in Figure 13-1. This visually flags a package as having one or more files that were altered.

The NetBeans CVS tool also provides a Versioning window that allows you to see what has changed, as shown in Figure 13-8. To open this window, right-click the name of the project and select CVS ➤ Show Changes.

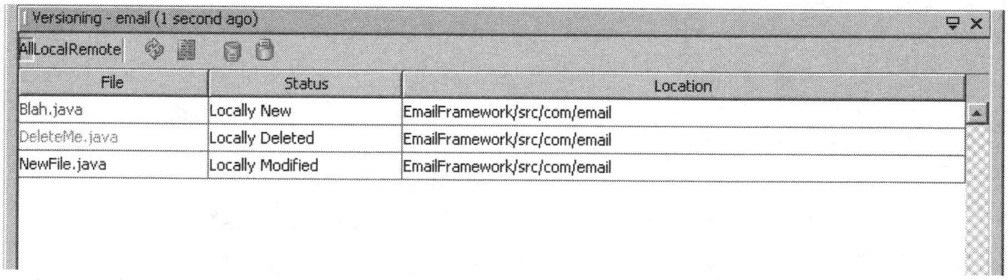

Figure 13-8. *The Versioning window displayed by the Show Changes option*

The Versioning window displays any files that were added, modified, or deleted. For each file listed, you can individually choose to commit the file, ignore the file and exclude it from the commit, or revert the file modifications back to the repository version. The Status column will contain one of the following:

Locally New: Files that were added have a status of Locally New. They exist in the NetBeans project, but have not yet been added to the code repository. If you right-click the file in the Versioning window, you can choose to open the file in the Source Editor or to commit the file, which adds it to the CVS repository.

Locally Deleted: Files that were deleted from the project have a status of Locally Deleted. You can right-click the deleted file and choose to commit it. This confirms the deletion with the CVS repository. You can also select to update the file, which downloads the latest version of the file from the repository, effectively undoing the deletion.

Locally Modified: Files that were modified have a status of Locally Modified. You can commit and update these files. If you commit a modified file, the changes that you made are saved into the CVS repository. If you update the file, the local changes you made are undone. You may also want to know what you changed in a file and compare the differences. (These CVS options are covered in the following sections.)

Another way to view changes is to select CVS ➤ Show All Changes. This shows all the changes to all the open projects that are CVS-enabled. You should be careful, since different projects may have files with the same name. It is safer to view CVS changes project by project, rather than by using the Show All Changes option.

Committing Changes

When you want to commit the changes made in your project, you have several options. You can commit a single file, multiple files, an entire package, or an entire project.

To commit a file that is locally new, right-click the file and select CVS ➤ Commit from the context menu. In the Commit dialog box, shown in Figure 13-9, you see the name of the file to commit, the status, the commit action, and the repository path. The commit action is the only option you can modify.

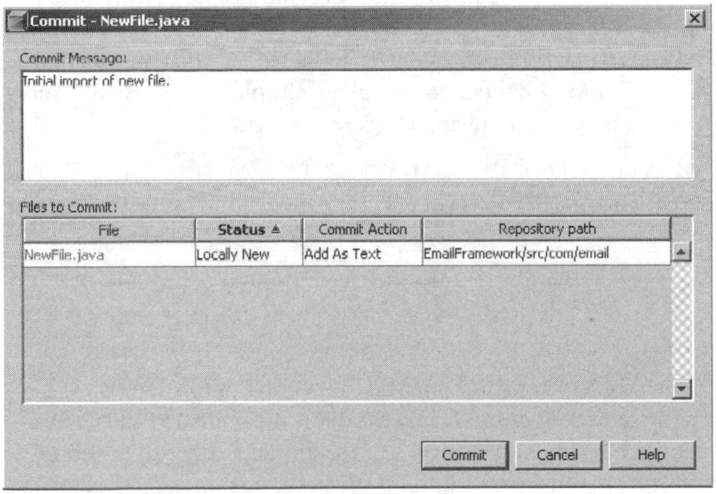

Figure 13-9. *Committing a new file*

By default, a Java source file's commit action is set to Add As Text. By clicking the field, you can change it to Add As Binary or Exclude from Commit. The Add As Binary option should be used for images, compiled class files, or other binary files. The Exclude from Commit option is useful when you are working with multiple files and want to exclude one or more of them from being committed, such as if you want to commit an entire project but exclude one file that you are still developing.

In the text box at the top of the Commit dialog box, you can add a commit message, which is intended to provide a clue to the changes being committed. It should be brief, but still convey the reason for the change to the code. The "Searching History" section later in this chapter explains how to view the history of a file and see the comments made for each version of a file.

To commit multiple files, hold down the Ctrl key (in Windows) and click each file one at a time. You can also commit an entire package or the entire project by selecting it, right-clicking, and choosing CVS ➤ Commit. The Commit All Changes option is available from the CVS main menu, but make sure you are certain that you know the ramifications of performing this action. All added, modified, and deleted files in *all* open projects will be committed if you use the Commit All Changes option.

■**Note** When you commit multiple files, the commit message that is entered is applied to all the files. If you want your files to have different commit messages, you should commit them in separate batches.

Updating Files

Performing a CVS update on a file can sometimes be a little confusing. A CVS update operation grabs the latest copy of the file from the CVS repository and tries to merge it with the local copy. If changes have not been made to the local copy, then the file is said to be *patched*. Updates on a code base should always be performed prior to making any local changes, so you are sure you are working with the latest code.

When code is updated and a merge performed, CVS tries to figure out the changes that differ between the two files (the local copy and repository copy). A simple scenario can demonstrate the functionality. Assume you have the following class named NewFile:

```
public class NewFile {

    public NewFile() {
        System.out.println("In the constructor");
    }
}
```

You have just retrieved a fresh copy of version 1.4 of the file onto your local machine. Another developer, John, does the same and immediately modifies the code. He adds a new method and commits the code, thereby creating version 1.5. He should really run the code through unit tests *before* committing it, but we'll let him off the hook this time. Here is the modified code:

```
public class NewFile {

    public NewFile() {
        System.out.println("In the constructor");
    }
```

```
    public void doNothing() {
        System.out.println("In the doNothing method");
    }
}
```

You still have the original code. If you modify the constructor and want to commit your changes, there is a problem. Your copy of the file does not have the new doNothing method. If you were able to commit the code, you would essentially overwrite John's changes and they would be lost. You could review the file's versions, but not if you didn't know John had made the changes.

Assume you went ahead and tried to commit the file. The commit will fail, and you will receive an error message similar to "Up-to-date check failed for file." This is warning you that the copy of the file in the CVS repository does not match what you have. This situation is where the CVS update function comes in handy.

When you choose CVS ➤ Update for the file, the CVS tool compares the files line by line to see what changed. Suppose you made the following change to the string in the println method in the NewFile class:

```
public class NewFile {

    public NewFile() {
        System.out.println("******** In the constructor ********");
    }
}
```

When you update the file, the tool sees that only one line differs in your local file and the three lines for the doNothing method differ in the remote file in the repository. It then combines these lines into one file:

```
public class NewFile {

    public NewFile() {
        System.out.println("******** In the constructor ********");
    }

    public void doNothing() {
        System.out.println("In the doNothing method");
    }
}
```

From a developer's perspective, this feature is fantastic. You no longer need to manually compare files to see changes, or copy and paste the new or updated code. However, it should be used with caution, since conflicts may occur. If you and the other developer modify the same line or lines, CVS cannot make automatic assumptions. It merges the files and warns of a conflict during the update operation, as shown in Figure 13-10.

Figure 13-10. *Merge conflicts warning during a CVS update operation*

The filename will be shown in red in the Projects and Files windows. You can open the file and see what conflicts occurred. The file now contains invalid Java syntax, since CVS inserted text into the file during the update operation to identify the conflicting lines, as shown in Figure 13-11.

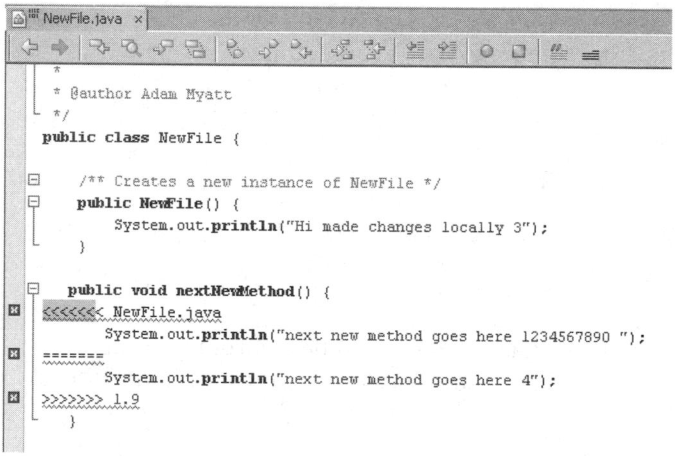

```
* 
* @author Adam Myatt
*/
public class NewFile {

    /** Creates a new instance of NewFile */
    public NewFile() {
        System.out.println("Hi made changes locally 3");
    }

    public void nextNewMethod() {
<<<<<<< NewFile.java
        System.out.println("next new method goes here 1234567890 ");
=======
        System.out.println("next new method goes here 4");
>>>>>>> 1.9
    }
```

Figure 13-11. *The line conflicts in the merged file*

In this example, both developers modified the text in the System.out.println statement in the nextNewMethod method. The text that was added identifies the following changes:

- <<<<<<< NewFile.java denotes the start of the section where text in the local file differs from that of the file in the repository.

- System.out.println("next new method goes here 1234567890 "); is the text that differs and is present in the locally modified file.

- ======= denotes the end of the section of text that differs in the locally modified file.

- >>>>>>> 1.9 denotes the end of the section of text that differs in the remote repository file.

If there were multiple consecutive lines of code, they would appear between the section delimiters. If lines of code differ in multiple sections of the file, these delimiters appear in each location of conflict. This allows you to review the conflicting code and attempt to choose which line you want to include in the file prior to committing it. The NetBeans CVS module also provides a Resolve Conflicts tool that attempts to help you in this process, as discussed in the next section.

Resolving Conflicts

When a filename shows up in red in the Projects window, as described in the previous section, right-click the filename and select CVS ➤ Resolve Conflicts. The Resolve Conflicts tool opens, as shown in Figure 13-12. This tool is a very convenient way to edit files that have conflicts. It takes out some of the guesswork of reading the CVS merge text that was inserted into the file. It also allows you to see a side-by-side comparison of the changes.

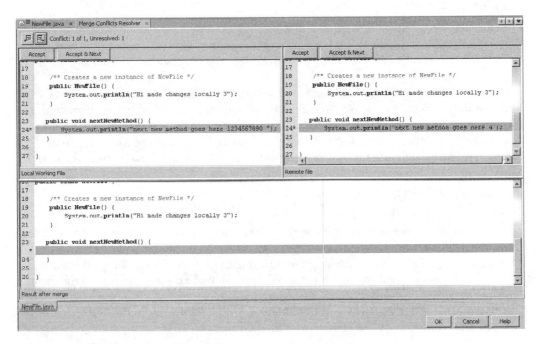

Figure 13-12. *The Resolve Conflicts tool*

It may not be easy to see all the text in Figure 13-12, since it is a wide screenshot, but I wanted to show the general screen layout. The top-left section shows the locally modified file with each conflict highlighted. The top-right section shows the CVS repository version (remote file). Each conflict is highlighted. The lower half of the window shows the results that occur after the merge operation. In either the top-left or top-right pane, you can review and accept each conflicting line, one at a time. If you decide to accept the locally modified file's changes, click the Accept or Accept & Next buttons in the top-left pane. If you want to accept the changes from the remote file, use the buttons in the top-right pane.

When you are finished accepting changes, click the OK button at the bottom of the window. The CVS merge text will be removed from the file. If you accepted any changes from the locally modified file, you still need to commit the file before the changes are saved into the repository.

You may also encounter conflicts when you attempt to commit changes to a file that was modified by another user. If you run a commit operation before an update operation, you may receive a warning like this:

```
cvs commit: Up-to-date check failed for `NewFile.java'
cvs [commit aborted]: correct above errors first!
```

This message means you need to run an update operation. After doing so, the NetBeans CVS tool should warn you that conflicts were created between the local and repository versions. After you resolve the conflicts, you will be able to commit the changes to the file.

Reverting Modifications

Programmers frequently write some code and then immediately want to undo what they changed. Whether it is incorrect code or you were just experimenting with some new algorithms, you need to be able to roll back one or more code changes. The NetBeans CVS tool allows you to do so.

If you have locally modified a file and need to undo the changes, right-click and select CVS ➤ Revert Modifications. You will receive a Yes/No prompt asking if you want to overwrite your locally selected files with the current versions from the repository. If you click Yes, the changes to your code are undone, and the file should match the latest version of code stored in the CVS repository. You can also use the Revert Modifications option at the package and project level.

Comparing Differences

One of the most important features of any CVS tool is the ability to compare the differences between two files. When you make changes to a local file, you may need to compare it against the remote version stored in the repository. This is useful if you modify a file and forget to commit it for a period of time. If you later come back to the file and need to know what changed, you can easily check it against the repository version. For this, you can use the Diff tool, which is my favorite of all the NetBeans CVS features.

To compare differences in locally modified files, right-click the file or files and select CVS ➤ Diff. The Diff window opens, as shown in Figure 13-13.

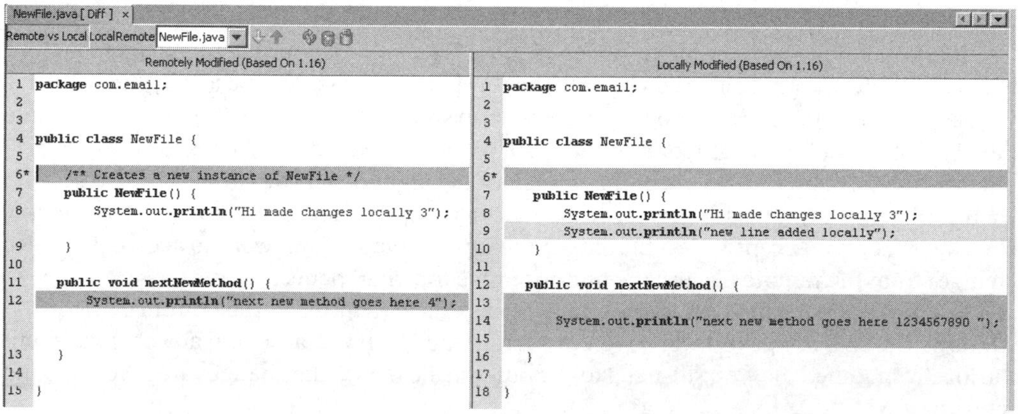

Figure 13-13. *The Diff window*

In the Diff window, the two files are compared side by side. Changes to the files are highlighted line by line. Different lines are highlighted in different colors. Typically, green lines were added, blue lines were modified, and red lines were removed. However, it has been my experience that the CVS color-coding in Diff tools is not an exact science and sometimes appears incorrectly.

In the Diff tool, you can use the up and down arrow icons along the top to navigate the differences between the files. You can also use the toolbar icons to either update the local file or commit it.

To compare differences in multiple files or the entire project, select CVS ➤ Diff All Files. In this case, the drop-down list with the filename at the top left of the Diff window will include all files that have been locally added, modified, or deleted. Choosing a file from the drop-down list will open the file's difference comparison.

Searching History

One of the nice features of the NetBeans CVS tool is the ability to search the history of files in the repository. Using the Search History tool, you can query versions of files for several parameters, and perform a variety of important operations.

To search the history of an individual file, package, or project, right-click the element and select CVS ➤ Search History. If you are searching using an individual file, the Search History tool automatically queries the repository and displays all the versions of that file. If you are searching multiple files at the package or project level, the Search History tool will open but not display results. You will need to manually enter search terms or just click the Search button to execute the search without any filtering parameters. Figure 13-14 shows the results of searching on the com.email package without any filtering parameters.

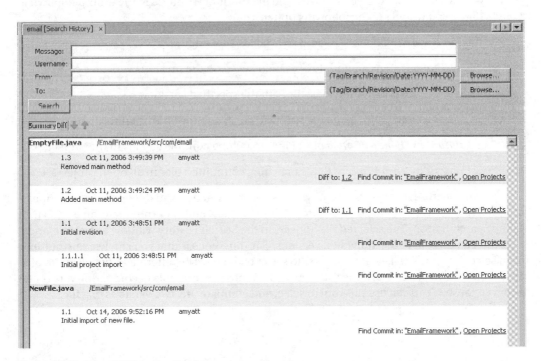

Figure 13-14. *The CVS history for the com.email package*

You can use the fields at the top of the Search History window to filter the search results:

- The Message field allows you to query the commit messages that were saved for each file in the range you are searching (package, project, and so on).

- The Username field allows you to query for all the versions that were added by a specific user in the CVS repository.

- The From and To fields allow you to query by revision date, branch, and tag.

These search filters are very useful if you are looking for a specific version of a file that might have dozens or hundreds of versions.

Each file and version that matches the filter parameters is displayed in the search results pane in the lower half of the Search History window. Versions are grouped under a file heading, and the version number, date, username, and commit message are listed.

For each version listed, several convenient links are listed on the right side of each row. The first link, Diff to #.#, allows you to perform a diff operation on the current version of the file against the previous version. This feature can help you understand what historic changes to a file took place over time. This is frequently used if something breaks in your application and you need to go back and see where it broke and who broke it. The other two links are for the Find Commit In feature. They allow you to query the current project or all open projects for any files that were committed during the same batch as the file you selected. This makes it easier to identify the five, ten, or two hundred files that were all committed simultaneously as a batch.

Right-clicking a version row in the Search History window opens a context menu with more options. For example, if you right-clicked the row for version 1.3 in the example shown in Figure 13-14, you would see the following options:

Diff to 1.2: Runs a diff operation between versions 1.3 and 1.2.

Rollback Changes: Runs an update operation based on the previous version's code.

Rollback to 1.3: Overwrites the local file with the specified version.

View 1.3: Downloads and opens the specified version in the Source Editor.

Find Commit in "Email-Framework": Finds matching committed files in the project.

Find Commit in Open Projects: Finds matching committed files in all open projects.

The one feature that may not be obvious is the ability to perform diff operations on nonsequential versions. Select a file in the Search History window and click the small Diff button next to the Search button. The selected file appears in the Search History window as a single node that you can expand to see individual versions. The difference is that you can use the multiple-item select key (the Ctrl key in Windows) to select two rows. The differences between the files appear in the two panes below the list. Figure 13-15 shows an example of comparing version 1.6 with version 1.3. You can use this tool to select and compare any two versions of a file.

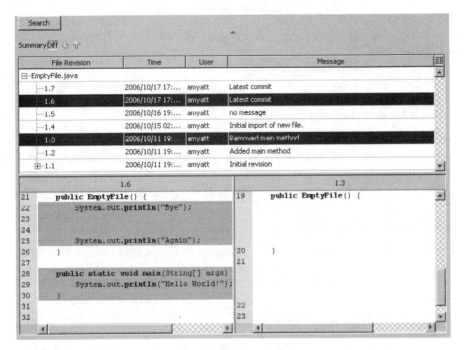

Figure 13-15. *Seeing differences in two nonsequential versions*

Adding Annotations

The Annotation tool is simple but powerful. It displays two important pieces of information on a line-by-line basis directly in the Source Editor window: the version number that the line was last modified and the username of who made that modification.

To view annotations, select a file in the Source Editor or the Projects window and select CVS ➤ Show "*File.java*" Annotations. In the example shown in Figure 13-16, the source file contains numerous modifications, ranging from version 1.1 to 1.18.

```
 NewFile.java  x

1.17 amyatt    package com.email;
1.1 amyatt
1.1 amyatt
1.1 amyatt     public class NewFile {
1.1 amyatt
1.1 amyatt □      /** Creates a new instance of NewFile */
1.1 amyatt □      public NewFile() {
1.12 amyatt            System.out.println("Hi made changes locally 3");
1.18 amyatt
1.18 amyatt
1.1 amyatt         }
1.1 amyatt
1.5 amyatt □      public void nextNewMethod() {
1.16 amyatt            System.out.println("next new method goes here 4");
1.5 amyatt         }
1.3 amyatt
1.1 amyatt     }
```

Figure 13-16. *The CVS annotations for a source file*

Being able to view these annotations can quickly help you understand when changes were made and who made them. This is much faster than manually reviewing each version of a file or performing numerous diff operations between the different versions.

To turn off the display of annotations, select CVS ➤ Hide Annotations.

Using Subversion

Subversion is rapidly becoming a popular version control system. CVS is probably still the leader as far as number of users, but Subversion is rapidly gaining ground. It was built in an attempt to replace CVS and improve on its functionality. For a tutorial on Subversion features and how it differs from CVS, refer to the Subversion web site at `http://subversion.tigris.org`.

Installing Subversion

To install the Subversion module, select Tools ➤ Update Center. Depending on the NetBeans version you are working with, the Subversion module is either at the NetBeans Update Center or the NetBeans Update Center Beta. Select the module, install it, and wait for NetBeans to finish activating the module. (See Chapter 2 for details on using the Update Center.) Once installation is complete, you should see a main menu item named Subversion. Starting with NetBeans 6.0, the Subversion module should come bundled with the IDE.

Unlike with the CVS module, this is only half the battle. You also need to install the actual Subversion client on your machine. You can download the Subversion software by visiting the Subversion web site at `http://subversion.tigris.org`. On the Subversion site, there is a section on the main menu titled Documents and Files. This contains several How-To documents that describe the installation steps, Subversion best practices, and also a CVS-to-Subversion Crossover Guide.

■**Note** For those of you on a Windows platform, the installation of the Subversion software is quite easy. Just click the Next button about seven or eight times. The Subversion installer takes care of the rest.

Once you have installed the Subversion client and the NetBeans Subversion module, you are ready to begin working with Subversion repositories.

Performing Common Subversion Operations

Many of the version control features for CVS and Subversion are nearly identical in NetBeans. The Update, Commit, Diff, and Search History tools function the same, have the same look and feel, and contain the same information. Here, we'll cover some of the areas where the two version control tools differ.

Checking Out Code

When you choose Subversion ➤ Checkout, the Subversion Checkout wizard starts. The first step to check out code is to specify the protocol. The Subversion module allows you to check out code using several protocols: File, HTTP, HTTPS, SVN, and SVN+SSH.

To check out the Subversion project code, use the URL http://svn.collab.net/repos/svn/trunk, as shown in Figure 13-17. After you enter the URL, you can optionally enter a username or password if you have one assigned, or leave the fields blank for anonymous access. Click the Next button to move to the Folders to Checkout window.

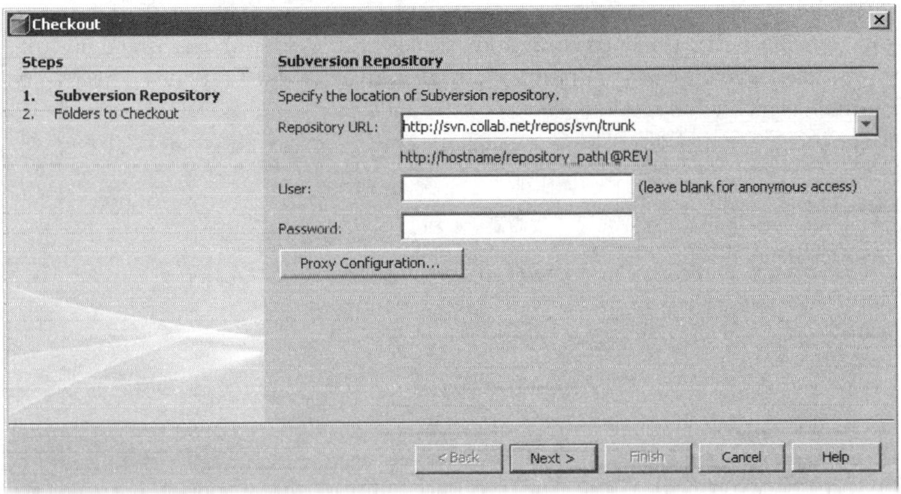

Figure 13-17. *Checking out a Subversion project*

In the Folders to Checkout window, specify the repository folder. You can manually enter the folder name in the Repository Folder field or click the Browse button to connect to the repository and browse the available options. You can also select the revision and the local folder to which to check out the code. Once you have the completed the fields, click the Finish button.

The Subversion module connects to the repository and attempts to download the code. In the Output window, you will see Subversion logging like the following:

```
co -r HEAD http://svn.collab.net/repos/svn/trunk@HEAD
D:\projects\trunk --non-interactive --config-dir
C:\Documents and Settings\adam\.netbeans\5.5rc2\config\svn\config

U    D:\projects\trunk\www\project_license.html
...
U    D:\projects\trunk\subversion\libsvn_client\compat_providers.c

Checked out revision 22009.

==[IDE]== Oct 17, 2006 7:11:35 PM Checking out... finished.
```

The first few lines of the output show the Subversion statements that have run, then the downloading of individual files, and finally some summary information.

Once the code is finished downloading, if it contains NetBeans project metadata, the tool attempts to open the project. Otherwise, you will see a dialog box that asks if you want to create a new project. If you click the Create Project button, the New Project wizard appears and prompts you through its steps.

Working with Branches

One of the features that differs between Subversion and CVS is working with branches. In the Subversion module, you can create a branch, or copy, of a file, folder, or entire project and place it in your repository. The previous commit messages and history for the copied file are linked to the original. You can then later merge changes between these branches if necessary.

In the NetBeans Subversion module, you can copy a file by right-clicking the name and selecting Subversion ➤ Create Copy. The Copy dialog box appears, as shown in Figure 13-18.

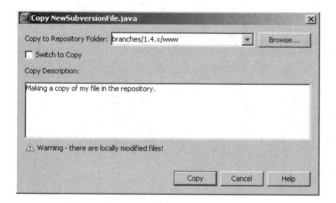

Figure 13-18. *The Subversion Copy dialog box*

In the Copy dialog box, you can select the destination folder in the repository for the copy of the file or files, or click the Browse button to view the existing tags and branches and choose where to copy the file. If you are branching an entire project, you can create a new folder under the branches node. You can also enter a description in the Copy Description text box. This description will be attached to the copy of the file. When the fields are set correctly, click the Copy button.

You can also choose to switch the local working copy of a file or project to a specific branch or tag. Right-click the item you wish to switch to and select Subversion ➤ Switch to Copy. The Switch dialog box opens, as shown in Figure 13-19. In the Switch dialog box, select to which branch or revision you want to switch. Once the switch is complete, you can edit and make changes to the file locally. The changes to the file occur to the branch you switched to, not to the original file.

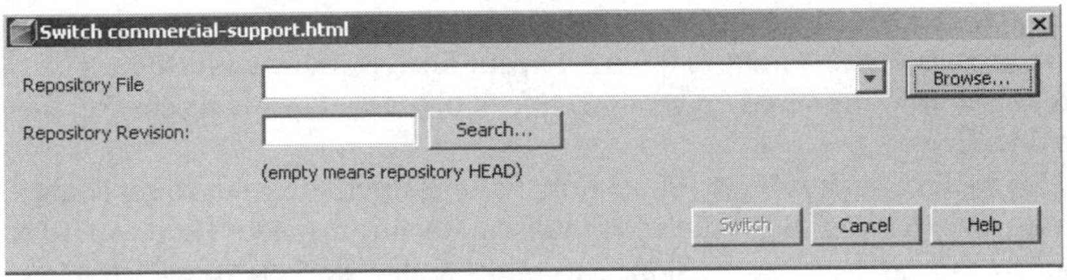

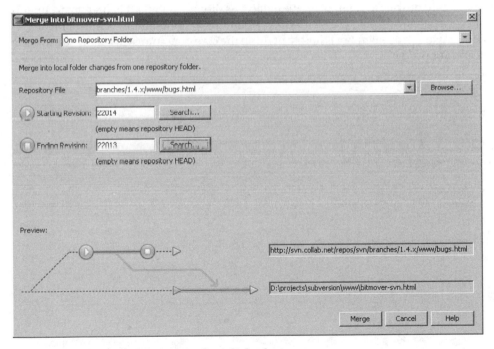

Figure 13-19. *The Subversion Switch dialog box*

Merging Changes

One of the other differences between the CVS and Subversion modules is the Merge Changes tool. This Subversion tool allows you to merge changes made in one or two different repository revisions and pull them into your local working code.

To merge changes, right-click a file and choose Subversion ➤ Merge Changes from Branch. If you select One Repository Folder from the Merge From drop-down list, you will see the fields in Figure 13-20. You must fill in the Repository File field or use the Browse button to query the repository and choose an item. You must also set the Starting Revision and Ending Revision fields. The Search button next to each field lets you query the repository and pick a revision from a list.

Figure 13-20. *The Subversion Merge Into dialog box*

When you are ready, click the Merge button. The Subversion tool grabs the changes from the specified revision or revisions and merges them into your local working code. If merge conflicts occur, you must follow the standard version control process of resolving conflicts, as discussed earlier in this chapter.

If you specify a Merge From value of Two Repository Folders, then the fields to set change slightly. First, you must specify a repository file and matching starting revision. Then you must pick a separate repository file and ending revision. This process allows you to merge changes from two separate revisions into your local working code.

If you specify a Merge From value of One Repository Folder Since Its Origin, only two fields need to be set: Repository File and Ending Revision. This allows you to merge changes in a local working file since it was first created until the ending revision that you specify.

Summary

In this chapter, we covered one of the core practices of software development: storing code in a source repository. This chapter gave a quick crash course in version control and how to perform specific operations using a version control module in NetBeans. There are many additional operations that we did not cover. I encourage you to experiment with the version control module of your choice to fully understand all its features.

Regardless of which version control software you use (CVS, Subversion, or another system), NetBeans tries to provide a standard user interface. As discussed in this chapter, many operations, such as update, commit, diff, search history, and show annotations, behave similarly. The important thing to remember is how to perform the core operations that allow you to store and retrieve your code.

CHAPTER 14

■■■

Managing Compilation and Projects with Ant

Many problems can occur while building and developing software. One of the biggest challenges is attempting to build and compile a software application on a platform other than the one for which it was developed. Imagine three programmers working on the same application on three different platforms: Linux, Windows, and Mac.

Many existing build tools work fine, but do not offer as much flexibility as some developers would like and are usually operating system-specific. It can also prove difficult to extend their functionality and integrate them with Java IDE tools.

Ant was created to address many problems in the arena of cross-platform source code compilation. Written in Java, tasks that are performed by Ant are executed by Java objects. Ant can also be extended using standard Java classes. This makes it an ideal tool for structuring cross-platform software builds (at least for the platforms that support a JDK).

Because Ant runs entirely in Java, there are no operating system-specific build configurations that need to be written. You can create and structure a single build configuration and execute it across multiple platforms. This helps ensure that a build process is reliable and repeatable, which is a key foundation to developing quality software.

Ant is tightly integrated with NetBeans. NetBeans makes full use of Ant and its capabilities for each type of project. In this chapter, we will explore how Ant works with NetBeans.

Ant Tasks and Targets

Ant uses XML files to store build configurations. Typically named `build.xml`, the build configuration file contains the definitions of specific tasks and targets. A *task* is a specific operation to be executed by an Ant Java class. A *target* is a group of one or more tasks that can then be executed by Ant.

One of the key things to remember regarding Ant targets is that they can be dependent on each other. For example, a target can contain an attribute named `depends` that directs Ant to process other targets first. This can lead to a cycle such as the following pseudo build configuration:

```
target = "build-full", depends on ➥
"compile source, create javadoc, package classes to jar"
target = "package classes to jar", depends on "compile source, create javadoc"
target = "create javadoc", depends on "compile source"
target = "compile source"
```

These targets contain dependencies on other targets. Ant resolves any conflicts in duplicate dependencies and does not execute the same target more than once. In the example, when build-full is executed, the three targets it depends on are executed in order from left to right. The first target could also be defined as follows:

```
target = "build-full", depends on "package classes to jar"
```

This line is valid since the build-full target depends on the package classes to jar target. In turn, that target depends on the create javadoc and compile source targets.

Needless to say, there are numerous ways you could structure targets and their dependencies, but this is just a very quick overview. For more discussion and information on Ant targets and semantics of dependencies, you can read *Pro Apache Ant* by Matthew Moodie (Apress, 2005).

As mentioned previously, targets are just groups of tasks. A task is basically a Java class that performs the actual processing and work. In the build configuration file, tasks can contain attributes and tags that further define how they function. See Table 14-1 for a partial list of Ant tasks with brief descriptions.

Table 14-1. *Some Common Ant Tasks*

Task	Description
java	Executes a Java file in the current JVM
javac	Compiles one or more source files
jspc	Compiles one or more JSP files into Java source files
javadoc	Runs the Javadoc tool for the specified Java source files
copy	Copies one or more files to a specific location
delete	Deletes one or more files
mkdir	Makes a new directory on the file system
move	Moves one or more files to a specific location
rename	Renames a file or directory
mail	Sends an SMTP email message
input	Interacts with the user to retrieve command-line input
jar	Packages a set of source or class files into a JAR file
unjar	Extracts the source or class files from a JAR file
war	Packages a set of files (an entire application) into a WAR file
unwar	Extracts a set of files from a WAR file

Table 14-1. *Some Common Ant Tasks*

Task	Description
zip	Packages a set of source or class files into a zip file
unzip	Extracts the source or class files from a zip file
ftp	Performs an FTP operation
scp	Transfers files to a remote machine via SSH
cvs	Performs various CVS operations
junit	Executes a set of JUnit test classes
junitreport	Creates a JUnit report based on JUnit test data

Many additional tasks are available for use in Ant. You can even extend Ant and implement your own custom tasks. Once you understand a few of the Ant tasks, you can write your
own build scripts like the one shown in Listing 14-1.

Listing 14-1. *Sample Ant Build Script*

```xml
<?xml version="1.0" ?>

<project name="pronetbeans" default="dist" basedir=".">

    <property name="dir.src" value="src" />
    <property name="dir.build" value="build" />
    <property name="dir.build.classes" value="${dir.build}/classes" />
    <property name="dir.dist" value="dist" />

    <target name="init">
        <mkdir dir="${dir.build}" />
        <mkdir dir="${dir.build.classes}" />
        <mkdir dir="${dir.dist}" />
    </target>

    <target name="compile" depends="init">
        <javac srcdir="${dir.src}" destdir="${dir.build.classes}" />
    </target>

    <target name="dist" depends="compile">
        <jar jarfile="${dir.dist}/pronetbeans.jar"
            basedir="${dir.build.classes}" />
    </target>

</project>
```

The build file in Listing 14-1 contains several important sections. The first section defines the project name.

```
<project name="pronetbeans" default="dist" basedir=".">
```

The project tag has an attribute named default, which defines the target that is executed by Ant if no target is specified on the command line when Ant is run. It also defines a basedir attribute, which specifies where the root directory for the project's files is located. Using the basedir attribute makes specifying directory paths easy, since you do not need to have a full path defined throughout the build file.

The property tags define a variable that can be specified once and referred to numerous times in the build file.

```
<property name="dir.src" value="src" />
<property name="dir.build" value="build" />
<property name="dir.build.classes" value="${dir.build}/classes" />
<property name="dir.dist" value="dist" />
```

This is a convenient and easy way to define directory paths, directory names, filenames, and so on. To refer to the value of a defined property, you can use the syntax ${*variable*}.

The first target that is defined is named init. This target contains three mkdir tasks.

```
<target name="init">
    <mkdir dir="${dir.build}" />
    <mkdir dir="${dir.build.classes}" />
    <mkdir dir="${dir.dist}" />
</target>
```

Each mkdir task will create the directory specified by the dir attribute. Many Ant build files contain a target that initializes the overall build by creating directories and setting up any needed configurations.

The compile target will perform the actual compilation of the source code. It lists a dependency on the init target that will execute before the compile target.

```
<target name="compile" depends="init">
    <javac srcdir="${dir.src}" destdir="${dir.build.classes}" />
</target>
```

The dependency ensures the build and build/classes directories are created. The javac task performs the compilation of the source and is essentially the same as calling the javac executable on the command line. The srcdir attribute specifies the location of the source code that will be compiled. The destdir attribute specifies the location where the compiled classes are placed.

The dist target serves as a wrapper for the jar task. It depends on the compile task, since the source code should be compiled before being packaged into a JAR file.

```
<target name="dist" depends="compile">
    <jar jarfile="${dir.dist}/pronetbeans.jar"
            basedir="${dir.build.classes}" />
</target>
```

The jarfile attribute specifies the location and name of the JAR file to create. The basedir attribute specifies the location of the class files that should be compiled and packaged.

Note Listing 14-1 is a very simple and basic example of a build file. A single target can wrap many tasks. Tasks can contain numerous subelements and other tasks. For further examples, see the Apache Ant documentation or any NetBeans project build.xml file.

When NetBeans creates a project, it also creates a build.xml file and supporting files for the project. It defines the targets and tasks it needs to manage the compilation and build of the project.

Configuring Ant Properties in NetBeans

You can configure several Ant properties directly in NetBeans. These allow basic control over several pieces of Ant functionality.

To access the Ant properties, select Tools ➤ Options. In the Basic Options window, click the Advanced Options button. In the left pane, select the Miscellaneous icon and expand the Ant node in the right pane. You will see the Ant properties, as shown in Figure 14-1.

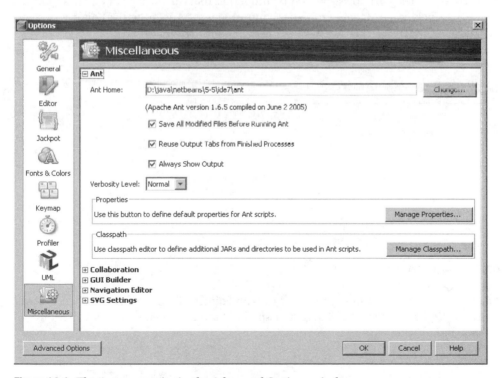

Figure 14-1. *The Ant properties in the Advanced Options window*

The following properties are available:

Ant Home: This defines the directory location where the Ant program executable and supporting files are installed. When NetBeans is initially installed, a distribution of Ant is installed along with it. You can also download and install a separate version of Ant and change the Ant Home property to reference that location.

Save All Modified Files Before Running Ant: If you are modifying several files at a time and need to execute a target, NetBeans will save each modified file before executing the Ant target specified. This can save you a lot of time and is also convenient.

Reuse Output Tabs from Finished Processes: This is a space saver. If you uncheck this option, every time you execute an Ant task, a new tab will open in the Output window. This doesn't sound too bad until you have spent several hours executing build targets and end up with dozens of tabs. If the property is checked, each time you execute an Ant target, NetBeans will reuse an existing tab for any target process that previously was complete.

Always Show Output: This directs NetBeans to bring the Output window to focus if it is not already and there is an error.

Verbosity Level: This specifies the amount of output that should be logged in the Output window. Several tasks, such as `copy`, `delete`, and `move`, have a `verbose` attribute that can be set. Your choices for this property are Quiet, Normal, Verbose, and Debug.

Properties: This section allows you to enter properties that can be used by all Ant scripts in NetBeans. Clicking the Manage Properties button opens the Ant Properties Editor, as shown in Figure 14-2. Here, you can enter properties in a *name=value* format. The properties can be used in your build files.

Figure 14-2. *The Ant Properties Editor*

Classpath: This section allows you to add JARs and directories that can be used by all Ant scripts in NetBeans. Click the Manage Classpath button to open the Classpath Editor.

NetBeans Project Build Files

NetBeans uses several related files to structure the build environment for a Java project. It uses targets and tasks, as in a normal Ant build file, but specific menu items and shortcuts are linked directly to targets, making for a tight integration between Ant and NetBeans.

Ant build files are not visible in the Projects window. NetBeans tries to abstract away the details of how projects are maintained and built during the normal day-to-day development tasks. You can view the Ant build files by switching to the Files window for a project. In this view, you can see the build.xml file for the project. Additional files are located in the nbproject directory. The following sections describe each of the project build files.

The build.xml File

The build.xml file is what Ant initially executes whenever a target needs to be executed. If you open the file, you will notice immediately that it contains very little information except for some comments. This is done to provide a flexible environment for you to work with NetBeans and Ant.

The targets that wrap Ant tasks are placed in the build-impl.xml file, which is explicitly referenced in the build.xml file via an import tag.

```
<import file="nbproject/build-impl.xml"/>
```

The import tag essentially makes the content of the build-impl.xml file function as if it were located in the build.xml file. Any targets defined in the imported file can be also overridden in the build.xml file.

The system-generated build-impl.xml file should never be modified (not that it can't be changed, but it's a best practice to leave it as is). If you need to modify or augment the behavior of a target, you can override it be redefining it in the build.xml file with a different set of tasks that it will perform.

You may want to override Ant targets for various reasons, such as to modify how an existing target works, add custom behaviors to the NetBeans build process, or integrate third-party tools into your Ant build scripts (such as a code coverage tool, as discussed in Chapter 16).

For example, for code I have written, I have needed to use the java.util.ResourceBundle class to read name/value pairs from a .properties file. In a project of type Java Application or Java Class Library, I will add the .properties file to the default package in the Source Packages node. When the code is compiled, the .properties file is compiled into the corresponding default package in the build/classes directory and is subsequently packaged into the JAR file. The problem arises when I do not want the .properties file to be included in the JAR, but I still want it copied into the build/classes and dist directories for easy access. I can arrange this in NetBeans by doing two things: excluding the .properties file from the JAR file and overriding a target defined in the build-impl.xml file.

First, to exclude the .properties file from the list of files that are included in the JAR file during the packaging process, I open the Project Properties window (right-click the project name and select Properties) and select the Packaging node on the left. The Exclude from JAR File field typically contains the value **/*.java,**/*.form. As shown in Figure 14-3, I add **/*.properties to the end of the value. Now when the JAR file is created, the .properties file will not be included.

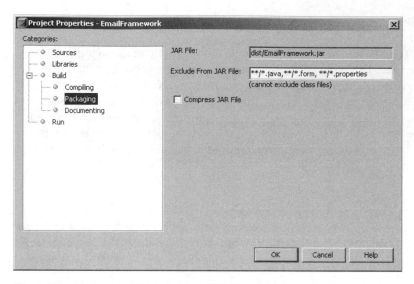

Figure 14-3. *Setting the Exclude from JAR File field for a project*

At this stage, the .properties file will also not be copied to the build/classes or dist directory. I remedy this by overriding the -post-jar target. If you open the build-impl.xml file and locate the target named jar, you will see its dependencies listed in the following order:

- init

- compile

- -pre-jar

- -do-jar-with-manifest

- -do-jar-without-manifest

- -do-jar-with-mainclass

- -do-jar-with-libraries

- -post-jar

The last target in the dependency chain is -post-jar. If you look at the definition of this target, you will see the following XML code:

```
<target name="-post-jar">
    <!-- Empty placeholder for easier customization. -->
    <!-- You can override this target in the ../build.xml file. -->
</target>
```

Notice that no tasks are in the -post-jar target. This is an empty placeholder target, provided so that you can define custom behaviors by overriding this task in the build.xml file. Here is the new -post-jar target I define at the bottom of the build.xml file:

```
<target name="-post-jar">
    <copy todir="${build.classes.dir}" >
        <fileset dir="${src.dir}" includes="**/*.properties" />
    </copy>
    <copy todir="${dist.dir}" >
        <fileset dir="${src.dir}" includes="**/*.properties" />
    </copy>
</target>
```

The new –post-jar target contains two copy tasks. Each task copies any .properties files from the source packages to the corresponding location in the build/classes directory and also into the dist directory.

The build-impl.xml File

The build-impl.xml file contains the core of the Ant tasks that NetBeans uses to execute and manage the project build. Project-related actions include Build, Clean and Build, Run Main Project, Run File, Test, and Generate Javadoc. Whether these actions are activated via menu items or keyboard shortcuts, they tie directly to Ant targets in the project build configuration.

As discussed in the previous section, the content of the build-impl.xml file is imported into the build.xml file. Any target can be overridden, but for the most part, you should not need to override the core targets. The build-impl.xml file for a Java Application or Java Class Library project is divided into several sections, as described in Table 14-2.

Table 14-2. *Sections of the build-impl.xml File*

Section	Description
Initialization	Initialize properties defined in the build file and in separate .properties files. Perform several conditional checks on project parameters and settings.
Compilation	Create build directories, compile the project code, or compile single files.
Dist	Create the distribution directory and package the compiled class files into a JAR file.
Execution	Execute the project class files or a single class file.
Debugging	Provide tasks for debugging projects and code in NetBeans.
Javadoc	Run the Javadoc tool against the project code and open a browser to view the generated report.
JUnit compilation	Compile all the project test files or a single test file.
JUnit execution	Execute one or all tests in a project.
JUnit debugging	Provide debugging tasks for project tests.
Applet	Provide Ant tasks for executing a Java applet.
Cleanup	Delete the build and dist directories and all the files inside them.

The build files for a Java Web Application project (and other project types in NetBeans) differ from those for a Java Application or Java Class Library project. The same types of files are created, but may contain different sets of targets and tasks. For example, the `build-impl.xml` file for a Java Web Application project contains targets for compiling JSP files, packaging the application into a WAR file instead of a JAR file, and deploying the code to the target application server. However, the core targets and tasks are similar across each of the project types.

The build-before-profiler.xml File

The `build-before-profiler.xml` file is only a backup of the `build.xml` file. When you first initiate the NetBeans Profiler for a project, the `build.xml` file is copied and named `build-before-profiler.xml`. The original `build.xml` file is modified with the addition of an `import` statement:

```
<import file="nbproject/ profiler-build-impl.xml "/>
```

■**Note** Chapter 2 described how to install the NetBeans Profiler, the code profiling tool that allows you to profile for memory, CPU, and performance problems, as well as monitor threads. For more information about using the NetBeans Profiler, visit `http://profiler.netbeans.org/`.

This `import` in the `build.xml` file allows the targets and tasks defined in the `profiler-build-impl.xml` file to be run during the normal project `build.xml` execution.

The profiler-build-impl.xml File

The `profiler-build-impl.xml` file defines the targets for profiling the project, a single file, applets, or tests, depending on how you activate the NetBeans Profiler. It is imported into the `build.xml` file so that the targets are part of the overall build configuration for a project. Similar to `build.xml`, the targets can be executed by using the menu items from the Profile menu. If you selected Profile ➤ Profile Main Project, then the `profile` target would execute.

```
<target name="profile" if="netbeans.home"
        depends="profile-init,compile"
        description="Profile a project in the IDE.">
    <nbprofiledirect>
        <classpath>
            <path path="${run.classpath}"/>
        </classpath>
    </nbprofiledirect>
    <profile/>
</target>
```

The `profile` target depends on the `profile-init` and `compile` targets to work correctly. You can't really profile code unless it compiles. It also wraps the `nbprofiledirect` task that defines the classpath for the classes to profile.

You can also profile a single source code file if there is a Main method defined in the class. With the file open in the Source Editor, select Profile ➤ Profile Other ➤ Profile "*MyFile.java*". You can also right-click the file in the Projects window and select Profile from the context menu. The profile-single target will then execute.

```
<target name="profile-single" if="netbeans.home"
        depends="profile-init,compile-single"
        description="Profile a selected class in the IDE.">
    <fail unless="profile.class">Must select a file in the IDE</fail>
    <nbprofiledirect>
    <classpath>
        <path path="${run.classpath}"/>
    </classpath>
    </nbprofiledirect>
    <profile classname="${profile.class}"/>
</target>
```

The profile-single target contains a fail clause that requires a class be selected for profiling. The profile task explicitly defines which class should be profiled via the classname attribute.

There are several other targets included in this file, but the only other two to note are -profile-pre-init and -profile-post-init. These two targets are initially blank. The profile target depends on the profile-init target, which, in turn, depends on the -profile-pre-init and -profile-post-init targets. You can override them in the build.xml file if there are additional tasks you need to execute before and after a profiling session executes.

The project.properties File

The project.properties file contains the name/value pairs of properties used throughout the various Ant build files. It contains project settings, project configuration details, and directory definitions. The build file will recognize the properties after execution of the following target from the build-impl.xml file:

```
<target name="-init-project" depends="-pre-init,-init-private,-init-user">
    <property file="nbproject/project.properties"/>
</target>
```

This target uses a property task to reference and load the information in the project.properties file. The properties can then be referenced in the usual format of ${propertyName}.

The following are some of the key values in the project.properties file:

```
build.dir=build
build.classes.dir=${build.dir}/classes
build.test.classes.dir=${build.dir}/test/classes
dist.dir=dist
dist.javadoc.dir=${dist.dir}/javadoc
javac.source=1.5
main.class=com.email.NewFile
src.dir=src
test.src.dir=test
```

Some of these properties define directory paths; others define project settings. The properties such as `java.source` and `main.class` can be set in the Project Properties window.

Working with Targets

You can activate the targets in the build configuration in several ways. The first and obvious is through the main menu items that correlate to specific targets. The second is by running the targets directly from the build files.

Locate the `build.xml` file in the Files window and right-click it to see the build file context menu. The context menu contains two relevant items: Run Target and Debug Target.

Running Targets

From the build file context menu, expand the Run Target submenu. You will see several target names displayed, as shown in Figure 14-4. If you click one of them, it will run that target. This is handy, especially if there is a target you want to run that performs a small chunk of work you need done without running the target that is at the beginning of a dependency chain.

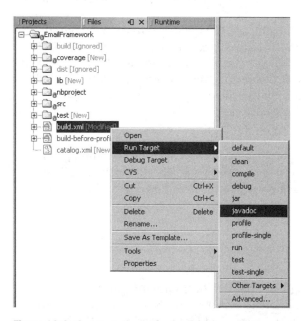

Figure 14-4. *Context menu for build files*

Clicking the Other Targets option displays a submenu that allows you to directly execute the remaining targets that are not in the first submenu. To see how to add keyboard shortcuts to a specific Ant target, check out the example in Chapter 16.

Debugging Targets

One of the many interesting features NetBeans provides is the ability to debug Ant files. Much in the same way you can debug Java source files, you can step through a build file line by line.

You can set a breakpoint in a build file, just as in a regular source code file: by clicking the line number in the glyph margin, as shown in Figure 14-5. You can then activate the debugging session for the target by right-clicking the build.xml file, selecting Debug Target, and choosing run from the submenu. This will trigger a debugging session for the run target and allow you to step through the build file.

```
336    <!--
337    ==================
338    EXECUTION SECTION
339    ==================
340    -->
341    <target name="run" depends="init,compile" description="Run a main class ">
       <j2seproject1:java>
343        <customize>
344            <arg line="${application.args}"/>
345        </customize>
346        </j2seproject1:java>
347    </target>
```

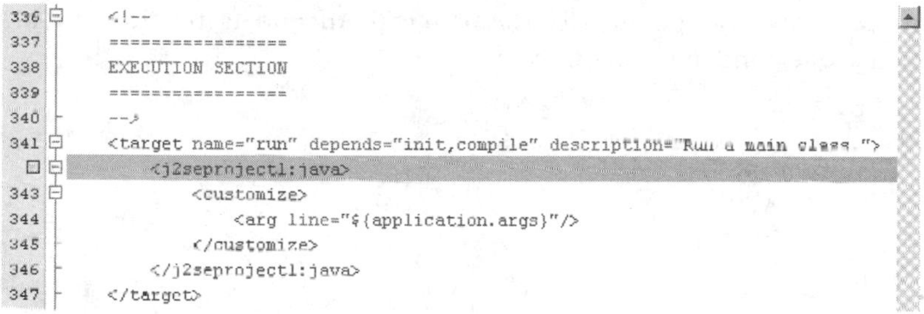

Figure 14-5. *Setting a breakpoint in an Ant build file*

Since Ant is so tightly integrated with NetBeans, you can access full debugging information using the IDE tools. For example, you can open the Local Variables window by selecting Window ➤ Debugging ➤ Local Variables or using the shortcut Alt+Shift+1.

As shown in Figure 14-6, a variety of variables are available during the debugging session. As you step through the build file, you can watch the values of those variables. This can be very useful if you need help debugging sporadic errors that occur while building your project code.

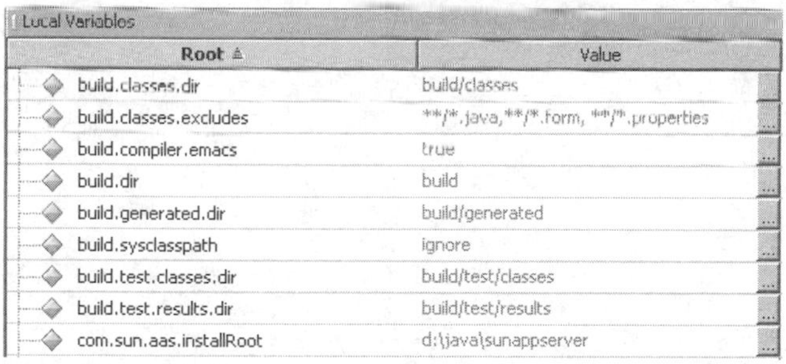

Root	Value
build.classes.dir	build/classes
build.classes.excludes	**/*.java,**/*.form, **/*.properties
build.compiler.emacs	true
build.dir	build
build.generated.dir	build/generated
build.sysclasspath	ignore
build.test.classes.dir	build/test/classes
build.test.results.dir	build/test/results
com.sun.aas.installRoot	d:\java\sunappserver

Figure 14-6. *Local variables during an Ant debug session*

Summary

This chapter provided a quick introduction to the Ant build tool. It covered the concepts of targets and tasks, and how they provide the necessary functionality to the build process of your application.

Ant offers a full array of tasks that provide functionality such as compiling source code, packaging class files, sending SMTP email, and sending files via FTP. Much of this functionality is created and inserted into build files when you create a NetBeans Java project. The generated build files are linked directly to menu items in NetBeans. As you use the build-related tools available in the NetBeans IDE, you are actually executing Ant targets. Even though NetBeans abstracts away many of the details, you should still be familiar with Ant and its functionality, in case you want to customize or extend the build process.

CHAPTER 15

JUnit Testing

Untested code has the potential to contain errors and bugs. Whether caused by an invalid assumption, an explicit coding mistake, or an otherwise unknown issue, bugs that appear in code cause problems. Developers lose time trying to find the mistake, organizations lose productivity, and companies lose money. For more critical systems, human lives can be lost if a software glitch occurs. This is why developers test code.

Testing should come as natural as breathing. Every time there is code being written, it should have a matching test. I won't go into the hotly debated topic of exactly when a test should be written. Some say after the code is finished, and some say before a single line of code is written. This chapter makes the general assumption that you write a class and then write a test. For those of you who write tests first, I will also review how to create empty JUnit test classes.

An industry-standard mechanism for testing code is via a framework called JUnit. This framework defines a simple API to extend to implement tests. JUnit tests can be executed via the command line, Ant tasks, or numerous Java tools.

Full support for JUnit is bundled directly into NetBeans. NetBeans provides various wizards and code-generation tools for the supported JUnit version (JUnit 3 at the time of this writing).

Note Currently, you can use JUnit 4 with NetBeans, but you will need to manually write your tests. NetBeans developers are working on the NetBeans wizards, Ant task support, and automatic test code generation of test classes for the newer version of JUnit.

Creating a JUnit Test Case

There are two scenarios for creating JUnit tests in NetBeans. The first is writing a test for a class that does not yet exist. The second is generating a JUnit class to test an existing Java source file.

Creating a New Test Class

NetBeans provides an option in the New File wizard for different types of JUnit classes. Here are the steps for creating a new empty test:

1. For any open Java project, right-click the project name in the Projects window and select New ➤ File/Folder.

2. In the wizard, select the JUnit category. In the File Types section on the right, select the Empty Test item. Then click the Next button.

3. In the New Empty Test window, shown in Figure 15-1, enter a class name. It is predefined as `NewEmptyJUnitTest`, but can be changed to whatever you need. Typically, JUnit tests follow a standard naming convention. If the class that will be tested is called `MyFile`, then the matching JUnit test is usually named `MyFileTest`. This is not required, but is a best practice.

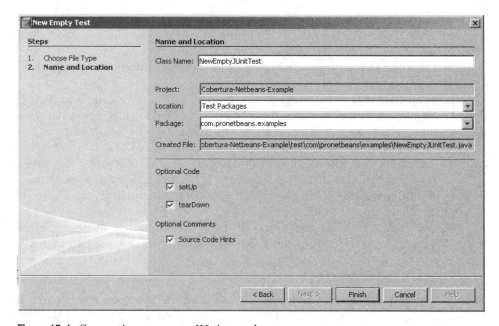

Figure 15-1. *Generating an empty JUnit test class*

4. If desired, you can change the values in the Location and Package fields. The Location field should be set to Test Packages, and the Package field is initially blank. If you right-click the name of a package that already exists in the Test Packages node and create a new empty test, this field is prepopulated with the package name.

5. You can select the check boxes to have the NetBeans New File wizard automatically generate method stubs for the `setUp` and `tearDown` methods. In simplest terms, these are generic utility methods used in a test class, but they are optional.

6. Optionally, select the Source Code Hints check box. If this is checked, NetBeans will insert some suggestions into the generated JUnit test file.

7. Click the Finish button to complete the file-creation process.

For ease of viewing, the comments have been stripped from the file, but the resulting code looks like the following:

```
package com.pronetbeans.examples;
import junit.framework.*;

public class NewEmptyJUnitTest extends TestCase {

    public NewEmptyJUnitTest(String testName) {
        super(testName);
    }
    protected void setUp() throws Exception {
    }
    protected void tearDown() throws Exception {
    }
    // TODO add test methods here. The name must begin with 'test'. For example:
    // public void testHello() {}
}
```

The NewEmptyJUnitTest class imports the standard junit.framework package. It also extends TestCase, which is the superclass for all JUnit tests. The empty method stubs for the setUp and tearDown methods have been generated and can be modified if desired.

Currently, there are no test methods in the NewEmptyJUnitTest class. If you selected the Source Code Hints check box in the wizard, you will see a TODO directive in the code (as in the preceding example), which will show up in the NetBeans To Do window.

Tip You can open the NetBeans To Do window by selecting Window ➤ To Do or using the keyboard shortcut Ctrl ı 6. The To Do window allows you to track all the TODO comments in your code. You can jump directly to them in the source by double-clicking any TODO listed in the window.

Creating a Test for an Existing Class

You can also create a new JUnit test class by modeling the test on an existing Java source file. The NetBeans JUnit module will examine the source file and generate method stubs and sample test code in each method. For example, suppose you have the following Calc class:

```
public class Calc {

    public int checkNum(int origVal) {

        int returnVal = 0;

        if(origVal > 10) {
            returnVal = origVal -1;
        }
```

```
        else {
            returnVal = origVal + 1;
        }

        return returnVal;
    }
}
```

This code contains a checkNum method, which takes a single parameter as an int primitive, performs a simple check comparison on it, and returns a modified value. To make sure this code functions as expected, you want to exercise the method using a variety of tests. You also want the tests to be repeatable, so you decide to create a JUnit test.

Using the Create Tests Dialog Box

To create the JUnit test based on the Calc class, right-click the Calc class name in the Projects window and select Tools ➤ Create JUnit Tests. With a class selected, you can also use the keyboard shortcut Ctrl+Shift+U. The Create Tests dialog box will appear, as shown in Figure 15-2.

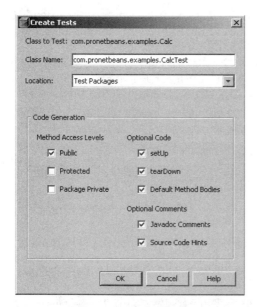

Figure 15-2. *The Create Tests dialog box for generating JUnit tests*

The Create Tests dialog box has several fields already filled out. The Class Name field contains a package and class name for the JUnit test. You can change this to whatever you want, but typically the package name should mirror the same package as the original source file.

■Note Remember the NetBeans project structure. The src directory contains the source packages, and the test directory contains the test sources. You can have a test with the same package name as its matching source class without having them in the same directory.

In the Create Tests dialog box, you can also specify the method access levels that will be included for the new JUnit class. These determine which methods in the original source file will have matching JUnit test methods generated.

The Optional Code section allows you to specify what is autogenerated in the test. You can have the wizard generate the setUp and tearDown methods, as well as the default method bodies for the methods that will be tested.

The Optional Comments section has check boxes for comments and hints. The Javadoc Comments option directs the wizard to generate standard Javadoc for the test methods that are created. The Source Code Hints option inserts TODO directives or other comments into the code as hints to the programmer of actions to take.

Once you have specified the options you want, click the OK button. The JUnit test will be generated.

Using the New File Wizard

An alternate method of creating a test for an existing class is to use the New File wizard. Select New ➤ File/Folder. In the JUnit category, select the Test for Existing Class option and click the Next button. You'll see the New Test for Existing Class window, as shown in Figure 15-3.

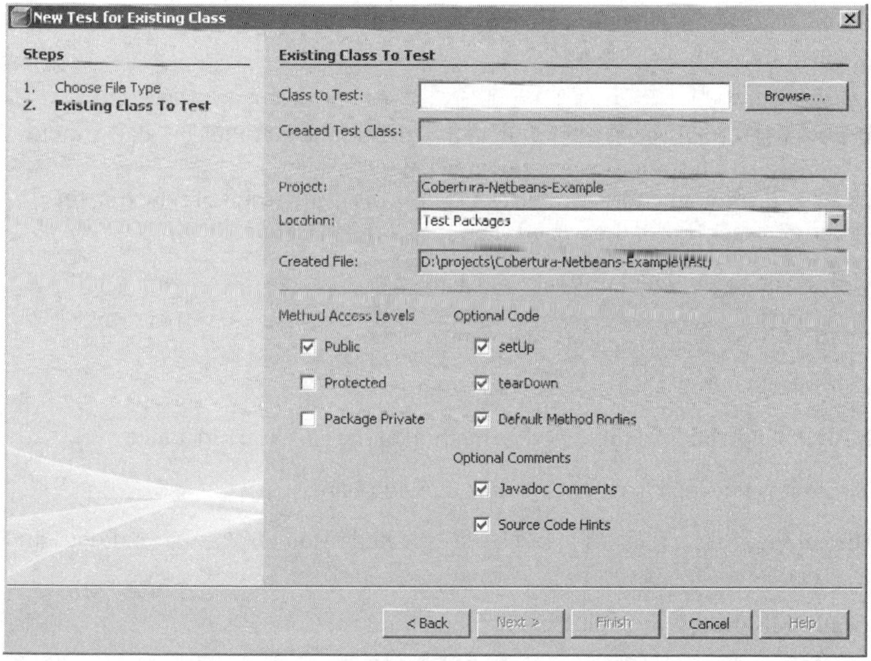

Figure 15-3. *Creating a JUnit test for an existing class*

This window looks very similar to the Create Tests dialog box (see Figure 15-2), but has two main differences. First, you need to specify the class you want to test. Click the Browse button and navigate the project package structure to find the class you want to test. Once you have selected which class to test, you will notice the other difference. In the Created Test Class field, you'll see that the wizard automatically named the JUnit test class for you based on the class you selected to test.

Viewing the Test

Whether you use the New File wizard or the Create JUnit Tests wizard, once the test class is generated, it will open in the Source Editor window. You will also see that the package and class are listed under the Test Packages node in the Projects window.

Here is an excerpt from the sample CalcTest class:

```
/**
 * Test of checkNum method, of class com.pronetbeans.examples.Calc.
 */
public void testCheckNum() {
    System.out.println("checkNum");

    int origVal = 0;
    Calc instance = new Calc();

    int expResult = 0;
    int result = instance.checkNum(origVal);
    assertEquals(expResult, result);

    // TODO review the generated test code and remove the default call to fail.
    fail("The test case is a prototype.");
}
```

The wizard analyzed the Calc class, determined that the public method checkNum should be included, and generated a test method for it named testCheckNum.

The testCheckNum method includes sample test code. This is the result of selecting the Default Method Bodies check box in the wizard. This test code does the following:

- Declares an int named origVal and sets it to zero

- Creates an instance of the Calc class named instance

- Declares an int named expResult and sets it to zero

- Passes the origVal variable to the checkNum method of the Calc class instance

- Sets the int that is returned to an int variable named result

- Calls a JUnit method assertEquals to test if the expected result (expResult) matches the actual result (result)

- Automatically fails the test by calling the JUnit method fail

The intention of this test is to pass a sample value to Calc.checkNum and compare the expected return result with the actual return result. The call to the fail method is automatically inserted into the test method to make sure that you at least review the method prior to running it. The fail and assertEquals methods are inherited from the TestCase superclass.

Tip In the test file in the Source Editor, you can press Ctrl+spacebar to open the code completion box. Here, you can review the numerous overloaded assertEquals methods and the other inherited JUnit methods available in the test class.

Modifying the Test

In this example, you will want to make a few changes to the code to make sure the test will pass. First, change the value of the origVal variable to 20. The Calc.checkNum method takes the value 20 and performs an if-else check on it. It should then subtract 1 from the value and return the value 19. Knowing what the method should return, you can set the expResult variable in the testCheckNum method to a value of 19. If you make these changes and remove the explicit call to fail, the resulting test method looks like this:

```
public void testCheckNum() {
    System.out.println("checkNum");

    int origVal = 20;
    Calc instance = new Calc();

    int expResult = 19;
    int result = instance.checkNum(origVal);
    assertEquals(expResult, result);
}
```

When the JUnit test classes execute, the testCheckNum method should now pass.

You do not have to use one of the assertEquals methods to pass or fail a test method. You can perform any manual comparison you like and explicitly fail the test case. Suppose you want the expected result to be 18. Based on an original value of 20, the actual result should be 19. You could write a test to check if the expected and actual results were equal and fail the test since they should *not* be equal, like this:

```
public void testCheckNumFail() {

    int origVal = 20;
    Calc instance = new Calc();

    int expResult = 18;
    int result = instance.checkNum(origVal);
    if(expResult == result) {
        fail("The expected result should NOT match the actual result.");
    }
}
```

Running JUnit Tests

Once you have written JUnit tests, you need to execute them. You can choose to run all the tests in a project or to run a test individually.

You can run the tests for an entire project in any of the following ways:

- Right-click the project name and select Test Project from the context menu.

- From the main menu, select Run ➤ Test "*Project-Name*".

- Use the keyboard shortcut Alt+F6.

You can run a single test in any of the following ways (using the `Calc` class test from the previous section as an example):

- Right-click the test class under the Test Packages node in the Projects window and select Run File. NetBeans knows it should be run as a JUnit test.

- If the test class is open in the Source Editor, right-click anywhere in the code and select Run File from the context menu.

- If the test class is selected in the Source Editor, Projects, or Files window, from the main menu, select Run ➤ Run File ➤ Run "Calc.java".

- If the test class is selected, use the keyboard shortcut Shift+F6.

- If the test's matching source class is open, select Run ➤ Run File ➤ Test "Calc.java". This will execute the matching JUnit test in the Test Packages node.

Viewing Test Results

After one or more JUnit tests have executed, you can view the results in the JUnit Test Results window. To open this window, select Window ➤ JUnit Test Results or use the keyboard shortcut Ctrl+Shift+6. Figure 15-4 shows an example of test results.

Figure 15-4. *The JUnit Test Results window after test case execution*

At the top of the JUnit Test Results window are two buttons that represent different views of the JUnit results and a button for filtering results. By default, the Statistics view appears. Clicking the Output button displays the standard output and error results from the JUnit test execution. If you used `System.out.*` or `System.err.*` in any of the tests or tested classes, the data will be listed.

The button to the right of the Output button allows you to filter the view to show only failed tests. If you click this filter button and execute the project tests, you will see lines displayed only for test classes that had at least one failure. This is a nice feature, especially if you are running hundreds of tests and only receiving a handful of failures. You can quickly see what is failing and not have to scroll down a long list of test classes that passed.

In the Statistics view for this example, you see the message "Both tests passed," since only two test methods were created. For each JUnit test class in the test package, you should see an individual line with the fully qualified class name and a pass/fail label next to it.

You can click the plus icon next to the class name to expand the class and display the individual method test cases. If a test method passed, it will be listed with a green "passed" label, along with the approximate time it took to execute.

To see what happens when a test fails, you can modify the CalcTest code from the previous section. In the testCheckNumFail method, change the code int expResult = 18; to read int expResult = 19;. The expected and actual results will then be equivalent, the if statement will pass, and the explicit call to the fail method will run, thereby failing the test case. After changing the code and running the JUnit tests, the JUnit Test Results window should display the results shown in Figure 15-5.

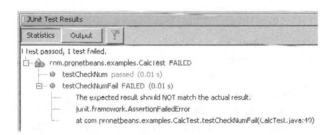

Figure 15-5. *The JUnit Test Results window after a test fails*

In this example, the Statistics view now shows the message "1 test passed, 1 test failed." Alongside the fully qualified class name is a red "FAILED" message. If numerous classes were listed, you could quickly pick out which class had at least one failure in it. Clicking the plus icon next to the class displays the individual test methods.

One of the nice features of the JUnit Test Results window is that, for any test method that failed, you can see error-related output by clicking the plus icon next to it. The message "The expected result should NOT match the actual result" was the text that was logged with the explicit call to the fail method in the CalcTest.testCheckNumFail method. You can double-click the line that lists that the testCheckNumFail method failed, and the CalcTest class will open in the Source Editor.

Generating Test Case Reports

An additional option for viewing JUnit results data is available. Since NetBeans projects are layered on top of Ant, you can use the JUnit Ant tasks to generate test case reports. (See Chapter 14 for more information about Ant tasks.)

Listing 15-1 shows a sample Ant task that allows you to execute the project test classes and generate a special output of JUnit test results.

Listing 15-1. *Ant Task for Executing Test Classes and Generating Test Result Output*

```xml
<target name="JUnit-Tests-With-Reports" depends="compile,compile-test">
    <junit fork="yes" dir="${basedir}" failureProperty="test.failed">
        <classpath location="${build.classes.dir}" />
        <classpath location="${build.test.classes.dir}" />
        <formatter type="xml" />
        <test name="${testcase}" todir="${reports.junit.dir}" if="testcase" />
        <batchtest todir="${reports.junit.dir}" unless="testcase">
            <fileset dir="${test.src.dir}">
                <include name="**/*Test.java" />
            </fileset>
        </batchtest>
    </junit>

    <junitreport todir="${reports.junit.dir}">
        <fileset dir="${reports.junit.dir}">
            <include name="TEST-*.xml" />
        </fileset>
        <report format="frames" todir="${reports.junit.dir}" />
    </junitreport>

</target>
```

The target is named `JUnit-Tests-With-Reports`, so it stands out as a custom Ant task in your build file. It depends on the NetBeans project targets of `compile` and `compile-test`, so that each time this target is executed, the code in the Source and Test Packages nodes are always compiled fresh.

It then uses the `junit` and `junitreport` Ant tasks. The script defines several classpath and directory properties to tell the Ant tasks where the source is located, which files to include, where to dump the output of the JUnit test execution, and where the final JUnit test results report is deposited. The property `${reports.junit.dir}` is defined higher up in the build file as follows:

```xml
<property name="reports.junit.dir" value="reports/junit/" />
```

I use a `reports` base directory, so that the other plug-ins I use can deposit results into subdirectories within it.

Once you have created the new target, you can trigger it to run the project tests and generate the JUnit report files any time you wish. The JUnit test result format is similar to a Javadoc-style web site. It lists the tests by package and class, and displays the pass/fail results for each individual method. Figure 15-6 shows a sample test results report.

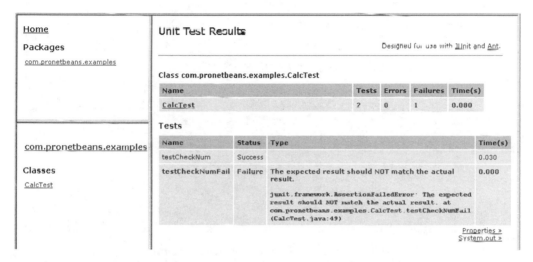

Figure 15-6. *A sample JUnit test results report*

As you can see, this report provides nearly identical information as the NetBeans JUnit Test Results window. However, with this approach, you can zip or tar the report files and catalog the results or send them to a colleague

Configuring JUnit Properties in NetBeans

You may have noticed that as you use the various JUnit wizards and tools, several properties are enabled or disabled by default (see Figures 15-1, 15-2, and 15-3).

As you create more and more test cases, you will not want to continually keep checking the same properties that you use most often. You can set which JUnit properties are enabled by default to save time when generating JUnit test classes.

To set the properties, select Tools ➤ Options. Click the Advanced Options button. In the left pane under the Testing folder, select the JUnit Module Settings option. The pane on the right will display the JUnit default properties, as shown in Figure 15-7. Using the check boxes, you can disable and enable properties as desired.

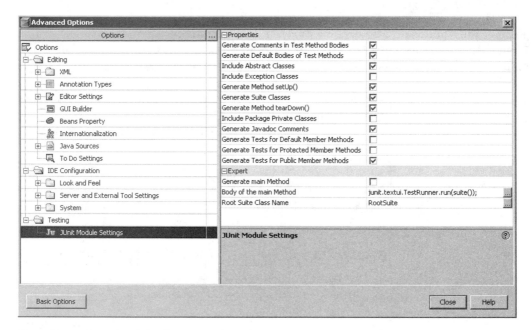

Figure 15-7. *The JUnit default properties in the Advanced Options window*

The properties in the Expert section offer additional settings:

Generate main Method: Specifies that a `main` method should be generated during the creation of the JUnit test.

Body of the main Method: Contains the default method body for the `main` method that is created. Adding a `main` method to your JUnit tests is necessary if you want to execute your tests from the command line.

Summary

This chapter covered how to run JUnit tests on your code. Writing tests that are thorough and repeatable provides a comfort level as source code evolves. Programmers can make enhancements to application code, run the set of project tests, and know what passes and fails.

The industry standard for testing is the JUnit framework. NetBeans provides support for JUnit via Ant build files and several integrated tools. You can use NetBeans to generate tests based on existing classes, execute all tests in a project, and directly view test results within the IDE.

CHAPTER 16

■■■

Using Code Coverage Tools

You know that it is important to write accurate and effective tests for your code. But how do you measure the effectiveness of your tests? In a perfect world, you would write a test for every class, every method, and every line of code. Depending on the complexity of your code base, this may be easy or extremely difficult.

How do you know when you've written enough tests? If you have 200 tests for your code, and they all pass, then you're finished, right? Not necessarily. You're finished writing tests only when you know for a fact how effective your tests are. Since testing often involves visual analysis by programmers and code-based test cases, it's difficult to know if 100 percent of your code has been tested. This is where code coverage tools come into play.

The first and obvious benefit of using a code coverage tool is being able to measure the coverage of your test cases (and, by association, the test case effectiveness). Untested code can lead to bugs, and bugs lead to many other problems.

Code coverage tools also help you identify areas in your code that are dead or unreachable. Suppose you have written test cases for all the public methods in your code. If your code coverage tool identifies one or more methods with private-level access that have never been executed, then you may be able to remove those methods from your source code. You can then use the NetBeans Safely Delete refactoring to check the method and make sure it is not called by any other code, as discussed in Chapter 11.

A good code coverage tool not only tracks if each line in each method was executed, but also how many times each line was executed. Using this data and the knowledge of what lines were and were not executed, you can understand the flow of program functionality and rearrange code blocks accordingly.

In this chapter, we'll focus on using Cobertura (Spanish for coverage), a free Java code coverage tool. At the end of the chapter, we'll take a quick look at the code coverage module available from the nbextras Update Center.

Getting Started with Cobertura

For a free tool, Cobertura provides a decent mix of functionality and usability. Several other free and fee-based code coverage tools, such as Emma and Clover, compete with Cobertura. These tools might contain more features, but they are more difficult to use or understand. One of the reasons I use Cobertura is that is generates easy-to-understand reports.

Using Cobertura, you can identify which parts of your Java program are lacking test coverage. It works by adding special markers, sometimes referred to as *instrumentation*, into the compiled classes using a library called ASM. ASM is a Java framework for bytecode manipulation from ObjectWeb.

Originally created by Mark Doliner at SAS, Cobertura is maintained by a variety of members of the open source community. It is based on the jcoverage tool and is hosted at SourceForge.net. The project web site contains a pretty good set of usage instructions and documentation.

Installing and Running Cobertura

You can download the files for Cobertura from the project web site at `http://cobertura.sourceforge.net`.

Once you have unpacked the install file, you will have the base batch/shell scripts, the Cobertura and supporting JAR files, and a sample application. I highly recommend setting an environment variable on your local system named `COBERTURA_HOME` that points to the root directory where these files are located. This allows you to reference the files in Ant build scripts and other locations, without having to hard-code a specific directory anywhere.

You can run Cobertura using two main methods. The first is via a set of handy batch files for a Windows platform and shell scripts for Unix-based users. These execute the Cobertura Java libraries and pass in the necessary command-line arguments that are required. The other main method of using Cobertura is via tasks in an Ant build script. This is an extremely useful way of integrating a code coverage tool directly into your build and test process. The "Using Cobertura Functions" section later in this chapter describes both methods.

Cobertura makes use of a special file typically named `cobertura.ser`. This file is where the execution data is stored and retrieved. It represents a set of serialized Java objects, and the Cobertura API uses it internally to read and write information.

Examining a Cobertura Report

The end result of running Cobertura is to generate a set of reports. The reports are formatted like Javadoc and arranged by packages and classes. Cobertura includes valuable information in the report, such as the percentage of lines and branches covered for each class, for each package, and for the overall project. You can also see the McCabe cyclomatic code complexity score, which helps you identify areas for focused unit testing.

■**Note** Code that has a high percentage of coverage is not necessarily effectively tested. You could have written hundreds of test cases to exercise one method and each line in that method. That does not mean your suite of tests handles every possible scenario that might occur in the actual code.

You can navigate through the report by clicking package names to view the list of classes in that package. You can then click the class name to view the individual class report.

Package-Level Report

Figure 16-1 shows a sample Cobertura report. In the upper-left area is a list of the packages that are included in the report. If you click a package name, the lower-left area changes to display just the classes in that package. The area on the right displays the classes in that package, along with some of Cobertura's class data.

The top table on the right side of the example in Figure 16-1 is the overall package summary. It lists the package name, the total number of classes included in the package, the average percentage of line and branch coverage for all the classes in the package, and the McCabe complexity score. The bottom table in the sample report displays similar information for individual classes. The name of the class is hyperlinked to a drill-down report for the class, as described in the next section.

The columns for line and branch coverage show the results as a red and green bar graph, percentages, and numbers of lines. In Figure 16-1, the NumLoop class has 58 percent line coverage. The red and green bar graph shows that 22 out of a total of 38 lines were covered or executed. This means that at least one test ran through the code that was covered. The branch coverage for the NumLoop class is shown as 64 percent, or 7 out of 11 branches. A branch is counted as any decision point, such as an if else or switch statement.

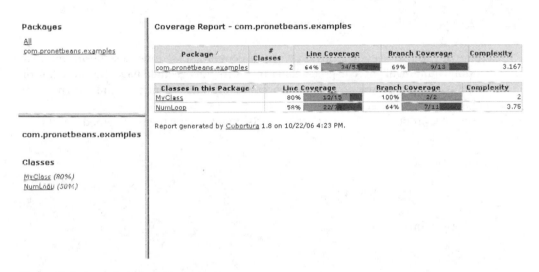

Figure 16-1. *Sample Cobertura report*

As mentioned previously, the Complexity column in the report represents the McCabe cyclomatic code complexity score. This is a basic calculation that estimates the overall complexity of the code based on the number of paths code execution can take and assigns it a score. The higher the score, the more complex the code is supposed to be. Complex code is more difficult to understand, and thus more difficult to maintain. This helps you identify these complex areas for more focused testing.

Source-Code Level Report

Figure 16-2 shows an example of a class-level coverage report. The table along the top of the figure shows the same general summary that is displayed in the package-level report. The rest of the report shows a specially formatted version of the source code of the file. The column of numbers along the left side represents the original line numbers from the source code. The second column of numbers represents the number of times each line was executed. In the example in Figure 16-2, line 7 was executed once, as was line 9. Lines 12 and 13 were not executed.

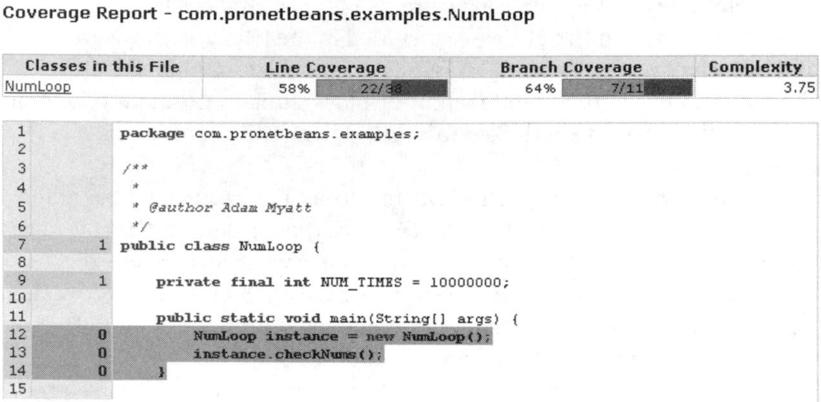

Coverage Report - com.pronetbeans.examples.NumLoop

Classes in this File	Line Coverage		Branch Coverage		Complexity
NumLoop	58%	22/38	64%	7/11	3.75

```
1              package com.pronetbeans.examples;
2
3              /**
4               *
5               * @author Adam Myatt
6               */
7         1    public class NumLoop {
8
9         1        private final int NUM_TIMES = 10000000;
10
11                 public static void main(String[] args) {
12        0            NumLoop instance = new NumLoop();
13        0            instance.checkNums();
14        0        }
15
```

Figure 16-2. *Cobertura drill-down report of source code*

The lines are also color-coded. Lines that were executed at least once have the line number and execution count highlighted in green. Lines that were not executed have the entire line of code highlighted in red. (However, Cobertura occasionally makes a mistake and does not always color-code lines correctly.)

For example, suppose you have a class NumUtils that defines a method named conditionalCheck:

```
public class NumUtils
{
    public int conditionalCheck(int i)
    {
        int iReturnVal = 0;

        if(i==0) {
            iReturnVal = i + 1;
        }
        else if (i>0 && i<8) {
            iReturnVal = i + 2;
        }
        else if (i==8) {
            iReturnVal = i + 3;
        }
        else {
            iReturnVal = i;
        }

        return iReturnVal;
    }
}
```

This method obviously doesn't do much, but it does provide a simple execution path to illustrate how you can see the code coverage results using Cobertura. The method takes an int parameter, performs several if-else checks, and returns a result. The execution path is simple and basically assumes the following:

- If the number passed in is 0, then add 1 and return the result.

- If the number passed in is between 1 and 7, then add 2 and return the result.

- If the number passed in is 8, then add 3 and return the result.

- If the number passed in is greater than 8, then return the original number.

Suppose you have the following JUnit test code for exercising the conditionalCheck method:

```
public void testconditionalCheck()
{
    NumUtils instance = new NumUtils();

    for(int i=0;i<1000;i++)
    {
        instance.conditionalCheck(8);
        instance.conditionalCheck(9);
        instance.conditionalCheck(10);
    }
}
```

This test method creates an instance of the NumUtils class, loops 1,000 times, and passes the values 8, 9, and 10 to the conditionalCheck method. It is indeed a silly test, but suppose this is somehow representative of real data requested by a customer. The important thing to note is that the conditionalCheck method should be executed a total of 3,000 times.

Once you have configured Cobertura to analyze your classes (covered in the next section), and you have executed your tests, you can see the source-level view of the conditionalCheck method, as shown in Figure 16-3.

```
24              public int conditionalCheck(int i)
25              {
26 3000             int iReturnVal = 0;
27
28 3000             if(i==0) {
29    0                 iReturnVal = i + 1;
30    0             }
31 3000             else if (i>0 && i<8) {
32    0                 iReturnVal = i + 2;
33    0             }
34 3000             else if (i==8) {
35 1000                 iReturnVal = i + 3;
36 1000             }
37                  else {
38 2000                 iReturnVal = i;
39                  }
40
41 3000             return iReturnVal;
42              }
43
44
45          }
```

Figure 16-3. *The Cobertura source-level report for the NumUtils class*

The report shows that line 26 was executed a total of 3,000 times, as expected. The if-else block starts at line 28 and the initial int comparison is made. The conditional check fails, since only the values 8, 9, and 10 are passed into the method. Thus, line 29 never executes, as indicated by the 0 in the second column and the red highlighting across the line. The same is true for the second conditional check. It fails and the code inside the else block never executes. The conditional check on line 34 succeeds. Since the value 8 was passed in 1,000 times, you see that line 35 has the execution count of 1,000 in the second column. Finally, the fall-through else clause was executed a total of 2,000 times, for the 1,000 values of 9 and the 1,000 values of 10.

The source-level report in Figure 16-3 not only looks pretty, but it also tells you some important information. First, you need to write several new tests. The conditional checks on lines 28 and 31 need to be met by at least one test so you can try out the code inside those blocks. As stated previously, it is a general assumption that untested code leads to bugs. You need to test the lines highlighted in red.

The report also shows where your code can be optimized. Out of a total of 3,000 executions, the fall-through else clause was hit 2,000 times, or approximately 66 percent of the time. The else clause that tests the parameter value to see if it is equivalent to 8 succeeds 1,000 times, or 33 percent of the time. Thus, you can assume that 99 percent of the time, the code performs the first two conditional checks on lines 28 and 31 unnecessarily. The execution time differences may be milliseconds (possibly nanoseconds), but depending on the execution path and complexity of your code, this type of optimization may pay off with better results.

Taking into account the optimizations suggested in the Cobertura report, you might reorganize the conditionalCheck method as follows:

```
public class NumUtils
{
    public int conditionalCheck(int i)
    {
        int iReturnVal = 0;

        if(i > 8) {
            iReturnVal = i;
        }
        else if (i==8) {
            iReturnVal = i + 3;
        }
        else if(i==0) {
            iReturnVal = i + 1;
        }
        else if (i>0 && i<8) {
            iReturnVal = i + 2;
        }

        return iReturnVal;
    }
}
```

■**Note** The newly formatted `conditionalCheck` method lacks an important check for negative values that the original method caught. I'll leave the implementation as an exercise for the reader, but suffice it to say that you should really make sure negative values are caught and handled appropriately.

Using Cobertura Functions

In this section, you will learn how to use the different functions of Cobertura via Ant targets and command scripts. Each core function possesses a set of parameters that need to be specified for the function to work correctly. Some parameters are required, and some are optional.

Instrument

The instrument function performs the physical modification of class files. The parameters you need to specify detail which classes should be instrumented and where those instrumented classes should be placed.

Here is an example of an Ant task for using the instrument function:

```
<cobertura-instrument todir="${instrumented.classes.dir}"
                             datafile="cobertura.ser">
    <ignore regex="org.apache.log4j.*" />
    <fileset dir="${build.classes.dir}">
        <include name="**/*.class" />
        <exclude name="**/*Test.class" />
    </fileset>
</cobertura-instrument>
```

In this Ant task, the `todir` attribute uses the build file property `${instrumented.classes.dir}` to define where it will place the instrumented class files. The `todir` attribute could also use a static value, such as a full directory path. The `datafile` attribute tells Cobertura the explicit name of the file that the instrumented classes use to collect and store data. Typically, it is named `cobertura.ser`, but you can change this to whatever you wish. You need to make sure that the name is consistent across the different Cobertura functions.

The other elements in the Ant task are pretty standard. It uses an `ignore` element, which directs the `cobertura-instrument` task to not instrument classes matching the regular expression specified. It also uses a `fileset` element to define a directory and a pattern of classes to instrument. The `exclude` element tells the `cobertura-instrument` task to not instrument classes that end with the characters `Test`. Your tests should not be in the same directory as your classes, but just in case, this `exclude` is helpful. You can remove it if you have actual classes that need to contain the word `Test`.

Here is an example of command-line usage of the instrument function:

```
cobertura-instrument.bat --basedir d:\project\MyApp\build\classes
--datafile cobertura.ser
--destination d:\project\MyApp\build\classes\instrumented
--ignore org.apache.log4j.*
*.class
```

In the command-line example, the cobertura-instrument.bat file is executed. It eventually ends up calling the same Java API that the cobertura-instrument Ant task calls. The parameters are just handled differently. In the command-line usage, the parameter --basedir tells Cobertura where to start looking for class files. The --datafile parameter allows you to optionally define the name of the data file. If you do not specify this property, it defaults to cobertura.ser.

The --destination property defines the directory where the instrumented classes are copied. The --ignore parameter is the same as the ignore element in the Ant task. It allows you to exclude a specific pattern of classes, regardless of physical location. The last value to pass in is the class files to instrument.

Check

The Cobertura check feature helps your development organization maintain a healthy level of code coverage. This feature can be used to check the line and branch coverage for your project and fail the build process if the desired levels are not met. This feature is especially useful if you use an automated build process or continuous integration server. If the developers have not written enough tests, the Cobertura check feature can warn you.

Here is an example of Ant task for using the check feature:

```
<cobertura-check branchrate="70" linerate="85" />
```

This Ant task tells Cobertura to enforce a branch coverage rate of 70 percent and a line coverage rate of 85 percent for *each class*. If the rates are not met, then the build process will fail.

Here is another example:

```
<cobertura-check branchrate="50" linerate="50">
    <regex pattern="com.pronetbeans.examples.utils.*"
                branchrate="80" linerate="90"/>
</cobertura-check>
```

In this example, the branch and line coverage rates are 50 percent. This means each class must have at least 50 percent coverage for both fields. Additionally, the task defines that for the classes in the com.pronetbeans.examples.utils package, the branch coverage rate is 80 percent and the line coverage rate is 90 percent. The Ant task provides quite a bit of flexibility for defining the acceptable levels of coverage per class, per package, or for the project overall.

Here is an example of command-line usage of the check feature:

```
cobertura-check.bat --datafile cobertura.ser
                                --branch 50
                                --line 50
                                --totalbranch 80
                                --totalline 80
```

For the command-line execution, the properties differ slightly from the Ant attributes. Table 16-1 lists the attributes for the check feature.

Table 16-1. *The Attributes/Parameters for the Cobertura Check Feature*

Command Line	Ant Name	Description
branch	branchrate	The percentage of branch coverage each class is required to meet
totalbranch	totalbranchrate	The percentage of branch coverage the entire code base is required to meet
line	linerate	The percentage of line coverage each class is required to meet
totalline	totallinerate	The percentage of line coverage the entire code base is required to meet
packageline	packagelinerate	The percentage of line coverage the package is required to meet
packagebranch	packagebranchrate	The percentage of branch coverage the package is required to meet
haltonfailure	haltonfailure	If set to true, Cobertura will fail the build if the line and branch rates are not met
failureproperty	failureproperty	Used if haltonfailure is set to false to indicate a check item failed
datafile	datafile	Typically cobertura.ser, but this is configurable

Merge

The Cobertura merge feature allows you to combine the analysis of multiple executions of instrumented code. You can merge the data from tests conducted on separate machines or separate directories. This can be useful if you need to test code across clustered servers or different environments, such as for a client/server program.

Here is an example of Ant task for using the merge feature:

```
<cobertura-merge datafile="cobertura.ser">
    <fileset dir="${instrumented.classes.dir}">
        <include name="clusternode1/cobertura.ser" />
        <include name="clusternode2/cobertura.ser" />
        <include name="clusternode3/cobertura.ser" />
        <include name="clusternode4/cobertura.ser" />
    </fileset>
</cobertura-merge>
```

In this example, you specify the base location of the cobertura.ser data files using the fileset element. The datafile attribute for the cobertura-merge task tells Cobertura the destination filename for the merged data files. You then need to specify two or more data files to merge together.

Here is an example of command-line usage of the merge feature:

```
cobertura-merge.bat --datafile d:\projects\MyApp\build\cobertura.ser
d:\projects\MyApp\build\clusternode1\cobertura.ser
d:\projects\MyApp\build\clusternode2\cobertura.ser
```

Report

The Cobertura report function takes all the aggregated data collected in one or more cobertura.ser files and generates the final report. It also allows you to point the tool at the original source code for the instrumented classes, so that Cobertura can generate the source-level reports.

Here is an example of an Ant task for using the report function:

```
<cobertura-report format="html"
destdir="${coveragereport.dir}"
srcdir="${src.dir}" />
```

In this example, the format attribute can be either HTML or XML. The destdir attribute specifies where you want the report files to be generated. The srcdir attribute specifies the location of the source code for the instrumented classes.

You can also format the cobertura-report Ant task like this:

```
<cobertura-report format="html" destdir="${coveragereport.dir}" >
    <fileset dir="${src.dir}">
        <include name="**/*.java" />
    </fileset>
</cobertura-report>
```

This format is useful if you need to specify multiple fileset elements for different source code locations or use include and exclude elements to filter different sets of Java files.

Here is an example of command-line usage of the report function:

```
cobertura-report.bat --format html
--datafile d:\projects\MyApp\build\cobertura.ser
--destination d:\projects\MyApp\reports\coverage
d:\projects\MyApp\src
```

In this command-line example, note that the location of the source code does not have an attribute name, but is merely a command-line value.

Once the task is finished executing, a set of files is created in the destination directory. The default homepage for the report is named index.html.

Using Cobertura in NetBeans

At the time of this writing, Cobertura does not have a plug-in to seamlessly integrate with NetBeans. You need to integrate with an Ant build.xml file. Since NetBeans projects are structured using Ant, this is easy to do.

Integrating with the Project Build File

As you learned in Chapter 14, the build.xml file is mostly empty. It allows you to define your own tasks or to override existing tasks. You can include the Cobertura tasks, wrap them with targets, and link them to NetBeans menus or toolbars. It's not perfect, but I found this to be an effective way for integrating tools that support Ant and do not have an actual plug-in for NetBeans.

To start, I define the following lines in the project build.xml file.

```
<property environment="env" />
<property name="cobertura.dir" value="${env.COBERTURA_HOME}" />
<property name="instrumented.classes.dir" value="build/test/instrumented/" />
<property name="reports.junit.dir" value="reports/junit/" />
<property name="reports.cobertura.dir" value="reports/cobertura/" />
```

These lines define an environment variable and several properties I use through the Cobertura tasks. The most notable is the cobertura.dir property, which points to the system environment variable COBERTURA_HOME, which was created during the installation of Cobertura. The rest of the properties simply define directory locations.

I then need to define the classpath for the Cobertura tasks so Ant recognizes Cobertura:

```
<taskdef classpathref="cobertura_classpath" resource="tasks.properties" />
<path id="cobertura_classpath">
    <fileset dir="${cobertura.dir}">
        <include name="cobertura.jar" />
        <include name="lib/**/*.jar" />
    </fileset>
</path>
```

This classpath definition also defines the location of the cobertura.jar file and supporting JAR files. I can then start defining my custom-named targets. First, I perform several initialization steps.

```
<target name="Cobertura-Init" depends="init">
    <mkdir dir="reports" />
    <mkdir dir="reports/junit/" />
    <mkdir dir="reports/cobertura/" />

    <delete file="cobertura.ser" />
</target>
```

This target creates the report directories if they do not already exist. It then tries to delete the cobertura.ser file so that the data that is read during the testing of the instrumented classes is fresh. It also lists as a dependency the NetBeans project init target defined in the build-impl.xml file. This is so the NetBeans project data is properly initialized. It isn't really necessary, but I do it anyway.

Next, I define the Cobertura-Instrument target, which performs the actual instrumentation of Java class files.

```
<target name="Cobertura-Instrument" depends="Cobertura-Init,compile">
    <delete dir="${instrumented.classes.dir}" />

    <cobertura-instrument todir="${instrumented.classes.dir}"
                                    datafile="cobertura.ser">
        <ignore regex="org.apache.log4j.*" />
        <fileset dir="${build.classes.dir}">
            <include name="**/*.class" />
        </fileset>
    </cobertura-instrument>
</target>
```

This target starts by deleting the directory that contains the instrumented classes. It then executes the `cobertura-instrument` task, which instruments the class files in the build directory. I marked the task as having a dependency of the NetBeans project task named `compile` so that the source files are correctly compiled and placed in the `build/classes` directory in the NetBeans project structure. This performs the instrumentation, but you still need to define for NetBeans and Cobertura how to execute the tests.

The target `Cobertura-Tests`, defined as follows, wraps up the actual execution of the JUnit tests into one task.

```
<target name="Cobertura-Tests"
        depends="Cobertura-Init,compile,compile-test,Cobertura-Instrument">
    <junit fork="yes" dir="${basedir}" failureProperty="test.failed">
        <classpath location="${instrumented.classes.dir}" />
        <classpath location="${build.classes.dir}" />
        <classpath location="${build.test.classes.dir}" />
        <classpath refid="cobertura_classpath" />

        <formatter type="xml" />
        <test name="${testcase}" todir="${reports.junit.dir}" if="testcase" />
        <batchtest todir="${reports.junit.dir}" unless="testcase">
            <fileset dir="${test.src.dir}">
                <include name="**/*Test.java" />
            </fileset>
        </batchtest>
    </junit>

    <junitreport todir="${reports.junit.dir}">
        <fileset dir="${reports.junit.dir}">
            <include name="TEST-*.xml" />
        </fileset>
        <report format="frames" todir="${reports.junit.dir}" />
    </junitreport>

</target>
```

The important thing to note is that the first classpath defined for the JUnit task references the instrumented classes. This is necessary for Cobertura to correctly execute the tests against the instrumented classes. The Cobertura-Tests target also generates the JUnit results in XML format and uses that XML data to generate an HTML-based JUnit report.

Finally, I use a target named Cobertura-Report to wrap the cobertura-report task.

```
<target name="Cobertura-Report">
    <cobertura-report destdir="${reports.cobertura.dir}" srcdir="${src.dir}" />
</target>
```

This task generates the HTML-based Cobertura report using the standard cobertura.ser file, links to the source files in the source directory, and places the report files in the specified directory.

That's all there is to it. It may seem a little complicated, but once you have added the Ant targets to the build.xml file, it is simple to execute the required Ant targets.

To use this implementation, all you need to do is execute the Cobertura-Tests target and the Cobertura-Report target. These two are separate, since you may want to retest your code several times before generating a complete Cobertura report.

You also have the option of integrating these steps into the standard Ant targets used by NetBeans. You can override the NetBeans project target named test as follows:

```
<target name="test" depends="Cobertura-Init,compile,compile-test, ➥
Cobertura-Instrument,-pre-test-run,Cobertura-Tests,-post-test-run,-test-browse, ➥
Cobertura-Report" description="Use Cobertura to compile, instrument, and test ➥
classes. Generates report."/>
```

The test target lists several NetBeans targets and Cobertura targets as dependencies in a specific order. This list tells NetBeans to execute this target each time you activate the Test Project item from the main Run menu. It compiles the source and test code, instruments the classes, executes the JUnit tests against the instrumented classes, displays the JUnit summary in the JUnit Test Results window, and generates the Cobertura reports.

Creating Shortcuts to Ant Targets

If you do not want to integrate directly with the Test menu item, you can create shortcuts to the Ant targets. Follow these steps to create a Cobertura toolbar with shortcuts:

1. Select Tools ➤ Options. In the Basic Options window, click the Advanced Options button. Under the Look and Feel node, right-click the Toolbars node and select Add Toolbar. Type in the name **Cobertura** and click the OK button. The Cobertura toolbar has now been added to the list, as shown in Figure 16-4. Exit the Advanced Options window.

2. In the Files window, find the build.xml file and click the plus sign next to the node to display the list of Ant targets. For the Cobertura-Tests target, right-click and select Create Shortcut from the context menu.

3. In the Create Shortcut to Ant Target window of the Toolbar wizard, click the Add a Toolbar Button check box, and then click Next. As shown in Figure 16-5, you need to select which toolbar you want the shortcut to appear on and name the shortcut. Once you have set the name and selected the toolbar, click the Finish button.

Figure 16-4. *The Cobertura toolbar in the Advanced Options window*

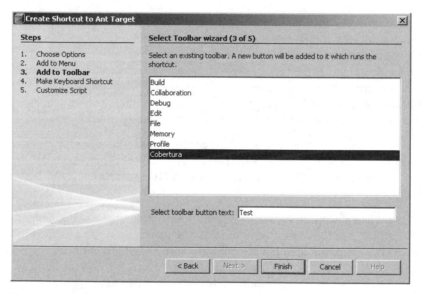

Figure 16-5. *Selecting the toolbar for the new shortcut*

4. Repeat steps 2 and 3 for the `Cobertura-Report` target and name the shortcut **Report**. You should then have a new toolbar that looks similar to Figure 16-6.

With these two toolbar shortcuts, you have quick access to the features Cobertura provides. The Test button allows you to instrument and test all your project classes. The Report button allows you to regenerate the Cobertura reports when you want to view the results of your tests and review the coverage.

■Tip The procedure described in this section can be used to create a shortcut for any Ant target. You can create a set of toolbars and shortcuts to provide quick access to the Ant targets you plan to use most often.

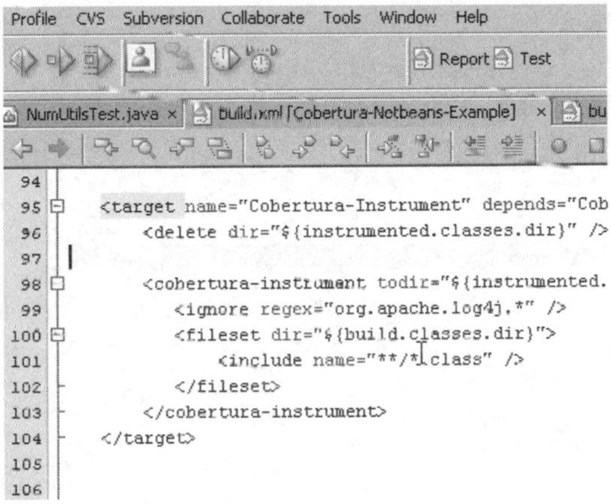

Figure 16-6. *The new Cobertura toolbar*

Using the Unit Tests Code Coverage Viewer

Fairly recently, a new module that performs code coverage inside NetBeans appeared on the nbextras.org site. This tool is based on Emma at the core and is listed as open source (however, the source code has been unavailable for quite some time).

Using the nbextras Update Center, you can install and evaluate the Unit Tests Code Coverage Viewer tool. The tool seems to hold great promise, so I will cover it briefly here.

The nbextras description of the plug-in describes it as a service that color-codes Java source files according to the unit tests coverage data. As you execute unit tests in NetBeans, the color-coding in the code displayed in the Source Editor is updated. This provides almost real-time data on the code coverage of a file.

Once installed, you can activate the tool by right-clicking the name of the project and selecting Coverage ➤ Activate Coverage Collection. There are no configurable parameters or options to set. Simply run your tests and open any tested source file. If the code in your source files is covered by a test, the lines should be highlighted. Lines that are not covered by tests are not highlighted.

Figure 16-7 shows the highlighted lines in the conditionalCheck method that we covered in the Cobertura section earlier in the chapter. The module highlights nearly the same lines as Cobertura, but does not list the number of times each line was executed. Its advantage is that the highlighting is built directly into the IDE, so you can modify your code, execute the tests, and get near-real-time feedback.

```
23
24        public int conditionalCheck(int i)
25   ⊟    {
             int iReturnVal = 0;
27
             if(i==0) {
29               iReturnVal = i + 1;
30           }
             else if (i>0 && i<8) {
32               iReturnVal = i + 2;
33           }
             else if (i==8) {
                 iReturnVal = i + 3;
             }
37           else {
                 iReturnVal = i;
39           }
40
             return iReturnVal;
42       }
43
```

Figure 16-7. *The highlighted code after test execution in the Unit Tests Code Coverage Viewer*

Summary

This chapter introduced using code coverage tools to measure the coverage of your test cases, as well as to gain information that helps you optimize your code.

Cobertura is a nice open source tool that provides a range of customizable features, but does not have an actual plug-in for NetBeans. Since it can be used in an Ant build script, you can easily integrate it with your project build process, whether you are working directly in NetBeans or externally in an automated build server environment. Cobertura provides easy-to-understand reports.

The Unit Tests Code Coverage Viewer module provides a standard plug-in integration with NetBeans. It allows you to display code coverage metrics directly in your source code, but does not provide as much overall information about the code coverage or as many configurable options as Cobertura does.

■ ■ ■

CHAPTER 17

Working with NetBeans Developer Collaboration Tools

In today's fast-paced global economy, a determining element for success is the ability to collaborate and share information among numerous teams. Being able to communicate complex sets of data, send email, chat online, and digitally share computer screens can give software development teams a significant advantage.

There are many models for collaboration between geographically separated development teams. Some teams hold phone conferences while looking at and discussing the same pieces of code. A problem arises when one side of the call changes code that the other side cannot see. For the two sides of the phone call to stay up-to-date, they need to email the changes or commit to a code repository. This can become time-consuming and cumbersome.

Other teams use sophisticated instant messaging software. This allows them to actually share the screen of one member with everyone on the team. As that person changes something on screen, everyone can see it. But this approach can create a bottleneck that can significantly slow the collaborative editing process. The person sharing usually has the ability to allow someone else to control the screen and make changes, but this, too, can be a slow process.

The NetBeans Developer Collaboration Tools address many of these problems. NetBeans allows you and your team to register for accounts, maintain lists of contacts, conduct online chat sessions, exchange messages, and share NetBeans projects and code. Your teams can even perform simultaneous edits on the same file. It facilitates a flexible, time-saving team-coding environment unlike any other approach.

Installing and Configuring the Collaboration Tools

The NetBeans Developer Collaboration Tools are not installed by default. To install them, select Tools ➤ Update Center and choose the NetBeans Update Center. Select the Developer Collaboration module and proceed through the Update Center wizard until the module is installed. Once it is installed, you will notice the new Collaborate menu item in the main menu bar.

The Developer Collaboration Tools have several properties you may want to set before beginning to use them. Select Tools ➤ Options and choose Miscellaneous from the pane on the left side of the window. Click the plus sign next to the Collaboration item, and you will see the available properties, as shown in Figure 17-1.

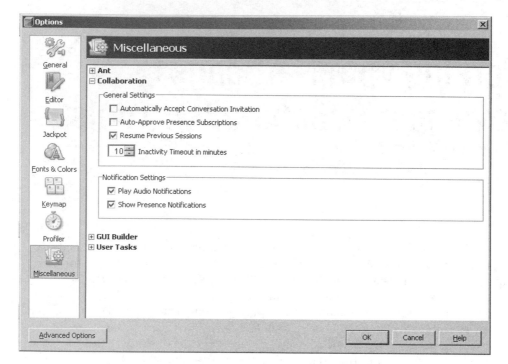

Figure 17-1. *Configuring Collaboration properties in the Options window*

The Automatically Accept Conversation Invitation option is usually a good option to activate. If you are working with a team throughout a given workday, it can get annoying to constantly need to accept conversation invitations. If you really don't want to be bothered or will be away from your computer, you can set your online status to Away.

I also recommend incrementing the Inactivity Timeout in Minutes to 10 minutes or more. This gives you adequate time while you are reading documentation or staring at a block of code without performing any actions. The timeout is initially set to 5 minutes, which is usually too short.

Set the other Collaboration properties according to your personal preferences. One option I do not recommend enabling is Auto-Approve Presence Subscriptions. If this option is checked, other users can add you to their contact lists without your approval (you won't see a dialog box asking you to approve or decline the request).

Managing Accounts

When you first choose Collaborate ➤ Login, the Collaboration Login window will open with a link to Manage Accounts. The first time you click Manage Accounts, you will be prompted to add a new account. After you create an account, you can add, edit, and remove accounts.

Creating a New Account

Follow these steps to create a new collaboration account:

1. Select Collaborate ➤ Login, and then click the Manage Accounts link in the Collaboration Login window.

2. In the initial Account Creation window, shown in Figure 17-2, you must tell NetBeans whether you want to create a new collaboration account on share.java.net, the general collaboration server run by NetBeans and Sun Microsystems, or on a different collaboration server. To use share.java.net, you'll need to also check the Accept check box. The third option is to configure NetBeans to use an existing NetBeans collaboration account, which is described in the next section. Click Next to continue.

Tip Your company, school, or group may want to use a private collaboration server to ensure the security of the data being transmitted. The Jabber open source project is a good resource for configuring and running an XMPP-compatible server. NetBeans Collaboration uses XMPP, which is a combination of plaintext XML messages and encoded data to transmit between clients and servers. For example, sharing a project would transmit usernames and filenames as plaintext embedded in an XML-like protocol, but the class data would be Base64-encoded for at least some security.

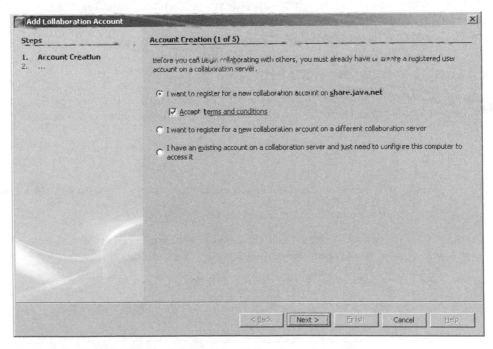

Figure 17-2. *The Add Collaboration Account wizard*

3. In the next step of the wizard, enter your account display name. This is the name that will appear in all account windows and lists of conversation participants. Then click the Next button.

4. The next step deals with connecting to the collaboration server. The first field, Server Hostname, asks for the server name and port of the collaboration server to which you need to connect. If you selected to use share.java.net, the server hostname and port are already set. There is also an option to specify the connection type: direct, HTTPS proxy, or SOCKS 5 proxy. Many universities and businesses use some sort of proxy, so the second option is what you would most likely use. Otherwise, select the first option to directly connect. Then click the Next button.

5. In the next step, you are asked to specify the account details. Enter your first name, last name, and email address. This information is not displayed in chat sessions or lists of users.

6. In the last step, enter your username and password. The username is what you use to log in with and is also viewable to other users. Click the Finish button.

NetBeans will immediately send the account information to the collaboration server. If the request succeeds, you should get a message saying "Congratulations! The account was successfully registered with the server."

Once the account has been added, it will be listed in the Collaboration Login window, which is docked on the right side of the NetBeans IDE by default. Your new account should be selected in the Account drop-down list. All you need to do is enter your password and select the Remember Password check box. If you are sure you will not need multiple accounts, then for convenience, you can also select the Login Automatically check box. You can always undo this action later, but it helps speed up the login process.

Setting Up Existing Accounts

If you have an existing NetBeans collaboration account, you can set up any system running NetBeans to use it. The steps to set up an existing account are similar to adding a new one.

1. Select Collaborate ➤ Login and click the Manage Accounts link in the Collaboration Login window.

2. Select "I have an existing account on a collaboration server . . ." and click the Next button.

3. Enter the display name for the account and click the Next button.

4. Enter the server hostname and port for the collaboration server (for example, share.java.net:5222 for the standard NetBeans collaboration server).

5. Select the type of proxy or nonproxy connection and click the Next button.

6. Enter the username for the existing account and click the Finish button.

The account will be listed in the Account Management window. However, it has not yet been validated by the collaboration server. To validate it, you need to actually log in. Open the Collaboration Login window, select the account from the drop-down list, and click the Login button. If the username/password is invalid, you will see a message to that effect. Otherwise, you will be logged in to the collaboration server.

Modifying Accounts

If you need to change the settings for an existing account, click the Manage Accounts link in the Collaboration Login window. In the Account Management window, select the account, and the corresponding properties should appear, as shown in Figure 17-3.

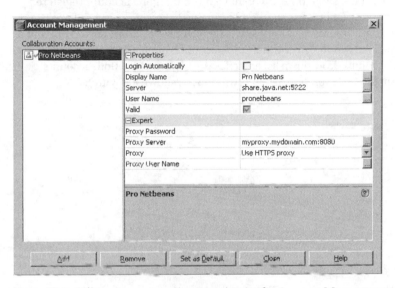

Figure 17-3. *Editing an account's properties in the Account Management window*

You can edit all the account settings. You can change the display name, server name, server port, and whether or not you use a proxy to connect to the collaboration server. For example, if you have NetBeans on a laptop and use an account both at work, behind a proxy, and at home, where you have a direct connection, you can edit the properties for either use.

■**Tip** You can actually register two accounts in the Account Management window for the same username and have one that uses a proxy and one that doesn't. This way, you can use one at home where a proxy is not required and one at work where a proxy is required. After creating the original account and naming it something like *MyDisplayName* (Proxy), just use NetBeans to register an existing account. Reregister the same username, but with a different display name, like *MyDisplayName* (No Proxy), and make sure the proxy fields are not set.

To remove an account, just highlight it and click the Remove button at the bottom of the Account Management window. You'll be asked to confirm that you want to remove the account and whether to unregister your username from the collaboration server. If you select this check box and click OK, the account is unregistered from the server, making it available to other people.

The Set As Default button in the Account Management window allows you to specify which account will be selected in the Collaboration Login window when you first attempt to start a collaboration session. If the Login Automatically option is set for an account, the default account is the one that will log in when you first start NetBeans.

Logging In with Multiple Accounts

Another interesting feature of the NetBeans Collaboration Tools is that you can log in and be active on multiple accounts at the same time. If you have more than one account registered, start by logging in to one account. Once it has successfully enabled a session, select Collaborate ➤ Login. The Collaboration Login window will appear with the current account grayed out and a message along the bottom of the window saying that "this account is already logged in." Select the second account from the Accounts drop-down list and click the Login button. Both accounts should then be displayed in the Collaboration Sessions window, as shown in Figure 17-4.

Figure 17-4. *Logging in with multiple accounts*

If you are logged in with one or more accounts, you may need to log out. You can log out by right-clicking the account name in the Collaboration Sessions window and selecting the End Session option or by selecting Collaborate ➤ End Session. The account should then be logged off the collaboration server and any conversations terminated. If you select Collaborate ➤ End All Sessions, all the accounts that were currently logged in are logged out.

Building Your Contacts List

In the NetBeans Developer Collaboration Tools, a *contact* is essentially a buddy, friend, or coworker who you save on a list for easy access. The concept here is very similar to many popular instant messaging programs. You can also assign contacts to different groups.

Adding Contacts

To add a contact, after you log in, click the Add Contacts icon next to the Online button in the Collaboration Sessions window. You can also right-click the account name and select Add Contacts from the context menu. The Add Contacts window will appear.

In the Add Contacts window, choose to search by display name or username in the Search For field. In the Search Text field, enter the name, characters, or phrase you want to search for and click the Find button. Any matches will appear in the Select User dialog box. Select the user that matches your search criteria and click the OK button. You can then continue to search for contacts and add them to your Contacts to Add list. When you are finished, click the OK button.

Each user you chose to add to your list will be sent an Authorize Subscription form, as shown in Figure 17-5. Users will not be added to your contact list until they approve your request. Obviously, users probably wouldn't accept this offer if they don't recognize your name.

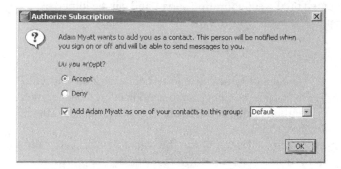

Figure 17-5. *The Authorize Subscription form*

Adding Groups

A *group* in the NetBeans Developer Collaboration Tools is defined as a collection of contacts. Just as in all popular instant messaging programs, a group allows you to arrange your contacts in logical or convenient ways based on group names.

NetBeans starts you out with one default group (coincidentally named Default). To add a new group to the list, log in using your account, right-click the account name, and select Add Contact Group. In the pop-up window that appears, type in the name of the new group and click the OK button.

The group will be added to your list of contacts and represented by a folder icon and group name. Once you have added a group, you can fill it with contacts in several ways:

- Click any contact in your list and drag-and-drop it into the new group.

- Right-click a contact name and select Copy. Then right-click the group name where you want the contact to appear and select Paste.

- Follow the process described in the previous section for adding contacts. Before confirming the final list of contacts to add, you can choose the group to which they belong by selecting it from the Add to Group drop-down list.

You can easily remove a group by right-clicking the name and selecting Delete from the context menu. Note that if you delete a group containing contacts, the contacts will be removed entirely from your list.

You can also rename a group at any time by right-clicking the name and selecting Rename from the context menu.

Conducting Collaboration Sessions

To get started using the Developer Collaboration Tools, you need to log in and initiate a session. During the session, you can start conversations with other people, join existing conversations, search for other users, share projects and files, and exchange messages in a variety of formats.

Joining Conversations

You can join two types of conversations in the Developer Collaboration Tools: public and private. Public conversations are defined on the collaboration server and can be joined by anyone. Private conversations take place between you and one or more people.

Joining a Public Conversation

To join a public conversation, you need to find it and subscribe to it. To begin, click the Subscribe to Public Conversation icon. You can also right-click the Conversations node in the Collaboration Sessions window and select Subscribe to Public Conversation from the context menu. The Subscribe to Public Conversation dialog box appears.

To search for a conversation, enter a word or character into the Name field and click the Find button. The search results appear in the Subscribe to Conversations box, as shown in Figure 17-6.

Figure 17-6. *Finding a public conversation*

If you do not know the partial or full name of a conversation, you can also browse the list of existing public conversations. Click the Browse button in the Subscribe to Public Conversation dialog box to see a list of available public conversations in the Select Conversation dialog box. You can click an individual name or Ctrl-click (in Windows) to select multiple names from the list. When you are finished, click the OK button.

Once you have searched or browsed for all the conversations you want to subscribe to, click the OK button. The conversation(s) will then appear in your list under the Conversations node in the Collaboration Sessions window.

Starting a Private Conversation

Starting a private conversation is easy. Simply double-click the name of a contact. You can also Ctrl-click multiple contact names, right-click any contact name, and select Start Conversation from the context menu.

If you initiate a conversation, the users you selected will receive a prompt asking if they want to join the conversation or decline the invitation. If the user accepts the conversation invitation, the Conversation window will open. If the user declined, you will receive a message to that effect.

Note If users configured NetBeans to automatically accept conversation invitations, as described earlier in this chapter, they will not receive a prompt, and the Conversation window will immediately open.

Creating a Public Conversation

The NetBeans Developer Collaboration Tools also allow you to initiate and manage public conversations. To create your own public conversation, log in to the collaboration server. In the Collaboration Sessions window, right-click the Conversations node and select Create Public Conversation from the context menu. In the dialog box that opens, type a name for the new conversation (without special characters or spaces). Click the OK button to create the conversation.

If the new conversation was successfully added to the collaboration server, it appears under the Conversations node. The Manage Public Conversation window also immediately appears, as shown in Figure 17-7.

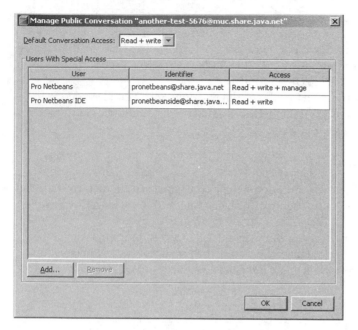

Figure 17-7. *The Manage Public Conversation window*

Using the Manage Public Conversation window, you can perform a variety of actions. First and most important, you should set the default access level for the conversation. This affects how the general public can access the conversation, as follows:

None: Users cannot subscribe to or join conversations. Users cannot even search for or browse the conversation. Even if one or more users has previously added the conversation to their list in NetBeans, the conversation manager can set the access level to None. Then the next time the user logs in, the conversation will be removed from that user's list.

Read: Users can subscribe to conversations and search/browse them. After joining a conversation, users can only watch other participants add comments and cannot contribute to the conversation.

Read + write: Users can subscribe to conversations and search/browse them. After joining a conversation, users can fully participate and add comments.

Read + write + manage: Users can subscribe to conversations and search/browse them. After joining a conversation, users can fully participate and add comments. Users can fully manage a conversation by assigning default access, adding users and setting their access levels, and removing users.

You can also assign special access privileges to specific users by using the Add and Remove buttons at the bottom of the Manage Public Conversation window.

You can manage the conversation at any time by right-clicking the conversation name and selecting Manage from the context menu. You can also unsubscribe by right-clicking the name and selecting Unsubscribe, but this doesn't make sense for the manager of a conversation. For safety purposes, users with the manage permission cannot modify their own access level for a conversation and cannot remove themselves from the list of special privileges.

■**Tip** Ownership for a public conversation can be transferred by adding a second user with the read + write + manage privilege. The second user can then remove the original manager and take over maintenance of the conversation.

The manager of a conversation can also permanently delete it from the collaboration server by right-clicking the conversation name and selecting Delete from the context menu. The manager will then see a warning message that the conversation is about to be deleted and all users unsubscribed from it, as shown in Figure 17-8. Once the deletion of the conversation is confirmed, it is unregistered from the server and removed from the Conversations node.

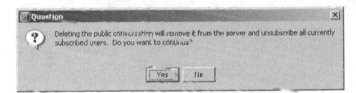

Figure 17-8. *Confirming the deletion of a public conversation*

Now that you have learned how to search for, browse, subscribe to, delete, and manage conversations, it is time to see what functionality the Conversation window provides.

Using the Conversation Window

Once you have initiated a conversation, you can commence chatting with your contacts and sharing projects and files. These activities are conducted through the Conversation window, as shown in Figure 17-9.

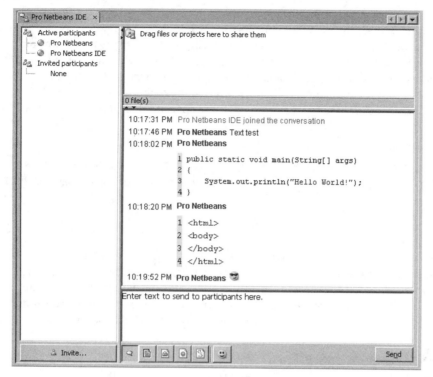

Figure 17-9. *The Conversation window*

The Conversation window is divided into four panes:

List of participants: In the left pane, the list displays all active and invited participants for the conversation. You can invite participants to the conversation by clicking the Invite button at the bottom of the pane. You can then search for users and send them a custom message inviting them to join the conversation. They then will have the option to accept or decline the invitation (unless they have previously configured NetBeans to automatically accept all invitations; in which case, they will immediately join).

Project and file-sharing: In the top pane, you can drag-and-drop files and projects to share with the participants in the conversation. The next section describes how to share projects and files.

Conversation transcript: In the middle pane, the input from all participants appears. Messages are also displayed when participants join and leave the conversation. The text displayed in the conversation transcript pane can be saved to a text file for archival purposes. Right-click anywhere in the pane and select Save from the context menu. Name the file and click the Save button. You will then have a record of the entire conversation up to that moment in time. Note that if the conversation continues, the newly added text will *not* be included in the saved file.

Conversation input: In the bottom pane, participants can enter various types of text and send it to the other participants in the conversation. What makes this section of the Conversation window unique is the ability of NetBeans to format the text as different types using the buttons at the bottom of the pane:

- Participants can send plaintext messages. The first icon is initially selected and represents plaintext. This type of text is used for general conversation.

- Participants can send formatted text by clicking the second icon. Using formatted text, you can send multiline text that is indented with spaces and tabs. The participants see the sent text exactly as you entered it.

- Participants can select to format their input as Java, HTML, or XML using the corresponding buttons. If the input type is set to one of these options, NetBeans provides some advanced functions.

- Last, but not least, participants can indicate tone and mood by inserting various smiley icons. By clicking the smiley face icon, participants can choose from several different icons to send.

If the type is set to Java in the conversation input pane, full usage of code completion is available. You can type Java source code into the input pane exactly as you would in the Source Editor. If you type the name of a package, NetBeans will attempt to suggest names.

Code templates are also available for use in the conversation input pane. Try typing psvm and pressing the spacebar. The abbreviation will expand into the definition of a standard main method. To send the Java code, click the Send button. You will see that the source code remains properly formatted in the conversation input pane. It also has line numbers applied, as shown in Figure 17-9.

Tip If participants intend to copy and paste the Java code you sent, they should probably disable line numbers by deselecting Show Line Numbers on the View menu. On the other hand, if the Java code shared in the conversation is to be used for discussion purposes, leaving the line numbers displayed can prove useful.

Sharing Projects and Files

In my opinion, the most powerful feature of the NetBeans Developer Collaboration Tools is the ability to share projects and files. Simply by dragging-and-dropping the name of a project, an entire list of participants can view and interact with the code. You can also decide to share everything in the Source Packages folder, the Test Packages folder, or just a single file.

To share a project or file, select it in the Projects or Files window and drag-and-drop it into the project and file-sharing pane of the Conversation window. Almost immediately, you should see the name of the user sharing the file as the top-level node. Below that is the name of the project, the location of the item you are sharing (Source or Test Packages), the package name, and finally the source filename. In the example in Figure 17-10, I shared a single Java source file named EmailClient. The other participants in the conversation will now be able to see the same file.

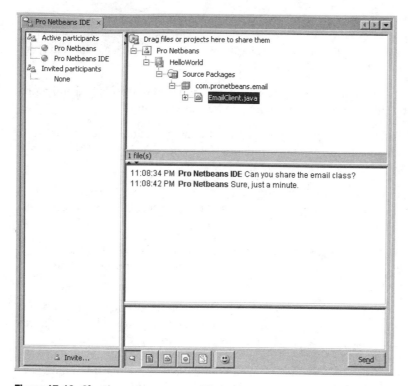

Figure 17-10. *Sharing a Java source file in the Conversation window*

Note Depending on the size of what you are sharing and the connection speed of each participant, the time it takes for the items to be visible will vary.

Once a file is visible to participants, they are immediately able to open the file. In the project and file-sharing pane of the Conversation window, you can double-click the name of a file to open it in a separate Source Editor window, like any standard Java source file. The main difference is that the tab containing the filename also includes the text "Shared." Participants can now edit the code in near real time.

The EmailClient source file initially contains the following code:

```
package com.pronetbeans.email;

import org.apache.commons.mail.Email;

public class EmailClient
{

}
```

If a participant opened the file, placed his cursor between the opening and closing brackets of the `EmailClient` class, and started typing text, several things would happen. First, tiny glyphs appear in the glyph margin, indicating that a participant is editing the line. The background color of the lines being edited also changes to visually flag to other participants that a section of code is being altered. In Figure 17-11, a participant has started to edit the specified line in the file. Once the participant finishes typing or pauses for several seconds, the change replicates through to the other participants, as shown in Figure 17-12.

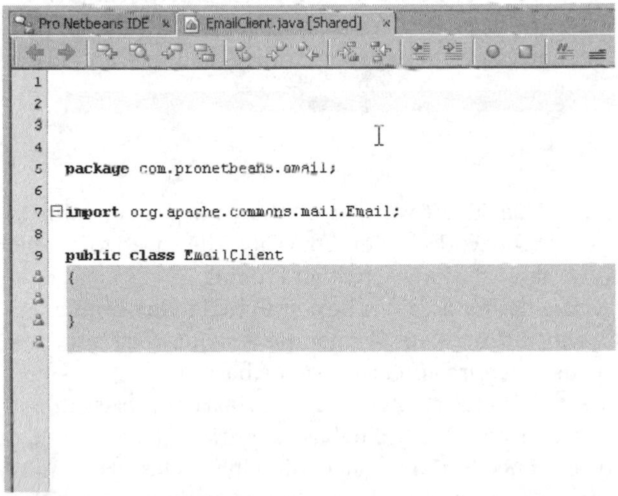

Figure 17-11. *The EmailClient source file being edited by a participant*

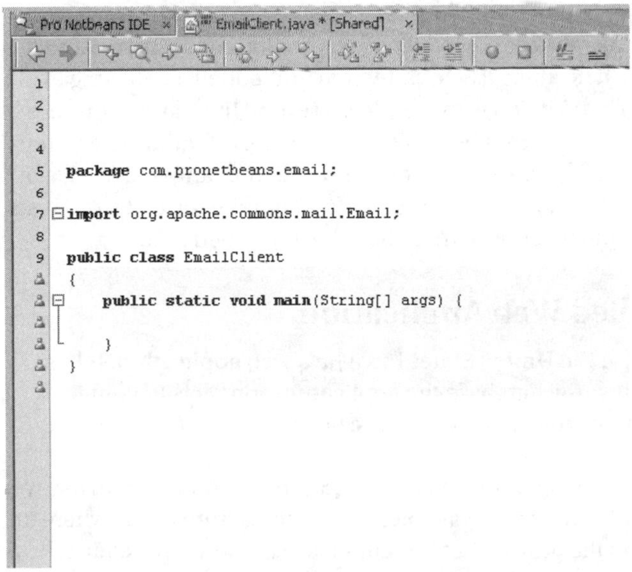

Figure 17-12. *The EmailClient source file after being edited by a participant*

While one participant is editing a line of code, it is locked so that no other participant can alter it. This prevents unseemly bugs or errors if two developers try to fix the same line in a different way.

Collaborative Tools Usage Scenarios

The capability to perform global collaborative coding opens the door to several interesting usage scenarios. Many development teams are spread out across multiple office locations. They also may need to adhere to corporate and legal restrictions, such as the designation of company internal intellectual property, country-specific export control regulations, and so on. Let's look at two typical scenarios.

Team Coding

In this scenario, two programmers, John and David, are working on the same project. John works out of an office in San Francisco, and David works in New York City. They need to be able to view the same code base and stay up-to-date on what each other is doing.

Their company has a strict policy that code should never be committed to the source repository (CVS, for example) without having been tested. The company requires all tests suites to run and a full integration run with the entire application code base.

John needs to fix a bug in a specific set of modules. There is a SalesTaxLookup class that uses Java Database Connectivity (JDBC) to query an Oracle database to retrieve the percentage of sales tax for a given customer locality. John needs to fix a calculation in the class. He is not very familiar with the JDBC code, and after a while, realizes he might be breaking some of the code. He logs in to the collaboration server and initiates a conversation with David, who is an expert in Java and JDBC.

Once David has joined the conversation, John drags the SalesTaxLookup class into the project and file-sharing pane of the Conversation window. With the shared file open, John starts to change the code. At one point, he alters a SQL statement embedded as a String in a particular method, but makes a small typo in it. He moves down several lines and continues coding. However, David spotted the typo and immediately corrected the offending characters. John sees the lines of code David is altering, since the background color changes. Once David is finished typing, John can see his changes. John can immediately compile the code, run tests for it, and run the entire application utilizing the changes both he and David made.

Fixing an Export-Controlled Web Application

Suppose a development team based in the United States has a Java web application. It has been determined by your company that the database the application connects to contains export-controlled information. As a junior developer, you have been tasked with fixing a bug in one section of the web application.

You have experience in Java, but your team's best Java programmer is on vacation for two weeks. Another programmer on your team, Vik, is available, but he works from India, where he is a citizen. You really need his help on the project, but he cannot access the source code repository since the project is marked as export-controlled.

You finally are able to determine which Java source file the bug is in, but the code is extremely complex. You get your manager to sign off stating that the specific file contains no export-controlled material. Rather than play the exchange-the-email-attachment-ten-times game, you decide to use the NetBeans Developer Collaboration Tools. You instant message Vik, and both of you log in to your collaboration server. You drag the specific file into the Conversation window and edit it together.

Just when Vik thinks he has the code right, you get a phone call and are distracted. Thanks to NetBeans, Vik does not have to wait for you to see if his change will compile and build with the rest of the project. In the project and file-sharing pane in the Conversation window, he can right-click the project and select Build Project from the context menu. The Output window will appear for both you and Vik (and all participants in the conversation). Any build errors or output is visible in the window, even though Vik has only been given access to a specific file. The build takes place on your machine, not Vik's. He cannot access any code, configuration files, or other sensitive data, but he can determine if the code he changed in the shared file will integrate and build along with the rest of the system.

The important thing to note is that any participant in a conversation can build and run the project that is shared, even if a single file is all that is shared. All participants can also see the output in the Output window.

Summary

This chapter covered one of the most unique features of NetBeans. The NetBeans Developer Collaboration Tools are amazingly simple to use, but allow you to perform some very powerful actions.

Using the Developer Collaboration Tools, you can register an account, log in to a chat-like server, search for and add contacts, and conduct different kinds of text-based chat sessions. Your chats can be specially formatted based on plaintext, Java, HTML, XML, and so on, making them more efficient and easy to understand.

One of the best features involves the ability to share files or projects inside a chat session. Programmers from around the globe can view and edit source code in near real time and compile it against the entire system.

These features not only allow global teams to work more effectively, but to also be more productive. Teams can work on different pieces of a project at the same time and integrate with the work of others almost instantly.

CHAPTER 18

Using NetBeans Database Tools

Programmers often require database access tools for the purposes of development and testing. All too often, developers need to be able to add or remove a record from a specific table in order to test some code.

Purists might argue that only database administrators (DBAs) should be accessing the database, with tools like Enterprise Manager for Microsoft SQL Server or Toad and Embarcadero for Oracle. However, in the real world, it is often the case that developers serve as DBAs, at least for basic development of their projects. It can save a lot of time and effort when programmers can also access the database, but the software to do so can be particularly costly to license across a large organization.

NetBeans provides several convenient tools for working with databases. Having the ability to access a database directly in a development environment is invaluable. Programmers can not only use their development environment for writing code, but can also save the cost of using additional software products. This makes programmers lives easier, since they can do their work, and makes managers happy, since they save on software license costs.

Connecting to Databases

The NetBeans database tools allow you to connect to a wide variety of database systems, create and view tables, work with custom SQL scripts, and view data. To get started, you need to add a driver and database connection.

Adding a Database Driver

The first step in working with databases is adding a new driver. This directs NetBeans to the correct set of JDBC classes that allow it to work with whatever vendor database you need to use.

To add a driver, follow these steps:

1. Open the Runtime window (Window ➤ Runtime).

2. In the Runtime window, expand the Databases node to see the Drivers node.

3. Right-click the Drivers node and select Add Driver from the context menu.

4. In the New JDBC Driver dialog box, click the Add button.

5. In the file system browser, select the JAR or zip file that contains the JDBC drivers for your database, and then click OK. The driver file will be displayed in the New JDBC Driver dialog box, as shown in Figure 18-1.

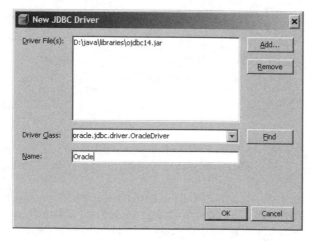

Figure 18-1. *The New JDBC Driver dialog box*

6. NetBeans will also attempt to preselect the main driver class and name the driver. If there is more than one driver class, the list of class names will appear in the Driver Class drop-down list. If necessary, select the correct class from the list. You can also use the Find button to query the selected driver files to locate the correct Driver Class value.

7. The Name field should be used to properly identify the type of driver. You can set this to whatever you wish, but it's useful to name the driver with the versions that the driver supports. This can be especially helpful if you have numerous versions of a database in your environment. Having a driver named Oracle 8 can help you avoid trying to use it to connect to an Oracle 9 database and experiencing issues.

■**Caution** According to Oracle's JDBC FAQ online, the Oracle 8.1.7 JDBC drivers can support Oracle database versions 10.1.0, 9.2.0, 9.0.1, 8.1.7, 8.1.6, 8.1.5, 8.0.6, 8.0.5, 8.0.4, and 7.3.4. Regardless of the listed support, the original JDBC drivers for Oracle 8 still seem to have issues when interacting with an Oracle 9 database in my environment.

---

8. When the driver is specified correctly, click OK to add it.

Adding the New Database Connection

After you've added a database driver, you can define a new database connection and then activate it.

Defining a Database Connection

Follow these steps to add a new database connection:

1. In the Runtime window, locate the name of the driver that you want to use.

2. Right-click the driver and select Connect Using.

3. In the New Database Connection dialog box, the Name and Driver fields should be prepopulated with the values you previously selected when adding the driver. In the Database URL field, enter the URL that NetBeans should use to locate and connect to your specified database. It is typically in the format of `jdbc:oracle:thin:@hostname:port:sid` or `jdbc:oracle:@hostname:port:sid`, as shown in Figure 18-2. You must also fill in the Username and Password fields. The Remember Password During This Session check box should be selected, so that you do not have to continually reenter your password.

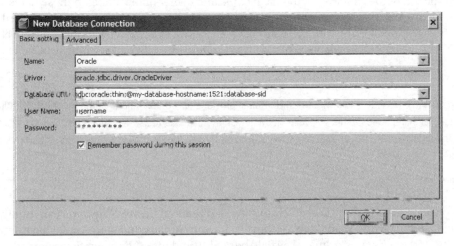

Figure 18-2. *The New Database Connection dialog box*

4. You can also search for database schemas using the Advanced tab of the New Database Connection dialog box. On that tab, click the Get Schemas button to connect to the database using the current settings and retrieve a list of available schemas.

5. Once you have set all the fields to the desired values, click the OK button to add the connection.

Activating the Connection

After the new connection is listed under the Databases node in the Runtime window, you can activate the connection and begin to use it. Simply right-click the connection and select Connect. If the connection was successful, the broken icon next to the connection should be replaced by a connected icon.

Click the plus sign next to the connection to see the Tables, Views, and Procedures nodes. These nodes allow you to interact with the database and perform specific operations.

Working with Database Tables and Views

Once you have defined a database driver, created a connection, and activated the connection, you can create and work with database tables. You can also use the NetBeans database tools to create a view.

Creating a Table

You can create tables directly in NetBeans using the database tools. To add a table, right-click the Tables node in the Runtime window and select Create Table from the context menu. The Create Table window will appear.

The Create Table window is a simple utility for defining columns in a table. Rather than typing out the CREATE TABLE SQL statement, you can define an entire table structure and set various parameters.

At the top of the window are the table name and owner name. Beneath those fields is the data grid for setting up the table columns. Initially, the data grid displays only one record with numerous columns. In the window, columns such as Key, Index, Null, Unique, Column Name, and Data Type should be visible. You can also scroll to the right and see other available fields.

Caution The Create Table window in NetBeans provides only a text field to name the table, without any validation for acceptable names or invalid characters. If there is a database-specific restriction to naming the table, the defined JDBC driver may cause an error to be thrown during the actual creation of the table in the database.

To add each column to the table, click the Add Column button. Then you can modify the fields to match the desired table definition for your project. In Figure 18-3, I have defined an EMPLOYEES table with a primary key field named ID and three character fields named FIRST_NAME, LAST_NAME, and EMAIL.

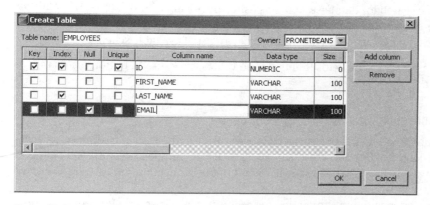

Figure 18-3. *The Create Table window with a new table defined*

For the ID field, I selected the Key and Unique parameters to flag the column as the unique primary key for the table. I also added indexes to the ID and LAST_NAME columns. You can set other options for columns, including comments, check constraints, and default values.

When you are finished adding table columns, click the OK button. The table will then appear under the Tables node in the Runtime window. Below it, you will see nodes for each column in the table, as well as folder nodes for the indexes and foreign keys.

If you later want to remove a table, right-click the table name and select Delete from the context menu.

Modifying a Table

As of the time of this writing, NetBeans provides limited functions for modifying a table (without re-creating it, as described in the "Re-creating a Table" section later in this chapter). Basically, you can add columns and add an index.

Adding a Column

To add a new column to a table, right-click the name of the table in the Runtime window and select Add a Column from the context menu. In the Add Column window, you can enter the information for the new column, including its name, data type, size and/or scale, and additional fields.

Tip To remove a column from a table, right-click the name of the table, save the table structure, delete the table, and re-create the table using the saved structure. As described in the "Re-creating a Table" section later in this chapter, you can manually remove the listing for a column in the CREATE TABLE SQL script before re-creating the table.

Adding an Index

To add an index to a table, right-click the Indexes node and select Add Index from the context menu. In the Add Index dialog box, specify the name of the index to be added and select which columns should be included, as shown in Figure 18-4.

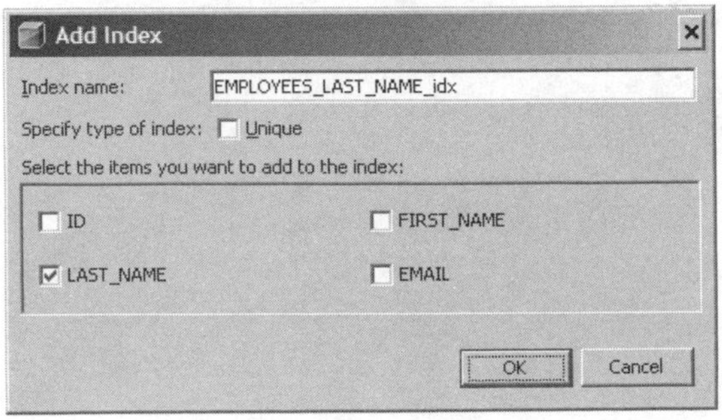

Figure 18-4. *The Add Index dialog box*

■Tip You can also modify an index. For example, if you wanted to modify the index shown in Figure 18-4 by adding the FIRST_NAME column to the index in addition to the LAST_NAME column, you could right-click the name of the index in the Runtime window and select Add Column from the context menu. This will open a dialog box in which you can select any of the other columns in the table.

Saving a Table Structure

If you make periodic changes to the structure of a table, you may want to save the state before-hand, in case you need to revert back to the previous structure.

To save the structure of a table, right-click its name in the Runtime window and select Grab Structure. You will be prompted to save a file named *TABLENAME*.grab somewhere on your system. This file contains the internal state of the table, in part text, part binary format.

Re-creating a Table

Sometimes tables need to be completely deleted and then re-created. In order to re-create a table, you need to first save the original table's structure, as described in the previous section. Then you can delete the original table (right-click the table name and select Delete) and reuse the copy of the structure you saved.

To re-create a table, right-click the Tables node, choose Recreate Table, and select the *TABLENAME*.grab file that you originally saved. The Name the Table dialog box appears, displaying the basic table creation script that will be run during the process of re-creating the table, as shown in Figure 18-5. The Name field shows the original name, which you can accept or change.

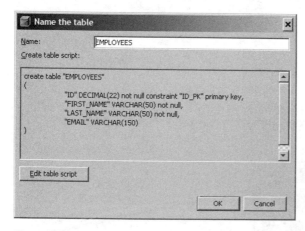

Figure 18-5. *Name the Table dialog box for re-creating a table*

You can also modify the script that will be run to re-create the table. Click the Edit Table Script button to activate the text box containing the CREATE TABLE SQL statement. Now you can edit the SQL. If you change your mind and want the table to be re-created based on the original table script, click the Reload Table Script from File button. The script box will turn gray and display the original script.

When you click the OK button in the Name the Table dialog box, the table will be re-created. It will once again be listed under the Tables node in the Runtime window.

During the table re-creation process, it is important to take note of any indexes, constraints, or other table-specific settings. For example, the original EMPLOYEES table (in the example in Figure 18-3) had an index for the LAST_NAME field. However, the index for the LAST_NAME field was not captured or re-created. You can add the index to the re-created table as described in the previous section (see Figure 18-4).

■**Tip** You can avoid table reconstruction issues by saving the CREATE TABLE script in .sql files in your project. You can have .sql files for re-creating any special indexes or constraints on the table. When you re-create the table, click the Edit Table Script button in the Name the Table dialog box and paste in the contents of the .sql file you saved.

Creating a View

A database view is similar to a table in that it displays data with columns and rows, but it is not a physical object in the same sense as a table. A view is a contrived result set of a query that allows you to repeatedly view the same results. It is also tied to the underlying data such that as the data in the matching table or tables changes, the results returned by the view update accordingly.

In the world of databases, a view can be very useful in organizing data. Views can be used to display limited sets of data to users who may not need full access to an entire table. Imagine a table of employee data that contains fields such as first name, last name, hire date, Social Security number, salary, and email address. Obviously, you might not want all users to have access to view every Social Security number. You may want one group of users to be able to query and look up the first name, last name, and email address fields, and another group to be able to separately look up the first name, last name, and Social Security number. These sets of data can be created as views and given separate access privileges.

In NetBeans, follow these steps to create a view:

1. In the Runtime window, right-click the connection under the Databases node and select Connect from the context menu.

2. Right-click the connection's Views node and select Create View from the context menu.

3. In the Create View window, type in a value for the View Name field, such as VW_EMPNAMES.

4. Enter a SQL statement in the SQL Expression to Create View field. This should be a valid SELECT operation, such as SELECT * FROM EMPLOYEES.

5. Click the OK button.

Once you have created the view, it will be displayed under the Views node in the Runtime window. Click the plus sign next to the name of the view to expand the node and display the list of columns that are included in the view.

To delete the view, right-click its name and select Delete from the context menu.

Displaying Table Data

The quickest way to display data in a table or view without writing SQL is by using the View Data option. Right-click the name of a specific table or view and select View Data from the context menu. You will see the SQL Command window (described in the next section) with a statement already executed, such as the following:

```
SELECT * FROM "PRONETBEANS"."EMPLOYEES"
```

The results from the SELECT statement will already be displayed in the data grid at the bottom of the SQL Command window.

Once you have viewed the data, you have several options for working with the values. You can retrieve the data from the data grid by highlighting a single cell, right-clicking, and selecting Copy Cell Value. This will put the value of the selected cell into the clipboard and allow you to paste it elsewhere. You can also right-click anywhere in a row in the data grid and select Copy Row Values. This allows you to copy and paste the values in the entire row.

One unique feature is the ability to reorganize the columns in the data grid. If you click and hold on the name of a column in the data grid, you can drag it left or right to reorder the display. The feature only moves the columns around in the NetBeans SQL Command window *display* (perhaps to make them easier to read). It does *not* change anything in the database itself.

Writing SQL

The ability to type your own SQL commands and have them executed by the database is extremely convenient (and necessary) for many developers. It allows you to perform custom queries, insert data, update data, and delete records from your database schema.

Like many popular database tools, NetBeans provides a command window for executing SQL statements. It also allows you to use SQL templates.

Using the SQL Command Window

To view the SQL Command window in NetBeans, open the Runtime window and connect to a database. Then right-click a database connection, table, or view and select Execute Command from the context menu. The SQL Command window will open in the Source Editor section of the IDE. This tool allows you to run any SQL script you choose against the database to which you are connected.

The SQL Command window contains several useful features:

Connection field: The drop-down list at the top of the window shows all available connections. This is a convenient feature, allowing you to easily toggle back and forth between databases as you write SQL scripts. The ability to quickly toggle database connections is especially useful for professional programmers who need to work in multiple identical databases. Say you need to make a change to a table. You can write the ALTER TABLE SQL once and execute it against your development database. You can then quickly change to your staging, test, and production databases to run the same script, without having to spend time copying and pasting SQL back and forth between different windows.

Select Connection in Runtime button: This button appears next to the Connection drop-down list along the top of the SQL Command window. Clicking the button will select the matching database connection in the Runtime window. This can be helpful in avoiding confusion if you have numerous database connections defined or numerous SQL Command windows open. The last thing you want to do is execute a DROP TABLE statement against a production database (especially if there is no way to roll back the change).

Run SQL button: Clicking this button executes the SQL that appears in the SQL Command window.

Results pane: Once the SQL has successfully finished executing, if it was a SELECT operation, any results that are generated will be shown in a results pane at the bottom of the window as shown in Figure 18-6. A results pane will not display for operations other than SELECT statements.

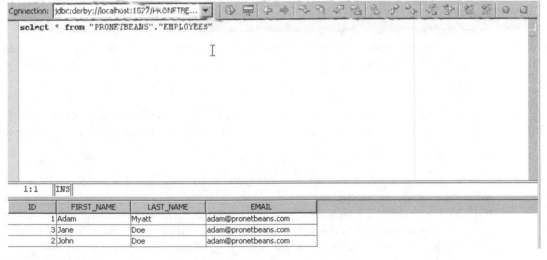

Figure 18-6. *The data grid results pane in the SQL Command window*

Suppose you need to execute a SQL operation like the following INSERT statement:

```
INSERT INTO EMPLOYEES(ID, FIRST_NAME, LAST_NAME, EMAIL, ADDRESS)
VALUES(1, 'Adam', 'Myatt', 'adam@pronetbeans.com', 'some place somewhere')
```

You can run this statement and then modify it to insert as many employee records as you want.

When the SQL statement finishes processing, the standard Output window appears and displays text results:

```
Executed successfully in 0.09 s, 1 rows affected.
Line 1, column 1
Execution finished after 0.09 s, 0 error(s) occured.
```

After inserting several other records, you have several ways of viewing the data. You can alter the INSERT INTO EMPLOYEES SQL to be a SELECT * FROM EMPLOYEES statement. You can also right-click the EMPLOYEES table name and select View Data from the context menu, as described in the previous section.

Using SQL Templates

As a developer, you may use NetBeans code templates (covered in Chapter 10) to save time. Just like code templates, NetBeans SQL templates allow you to type an abbreviation and have it expanded into a complete statement. You can add your own SQL templates to save time and typing.

To set up SQL templates, select Tools ➤ Options ➤ Editor and click the Code Templates tab. From the Language drop-down list, select SQL. The list of available SQL templates is empty by default. Add SQL templates using the procedure described in Chapter 10. After you've defined a SQL template, it will be available for use in the SQL Command window.

For example, I can never remember the exact name or format of some Oracle database date and character conversion functions, so I use SQL code templates. Here is a statement I use often:

```
SELECT TO_CHAR( HIRE_DATE, 'Mon, DD, YYYY') AS HIREDATE FROM EMPLOYEES
```

I define a SQL template named datetochar in the Code Templates tab in NetBeans. Once I have added the template abbreviation, I can assign the expanded text value to be as follows:

```
TO_CHAR(${name}, 'Mon DD, YYYY'),${cursor}
```

Then when I type the statement SELECT DATETOCHAR in the SQL Command window and press the spacebar, the abbreviation expands to SELECT TO_CHAR(NAME, 'Mon DD, YYYY'). The text name is highlighted, allowing me to immediately start typing the name of the actual date field that needs to appear in the SQL. After I've typed the name of the date column, I press the Tab key, and the cursor jumps to the end of the TO_CHAR function, as I originally defined in the SQL template.

Another convenient block of SQL might be to use the abbreviation countone with the following expanded SQL text:

```
SELECT COUNT(*), ${name} FROM ${table} GROUP BY ${name} ORDER BY COUNT(*)
```

This SQL allows you to quickly enter a column name that you want to query and list a summary of the number of times a particular value appears in a column. If this SQL were used to query the LAST_NAME field of the EMPLOYEES table described earlier in this chapter, you could view a list of the number of people with the same last name.

If you work frequently on a specific set of tables, it might be worthwhile to save several table-specific SQL code templates. Suppose you have a table with more than a dozen columns. If you need to frequently write various SELECT statements that use most but not all of the columns, you could create a SQL code template something like this:

```
SELECT COL1, COL2, COL3, COL4, COL5 FROM TABLE
```

This saves you from having to retype all of the column names. You can quickly delete the columns you don't want to appear in the SELECT statement, and you don't have to copy and paste the SQL from some other location.

Linking a Database Schema to a Project

One simple and powerful feature of NetBeans is the ability to capture the schema of a database and link it to a project. This means that you don't need to use external database tools to export SQL scripts containing the Data Definition Language (DDL) for your application to files and then copy those files into your project or CVS. The only negative of the feature is that the schema is saved to a file as XML, not DDL, so you can't really open the file and use it elsewhere.

Note The XML format was probably chosen due to the slight differences in DDL and SQL among different database vendors. For example, the CREATE TABLE syntax on Microsoft SQL Server can differ from that of Oracle and MySQL.

To save a database schema, follow these steps:

1. Select New ➤ New File. In the New File window, select the Persistence category, and then choose Database Schema.

2. The wizard will prompt you to enter the filename of the database schema you wish to save and to select a folder for the file. Typically, I specify src/conf for storing my schema files. Click the Next button to continue.

3. In the next step of the wizard, select a database connection from a list of previously defined connections. You can select one of the existing database connections or choose New Database Connection from the drop-down list.

4. The final step in the wizard allows you to select which database objects you want to persist. Select all the tables and views you wish to save using the Add button. You can also simply click the Add All button to include the entire database schema. Click the Finish button. The schema is then saved in your project as a .dbschema file.

If you selected a Java Web Application project and a folder location of `src/conf`, you can view the schema in the Projects window. Click the plus sign next to the Configuration Files node. The database schema should be listed along with the other project configuration files.

What makes this feature unique is that you can drill down through the schema and view the table, views, indexes, and so on directly in the Projects window. You don't need to use the Runtime, SQL Command, or View Data window to see the structure of a table.

The database schema file can also be stored in your source repository. This is a great advantage for the purposes of project documentation. The schema in the database can change, but you will have a snapshot of the schema from the date and time you originally linked the schema. You can easily save the schema in a CVS repository. Right-click the schema node and select CVS ➤ Commit. The entire schema for the database is then saved along with your project's source code.

During the lifetime of your project, the database schema might change. This happens frequently during the initial stages of some development projects as team members or DBAs access the database and make schema changes. NetBeans has a convenient feature that allows the schema to stay up-to-date (through direct user action—not automatically). Right-click the schema in the Projects window and select Recapture Schema from Database. This will trigger the associated database connection to become active, connect to the database, and grab the latest structure. The newly updated schema is then available directly in the Projects window to view or commit to CVS.

Configuring Database Connection Pools

A database connection pool allows you to conserve resources and reduce load. Connection pools are predefined queues of connections that have already been initialized. When a request comes in, if there is an available connection, it is retrieved from the queue. If a connection is not available, a new one is created (up to a set limit). When a connection is no longer being used, it is returned to the pool for use by another process.

NetBeans provides the capability to define a connection pool for any vendor database that supports the pool functionality. You can add a connection pool file to any Enterprise or Web project. To add a new connection pool, follow these steps:

1. Select New ➤ New File. In the New File window, select Sun Resources as the category and JDBC Connection Pool as the file type.

2. The New JDBC Connection Pool wizard will prompt you for the name of the connection pool and the database, as shown in Figure 18-7. You can choose an existing connection or define a new connection. Once you have set the specified parameters, click the Next button.

3. In the next step of the wizard, you will need to set several properties. When you define the connection the pool applies to (and thus the set of JDBC drivers it uses), NetBeans attempts to populate the Datasource Classname field for you. You can also add or remove additional properties. By default, the serverName, PortNumber, DatabaseNameURL, User, and Password properties should be displayed, as shown in Figure 18-8. By clicking the Add button, you can also specify properties for defining the description, network protocol, and so on. Once you have set the properties, click the Next button.

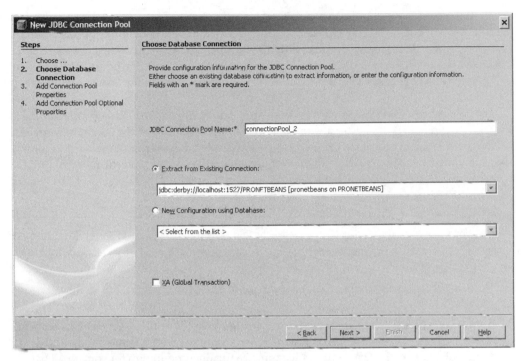

Figure 18-7. *Choosing a database connection in the New JDBC Connection Pool wizard*

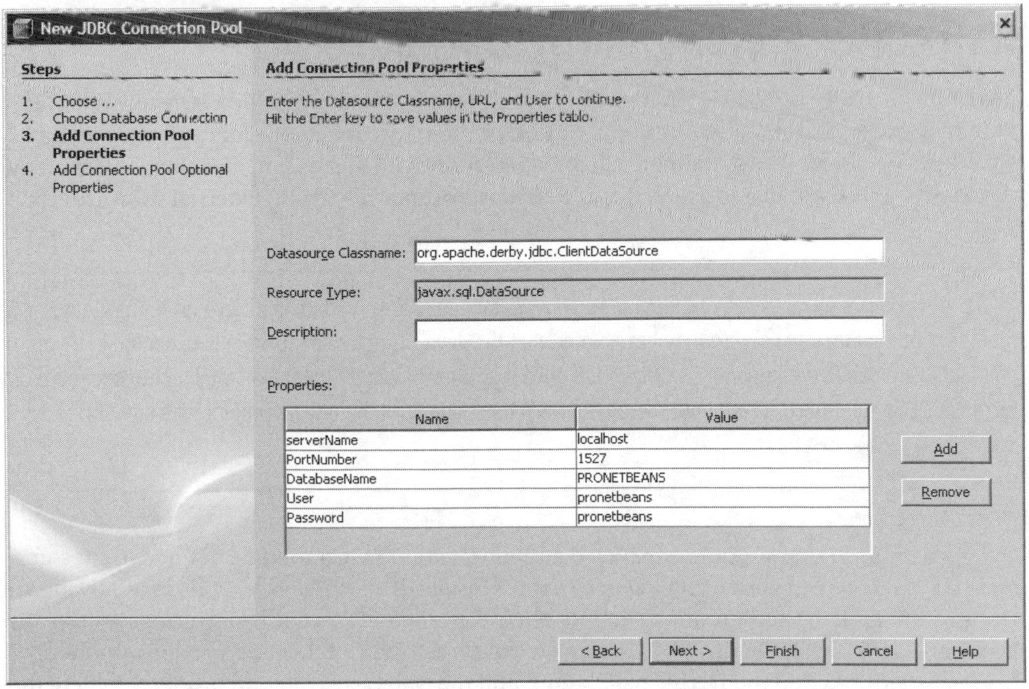

Figure 18-8. *Adding connection pool properties*

4. In the last step of the wizard, you can set additional parameters, such as the maximum size of the connection pool, the initial steady size of the connection pool, the idle timeout, and more. If you are not familiar with these properties, it is usually best to leave them set to their default values. Click the Finish button, and the connection pool will be added to your project and viewable under the Server Resources node in the Projects window.

For those of you using the Sun Java System Application Server, the next step after adding a new connection pool is to register it with the application server. Under the Server Resources node, right-click the name of the Connection Pool and select Register from the context menu. A pop-up window will list the name of the resource to register, along with the name of the server instance. To continue, click the Register button.

Note When you're using an application server like the Sun Java System Application Server, to register the connection pool, it must first be started. The connection pool register function does not automatically trigger the server to start.

If your web application is configured to use a different application server, such as Tomcat, you must manually register the connection pool and resources. In the Tomcat web-based admin console, look in the Data Sources section. See the documentation for your specific application server for details on registering a connection pool.

Using the Apache Derby Database

NetBeans provides built-in support for the Apache Derby database, which is installed along with most newer NetBeans distributions. This is extremely convenient for users who do not have their own database system installed. Using Derby, you can design, develop, and test any database-backed application directly in NetBeans, without relying on external software.

Tip If you have never heard of the Apache Derby database, you should keep an eye on it. Currently, members of the Sun Java community have stated that the Java DB database (Derby) is expected to be an optional downloadable component of Java SE 6 once it is available as a final release. Expect to see more of the Java DB in the future. To find out more about this database, visit the official project web site at `http://db.apache.org/derby/`.

By default, Derby should be installed and the location to it should be defined. If for some reason it is not, or you need to alter where Derby is installed, select Tools ➤ Options ➤ Advanced Options. In the IDE Configuration section, select Server and External Tool Settings ➤ Java DB Database, as shown in Figure 18-9. Here, you can set the Java DB Location property (where NetBeans looks to find the Derby installation) and the Database Location property (where the data files for the actual database schema are stored).

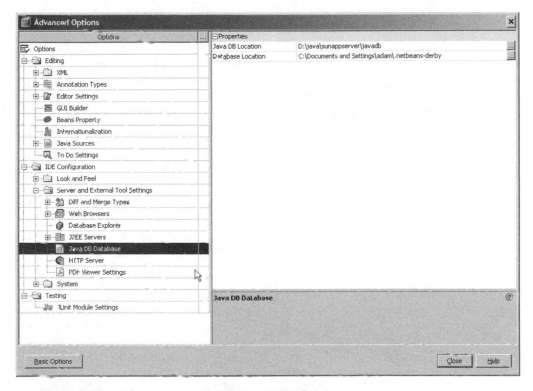

Figure 18-9. *Editing the properties for the Java DB (Derby)*

When you are ready to actually use Derby, select Tools ➤ Java DB Database. The submenu has the options Start Java DB Server, Stop Java DB Server (if it has previously been started), and Create Java DB Database. The Create Java DB Database menu item allows you to create multiple database schema, each with a separate username and password for defining connections. After a database has been created, you can connect to it and work in it using the Databases node in the Runtime window. A new database connection will also be listed in the Runtime window under the Databases node.

Summary

In this chapter, you saw that NetBeans provides a variety of tools for working with databases. This can help an application developer who is programming a database-dependent project. During application development, it is often useful to be able to view, query, and modify the data in a database. Normally, you would need a separate tool to perform these actions, but NetBeans has built-in support for them.

This chapter covered how to specify a database driver, create and configure a connection to a database, and work with various database objects. You learned how to create tables, drop and re-create tables, add an index, and create views—all from within the NetBeans IDE.

Next, you saw how the SQL Command window allows you to write and execute custom SQL queries against the database. You can write and run almost any standard piece of SQL in this window and view the results from the operation (assuming a SELECT query was performed).

You can also use SQL templates directly in the SQL Command window. Doing so allows you to save long snippets of frequently used SQL and recall them using a shortcut.

Another useful feature is the ability to link a database schema to a project. This is valuable because you can link a schema to a Java project and thus view the associated tables and columns directly in the Projects window. You can also save the schema snapshot in a code repository like CVS along with your code.

Then you learned how to establish a connection pool, if the database supports pooling. Finally, we discussed how to use the built-in support for the Derby database. This is handy if you don't have a database system, such as Microsoft SQL Server, Oracle, or MySQL, installed.

Index

You Need the Companion eBook

Your purchase of this book entitles you to buy the companion PDF-version eBook for only $10. Take the weightless companion with you anywhere.

We believe this Apress title will prove so indispensable that you'll want to carry it with you everywhere, which is why we are offering the companion eBook (in PDF format) for $10 to customers who purchase this book now. Convenient and fully searchable, the PDF version of any content-rich, page-heavy Apress book makes a valuable addition to your programming library. You can easily find and copy code—or perform examples by quickly toggling between instructions and the application. Even simultaneously tackling a donut, diet soda, and complex code becomes simplified with hands-free eBooks!

Once you purchase your book, getting the $10 companion eBook is simple:

❶ Visit **www.apress.com/promo/tendollars/**.

❷ Complete a basic registration form to receive a randomly generated question about this title.

❸ Answer the question correctly in 60 seconds, and you will receive a promotional code to redeem for the $10.00 eBook.

2560 Ninth Street • Suite 219 • Berkeley, CA 94710

eBookshop

THE EXPERT'S VOICE™

Offer valid through 9/26/07.